RAYMOND KLIBANSKY
and the Warburg Library Network

Portrait of Raymond Klibansky, signed E[lise] Saxl, London, late 1930s (private collection)

RAYMOND KLIBANSKY
and the Warburg Library Network

Intellectual Peregrinations from Hamburg to London and Montreal

Edited by Philippe Despoix and Jillian Tomm

with the collaboration of Eric Méchoulan and Georges Leroux

McGILL-QUEEN'S UNIVERSITY PRESS

Montreal & Kingston • London • Chicago

ISBN 978-0-7735-5463-4 (cloth)
ISBN 978-0-7735-5606-5 (ePDF)
ISBN 978-0-7735-5607-2 (ePUB)

Legal deposit fourth quarter 2018
Bibliothèque nationale du Québec

Printed in Canada on acid-free paper that is 100% ancient forest free (100% post-consumer recycled), processed chlorine free

This book has been published with the help of a grant from the Canadian Federation for the Humanities and Social Sciences, through the Awards to Scholarly Publications Program, using funds provided by the Social Sciences and Humanities Research Council of Canada. Funding has also been received from the Université de Montréal.

Funded by the Government of Canada | Financé par le gouvernement du Canada | Canada

Canada Council for the Arts | Conseil des arts du Canada

We acknowledge the support of the Canada Council for the Arts, which last year invested $153 million to bring the arts to Canadians throughout the country.

Nous remercions le Conseil des arts du Canada de son soutien. L'an dernier, le Conseil a investi 153 millions de dollars pour mettre de l'art dans la vie des Canadiennes et des Canadiens de tout le pays.

Library and Archives Canada Cataloguing in Publication

Raymond Klibansky and the Warburg Library network : intellectual peregrinations from Hamburg to London and Montreal / edited by Philippe Despoix and Jillian Tomm with the collaboration of Eric Méchoulan and Georges Leroux.

Includes bibliographical references and index.
Issued in print and electronic formats.
ISBN 978-0-7735-5463-4 (cloth).–ISBN 978-0-7735-5606-5 (ePDF).
–ISBN 978-0-7735-5607-2 (ePUB)

1. Klibansky, Raymond, 1905–2005 – Friends and associates. 2. Klibansky, Raymond, 1905–2005 – Influence. 3. Warburg Institute. Library – History. 4. Warburg Institute – History. 5. Humanities – Research. I. Leroux, Georges, 1945–, editor II. Méchoulan, Éric, 1959–, editor III. Despoix, Philippe, editor IV. Tomm, Jillian, editor

B995.K547R39 2018 191 C2018-903775-X
C2018-903776-8

CONTENTS

FIGURES

FOREWORD

Hosting the "Raymond Klibansky and the Warburg Library Network" conference in June 2015 at the Warburg Institute was one of the most rewarding moments of the year during which I was acting director of the institute. As the reader will understand from the subsequent chapters, which grew out of that exchange, the conference depicted a fascinating landscape of the Warburg Library network from the mid-1920s through the mid-1960s. The authors recount the history of the scholars whose intellectual contributions helped to steer the directions of the library created by Aby Warburg in Hamburg: the history of ambitious publication projects, of demanding intellectual research; the history of people adapting to a greater history but maintaining their will to offer outstanding publications, lessons to the international community of scholars.

Scholars known individually from their publications are studied here with particular attention to the way they worked together, creating and researching together, and also facilitating others' research: Ernst Cassirer, Erwin Panofsky, Lotte Labowsky, Fritz Saxl, Gertrud Bing, Edgar Wind, Walter Solmitz, and especially Raymond Klibansky. Studying Klibansky's major works and research – the ambitious *Corpus Platonicum* series, for instance, or the collaborative *Saturn and Melancholy* – not as part of an isolated path but as an *œuvre* born of his encounters with the scholars who influenced him and from the results of multiple interactions with his colleagues – brings a clearer understanding of his complex projects and of the "something of a 'genius'" that was seen in him before he reached the age of thirty.

Raphaële Mouren
Librarian of the Warburg Institute and Reader

ACKNOWLEDGMENTS

We would like to thank the Warburg Institute for their collaboration and support for this project, in particular Raphaële Mouren, Warburg Librarian and also acting director of the institute during the period of most intense collaboration, and Claudia Wedepohl, archivist of the Warburg Institute, who continues to be a constant source of assistance to researchers and editors. Our thanks go also to the other main holding institutions of Klibansky's archives: to McGill Library Rare Books and Special Collections, with special thanks to Sophie Trolliet-Martial; and to the Deutsches Literaturarchiv Marbach, in particular to Roland Kamzelak for his valuable addition of a common database for archival data pertaining to Klibansky's dispersed correspondence.

We cannot overstate our appreciation for the assistance of Elisabeth Otto and Caroline Bem of the Centre de Recherches Intermédiales sur les arts, les lettres et les techniques (CRIalt) at the Université de Montréal. And we are equally grateful for the generous support provided by Le Centre canadien des études allemandes et européennes/The Canadian Centre for German and European Studies (CCEAE/CCGES) and IRTG Diversity, also at the Université de Montréal, with particular thanks to Elisabeth Tutschek, coordinator of IRTG Diversity, and Morgan Gaulin, postdoctoral researcher at CCEAE/CCGES.

And finally, we offer our deepest gratitude to Ethel Groffier, whose unflagging support and ready responses to countless questions and requests have been invaluable.

RAYMOND KLIBANSKY
and the Warburg Library Network

INTRODUCTION

Raymond Klibansky and the Warburg Library Network: From Hamburg to London and Montreal

PHILIPPE DESPOIX, GEORGES LEROUX,
AND JILLIAN TOMM

S'il est vrai … que, comme la plupart des amours, l'amour des bibliothèques s'apprend, pour Raymond Klibansky, cet amour doit être né dans le labyrinthe enchanté de la bibliothèque d'Aby Warburg, à Hambourg.
Ethel Groffier, "De l'amour des livres à l'amour des bibliothèques"

Among the numerous scholarly approaches that have enquired into the place of ideas, representations, and images within the history of culture and the modalities of their transmission emerged a distinct set of methods that still today continue to be perceived as highly pertinent to the humanities and social sciences. These were developed in the twentieth century by the various members of a circle of scholars who gravitated around the library founded by German Jewish art historian and cultural theorist Aby Warburg. The famous Kulturwissenschaftliche Bibliothek Warburg (KBW) was conceived in Hamburg as a "laboratory" that went beyond contributing to a redefinition of interdisciplinary standards in the cultural sciences, among which the iconological method remains the most widely familiar to date; it also revealed, for instance, the determining importance of Arab cultural transmission in the endurance of representations and knowledge from Greco-Roman antiquity to the European Renaissance, which would in turn set the scene for the modern scientific revolution.

The writings of the library's prestigious founder, Aby Warburg, are widely studied, but little attention has been paid until now to the network of collaborators who, as a network – beyond their work as individuals – participated directly in the immense learned production of this institution during the 1920s and after. Yet, it was this exceptional constellation of researchers – Fritz Saxl, Gertrud Bing, Ernst Cassirer, Erwin Panofsky, Edgar Wind, Raymond Klibansky, and others – who preserved, transmitted, and further developed the Hamburgian KBW heritage. When, in order to escape the persecutions of the Nazi regime in Germany, the group's members fled to London and founded the Warburg Institute, they continued to develop core collective research projects in spite of the subsequent dispersion of some members to the United States, Sweden, and Canada. From the 1920s until well after the Second World War, the KBW, and subsequently the Warburg Institute, owed its unique politics of publication to the close-knit network that grew especially around Fritz Saxl (1890–1948) and Gertrud Bing (1892–1964) – a network of collaborators in which Raymond Klibansky played a crucial role.

In May 2013 an international workshop paying homage to Raymond Klibansky was organized at the Université de Montréal in parallel with an exhibition devoted to his library, curated by Georges Leroux at the Bibliothèque et Archives nationales du Québec.[1] Both events explored Klibansky's editorial work and his connection with the Warburg Library, which he and Edgar Wind were instrumental in saving by strongly supporting its move to London. Titled "Raymond Klibansky and the Warburgian Legacy of the Cultural Sciences," the workshop brought together international experts on different aspects of the Warburg network, as well as findings from material newly available for research through the acquisition, in 2005, of Klibansky's fonds by the Deutsches Literaturarchiv Marbach (DLA), and through the acquisition of Klibansky's library by McGill University, Montreal.[2] Discussions led to further archival research and to a subsequent colloquium held in June 2015 at the Warburg Institute, London, under the title "The Warburg Library Network: Geography and History of an Intellectual Afterlife. From Hamburg to London, and to Montreal – the contribution of Raymond Klibansky."[3] The tenth anniversary of the death of Klibansky was an occasion for reflecting on his exceptional contribution to the great collective ventures of the

Warburg Institute, which profoundly altered our perception of occidental intellectual history through publications like the Latin and Arabic *Corpus Platonicum Medii Aevi* (1940–62), the journal *Mediaeval and Renaissance Studies* (1941–68), and the belated but all the more famous *Saturn and Melancholy* (1964). In each of these projects, he was a central contributor. The chapters here present studies that evolved from these symposia and discussions.

Raymond Klibansky (1905–2005) – A German Education: Heidelberg and Hamburg

While Klibansky's intellectual biography has not yet been written, it is nonetheless possible to sketch the life circumstances and peregrinations that led him from France to Germany, and from exile in England to Canada.[4] Born in Paris in 1905 to a practising Jewish bourgeois family of German-Lithuanian origin, Klibansky was uprooted at the outbreak of the First World War when he fled with his family to Frankfurt am Main, the home of his paternal family. The bulk of Klibansky's developmental period coincided, then, with the years of the Weimar Republic (1918–33), and – both as a person born in France and as a Jew – he became something of an outsider from an early age. Thus, it is hardly surprising that, finding himself in "two Germanies: the Germany of military swagger, abject submission to authority, aggressive foreign adventure, and obsessive preoccupation with form, and the Germany of lyrical poetry, humanist philosophy, and pacific cosmopolitanism," he gravitated to the humanist "way of Goethe and Humboldt."[5]

At fifteen, having received a strong education in Greek and Latin at the Goethe Gymnasium in Frankfurt, Klibansky requested his father's permission to transfer to the Odenwaldschule, a progressive school founded near the city of Stuttgart by psychologist Paul Geheeb (1870–1961). Favoured by writers and intellectuals like Thomas Mann and his contemporary Ernst Cassirer (1874–1945), whose children attended the school, Odenwald opted for a liberal and humanistic approach to education. It was here that he met Walter Solmitz (1905–1962), who would remain always a dear friend.

Klibansky began his university years in 1923 at the age of eighteen in Heidelberg, a city that was to remain the intellectual and spiritual heart of his entire life.[6] This was Germany's oldest university, praised by Hölderlin, where Hegel and Max Weber had both taught, and which was then one of the centres of Weimar intellectual culture. Among Klibanky's early professors were Heinrich Rickert (1863–1936) and Karl Jaspers (1883–1969), both of whom provided models of republican ideals that contrasted with the *Kulturpessimismus* of the conservative thinkers of the time. Yet, while imposing figures such as these dominated Heidelberg and peopled Klibansky's education, he became the disciple of none.[7]

Beyond the walls of the university, he had the opportunity to meet local and visiting intellectuals at regular *jours* in the homes of archaeologist Ludwig Curtius (1874–1954) and, especially, Marianne Weber (1870–1954), widow of the sociologist Max Weber (1864–1920). Ever present in debates at the house, the Weberian critique of subjectivity influenced the young Klibansky, with its argument in favour of *Wertfreiheit* and against the dangers of personal charisma. Equally influential in his development, perhaps, was literary scholar Friedrich Gundolf (1880–1931), Klibansky's senior by twenty-five years. They met in 1928 and enjoyed a short but intense friendship, sharing especially a love of poetry and of books. Some years earlier, Gundolf had been very close to the lyric poet and cult figure Stefan George, whose following at the time rivalled that of Rilke. But despite acknowledging the importance of George's poetry, Klibansky never joined in the circle of his followers.[8]

Klibansky's studies took him out of Heidelberg on two occasions. During the hyper-inflation of 1923–24, Jaspers selected him from among the students at Heidelberg to attend a scholarship program in the northern city of Kiel that aimed at developing a new class of leaders for Germany. Klibansky stayed only a few months, but during that time he studied under the pioneering sociologist Ferdinand Tönnies (1855–1936), through whom he gained an insight into statistics that he would later use in his war work for England.[9] In 1926 he left Heidelberg again, this time after accepting an invitation to study for a year in Hamburg with the eminent Neo-Kantian Ernst Cassirer. Klibansky was introduced to the philosopher by Cassirer's son Heinz (Heinrich), who was a school friend, and he lived for several weeks with the family. The time he spent in Hamburg was crucial for the young scholar, for it was then, through Cassirer, that he gained entry into the world of the Warburg Library and its circle.

Sitzungsberichte
der Heidelberger Akademie der Wissenschaften
Philosophisch-historische Klasse
Jahrgang 1928/29. 5. Abhandlung

Ein PROKLOS-Fund
und seine Bedeutung

Von

RAYMOND KLIBANSKY

Eingegangen am 19. Februar 1929

Vorgelegt von Ernst Hoffmann

Heidelberg 1929
Carl Winters Universitätsbuchhandlung

Verlags-Nr. 2133

Fig. 0.1 Klibansky's doctoral dissertation, supervised by Ernst Hoffmann, which presented a little-known Latin translation of Proclus's *Commentary* on Plato's *Parmenides.*

After returning to Heidelberg in 1927, Klibansky completed his doctoral dissertation, *Ein Proklos-Fund und seine Bedeutung* (fig. 0.1), which was supervised by Cassirer's friend, the philosopher and classicist Ernst Hoffmann (1880–1952). The thesis constituted an important study on Proclus, the main Greek Neoplatonic source of Nicholas of Cusa, based on a manuscript he discovered in Cusa's library.[10] Once his doctoral work was complete,

Klibansky immediately pursued the *Habilitation* necessary for becoming a professor, which was yet again overseen by Hoffmann. This work, presented to the University of Heidelberg in 1932, brings together several texts from the Chartres Cathedral school in the twelfth century, examining the Platonic tradition as connected to this "Chartrian Academy." These two studies were first steps toward the larger project that would engage Klibansky for decades, outlined in his very short but dense 1939 publication of the Warburg Institute, *The Continuity of the Platonic Tradition during the Middle Ages: Outlines of a Corpus Platonicum Medii Aevi.*[11]

The introduction to Ernst Cassirer proved catalytic for Klibansky's future, since it would usher in his affiliation with the Kulturwissenschaftliche Bibliothek Warburg (KBW).[12] Within weeks of his Hamburg stay in 1926, Klibansky had gained Cassirer's support to provide a modern edition of a little-known Renaissance Latin text to be included in appendix to the latter's *Individuum und Kosmos in der Philosophie der Renaissance.*[13] Over a period of a few months, the doctoral candidate completed an edition of French humanist Charles de Bovelles's (1479–1567) *Liber de sapiente* – in Cassirer's words "perhaps the most curious and in some respects the most characteristic creation of Renaissance philosophy," which had not been printed since the sixteenth century.[14] Cassirer's book on the Renaissance was dedicated to Aby Warburg and issued in the series of *Studien der Bibliothek Warburg*; and the library was active in the support and preparation of Klibansky's Bovelles edition.

By the time of Klibansky's arrival in 1926, the KBW was established not only as a library but also as a research centre that featured numerous lectures, seminars, exhibitions, and publishing projects. Even though he was physically present, Warburg was at that point more a leader in spirit, while art historian Fritz Saxl and historian of philosophy Gertrud Bing oversaw the organization of the new library building. They hired students to assist in library work, and Klibansky and his friend Solmitz were among those taken on. Both became firmly rooted in this milieu – indeed they quickly also became friends with Saxl and Bing – and for Klibansky in particular this relatively brief time in Hamburg would prove fundamental to his path for many years to come.

The inspiration for Bovelles's work on the place of man in the cosmos and culture came from Nicholas of Cusa, who was central to Cassirer's book

Individuum und Kosmos. It was the exploration of this interest at the Warburg Library that would provide the main impulse for the project of a new edition of the works of Nicholas of Cusa that was to absorb much of Klibansky's attention.[15] His interest in Cusa progressed concurrently with his doctoral work, both of which were overseen by Hoffmann. The invitation to Klibansky by Hoffman to join in 1928 the *Opera omnia* edition of Cusa, an invitation made with Cassirer's support, launched a long and fruitful collaboration, colossal in scope – the project was only completed in 2005, having passed through many hands (with twenty volumes in over forty parts).[16]

It was not only Cassirer and Hoffmann who admired Klibansky's exceptional ability in carefully retracing texts and their reformulations through centuries and across linguistic and cultural boundaries; Panofsky (1892–1968) and Saxl also noticed his talent and invited him to collaborate in a new edition of their 1923 study, *Dürers 'Melencolia I.' Eine quellen- und typengeschichtliche Untersuchung* (A Historical Investigation of Sources and Types). Active in the revision of this text from 1927, Klibansky sent frequent notes, or *Zettel*, from Heidelberg – dealing primarily with ancient Greek and Latin philosophy, literature, and medicine, as well as medieval thought[17] – back to Saxl and Panofsky at the KBW, who worked through them, integrating them into the text that was later to become the celebrated *Saturn and Melancholy.*[18]

During what was an extremely productive period for Klibansky at the end of the twenties and early thirties in Germany, he also initiated with Heidelberg University an edition of the complete Latin works of the medieval theologian and mystic Meister Eckhart (1260–1328).[19] A logical focus for Klibansky, given his interest in the Platonic tradition, Eckhart was particularly intriguing because of his influence on Cusa and for his range of sources, which included Jewish and Arab thinkers. Within this beginning, one notes several avenues – from the Platonic tradition to ideas of pluralism and tolerance – that already dominated Klibansky's life work; indeed, for the most part, his orientation had reached maturity while he was still in Germany. By 1933, when Hitler became chancellor and Klibansky was forced to emigrate, the Eckhart edition, the Cusa edition, and the project with Saxl and Panofsky on melancholy had all become works in progress.

Years of Exile: From London/Oxford to Montreal

From 1933 onward, events in Germany quickly precipitated the move of the KBW and most of its staff to London.[20] Racial laws forced Klibansky, like countless others, to leave his post. Panofsky opted to move to the United States, and Klibansky, having been warned of imminent arrest, helped his family to leave the country, remained for a commemorative ceremony on the anniversary of his friend Gundolf's death, and finally crossed the border in July 1933. After stopping in Holland and Paris, he reached London in August, just months before the Warburg Library moved there in December.

Like many others with connections to the Warburg circle who came to England in those years, Klibansky was helped in England by the Academic Assistance Council (AAC), which was formed in 1933 precisely in response to racially and politically based dismissals of academics.[21] Saxl was among those who wrote in support of his continued stay in the country – a particularly close collegial relationship had developed between these two scholars in Germany – a further testimony to the desire of the Warburg Institute to find some means of keeping Klibansky in England.[22] In several ways, then, the newly founded institute, with its publications, networks, and activities, helped Klibansky to flourish in this new environment.

Among the first Warburg Institute publications in their new home was *A Bibliography on the Survival of the Classics* (1934), a reprint of the German original entitled *Kulturwissenschaftliche Bibliographie zum Nachleben der Antike*, co-edited by librarian Hans Meier (1900–1941) and art historian Edgar Wind (1900–1971), with their colleague the literature historian Richard Newald (1894–1954).[23] Klibansky had contributed copiously to the first volume of the *Bibliography*, and the summary of contributors lists his name alongside those of Gertrud Bing, Ernst Cassirer, and several other Warburg intimates, including Klibansky's close friend and contemporary Lotte Labowsky (1905–1991). This summary (fig. 0.2) provides an efficient way of learning who contributed to this shared effort, how much, and on what.

Klibansky obtained temporary teaching posts at King's College, University of London (1934–36), Oriel College, Oxford (1936–48), and the University of Liverpool (1938–39). He always maintained a connection with the Warburg Institute, where he gave lectures on medieval philosophy (1936) and on religion and science in the twelfth century (1937).[24] Throughout this

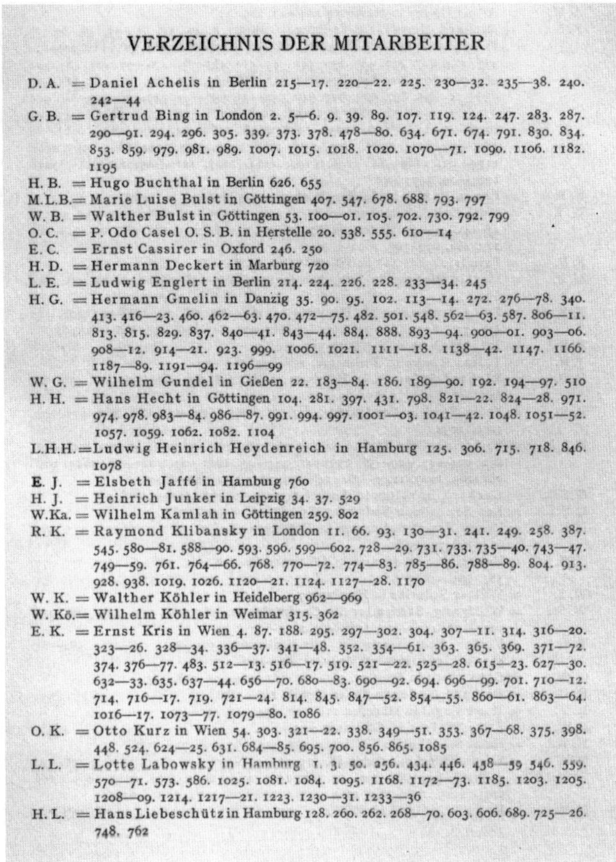

VERZEICHNIS DER MITARBEITER

D. A. = Daniel Achelis in Berlin 215—17. 220—22. 225. 230—32. 235—38. 240. 242—44
G. B. = Gertrud Bing in London 2. 5—6. 9. 39. 89. 107. 119. 124. 247. 283. 287. 290—91. 294. 296. 305. 339. 373. 378. 478—80. 634. 671. 674. 791. 830. 834. 853. 859. 979. 981. 989. 1007. 1015. 1018. 1020. 1070—71. 1090. 1106. 1182. 1195
H. B. = Hugo Buchthal in Berlin 626. 655
M.L.B.= Marie Luise Bulst in Göttingen 407. 547. 678. 688. 793. 797
W. B. = Walther Bulst in Göttingen 53. 100—01. 105. 702. 730. 792. 799
O. C. = P. Odo Casel O. S. B. in Herstelle 20. 538. 555. 610—14
E. C. = Ernst Cassirer in Oxford 246. 250
H. D. = Hermann Deckert in Marburg 720
L. E. = Ludwig Englert in Berlin 214. 224. 226. 228. 233—34. 245
H. G. = Hermann Gmelin in Danzig 35. 90. 95. 102. 113—14. 272. 276—78. 340. 413. 416—23. 460. 462—63. 470. 472—75. 482. 501. 548. 562—63. 587. 806—11. 813. 815. 829. 837. 840—41. 843—44. 884. 888. 893—94. 900—01. 903—06. 908—12. 914—21. 923. 999. 1006. 1021. 1111—18. 1138—42. 1147. 1166. 1187—89. 1191—94. 1196—99
W. G. = Wilhelm Gundel in Gießen 22. 183—84. 186. 189—90. 192. 194—97. 510
H. H. = Hans Hecht in Göttingen 104. 281. 397. 431. 798. 821—22. 824—28. 971. 974. 978. 983—84. 986—87. 991. 994. 997. 1001—03. 1041—42. 1048. 1051—52. 1057. 1059. 1062. 1082. 1104
L.H.H.= Ludwig Heinrich Heydenreich in Hamburg 125. 306. 715. 718. 846. 1078
E. J. = Elsbeth Jaffé in Hambuig 760
H. J. = Heinrich Junker in Leipzig 34. 37. 529
W.Ka. = Wilhelm Kamlah in Göttingen 259. 802
R. K. = Raymond Klibansky in London 11. 66. 93. 130—31. 241. 249. 258. 387. 545. 580—81. 588—90. 593. 596. 599—602. 728—29. 731. 733. 735—40. 743—47. 749—59. 761. 764—66. 768. 770—72. 774—83. 785—86. 788—89. 804. 913. 928. 938. 1019. 1026. 1120—21. 1124. 1127—28. 1170
W. K. = Walther Köhler in Heidelberg 962—969
W. Kö.= Wilhelm Köhler in Weimar 315. 362
E. K. = Ernst Kris in Wien 4. 87. 188. 295. 297—302. 304. 307—11. 314. 316—20. 323—26. 328—34. 336—37. 341—48. 352. 354—61. 363. 365. 369. 371—72. 374. 376—77. 483. 512—13. 516—17. 519. 521—22. 525—28. 615—23. 627—30. 632—33. 635. 637—44. 656—70. 680—83. 690—92. 694. 696—99. 701. 710—12. 714. 716—17. 719. 721—24. 814. 845. 847—52. 854—55. 860—61. 863—64. 1016—17. 1073—77. 1079—80. 1086
O. K. = Otto Kurz in Wien 54. 303. 321—22. 338. 349—51. 353. 367—68. 375. 398. 448. 524. 624—25. 631. 684—85. 695. 700. 856. 865. 1085
L. L. = Lotte Labowsky in Hamburg 1. 3. 50. 256. 434. 446. 458—59 546. 559. 570—71. 573. 586. 1025. 1081. 1084. 1095. 1168. 1172—73. 1185. 1203. 1205. 1208—09. 1214. 1217—21. 1223. 1230—31. 1233—36
H. L. = Hans Liebeschütz in Hamburg 128. 260. 262. 268—70. 603. 606. 689. 725—26. 748. 762

Fig. 0.2 Page from the list of contributors to the Warburg Institute's *A Bibliography on the Survival of the Classics*, Vol. 1 (1934).

period he also kept up a continual correspondence with Saxl and Bing which abounds with both personal exchanges and details about Warburg projects – such as the *Corpus Platonicum* – and other activities.

Throughout, Klibansky developed his ideas on tracing the paths through which the Platonic tradition reached and became understood in the Middle Ages and early Renaissance. What he had uncovered through the Latin manuscript segment of Proclus's commentary on Plato's *Parmenides* was central. Most particularly, the text contained more of Proclus's commentary than had survived in Greek manuscripts, providing evidence that, from the late thirteenth century, more of both the commentary and the *Parmenides* were known than was generally thought.[25] Klibansky's subsequent work, presented toward his *Habilitation* in 1932, had examined the relationship between the medieval Platonism in what he understood as a distinct School of Chartres, centred particularly around Thierry and Bernard, and the tradition of Proclus, of which Meister Eckhart and Nicholas of Cusa were important tributaries. But from Proclus and Damascius to Cusa and Marsilio Ficino, in order to understand the transmission more fully, it now became necessary to reconstitute links and various conduits of Plato's thought, not only in the West but also in the Arab world.

Klibansky aimed in fact to reconstitute the full chain of transmission from Platonism to German idealism; thus was born the *Corpus Platonicum Medii Aevi* project, which he developed in London with the Warburg Institute as early as 1934–35.[26] The project was to comprise two series, the *Plato Latinus* and the *Plato Arabus* (fig. 0.3), each of which was to bring together the complete set of known texts in the medieval Platonic tradition. The scope of the project required the participation of a great many scholars and, though it never reached completion, seven volumes were published, beginning in 1940. Here, in the third volume of the *Plato Latinus*, the fragment of Proclus's commentary on the *Parmenides* studied by Klibansky for his doctoral work is edited with Labowsky, who soon afterward produced her well-known work on the library of the fifteenth-century Cardinal Bessarion.[27]

Like Klibansky, several other researchers who had been connected with the KBW moved to England in the 1930s, often receiving help from within the Warburg circle. Ernst Cassirer was for a couple of years among this group, having accepted a teaching post at Oxford before becoming a professor at Göteborgs universitet in Sweden. While there, he was celebrated by the Warburg Institute in *Philosophy and History*, the *Festschrift* published in 1936 and co-edited by Klibansky, now at Oxford, with Scottish professor of philosophy H.J. (Herbert James) Paton (1887–1969).[28] As much as it is a homage to Cassirer, this volume honours the progressive culture of Weimar and the Warburg approach to borderless culture and ideas. We find here Warburg intimates such as Saxl, Panofsky, and Wind, who contributed some of their finest studies to this *Festschrift*, alongside other continental thinkers, including Johann Huizinga, Émile Bréhier, Étienne Gilson, Bernard Groethuysen,

- 4 -

B. PLATO ARABUS

The plan of the Plato Arabus, as outlined in agreement with Dr.Walzer, is as follows:

(1) Vitae

The Arabic Vitae Socratis et Platonis. This fascicule will contain all biographical material as well as lists of Plato's works which are to be found in certain Arabic encyclopaedias. Dr.Walzer is prepared to take over this part.

(2) Platonica

I. Description of Mss.containing extracts of Plato's works (Phaedon, Phaedrus etc.)
II.Collection of quotations from Plato to be found in early Arabic authors: a) in the works of philosophers and scientists (al-Kindi and Gabir); b) in the works of historians.
III. Sayings attributed to Plato.

(3-5)Paraphrases of Plato's writings.

(3) Galen's paraphrase of the Timaeus: edition being prepared by Dr.Walzer and Dr.P.Kraus, Paris.

(4) Al-Farabi: paraphrase of the Nomoi: edition being prepared by Dr.P.Kraus, Paris.

(5) Averroes: paraphrase of the Republic. Edition of the Hebrew translation of the Arabic text being prepared by E.Rosenthal, London (see Journal of the Royal Asiatic Society, 1934).

(6)Pseudo-Platonica.

I. Plato Alchemicus: Gabir, etc.; to be edited as far as possible, in connection with the Plato Alchemicus Latinus.
II.Plato Magus.
III. Alia Pseudo-Platonica.

(7-8)Arabic recasting of Neoplatonic works.

(7) "Theologia Aristotelis" founded on more reliable manuscripts than those used by Dieterici, with a translation and interpretation of the respective parts of Plotinus.

(8) "Liber de Causis" (to be confronted with Proclus' Elementatio theologica).

Fig. 0.3 Early unpublished plan for the *Corpus Platonicum Medii Aevi*, c. 1934–35.

and Giovanni Gentile, as well as British scholars such as C.C.J. Webb and Samuel Alexander. The posthumous contribution of Friedrich Gundolf would have been particularly poignant for Klibansky, who had lost this friend in such an untimely manner. The bibliography of the volume was also a very personal enterprise, with the work shared between Klibansky and his long-time friend Walter Solmitz.

Klibansky's own contribution was an English version of his *Antrittsvorlesung*, or inaugural lecture as a *Privatdozent*, presented to the University of Heidelberg in 1932.[29] Originally titled "Der philosophische Charakter der Historie," it provides us with one of Klibansky's few more speculative essays. In this text on the philosophical dimension of history he pays homage to Cassirer's Kantian ideal and vision of the logic of symbolic forms – it calls for an unrelenting effort toward an *Objektivierbarkeit* (objectifiability) that would permit the integration of historical knowledge into the sphere of sciences as detached from myth and magic.[30]

Like many other scholars in exile at this time, Klibansky contributed directly to the British effort in the Second World War. A British citizen as of 1938, he joined the secret Political Warfare Executive (PWE) of the Foreign Office from 1941 to 1946. Concentrating first on analyzing intelligence and propaganda from Germany, from late 1942 he oversaw the intelligence unit of the PWE for Italy.[31] Also working at the PWE as an archivist in intelligence was paleographer Richard Hunt, who had met Klibansky shortly after his arrival in London and with whom he became co-editor of a new Warburg Institute journal, *Mediaeval and Renaissance Studies*, which put out six issues between 1941 and 1968.[32]

Although Klibansky and Saxl remained very close in England – as their copious correspondence during that period makes clear – and were to pursue many joint initiatives under the auspices of the Warburg Institute, Panofsky's move to the United States complicated their common project on melancholy. Klibansky took over the final stages of the proofs for the work in German, but by the time of printing in autumn 1939 the venture had become impossible because of the war, and the plates were eventually lost. From across the Atlantic, Panofsky had lost much of his interest in the project, but Klibansky and Saxl continued to pursue options for publication. In the meantime, Klibansky too decided to move to North America, henceforth making his home in Montreal.

From Montreal he kept up a close and regular exchange with Bing and Saxl. He at first divided his time between England and Canada, and was uncertain of remaining in Montreal but, once invited to join McGill University's Department of Philosophy in 1946, he made the move permanent as Frothingham Professor of Logic and Metaphysics in 1948.[33] In addition to his responsibilities at McGill, Klibansky took on the role of visiting professor at the Institut d'Études Médiévales de l'Université de Montréal from 1947 to 1968, trying to increase communication between the two schools and their anglophone and francophone cultures, communities rarely in contact during those years.[34]

His interest in the work on melancholy did not flag, however, and Klibansky now had access at McGill to the resources of the William Osler Library of the History of Medicine, whose creator had also been interested in the subject. Reworked in English, first with Saxl's support and then by Klibansky alone after Saxl's death in 1948, *Saturn and Melancholy* did finally emerge in 1964, but with only grudging acceptance by Panofsky, with whom Klibansky faced off for years in a struggle for recognition as its full co-author. His correspondence with Saxl, and especially Bing, testifies to the difficult negotiation.[35] A German edition appeared only in 1990 (after the Italian and French versions), again under Klibansky's care, with a new foreword and slight modifications from the English edition.[36]

In Montreal, Klibansky's contributions to other early projects were also picked up anew. His participation in the Cusa edition restarted after a time with, for example, the texts of *De pace fidei* (1959) and a new edition of *De docta ignorantia* (1977), but the Eckhart project could not be salvaged.[37] And yet the war as a whole, and Klibansky's intelligence work in particular, had an impact on the direction of his subsequent scholarship. While he remained active in areas of early interest, with the ongoing publication of the *Corpus Platonicum* or the journal *Mediaeval and Renaissance Studies* through 1968, he also turned more of his attention to explicit expressions of a drive to disseminate and cultivate notions of tolerance and liberty.

Beyond the Warburg Networks

Once Klibansky had decided on Montreal as a base, he embarked on establishing new networks, while continuing to maintain contact with the Warburg circle, primarily through Bing and Labowsky. A founder (1959) and president of the Canadian Society for the History and Philosophy of Science, and at the end of the 1960s president of the Société internationale pour l'étude de la philosophie médiévale, he was most active with the Paris-based Institut international de philosophie (IIP).[38] The IIP counted among its members

Bertrand Russell, Jean-Paul Sartre, and Jean Piaget, as well as McGill philosophers Mario Bunge and Charles Taylor.[39] Klibansky was involved in particular with Paul Ricoeur, Max Black, Guido Calogero, and Hans-Georg Gadamer, some of whom he had known from Germany and with whom he shared the aim of building a community of dialogue across ideological and cultural lines. He took action in support of Czech philosopher and activist Jan Patočka who, despite the efforts of all, died in custody in Prague in 1977, and of Leszek Kołakowski, whom he welcomed at McGill for a time in the late 1960s.[40]

It was with the IIP that Klibansky expressed, through action more than through his own texts, his belief in the importance of tolerance and dialogue.[41] As president and honorary president of the IIP during and after the Cold War, Klibansky oversaw initiatives to increase the bibliographic control and dissemination of contemporary philosophical writings, and to produce translations of key texts on tolerance and liberty. A series titled Philosophy and World Community was launched with a German-English edition of Locke's *Letter on Toleration* (*Ein Brief über Toleranz* [1957]).[42] Subsequently appearing in several other languages, the collection included writings of, among others, Spinoza, Sébastien Castellion, Anthony Collins, and the Buddhist emperor Asoka of the third century BCE. Klibansky is also credited with playing a role in opening the doors of the IIP to Asian philosophy.[43]

Adding to this his large-scale project as general editor of the Nelson Philosophical Texts series, mainly on modern philosophy, his work during this period spanned the entire sweep of Western thought. Rooted in his beginnings at the KBW, Klibansky's intellectual journey not only brought to attention the tradition of tolerance of Cusa or Locke but it also opened an avenue into an erudite transmission of thought that recalls and affirms a radical pluralism, calling for open philosophical dialogue.

After he retired from McGill in 1975, Klibansky continued to live in Montreal but returned regularly to Oxford and to the Herzog August Bibliothek Wolfenbüttel, where Leibniz and Lessing had both once been librarians. He remained a frequent visitor to libraries all over Europe, especially, pursuing research into his last years. He was married for the first time in 1995 to Ethel Groffier, a professor of law, who collaborated on many of his later publications and projects.[44] His co-authored book on Apuleius's manuscripts is but one example, and is one manifestation of his ongoing interest in and attention to themes that he embarked upon in his earliest years of scholarship.[45] Patience, as well as philological, codicological, and paleographical abilities – these skills were cultivated in the years in which Klibansky was surrounded by the KBW and the diverse set of researchers it attracted. And these skills led to many discoveries, including his recognition, in a Vatican manuscript, of a forgotten text on Plato's works that he named the *Summarium Platonis librorum atque placitorum* (fig. 0.4), and which he was preparing for publication even in his final years.[46] An avid frequenter of libraries himself, Klibansky created in turn his own large and very rich library, which he ultimately donated so that it might be explored by others.[47] This library has become a valuable resource for a better understanding not only of Klibansky's intellectual universe but also of the heritage of the Warburg Library that is so strongly embedded within it.

The Warburg Library Network Project

The 2015 colloquium at the Warburg Institute was an important step toward such an understanding. Contributions were invited on three main topics: Raymond Klibansky and the Warburg Library network; the continuity of the Platonic tradition and the *Corpus Platonicum Medii Aevi*; and the *Saturn and Melancholy* project. These topics also form the general thematic sections of this volume, and their totality features a range of approaches, from source-based history to theoretical (re)think-pieces.

The first section, "Raymond Klibansky and the Warburg Library Network: Early Years and Exile," highlights the history of Klibansky's connections with and around the KBW and the Warburg Institute. Elizabeth Sears (University of Michigan) brings to light the role of Gertrud Bing at the centre of Warburg Library projects and communication, while also emphasizing the less-known figure of Walter Solmitz. Her chapter "Keepers of the Flame" focuses on shared thoughts and strategic endeavours of the three with respect to maintaining the Hamburg Warburgian tradition in the postwar era, even as a new generation came to maturity and figures including Ernst Gombrich played an ever-greater role in shaping the institute's future.

Quoting Gershom Scholem's provocative observation about the KBW being one of the most remarkable "Jewish sects" that German Jewry produced, Martin Treml (Zentrum für Literatur- und Kulturforschung Berlin)

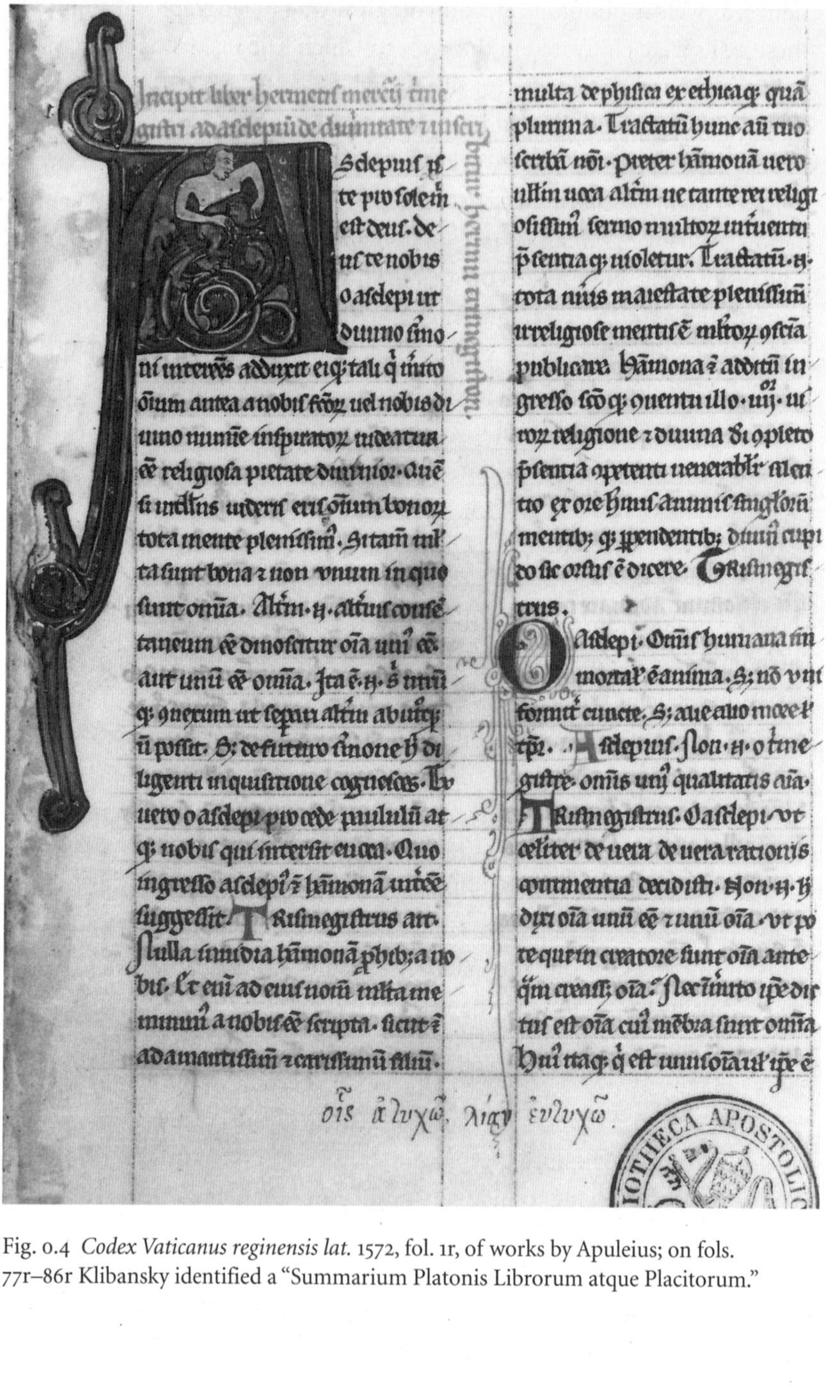

Fig. 0.4 *Codex Vaticanus reginensis lat.* 1572, fol. 1r, of works by Apuleius; on fols. 77r–86r Klibansky identified a "Summarium Platonis Librorum atque Placitorum."

considers, in "The Warburg Library within German Judaism," the role of Jewish identity and being, in the structure, dynamics, and trajectories of the self-declared (at least by Warburg) non-observant Warburg circle.

Graham Whitaker (University of Glasgow), in his chapter "The Warburg Institute Reaches Out," sheds new light on Klibansky's British networks, tracing their development and revealing their essential role in his career and the successful materialization of several Warburg Institute projects – including the Cassirer *Festschrift* and the initial volumes of the *Corpus Platonicum*.

Subsequently, Jillian Tomm (Université de Montréal) proposes, in "Tracing an Intellectual Afterlife in Library and Archival Sources," an overview of major kinds and locations of source materials available for the study of Klibansky's links with the Warburg Library network, with examples from the Raymond Klibansky Collection of McGill University, the most thoroughly documented repository to date.

Part 2 of this volume addresses the history and significance of Klibansky's publication of *The Continuity of the Platonic Tradition* (1939) and his subsequent edition of the *Corpus Platonicum Medii Aevi* (1940–62). Regina Weber (Deutsches Literaturarchiv Marbach), in her chapter, "From the Cusanus Edition to the *Corpus Platonicum*," shows how, from early on, Klibansky's mentors and colleagues – Ernst Hoffmann, Ernst Cassirer, and Fritz Saxl – were deeply invested in the path he negotiated through different ancient traditions and periods to arrive at this complex and immense project.

In "Raymond Klibansky and the *Corpus Platonicum Medii Aevi*," Georges Leroux (Université du Québec à Montréal) discusses the project launched as a vast program of edition, translation, and commentary of all known texts bearing witness to the vitality of the Platonic tradition prior to the Renaissance. In particular, he considers the *Plato Latinus* series and the quality and impact of J.H. Waszink's edition of Calcidius's commentary on Plato's *Timaeus*, and Klibansky's own edition of the *Parmenides*.

In a contribution finishing this section, Eric Méchoulan (Université de Montréal) invites us to consider the scholar as a transmitter and to look at Klibansky's agency in his publication projects as an active orientation toward an ethics of edition, a manifestation of his discourse and later work on tolerance. Thus, this text also offers an insight into more general questions of the value and relevance of intellectual history within contemporary society.

Part 3, the final section, puts together for the first time a full history of an iconic book within the history of ideas and culture, *Saturn and Melancholy* (1964), which brings different perspectives to bear on this long, complex, and personally charged story. The section is first introduced with a schematic overview of the material history of the publication of the "Melancholy Project" by Elisabeth Otto (Université de Montréal). Claudia Wedepohl (Warburg Institute London) subsequently initiates the discussion in "The Genesis, Writing, and Re-Writing of Erwin Panofsky and Fritz Saxl's *Dürers 'Melencolia I'*" by establishing the origins of their 1923 study on the famous engraving and, laying out key elements of accord and disagreement between the authors and their precursors, Karl Giehlow and Aby Warburg himself. Wedepohl also highlights the role of the friendship between Saxl and Klibansky, which led to a close scholarly collaboration and to the joint work on the revision of the book on Dürer that finally came out as *Saturn and Melancholy* in 1964.

Philippe Despoix (Université de Montréal) takes a close look at the basis for the 1923 analysis of the engraving (by Panofsky and Saxl) in its relation to that of Warburg, and charts the evolution of the argument, and of the volume overall, through the new German edition titled *Melancholie und Saturn* (fully prepared with Klibansky by 1939 but not published), the English version of 1964, and subsequent translations into French and German.

In his chapter "The Melancholy of the (Co-)Author," Davide Stimilli (Boulder University) sheds light on the genealogy of the "three-headed" *Saturn and Melancholy*, which relies heavily on Panofsky's correspondence. He illuminates the imperative role played by Panofsky's character in anxieties about the authorship of this *livre maudit* and in the shifting and fugitive nature of attribution.

Finally, Jean-Philippe Uzel (Université du Québec à Montréal) brings forth, through a reflection on "The Theme of Melancholy," a more complete picture of Klibansky's own position and imprint on this work after he had taken charge of the publication and translations of *Saturn and Melancholy* from 1964 forward. In particular, Uzel's chapter focuses on the forewords written for the French and German editions, in which Klibansky in some sense rehabilitated Aby Warburg's own work on Dürer's 1514 engraving, thus implicitly opposing Panofsky's strict iconological reading of *Melencolia I.*

This section offers a long-overdue understanding of methodological disputes at the centre of one of the twentieth century's flagship studies in cultural and art history.

The chapters in this volume thus give a unique overview that allows us to recontextualize several major works by Raymond Klibansky within their original institutional and intellectual network. These, and indeed Klibansky's lifelong endeavours and later activities in promotion of the values of tolerance and dialogue, are rooted and embedded in the philosophical erudition born of his Weimar education and connection with the Warburg circle. Exploration of the Warburg Library network, its output and its dynamics, illuminates part of the complex transfer that played an underlying yet decisive role in the development of the humanities after the Second World War. Reconstructing Klibansky's role as a crucial "node" within this network is but one example of the research that is necessary in order to understand the historical significance of the Warburg Library and its legacy.

Philippe Despoix, Georges Leroux, and Jillian Tomm

NOTES

1 Georges Leroux, curator, "Raymond Klibansky (1905–2005) – La bibliothèque d'un philosophe/A Philosopher's Library." Exhibition at the Grande Bibliothèque, Montréal (BAnQ), 13 November 2012–25 August 2013.

2 Philippe Despoix and Georges Leroux, organizers, "Raymond Klibansky and the Warburgian Legacy of the Cultural Sciences." International Workshop, Canadian Centre for German and European Studies (CCEAE, Université de Montréal), with the support of Bibliothèque et Archives nationales du Québec (BAnQ), 17–18 May 2013.

3 Philippe Despoix, Eric Méchoulan, and Jillian Tomm, organizers, "The Warburg Library Network: Geography and History of an Intellectual Afterlife. From Hamburg to London, and to Montreal: The contribution of Raymond Klibansky (1905–2005)," colloquium, the Warburg Institute, London, 18–19 June 2015. With

the support of the Centre de Recherches Intermédiales sur les arts, les lettres et les techniques (CRIalt), and CCEAE-IRTG Diversity (Université de Montréal), McGill Library, the Warburg Institute London, and the Quebec Government Office in London.

4 For a recent attempt at such an intellectual biography, see the introductory chapter to Klibansky, *Tradition antique et tolérance moderne*, 7–41. The main biographical source is Klibansky, *Le Philosophe et la mémoire du siècle.*

5 Gay, *Weimar Culture*, 1.

6 On Klibansky's experience in Heidelberg, see: Klibansky, *Le Philosophe et la mémoire du siècle*, chapters 1–4; Klibansky, "L'université allemande dans les années trente," 139–57; and a later version, "Aus dem Heidelberger Geistleben," in *Heidelberg. Geschichte und Gestalt* (Heidelberg: C. Winter, 1996), 270–83; see also "Raymond Klibansky. 15 Mai 1994" in *Erlebte Geschichte erzählt*, vol. 1, 1994–1997, *Michael Buselmeier im Gespräch mit Raymond Klibansky*... [et al.] (Heidelberg: Wunderhorn, 2000–), 8–29.

7 In his early student years, Klibansky's interest in history was also honed by his attendance at the seminars of archaeologist Ludwig Curtius (1874–1954) and philologist Otto Regenbogen (1871–1966).

8 On the character and influence of the George circle see, for example: Osterkamp, "Art History and Humanist Tradition"; Norton, *Secret Germany*; and Gay, "Secret Germany," in his *Weimar Culture.*

9 See Klibansky, *Le Philosophe et la mémoire du siècle*, 27–30.

10 Klibansky, *Ein Proklos-Fund und seine Bedeutung.*

11 Klibansky, *The Continuity of the Platonic Tradition during the Middle Ages.*

12 Some brief reflections by Klibansky on meeting Cassirer and on his relation to the Warburg Library can be read in Klibansky and Patrick Conley, "Die Grenzen des akademischen Lebens sprengen: Ein Gespräch über Ernst Cassirer und die Bibliothek Warburg," *Merkur* 50 (March 1996): 274–77.

13 Klibansky edited Charles de Bovelles's [Carolus Bovillus's] *Liber de sapiente* (Book of the wise), also known simply as *De sapiente*, as an appendix to Cassirer's *Individuum und Kosmos in der Philosophie der Renaissance*, 299–458.

14 Cassirer, *The Individual and the Cosmos in Renaissance Philosophy*, 88.

15 See Watanabe, "An Appreciation," 16–17.

16 See Nicolai de Cusa [Nicholas of Cusa], *Opera omnia*, vol. I, *De docta ignorantia*; vol. II, *Apologia Doctæ ignorantiæ*. After Klibansky had co-edited these first two volumes, the political upheaval of the 1930s interrupted his participation, but

he contributed again to the Cusa edition from the 1950s through to the 1980s. For more on the origins of the project, see Watanabe, "The Origins of Modern Cusanus Research"; on Klibansky's involvement, 33–42.

17 Klibansky, "Raymond Klibansky, philosophe et historien. Entretien avec Yves Hersant et Alain de Libera," 132.

18 Klibansky, Panofsky, and Saxl, *Saturn and Melancholy*.

19 See Eckardi, *Opera Latina*, Fasc. I, *Super oratione dominica*; and Eckardi, *Opera Latina*, Fasc. XII. *Quæstiones Parisienses*.

20 For an internal account, see Saxl, "The History of Warburg's Library," 336.

21 In 1936 the council became the Society for the Protection of Science and Learning (SPSL), which still exists.

22 See, for example, WIA, Ia.2.1.2. (Copy 1). Warburg Institute / Report [1933, unpublished draft], p. 7: "It would be of the greatest importance for the Library to secure the further sojourn of [Ernst Cassirer and Raymond Klibansky] in England."

23 See Meier, Newald, and Wind, eds., *A Bibliography on the Survival of the Classics*, vol 1. Hans Meier was a close colleague of Saxl's, and Edgar Wind, a former student of Panofsky, was also close to Cassirer and Warburg. Richard Newald's work as an important user of the KBW in part motivated the series.

24 Cf. McEwan, *Fritz Saxl*, 290.

25 See Proclus, *Commentaire sur le Parménide de Platon*, 1: vii.

26 The Warburg Institute Archive contains a great deal of evidence regarding the development of this program, among which is an early plan from 1934–35: WIA, [*Corpus Platonicum*, First Edition Plan].

27 Hendrik Waszink (1908–1990) should be also noted for his much-lauded work on the Latin version of *Timaeus* (*Plato Latinus* IV).

28 Klibansky and Paton, *Philosophy and History*.

29 The German original of this lecture was discovered in the archival material of Raymond Klibansky Collection of McGill Library (Montreal) during research for Klibansky, *Tradition antique et tolérance moderne*.

30 Klibansky defends here a post-critical conception of science, showing full philosophical fidelity to Cassirer. For the English version of this text, see "The Philosophical Character of History," 323–37. See also Groffier, "Raymond Klibansky et la quête de l'objectivité," 151–61.

31 Klibansky is circumspect about his work during the war; the most elaborated discussion is found in chapter 5 of *Le Philosophe et la mémoire du siècle*.

32 Klibansky and Hunt (eds.), *Mediaeval and Renaissance Studies*.

33 Klibansky is singled out in Stanley Frost's history of McGill for his "erudition and his sensitivity to modern currents of thought" during the 1950s and '60s, years in which questions of philosophy were themselves being much questioned: Frost, *McGill University: For the Advancement of Learning*, vol. 2, 1895–1971 (Montreal: McGill-Queen's University Press, 1984), 277.

34 See *Le Philosophe et la mémoire du siècle*, 176–84 passim, where Klibansky gives some information about Montreal's community of scholars. On Quebec thinkers, see also: his introduction to Klibansky and Boulad-Ayoub, *La pensée philosophique d'expression française au Canada*, 11–39; and his "Rencontres avec Benoît Lacroix," in *Dits et gestes de Benoît Lacroix. Prophète de l'amour et de l'esprit*, edited by Giselle Huot (Saint-Hippolyte: Éditions du Noroît, 1995), 143–5.

35 See Weber, "Aktivitäten der Warburg-Bibliothek," 100–14; and Davide Stimilli's chapter (11) in this volume.

36 Klibansky, Panofsky, and Saxl, *Saturn und Melancholie*. The Italian edition was published in 1983, and the French in 1989 with a new foreword; see Part Three of this volume.

37 Reasons for the termination of Klibansky's Eckhart edition project included his dismissal as a Jew from Heidelberg University, the seizure of his papers, his move to England, and obstructive measures taken by German authorities against his use of German-held manuscripts. In the 1930s, a second team was assembled within Germany to produce a complete edition of Eckhart's works, in this case with the approval of the government. This edition, the "Stuttgart edition," produced the now standard critical edition of Eckhart's works: Eckhart, *Die deutschen und lateinischen Werke*.

38 The most complete discussion on Klibansky's activities with the Institut international de philosophie is his *Idées sans frontières*, which contains his personal account of the institute; see also Klibansky, *Le Philosophe et la mémoire du siècle*, chapter 10. During this period Klibansky was equally active on the international stage; his teaching and research often took him abroad, and he was a visiting professor or fellow at universities in North America, Europe, Asia, and the Middle East (Indiana, 1949–50; Louvain, 1956; Rome, 1961; Genoa, 1964; Paris, 1967 and 1972; Tokyo, 1971; Tehran, 1974; Oxford, 1976–78; and Venice, 1996).

39 The IIP was of limited membership by invitation; for a complete list of members to 2004 see Klibansky, *Idées sans frontières*, 196–204.

40 Cf. Imamichi, introduction to "À la mémoire de Raymond Klibansky," 233.

41 For a collection of brief texts by Klibansky that articulate his reflections on tolerance and related topics, see Park, "Humanité et tolérance chez Raymond Klibansky," 141–9.

42 Locke, *Ein Brief über Toleranz* (bilingual English and German).

43 A summary of IIP publications is provided in the annexes of Klibansky's *Idées sans frontières.* See in particular Annex 8, 228–31 for the titles on tolerance and liberty published in the series "Philosophie et communauté mondiale/Philosophy and World Community."

44 See, for example, Groffier, "De l'amour des livres à l'amour des bibliothèques," 159–61.

45 See Klibansky and Regen, *Die Handschriften der philosophischen Werke des Apuleius.*

46 See Plato, *Summarium Platonis librorum atque placitorum.* Klibansky's discovery of the manuscript, which was previously owned by Christina of Sweden, was made shortly after the war. The manuscript was to be published, but the task was not completed. See also Klibansky, "La découverte d'un texte platonicien inconnu de l'antiquité classique," 41–51; reprinted in *Tradition antique et tolérance moderne*, 85–99. Cf. James Hankins, *Plato in the Italian Renaissance* (1: 4), where Hankins provides an alternative name for the manuscript (*De Platonis pluribus libris compendiosa expositio*); references to literature on this manuscript are in Pellegrin, *Fonds Paletta et fonds de la Reine*, 294–6.

47 On Klibansky's appreciation of the legacy of personal libraries through the centuries, see Georges Leroux's interview with Klibansky, "Des bibliothèques privées aux institutions publiques. Un parcours dans l'histoire des bibliothèques," with the collaboration of Steve Maskaleut, *L'Action nationale* 89, 7 (1999): 57–74. See also Jillian Tomm and Georges Leroux, "La collection Raymond Klibansky conservée à l'Université McGill. Présentation de la bibliothèque d'un humaniste montréalais," *Mémoires du livre / Studies in Book Culture* 5, 1 (2013), http://dx.doi.org/10.7202/1020226ar.

PART ONE

Raymond Klibansky and the Warburg Library Network: Early Years and Exile

Fig. 1.1 Gertrud Bing (in centre) celebrated as she becomes director of the Warburg Institute, 1955. Ernst Gombrich (10th from left), Otto Kurz (12th), Frances Yates (13th), Charles Mitchell (18th), Rudolf Wittkower (20th), Walter Solmitz (23rd), Hugo Buchthal (25th).

ONE

Keepers of the Flame: Bing, Solmitz, Klibansky, and the Continuity of the Warburg Tradition

ELIZABETH SEARS

In 1955, just three years short of mandatory retirement, Gertrud Bing was made director of the Warburg Institute (fig.1.1).[1] It was a strategic appointment. The institute had been jolted by rapid changes in leadership in the immediate past: Fritz Saxl, successor to the founder, Aby Warburg, had died suddenly in office in 1948, and his friend and successor, Henri Frankfort, had taken ill and died in 1954, just five years into his tenure. Bing would act as a stabilizing force: a member of the original inner circle in Hamburg, she was at once a proven administrator and a bearer of memory. Originally appointed by Saxl, she had come permanently onto the staff of the Kulturwissenschaftliche Bibliothek Warburg (KBW) in Hamburg in 1922 and had served as Warburg's research assistant in the years just before his death in 1929. Then and later, as Saxl's partner, she had worked unceasingly to preserve Warburg's intellectual legacy. After the Nazi *Machtergreifung*, applying her energies to practicalities, she had played a significant role in the physical transfer of the KBW to London in 1933, and in the years that followed she had been intimately involved in the business of integrating the newly named Warburg Institute into an alien, if welcoming, academic culture – a process ongoing even in 1955.

The library had kept moving, building to building, in a remarkable way, and a brief history of its transfers effectively reveals times and tensions. Bing would oversee each major reinstallation of property – books, photos, archive, equipment, furnishings – beginning with the first move. In 1925–26 a new library building, purpose-built and expensive, funded by the Warburg family, had gone up in the empty lot beside Aby Warburg's private home in Hamburg.[2] As the books were shifted next door, much collective thought was given as to how Warburg's methodological purposes might best be facilitated. On four floors – dedicated respectively to image, orientation, word, and action – primary and secondary sources were placed in meaningful sequences, under headings and subheadings conceived so as to demonstrate the interconnectedness of domains of knowledge and lead the scholar to reflect upon the processes of cultural memory and the changing orientation of man to the world, from antiquity to the European present. Bing worked with Saxl and Edgar Wind (appointed to the staff in 1928),[3] as well as with favoured assistants, including Walter Solmitz and Raymond Klibansky, to refine the system.

Soon came the hushed move from Hamburg to London, where the library reopened in May 1934, in a long suite of rooms on the ground floor of Thames House, a new office block in Westminster.[4] The next transfer took place after an especially anxious time: the initial three-year guarantee of space and funding was scheduled to come to an abrupt end in December 1936. Only after a new seven-year plan had been crafted could the library be rehoused in a curious set of rooms in the Imperial Institute Buildings, a Victorian structure in South Kensington that was partly managed by the University of London. With the war came the need to evacuate the holdings. During the Blitz, the German staff and some friends moved outside London to a country house, The Lea, in Denham. There work continued: a library of some ten thousand books, organized in Warburg fashion, had been cobbled together, largely from private libraries. Bing would write in September 1941: "I do not think that there is any other place in England at the moment where you will find 3 or 4 scholars of an evening, seriously engaged on research as if the world was not at all in the topsy-turvy state that it actually is in."[5] In November 1944, the seven-year plan having expired, the Warburg Institute was officially incorporated into the University of London. After war's end, beginning in August 1945, books were retrieved and reshelved in the Imperial Institute Buildings, on the understanding that the library would one day move to purpose-built quarters on the university site in Bloomsbury in north London. This promise was to be fulfilled during Bing's tenure as director. In accepting the post, she was in fact agreeing to orchestrate one final move, this time with a measure of control over design and outfitting. The new reading room opened in May 1958.

Bing took the reins at a critical historical juncture. The roots and purpose of the enterprise were fading from collective memory as the number of affiliated scholars who had known Warburg or worked in the KBW dwindled. In a letter of January 1957 to the prominent British art historian Kenneth Clark, who had heard Warburg speak in Rome in January 1929, Bing grumbled: "It is a little annoying to see how every scribbler on iconography thinks he is doing what Warburg did."[6] The imperative that had driven the prewar institute staff had, of course, lost urgency: a library of books and a tradition of learning had been saved from Nazi depredations. Now, in rather dreary postwar Britain (where food rationing persisted as late as 1954), the task to be undertaken was that of maintaining a defining mission, keeping on point, even while adapting to rapidly changing cultural conditions – a tension in the trajectory of any long-lived institution. For Bing, of course, friendships with members of the Hamburg circle took on importance. Among these colleagues were Walter Solmitz and Raymond Klibansky, two students of philosophy and philology who had worked at the KBW in the mid-1920s and whose own friendship reached back even further, to their schooldays: they had met in 1918 at the experimental Odenwaldschule, where they bonded while reading Homer and Plato together.[7] Remaining true to the Warburg cause across the years, from a distance, they were perhaps more conservatively loyal to the tradition than Bing herself. In the 1950s, as correspondence reveals, all three gave thought to ways of keeping the Hamburgian flame alive.

In the Inner Circle: Gertrud Bing, Walter Solmitz, and Raymond Klibansky at the KBW

Bing

Saxl appointed Gertrud Bing to the post of librarian of the KBW not long after she had completed a doctorate in philosophy at the newly founded University of Hamburg. Supervisors for her dissertation, "The Concept of the

Necessity in Lessing: A Contribution to the Intellectual-Historical Problem Leibniz-Lessing," were Robert Petsch (known especially for his work on dramatic form) and Ernst Cassirer (who played a pivotal role in Warburg's thinking through his work on symbolic forms).[8] The fact that Bing had demonstrated a broad intellectual range, touching upon issues including aesthetics, the philosophy of history and religion, and dramatic theory in her investigation, would from Saxl's point of view have been a good, indeed necessary, credential for the post.

Bing arrived at the KBW when Warburg himself was absent from Hamburg: suffering from severe mental illness, he had been placed by the family in Ludwig Binswanger's clinic in Kreuzlingen.[9] In 1919 Saxl, a Viennese art historian who had himself first come into Warburg's orbit in 1910, had agreed to direct the library as an interim measure. He had soon energetically effected change, inaugurating two publication series, *Studien* and *Vorträge* (*Studies* and *Lectures*), and seeking to rationalize the library's acquisition policy and its cataloguing system. When in 1924, against expectation, Warburg returned to Hamburg to take control of his library, Bing was there and, during the scholar's last five years, came to occupy a special place. As his assistant, she supported his research, thought with him, and even accompanied him on two trips to Italy, all the while being tutored in his methods. After Warburg's death, fittingly enough, the family put her in charge of preparing an edition of Warburg's collected writings (*Gesammelte Schriften*), which, ambitiously, was to include the unpublished fragments of unfinished works. Things started well: in 1932, shortly before Hitler came to power, Bing saw through press a thoroughly annotated re-edition of writings that Warburg had published during his lifetime.[10] But in the difficult times ahead the project faltered and would weigh on her conscience over the decades.

Tough-minded, critical, generous, and loyal, Bing played an essential role in sustaining the Warburg enterprise. Aby's nephew Eric would later say that Saxl and she, especially after Warburg's death, gave "Leben, Sinn und wissenschaftliche Bedeutung" ("life, meaning, and scholarly significance") to the Warburg Library.[11] She was apparently effective as a gatekeeper, judging whether a given scholar merited effort and attention.[12] Once admitted into the circle, the scholar would receive every help, and favours would be expected in return. The Warburgians were convinced that the way to learn method was to tackle an authentic scholarly problem, using the library, with their help. Promising young men and women, many of them studying art history at the university under Erwin Panofsky, Saxl's long-time collaborator, were taken on as assistants and trained. They learned method by cataloguing books or undertaking any of the myriad tasks associated with in-house publishing: checking facts and footnotes, compiling bibliographies, reading proofs, acquiring photographs, sometimes making far-flung research trips. Solmitz and Klibansky were two of the young recruits, welcomed with particular enthusiasm because they were students of classical philology and philosophy rather than art history, and therefore could support the library's wider interdisciplinary initiatives. At the KBW it was an article of belief that the afterlife of classical antiquity could be effectively tracked only along multiple, intersecting paths.[13]

Solmitz

Walter Solmitz came to the KBW through Cassirer.[14] Edith Geheeb, the wife of Paul Geheeb, who had founded the Odenwaldschule in 1910, was a cousin of Cassirer and, seeing that Walter was keen on philosophy, arranged the introduction. Solmitz visited Hamburg in 1922, met Cassirer, attended lectures, and left impressed. Although Solmitz, with Klibansky, started his university study at Heidelberg and later spent periods there and in Berlin, his primary intellectual home from the winter semester of 1924 was Hamburg. Later he would claim that his most significant teachers were Cassirer (Philosophy), Warburg (Cultural Study and Historical Psychology), and, at Heidelberg, Otto Regenbogen (Classical Philology).[15] A gentle soul who seems always to have engendered trust and liking in the people around him, Solmitz would spark the admiration of Warburg, who saw in him a future collaborator, a scholar who might "bear the torch of German-Jewish intellectuality."[16]

Solmitz was quickly integrated into the life of the KBW. His work in the library, beginning in 1927, was deemed exemplary, and he was accordingly entrusted with decisions about the placement of books. In the winter semester of 1927–28, with Bing, he sat in on Warburg's seminar on methods for an art-historical cultural science.[17] He also received private initiation into the most esoteric reaches of Warburg's thought. On a July morning in 1928,

Warburg, using one of his composite pictorial plates, instructed Solmitz on what he called "the two-fold nature of the artistic shaping process" – in the background a setting of the boundary by means of the material type (*Typus*) and in the foreground a dynamic pointing to the future through the momentary physiognomic sign.[18] By such means Solmitz acquired the expertise to interpret Warburg's theory of expression. Increasingly included in Warburg family events, he was invited in August 1928 to attend an in-house demonstration that Warburg gave of his culminating endeavour, the unfinished pictorial atlas called *Mnemosyne* (*Memory*).[19] He was the one student who would speak at Warburg's funeral in October 1929.[20]

In the new era, after Warburg's death, the KBW staff continued to enlist Solmitz's aid. Saxl relied on him when preparing a talk for the German Society for Psychology on a key aspect of Warburg's thought, "Die Ausdrucksgebärden in der bildenden Kunst" ("Expressive Gestures in the Pictorial Arts").[21] Solmitz, too, became involved in Bing's project of re-editing Warburg's published writings. In 1931, when she was in Florence, letters shuttled back and forth. Once Saxl, Wind, and Solmitz had received the ungainly set of trial proofs back from the publisher Teubner, they ruminated together about layout: how could the two sets of annotations (Warburg's own later comments and Bing's updating commentary) best be displayed in relation to the texts?[22] Solmitz also became engaged in questions of content. A surviving typed text likely belonged to the bundle (*Konvolut*) that Bing received from him in Florence: here he reflected on the nature of the edition (historical-critical) and put his mind to the meaning of the enigmatic set of precepts, the "Vier Thesen" ("Four Theses"), that Warburg had appended to his doctoral dissertation on Botticelli's *Birth of Venus* and *Primavera* (1893).[23] Bing expressed her gratitude to all of her "stern redaction committee" back in Hamburg but singled out Solmitz, thanking him for the effort he had put into his well-reasoned critique and worrying, too, that he had again delayed his own work.[24]

Modest to the point of crippling self-doubt, Solmitz would in fact rarely bring projects to completion. He long struggled, unsuccessfully, to write a dissertation under Cassirer on the problem of the symbol. In February 1929, he still hoped to finish by the autumn,[25] and in the summer of 1931 a concerned Saxl arranged that he be supported by a monthly stipend from the Warburg Bank: two years of intense work, secluded in the Bavarian countryside, yielded much thought but no dissertation.[26] The lack of a degree, and all that it implied, would complicate Solmitz's later life. He would again be employed by the KBW from 1 October 1933 to the end of January 1934. At this poignant juncture, his task was to help Bing dismantle the library and pack it up for shipment to London. Solmitz stayed behind in Germany as others of the Warburg circle emigrated: the KBW staff, Cassirer, Panofsky, and his friend Klibansky.

Klibansky

If less constant a presence at the KBW than Solmitz, Klibansky was the greater force. Like Solmitz, he had entered the circle at a young age. Invited by Cassirer to study in Hamburg for a time, he lived during the academic year 1926/27 in the Cassirer domicile, was introduced to Warburg, and became committed to the cause. Klibansky was productive, proactive, entrepreneurial, quick to offer opinion. He finished his degrees at Heidelberg with lightning speed: doctorate 1928, *Habilitation* 1932. When he became a *Privatdozent* at Heidelberg at age twenty-six, even Saxl, full of admiration for his gifts, worried that this was too young.[27] Through his editorial work on the writings of the fifteenth-century Dominican theologian Nicolaus Cusanus (Nicholas of Cusa), and the Latin texts of the fourteenth-century mystic Meister Eckhart, and texts by the twelfth-century members of the "School of Chartres," Klibansky became aware of the persistence of the Platonic tradition in European thought, and he would in time work with Saxl to launch a collaborative endeavour to recover and re-present crucial texts.[28] He would always be more Saxl's man than Warburg's, but he would regard Warburg as one of his teachers, and Warburg would recognize his capacities. In September 1929, Warburg inserted a striking encomium in the institutional diary: "Klibansky has universally vibrating thought-tentacles."[29]

Like other recruits, Klibansky learned Warburg's method through work in the library and assistance with publications. When in 1926 the books were transferred to the new building, he was given the task of arranging the core sections devoted to Philosophy, Encyclopedias, and Classical Studies.[30] More confidently assertive than Solmitz, Klibansky would point out lacunae in the library holdings, suggest lectures, propose initiatives. Saxl was pleased to draw on Klibansky's critical acumen and prodigious learning, which lay in areas crucial to the Warburg enterprise, including the history of philosophy, religion, and science. When in 1927 the KBW published Cassirer's *Individuum und Kosmos in der Philosophie der Renaissance* (*Individual and Cosmos in Renaissance Philosophy*), Klibansky, then aged twenty-one, provided as an appendix an edition of Charles de Bovelles's *Liber de sapiente*.[31] It was to Klibansky that Saxl turned when he and Panofsky embarked on a revised version of their co-authored book of 1923, *Dürers 'Melencolia I': Eine quellen- und typengeschichtliche Untersuchung*.[32] Klibansky attributed the invitation to his criticism that the authors had failed to do justice to the philosophical and theological roots of the concept of melancholy.[33] By 1928 he was periodically sending packets of relevant information to be integrated into the new edition.[34] All along, even while working in Heidelberg on his editorial projects, Klibansky continued to take on tasks for the KBW. In 1931 he helped correct proofs of Bing's edition of Warburg's writings.[35] When in 1934 the KBW launched its *Kulturwissenschaftliche Bibliographie zum Nachleben der Antike* – a series offering brief reviews of publications relevant to the greater Warburg project – Klibansky was a chief contributor. For the first volume, treating publications that had appeared in 1931, he supplied eighty-one entries, Bing forty-three, and Solmitz one.[36]

In the summer of 1933 Klibansky made a significant intervention in institutional history. The fallout from the promulgation of the "Aryan Paragraph" in April of that year, prohibiting persons of Jewish descent from working in state-run institutions, had been great. Owing to dismissals and resignations from the university, the KBW circle dissolved, and Klibansky lost his teaching post at Heidelberg in early August.[37] Saxl would later credit Klibansky with the notion of pulling up institutional stakes: "The idea of moving the Warburg Library from Hamburg to another intellectual centre, in which it could continue as a living source of scientific research and provide for a group of scholars a centre of culture and learning, emanates from Dr. Klibansky."[38] Corroborative testimony comes from Klibansky who, early in 1935, precariously established in England, declined a two-year research post at the University of Glasgow:

> It is in the first instance the collaboration with the Warburg Institute that determined my resolution: As it is partly owing to my own initiative that the Warburg Library has been transferred to London, with a

> view of trying to establish an Anglo-German school of history and philosophy of civilisation, I must not now leave it in the present primary stages of this development.[39]

Others, of course, had determined where and how the library might move. Saxl, Wind, and the Warburg family, along with a cohort of English friends, undertook the complex negotiations that resulted in the KBW coming to London.[40] The nascent Academic Assistance Council (AAC) – founded to help displaced German scholars, "refugees from Nazi oppression" – became involved early on: the Warburg Library was an agenda item for the first two meetings, held in June 1933.[41] The Warburgians would subsequently work with and through this organization – which in 1936 would be restructured and renamed the SPSL (Society for the Protection of Science and Learning) – smoothing the path for many refugees. Klibansky and, later, Solmitz were among the beneficiaries.

Hard Times and the Help of the Academic Assistance Council

At the time of the move, Saxl's aim had been to bring as many of the inner circle over to Britain as possible, and not only staff members. Saxl took a special interest in the fates of Cassirer and Klibansky. In September 1933, when Cassirer was about to accept an invitation to become a Chichele Lecturer at All Souls College for the following year, Saxl journeyed to Oxford with him,[42] and he also lobbied hard for Klibansky, who had arrived in London, via Paris, in August.[43] In January 1934, Klibansky was made a member of the Senior Common Room at Oriel College, Oxford, and in March he was given an Honorary Lectureship at King's College, University of London.[44] Saxl included him in the Warburg Institute's activities: in June 1935, Klibansky offered the course "Platonism in the Middle Ages and Renaissance" and in the spring of the following year, the class "Readings in Medieval Philosophy."[45] Saxl backed his initiatives, chief among them the *Corpus Platonicum Medii Aevi*, offering learned editions of neglected Latin and Arabic texts. The AAC/SPSL would long support this series: Klibansky received the first of the grants on 1 November 1933.[46] Through the *Corpus Platonicum* later refugees would be helped, including members of the Warburg circle, not only

Klibanksy's Heidelberg colleague Lotte Labowsky[47] but also, when he most needed it, Solmitz.

The circle around the Warburg Institute slowly expanded in the pre-war era as British friendships were forged and continental scholars unable or unwilling to work in their homelands passed through or settled in England. Saxl, of Viennese origin, monitored conditions in Austria with growing alarm. His friend Ernst Kris, an art historian and Freudian analyst, recommended Ernst Gombrich as promising: a student of Italian Renaissance art, he was collaborating with Kris on the subject of caricature, its origins, and principles – a topic attractive to the Warburgians, who were keen on the study of physiognomy, gesture, and expression. Bing needed help with the editing of Warburg's writings, especially the incomplete Atlas; Gombrich arrived in 1936 for a temporary stay, took up the task with interest, and in 1937 made England his home. Surveying Warburg's chaotic literary remains, he soon came to the unsettling opinion that an edition would be impossible, that it would be better to try to characterize and contextualize Warburg's thinking, drawing on the fragments.[48] The project was suspended at the outbreak of war, and Gombrich worked for six years monitoring German broadcasts at the BBC listening post, becoming something of an expert on propaganda. During the war, he kept in sporadic touch with the Warburgians, visiting Denham from time to time and returning to the institute in December 1945.[49]

Solmitz's history in these same years was a harsh one. Until it was prohibited, he taught some introductory courses in philosophy at the Jüdisches Lehrhaus (Jewish School) in Hamburg; in 1935, he returned to Bavaria, where he continued to study and write. Klibansky, co-editing *Philosophy and History*, a *Festschrift* in Cassirer's honour, had his friend help compile the bibliography of the philosopher's writings appended to the text.[50] In April 1936, Solmitz acquired a travel visa and was able to make a brief trip to England.[51] But later, even when an American uncle had provided an affidavit for him to enter the United States, it proved impossible to leave. In November 1938, Solmitz was arrested in an "action against the Jews" and taken to the concentration camp at Dachau. Klibansky and the Warburgians were desperate and took a series of steps to facilitate his release: they composed an invitation for him to join them in their work on the *Corpus Platonicum*, provided a guarantee, and pressed the British Consulate in Munich as well as the Home Office to issue a transit visa. Six weeks after his arrest, Solmitz was released from camp, and the Solmitzes escaped from Germany.[52] Bing met them at the airport one day in January 1939 and helped them settle while they waited to continue their travels. In time, Solmitz would be awarded a grant from the SPSL to work on the *Corpus Platonicum*; it was renewed four times.[53] In May 1940, with the world at war, the American visa at last came through, valid for just one month, and the Solmitzes scrambled to book a cross-Atlantic passage. Dismayingly, the tickets they had purchased in Germany proved invalid, and to pay their way they were forced to rely on a loan from the SPSL. After an unsettled period, in 1941 Solmitz received a fellowship from Harvard, where he was awarded an MA in 1943, after which he worked occasionally as a teaching fellow. Only in the summer of 1946, with the help of a Hamburg friend, Fritz Koelln, professor of German, would he land at peaceful Bowdoin College in Brunswick, Maine, as an instructor, and later as assistant professor, teaching German and in time philosophy as well. The final repayment of the loan to the SPSL in the summer of 1949 marked the effective end of an era.[54] By this point he would be back in touch with the Warburgians.

Klibansky had quite a different war. Having become a British citizen in 1938, he was brought into the Secret Service as a political intelligence officer and given major responsibilities. First dealing with the German theatre, he applied his "historico-logical method" to propaganda received so as to derive enemy intentions. In 1942, with the invasion of Italy in view, he was placed in charge of creating an Italian Intelligence and spent the next two years relentlessly engaged in this task.[55] He nevertheless managed sporadically to keep in touch with the Warburg circle. Work on the *Corpus Platonicum* naturally lagged, although Klibansky's introduction, *The Continuity of the Platonic Tradition*, was published in 1939, and the first volume of the series appeared in 1940.[56] Another Klibanskian project that Saxl endorsed, however, the launch of a new journal, *Mediaeval and Renaissance Studies*, made surprising headway. Saxl defined it as being "concerned with the classical tradition in pure thought and religion," comparing it to the recently inaugurated *Journal of the Warburg and Courtauld Institutes*, which had to do with the "classical tradition in the creative arts."[57] The first number, reprinted in England after the German invasion of Belgium had halted production in Bruges, appeared in 1941, and the second followed in 1943.[58] Five more volumes would see the light of day – in 1950, 1954, 1958, 1961, and 1968 – one of the pre-war projects that Klibansky doggedly pursued into the postwar era.

Keepers of the Flame

When the Warburg Institute reopened in 1945, it was as a part of the University of London with new curricular responsibilities. Just which of the scattered friends would return to the fold and precisely what role the institute would play in the new era remained to be seen. An exhausted Saxl summoned the energy to promote an ambitious collaborative enterprise, a twenty-year project to produce an encyclopaedia of the Middle Ages and the Renaissance. In 1945, and again in 1946, he travelled to the United States to drum up interest and funding, neither of which was ultimately forthcoming.[59] But there he was able to renew friendships and meet up with colleagues who had immigrated, including Solmitz and Wind. The meeting with the latter hardly went as planned. Wind, who had been caught in the United States at the outbreak of war, was then living in Northampton, occupying a temporary visiting position at Smith College, having resigned a professorship at the University of Chicago with the intention of returning to London and the Warburg Institute.[60] Now, in June 1945, he and Saxl looked to the future of the institute, and Wind, unimpressed by the encyclopaedia project ("a flight into conventionality"), and unhappy with the place he was to be assigned in the structure of the postwar institute, dramatically severed ties in a letter addressed to Bing. A parting shot: "the moment may come when the Warburg Institute is no longer the most suitable place for developing Warburg's methods and ideas."[61]

Not long afterward, in December 1945, Bing wrote a lengthy letter, in German, to Solmitz, in which she ruminated about the postwar state of things. She made mention of Wind's decision, which hurt, especially as the Warburg-Saxl-Wind succession had seemed to her the most logical.[62] She spoke of other acquaintances, including Klibansky, who was at a crossroads, having to decide whether to leave a highly paid government job, in which he had great responsibility and a certain influence, or to serve scholarship in a more modest position.[63] Her worries were great. She sensed that many of the best, most humane "Warburg" traditions were now hanging in the balance, that the temptation was too great to get along with less than the best – though she placed hope in the enthusiasm of the young English recruits, Frances Yates and Charles Mitchell. Inevitably turning to the problem of the publication of Warburg's collected writings, she noted how happy she was that Solmitz was rekindling his interest in Warburg's unpublished "Aesthetic Fragments." Her own path was not clear. She knew she could not go it alone. Could someone else? Was Gombrich the right man? Would the biography Saxl was writing accomplish what was hoped? She was coming to wonder if, beyond personal obligations, it was really still necessary to edit the Atlas and the other fragments. Current "Warburgian" scholarship was distant from the person of Warburg. Perhaps, she reflected, he would simply be one of those many whose true image lived on only in the hearts of their friends and died with them. Still, as she wrote to Solmitz, "for us," it remained a personal obligation to make at least one more attempt to edit his writings according to the original plan.

Wind's defection having thrust the succession into disarray, it seemed increasingly important to keep Klibansky involved in institute affairs. Saxl tried to enlist his aid in the encyclopaedia, just as he was leaving his government post in 1946.[64] In 1947 the Warburgians offered him the post of Director of Studies and Reader in the History of the Classical Tradition and did their all to encourage him to take it. Bing wrote that Saxl would then "feel the Institute was safe, in strong hands."[65] But Klibansky had decided to try out a teaching position at McGill University. When, after six months back at the Warburg Institute, he chose to accept a permanent post there, as the Frothingham Professor of Logic and Metaphysics, Warburgian disappointment was acute.[66] Still Saxl steadfastly supported Klibansky's several projects – the *Corpus Platonicum*, *Mediaeval and Renaissance Studies*, and the postwar English reworking of *Dürers 'Melencolia I'* – thereby committing the Warburg Institute to vast editorial labour in the coming two decades. Klibansky was made an Honorary Fellow of the Institute in 1949 and would typically spend a part of every year in London. When in Canada, he kept up a steady correspondence, sending a staggering quantity of directives concerning editorial minutiae. Following a practice that had begun in 1940–41, he would each year append a statement on the progress of the *Corpus Platonicum* to the Warburg Institute Annual Report.

In October 1945 Solmitz had tentatively renewed contact with Klibansky. Aware of his friend's stressful wartime activities, calling himself an *Etappenschwein* ("a soldier with a job safe from danger"), he wrote: "Without the slightest rational justification, I am counting on meeting you again, some time. I really count on that."[67] Soon the friends were living just 250 miles apart, Solmitz in Maine, and Klibansky in Montreal, and the old friendship was revived. Klibansky again began involving Solmitz in his projects. When, for example, in the early 1950s he made an effort to help the ailing Odenwaldschule, he enlisted Solmitz's aid in fundraising; and he kept Solmitz informed when, in 1952, he nominated Paul Geheeb, the school's founder, for a Nobel Peace Prize, even though fairly certain that Albert Schweitzer would get it that year (which he did).[68] To serve Warburg's legacy, and to give Solmitz direction, Klibansky began conspiring with Bing to bring him over to the Warburg Institute for a year. Solmitz duly applied for a Fulbright fellowship (unsuccessfully) and then (successfully) for a grant from the American Philosophical Society.[69] In the latter, he gave this account of his proposed project:

> *Volume III* (unpublished writings) is supposed to include some of Warburg's more theoretical work as distinguished from the historical studies of the first two volumes. In addition to, though in close connection with, his historical work, Warburg worked, from 1890 on throughout his life, on a general "Pragmatic Theory of Human Expression" (*Pragmatische Ausdruckskunde*), and, in fact, regarded his historical studies as material for such a general work the conception of which led him to extending his research into the fields of ethnology, anthropology, social (historical) psychology, and philosophy. One of his "pragmatic" interests was that of freeing the human mind from some dangerous forms of superstition by understanding thoroughly their roots and their propagation throughout the ages. His general theory was to clarify the role which symbolic thought plays in the various stages and the various fields of human activity, in every day life as well as in social, artistic, and intellectual endeavours.

Solmitz supplied his credentials and indicated that Saxl's successor, Henri Frankfort, had been brought on board: "I have had the good fortune of having both Professor Warburg and Professor Cassirer as my teachers during the time of their closest collaboration. Professor Frankfort, the present Director of the Warburg Institute, has expressed the wish that at some time a study be made of Warburg's way of thought, similar to the one which I published on Cassirer's way of thought." Solmitz was referring to a ruminative essay that he had recently published – "Cassirer on Galileo: An Example of Cassirer's Way of Thought" – in which he sought "to sketch briefly the formal schematism by which Cassirer's thought proceeds."[70]

Bing had been keen that Solmitz, as interpreter of the tradition, meet Frankfort. The Dutch scholar, an illustrious specialist in ancient Near Eastern art, Saxl and Bing's friend, was leaving a post at the Oriental Institute of the University of Chicago to come to the Warburg Institute as director and "Professor of the History of Pre-Classical Antiquity."[71] Solmitz and Frankfort arranged a rendezvous in New York in March 1949 and clearly hit it off. Afterward Bing wrote to Klibansky that Solmitz had "in his old way which I know and like so well, evidently succeeded in giving Frankfort a picture of Warburg which was new to Frankfort, and which stimulated him a great deal."[72] Solmitz for his part left hopeful. To Klibansky he wrote: "I personally felt greatly relieved and encouraged by the fact that a man was found who impressed me as the man 'born' for the job of continuing Saxl's work (just as Saxl never 'replaced' Warburg, but continued and carried *on* his work in a manner completely unforeseeable at the time of Warburg's death in 1929)."[73]

In the meantime, Gombrich's star had been rising, and ultimately, of course, it would be his position with respect to the Warburg tradition that would determine the future of the institution. He, like Klibansky, had had a choice to make: in his case to continue at the BBC, fairly lucratively, or, as the Warburgians hoped, return to the Warburg Institute and take up his academic career.[74] Provided with a three-year senior research fellowship (1946–48), he rejoined the community in December 1945, on the understanding that he would continue to work on Warburg's papers while pursuing his own scholarly interests. By the end of the following summer, Gombrich had completed four chapters of a book on Warburg's method; simultaneously, Saxl was making progress on his own biography of Warburg (reaching the year 1915).[75]

Before Saxl died in 1948, Gombrich had finished a draft. His interpretations made Saxl and Bing most uneasy, however, and it was ultimately decided to suspend publication until Gombrich's book could be "integrated with the other publications on Warburg" under preparation.[76] At the same time, he was one of their own: in 1948, he was appointed a lecturer and became involved in the teaching activities now required of the institute. His reputation would begin to skyrocket with the publication of the blockbuster survey, *The Story of Art* (1950), and he was becoming known in the United States. With Kris's support, Gombrich won a Rockefeller fellowship for a three-month visit in 1949, with the purpose, as Kris put it, of learning about new currents and, more specifically, seeing how psychological study might be integrated into art criticism.[77] In 1954 Gombrich was offered a post at Columbia University, which he declined, citing in part the freedoms allowed him in London and his loyalty to the Warburg Institute.[78] Accolades continued to come his way. Always retaining a home base at the institute, he served as Slade Professor at Oxford (1951–53) and then as Durning-Lawrence Professor at the Slade School of Fine Art, University College, London (1956–59). In 1956 he delivered the A.W. Mellon Lectures in the Fine Arts at the National Gallery of Art in Washington, lectures that would lead in time to his classic *Art and Illusion: A Study in the Psychology of Pictorial Representation* (1960). Gombrich was a possible successor to Frankfort as director of the Warburg Institute in 1955 and the obvious successor to Bing in 1959.[79] But his stance with respect to Warburg's legacy was inevitably distinct from that of KBW alumni.

Solmitz and family arrived in London for the 1954/55 academic year, when Bing was acting director, not long after tragedy had struck: Frankfort, diagnosed with a brain tumor, had died in mid-July 1954. Solmitz was present to observe Bing's surprise when she was chosen to be director and professor of the classical tradition, even though (as all were aware) she had published little and had never taught. Bing wrote to Klibansky that she took her unconventional appointment to be a sign that the university thought the tradition worth preserving: "All I can, and want to, achieve is to concentrate on essentials and consolidate the development which Saxl's premature death had interrupted and even threatened to shatter."[80] Solmitz and Klibansky agreed that her appointment was a good interim solution, Solmitz noting that "continuity was preserved."[81]

In London, Solmitz was given access to Warburg's papers and directed his attention to how Volume III might be conceived. As is clear from surviving notes and letters, he discussed Warburg's method with the strong-minded Gombrich, who, of course, had spent more time than Solmitz with Warburg's papers, and more recently. The conversations clearly shook him. Solmitz writing (in German) to Klibansky, was prepared to praise Gombrich as "very intelligent, well-read, versatile, with a markedly journalistic aptitude that also manifests itself in his teaching." He acknowledged that Gombrich had an impressive intellectual reach: an overview of the most diverse areas of institute inquiry. But Solmitz was deeply unsettled by Gombrich's skepticism, wondering whether his position was owed to Popperian positivism or to his Vienna lineage or both.[82] He indicated that he was trying to turn the newfound "methodological doubt" to advantage. Sheets and sheets of notes survive in his hand, presumably from just this time, in which he struggled to organize his observations and find criteria for assessing the value and validity of Warburg's thought. He worried about how powerful Warburg's actual presence had been: "Was the listener, perhaps, so much under the spell of Warburg's personality that he mistook for objectively significant something that was only the powerful expression of a subjective, personal experience?"[83] Here, a representative sequence of Solmitz's thoughts, which he wrote out in English:

> Warburg "enacted" as it were the drama he had written about humanity, and the drama he had written about humanity was the dramatization of his own conflicts. The dramatization of a personal conflict, both objectifies it and puts it on a larger scale. The enactment, the performance of the drama makes it more impressive than the mere reading of it … Will the writings be valid even without the presence of the "living proof"?[84] And is the impression justified that Warburg's personal experience corresponds, in a sense, to that of humanity itself? – Or are his teachings only a "projection" of his own personal emotions into history? … More generally: there is no doubt any longer that Warburg's approach to historical investigations has been fruitful and has inaugurated a new kind of historical research. Still, what about his own thought – the way in which he interpreted the factual relationships he discovered? … It is a singular kind of thought and quite unusual …

Its very "unusualness" and "singularity" and "extraordinariness" is apt to lead to several kinds of reserve with regard to it – a reserve from respect or a reserve from doubt. Both kinds of reserve may lead to indifference. An analysis of Warburg's way of thought may serve to overcome this indifference.

It was Warburg's style of thinking, his singular *Denkweise*, that interested Solmitz, and he earnestly endeavoured to map out the projected edition and find ways to present his sense of Warburg's intellectual contribution.[85] Yet, little tangible progress was made.[86]

Doubtless making Solmitz's task more difficult was his sense that the Warburg Institute was moving away from him. In a letter to Klibansky he broke the problem down, putting "we" and "the Institute" in opposition. Under the first heading, "Wir und das Institut," he drew an extended sartorial metaphor, distinguishing between shirt and jacket, *Hemd* and *Rock*: "The shirt lies closer to our own being than does the jacket of the Institute, however prized and useful. So long as the Institute does not identify with our shirt, we cannot fully identify with its jacket, which doesn't mean that the jacket as jacket can't still play an essential role." Turning to "Das Institut und wir," he observed: "Bing is at the moment, I believe, the only person who is *really* concerned about us (perhaps Mitchell as well)." For him, Popperianism was the issue. He concluded: "Objectively (!) seen, it would be good for the Institute, and fitting, if beyond 'Vienna' and 'England,' 'Hamburg' too (and not only through Bing) showed to greater advantage."[87] Solmitz planned to visit, albeit rarely, in the future.

In a letter that crossed Solmitz's in the mail, Klibansky, encouraging Solmitz, showed contrasting decisiveness: "I wish I had time to outline a constructive programme which I have in mind. – The centre of gravity is now much on the Art Historical side. I am sure you perform an important function in reminding the Institute that art is one of the facets of interest, but that a very idea of the Institute requires that other manifestations of *psyche* and other activities of *nous* – not the least that of thought – be studied in their own right and in their relation to the 'grand total.'"[88] Neither Saxl, nor Bing, nor Gombrich would have disagreed.

When Bing wrote to Solmitz that Gombrich had been designated as her successor, and that she thought this much the best alternative, he responded in a lengthy letter. If he felt some regret that "ein newcomer to the family" had been chosen, Solmitz acknowledged Gombrich's capacities. He was also aware of the "(sociological) natural history of 'academies,'" where inevitably the following generations overemphasize and pursue one side, and then the schisms occur, "etc. etc." Above all he knew that, gradually, he and Bing had come to an age where they had to see themselves as "historical." The Warburg Institute could not be a fortress: "ein feste Warburg" (playing on the words of Martin Luther's hymn); rather it must be understood as a nursery (*Pflanzstätte*); and the seeds, Solmitz reflected, were already far flown.[89] Bing concurred. While they might look back and lament what had been, it was necessary also to have faith in the possibilities of a new unfolding.[90]

Epilogue

Solmitz did not visit the Warburg Institute again. In 1962 this fragile soul took his own life.[91] Klibansky, ceaselessly active on the international academic stage, working for the cause of global tolerance, would diligently maintain ties with the institute through the 1960s. During the Gombrich era after 1961, guaranteed funding for the *Corpus Platonicum* ceased, but the final volume – an edition of Calcidius's *Timaeus* in which the entire scholarly apparatus (introduction and notes) was composed in Latin – can be considered a monument to pre-war standards of learning.[92] In 1964, bringing things full circle, Klibansky saw through to completion the revised second edition of Panofsky and Saxl's *Dürers 'Melencolia I,'* a project undertaken by 1928, stalled in 1939, and restarted in 1945, which would appear ultimately as *Saturn and Melancholy: Studies in the History of Natural Philosophy, Religion and Art*, with its authors listed, alphabetically, as Klibansky, Panofsky, and Saxl.[93] That year, 1964, was also the year of Bing's death. She would leave much unfinished, not only the later volumes of Warburg's collected writings but also the biography of Warburg that she had undertaken to write in her last years, supported by the Warburg family.[94] Her last piece, published posthumously, would appropriately enough be an introduction to the Italian translation of the volumes of Warburg's writings that she had published in 1932.[95] Only in 1970, after the generational shift had occurred, during Gombrich's own tenure as director, would his *Aby Warburg: An Intellectual Biography* be published by the Warburg Institute. Edgar Wind, who had returned to England in 1955 to take up the new chair of art history at Oxford University, would shortly before his own death write a notoriously scathing review of Gombrich's book for the *Times Literary Supplement*, drawing on his inner-circle memories of Warburg's perspectives.[96] Yet, as history has shown, the "newcomer's" ambitious and intelligent book, rooted in the archive, would then and later serve as the essential gateway to Warburg's thought.

Ultimately it was Bing, as much as anyone, who may be said to have provided the means for ensuring the continued vitality of the tradition she inhabited. It was she who worked to reproduce the original logic of the Hamburgian library as the institute moved to its present home in Bloomsbury, where its four floors allow the visitor to move through image, word, orientation, and action – from one domain of knowledge to another. She would foster the culture of assiduous documentation of institute history inaugurated by Warburg, which makes the Warburg Institute Archive the remarkable repository it is.[97] Moreover, near the end of her life, she set herself the task of readying Warburg's papers for later use. In 1964 William Heckscher, a Hamburgian student of Panofsky and Saxl, came to study the unpublished fragments so as to write a cultural historical account of the development of Warburg method.[98] Bing responded to Heckscher's note of thanks, just six weeks before her death, saying she was pleased that his search had borne fruit, noting: "It was the first time that my attempt at getting some order into Warburg's papers has undergone a test by someone from outside and I am glad to feel that his records are now open to scholarly inspection. It promises well for the future because there is certainly more in them than has appeared so far."[99] The library continues to model method, while the archive has been the essential source of the current Warburg revival, as the project of preparing an edition of Warburg's collected writings, undertaken in 1929, is pursued. "Hamburg" thus continues to play its part in contemporary scholarly culture.

NOTES

1 The greater part of the primary sources on which I have drawn are housed at the Warburg Institute Archive, London (hereafter WIA) as General Correspondence (hereafter GC); the Bodleian Library, Oxford, which preserves the papers of the Society for the Protection of Science and Learning (SPSL); and the

Deutsches Literaturarchiv Marbach (DLA), where the contents of 185 boxes of Klibansky's papers, including extensive correspondence, are roughly sorted by name and theme (https://www.dla-marbach.de/katalog/handschriften/, accessed 5 October 2016). I am grateful to those who hold copyright for permission to quote passages from unpublished documents: David Freedberg as director of the Warburg Institute, Ethel Groffier, David O. Solmitz, the executors of the Estate of Edgar Wind, and CARA (Council for At-Risk Academics). My thanks to Claudia Wedepohl, archivist at the WIA, for steadfast help and productive collaboration.

2 For the construction of the library at 116 Heilwigstrasse, see von Stockhausen, *Die Kulturwissenschaftliche Bibliothek Warburg*; for the history of its transfers: Sears, "The Warburg Institute, 1933–1944"; on the prominent banking family: Chernow, *The Warburgs*.

3 Wind, who had completed a doctorate on art-historical method under Erwin Panofsky in Hamburg in 1922, met Warburg during a visit to Hamburg in 1927 and was soon invited to join the KBW staff; his anti-Kantian *Habilitation*, "Das Experiment und die Metaphysik: Zur Auflösung der kosmologischen Antinomien," was finished in 1929 and accepted in 1930. See Balavoine, "Edgar Wind"; Lloyd-Jones, "A Biographical Memoir."

4 Bing provided an account of the newly installed library in "The Warburg Institute."

5 WIA, GC: Bing to Elly and Walter Solmitz, 5 September 1941. The move to Denham had been triggered by the sad events of 17 April 1941: Hans Meier, who had been with the library for some twenty years, was killed in an air raid and the same night the duplicate copy of the library's alphabetical catalogue, on loan to the National Central Library, had been destroyed.

6 WIA, GC: Bing to Lady Clark and Sir Kenneth, 31 January 1957. For the entire correspondence, triggered by the appearance of Clark's *The Nude: A Study in Ideal Form* in 1956, which Bing found far more Warburgian than "much that now sails under Warburg's flag"; see Sears, "Kenneth Clark and Gertrud Bing."

7 Klibansky, *Le Philosophe et la mémoire du siècle*, 11.

8 Bing, "Der Begriff des Notwendigen bei Lessing"; copy in Warburg Institute. Hamburg-born, Bing trained first as a primary and secondary school teacher, taught briefly, passed the *Abitur* in 1916, undertook university study for two years in Munich, and then completed the degree at Hamburg. In her dissertation she thanked Petsch for extraordinarily gracious responsiveness, and Cassirer for

all manner of stimulation, assistance, and encouragement. See Bing, "Auszug aus der Inaugural-Dissertation," 10 (*Lebenslauf*). See also the CV she completed in February 1942 (MS SPSL 184, fol. 476).

9 For an assemblage of documents describing the course of Warburg's illness, see Marazia and Stimilli (eds.), *Ludwig Binswanger–Aby Warburg*.

10 Warburg, *Die Erneuerung der heidnischen Antike* (*The Renewal of Pagan Antiquity*).

11 Eric M. Warburg to L.G.T. King, 17 August 1957, Hamburg Staatsarchiv, Bestandnr. 361–6, Sig. I, 126 – a letter in support of Bing's *Wiedergutmachung*.

12 As recalled by Claire Lachmann, who assisted Bing on the edition of Warburg's collected writings in 1930; interviewed by Ulrike Wendland (Zürich, 25 July 1983): "Man stellte sich erst 'der Bing' vor, die sich offenbar rasch ein Urteil darüber bildete, ob es sich menschlich und fachlich lohnte, den Neuling zu unterstützen. Hatte man diese 'Prüfung' bestanden, dann wurde man von ihr und von Saxl, der die 'Seele des Geschäfts' war, 'in jeder Notlage unterstüzt.'" Recorded in the unpublished "Chronik des Kunsthistorischen Seminars der Hamburgischen Universität," edited by Heinrich Dilly et al., entry for 22 February 1930.

13 See, for example, Bing's statement in the institutional diary, *Tagebuch der Kulturwissenschaftliche Bibliothek Warburg*, 7 February 1927, 51.

14 For Solmitz's life, see Grolle, *Walter Solmitz*; also important are the autobiographical reflections of his son David O. Solmitz, *Piecing Scattered Souls*.

15 MS SPSL 320, fols. 314–17 (materials submitted March 1939). Solmitz would identify his fields as philosophy, philology, and psychology, and his interests as theory of knowledge, social psychology, and the study of the symbol.

16 Warburg, *Tagebuch*: "29 November 1927," 150–1; "30 May 1928," 263.

17 See: WIA III.113.4 ("Einführung in die Methode der kulturwissenschaftlichen Kunstwissenschaft" or, in short form: "Kulturwissenschaftliche Methode"). Warburg, in the *Tagebuch*, "30 November 1927," 151, described it as: "Allgemeine Einführung in das Problem: die Funktion des sozialen Lebens als stilbildende Macht auf dem Gebiete der geistigen Orientierung wie der realen Gestaltungen in Tracht, Sitte und Gebrauch" (General introduction to the problem of the function of social life as a style-forming power in the domain of spiritual orientation and in the actual shaping of costume, custom, and use). In WS 1928–29 Solmitz attended a seminar given by Panofsky. Grolle, *Walter Solmitz*, 11.

18 Warburg, *Tagebuch*, "3 July 1928," 292: "Vormittag Solmitz die Duplizität des

künstlerisch gestaltenden Process an einer der Tafeln gezeigt: Umfangsetzung und Zukunftsweisung = Typus der Materiellen Gestaltung im Hintergrund und im Vordergrund das Physiognomische Augenblickszeichen als dynamische Zukunftsweisung."

19 WIA, Family Correspondence (hereafter FC): Warburg, "12 August 1928"; *Tagebuch*, 328; Also: letters from Mary to Aby Warburg, 29 April 1929; Mary to Frede Warburg, 17 July 1929.

20 *Worte zur Beisetzung von Professor Dr. Aby M. Warburg*. Others who spoke were Erich Warburg, Ernst Cassirer, Gustav Pauli (director of the Kunsthalle in Hamburg), and the Hamburgian Carl Georg Heise (director of the St Anne's Museum in Lübeck); obituaries written by Panofsky and Saxl were included in the privately printed brochure.

21 Delivered in April 1931, accompanied by a small exhibition of photographs from Warburg's Atlas. The evening was deemed successful: Cassirer moderated and discussion lasted into the night. See: "Bericht über die Tätigkeit der Bibliothek Warburg in den Jahren 1930 und 1931," 21–2, WIA. Saxl's talk, originally published in the conference proceedings, has now been reprinted with comment by Pablo Schneider in Saxl, *Gebärde, Form, Ausdruck*.

22 WIA, GC: Saxl to Bing, 5 March 1931.

23 Solmitz papers, WIA, uncatalogued. Bing printed the original four theses (later reworked) in the *Gesammelte Schriften*, I: 58, 328, but postponed their treatment to a later volume with other "Fragmente zur Ausdruckskunde." See Warburg, *Fragmente zur Ausdruckskunde*.

24 WIA, GC – KBW: A nine-page letter from Bing beginning "Liebes und gestreng eres Redaktionskomitee," 12 March 1931.

25 WIA, GC; Grolle, *Walter Solmitz*, 10–11. On 18 February 1929, Saxl wrote to Warburg in Italy that Solmitz could do no more than ten hours a week cataloguing books since he hoped to complete his dissertation by the autumn.

26 Grolle, *Walter Solmitz*, 17.

27 Saxl to General Secretary (AAC), 19 November 1934, MS SPSL 316, fols. 296–8. This lengthy testimonial is an important biographical source for Klibansky's early career. Both Klibansky's doctoral thesis ("Ein Proklos-Fund und seine Bedeutung") and his *Habilitation* ("Die Schule von Chartres und die Philosophie des XII. Jahrhunderts") concerned the afterlife of Platonist thought.

28 For the significant difficulties that Klibansky encountered as a "non-Aryan" working on the texts of Meister Eckhart, a Nazi-era hero, see: Regina Weber,

"Raymond Klibansky (1905–2005)," in *Deutschsprachige Exilliteratur seit 1933*, vol. 3: USA, edited by John M. Spalek, Konrad Feilchenfeldt, and Sandra H. Hawrylchak (Berlin: De Gruyter, 2010), 111–19.

29 DLA, A, KLIBANSKY: "Klibansky hat universal vibrierende Denk-Tentakeln"; Warburg, *Tagebuch*, "25 September 1929," 533. Warburg wrote letters of introduction to open doors for Klibansky in Italy, 25 September 1929: "Herr Dr. Klibansky, der ein 'Iter Italicum' antritt, um für die Heidelberger Akademie nach Nicolaus Cusanus zu forschen, hat sich schon seit einer Reihe von Jahren als ein hervorragend tüchtiger Mitarbeiter an den Publikationen der Kulturwissenschaftlichen Bibliothek Warburg erwiesen."

30 Klibansky, *Le Philosophe et la mémoire du siècle*, 34–5. See also Warburg, *Tagebuch*, "25 and 26 August 1926," 5–6.

31 The *Liber de sapiente* by Charles de Bovelles (Carolus Bovillus) was volume 10 in Saxl's series, *Studien der Bibliothek Warburg*. Klibansky would win Saxl and Bing's esteem by preparing an "exemplary" index for the volume. See Warburg, *Tagebuch*, "24 June 1927," 102.

32 Saxl and Panofsky began considering an amplified edition at an early date. See Warburg, *Tagebuch*, "28 September 1926," 19.

33 Klibansky, *Le Philosophe et la mémoire du siècle*, 35.

34 For the extraordinary history of the edition, which would appear only in 1964, and in English, see Weber, "Aktivitäten der Warburg-Bibliothek," 100–13.

35 DLA, A, KLIBANSKY: Bing to Klibansky, 18 October 1932.

36 The first volume of the bibliography, with an introduction by Wind, was published by Teubner in 1934, by which time the KBW had emigrated; accordingly, a version with a modified introduction in English was published in England, by Cassell, titled *A Bibliography on the Survival of the Classics*.

37 Officially called the Gesetz zur Wiederherstellung des Berufsbeamtentums (Law for the Restoration of the Professional Civil Service), it was enacted 7 April 1933. A copy of Klibansky's letter of dismissal, dated 8 August 1933, survives as MS SPSL 316, fol. 363.

38 Saxl to the AAC, 5 October 1933, MS SPSL 316, fols. 333–5.

39 Klibansky to Walter Adams (AAC), 3 March 1934, MS SPSL 316, fol. 366.

40 See Sears, "Warburg Institute," 7–9.

41 MS SPSL 1, fols. 150–1, 228. A subcommittee consisting of W.G. Constable, C.S. Gibson, and Charles Singer was formed on 14 June "to consider the possibility of the removal of the Warburg Library to London," MS SPSL 131, fol. 88.

42 Saxl to Adams, 17 September 1933, MS SPSL 131, fol. 97.

43 Saxl's testimonials: 5 October 1933, MS SPSL 316, fols. 333–5; 19 November 1934, fols. 296–8.

44 As indicated on Klibansky's CV, MS SPSL 316, fol. 287.

45 The Warburg Institute, "Courses to be held during the Lent and Trinity Terms, 1935" and WIA: "Lectures, Courses and Classes, January–June 1936," WIA. In winter 1935 Cassirer would give the course "The New Ideal of Truth in the Seventeenth Century."

46 The funds were insufficient for Klibansky's survival. A Warburg Institute friend, Sir Percival David, supplied some further support (MS SPSL 316, fols. 377, 404); for three years beginning 1 October 1934, Klibansky also received a grant from the Rockefeller Foundation to cover part of his salary at King's College (MS SPSL 316, fols. 385-402, 412–20). From 1936 the project would be backed by the British Academy.

47 A classical philologist, Labowsky completed her dissertation at Heidelberg in 1932 and worked as a volunteer at the KBW in 1933. For her life, see Weber, *Lotte Labowsky (1905–1991), Schülerin Aby Warburgs, Kollegin Raymond Klibanskys*.

48 For the entire history, see Wedepohl, "Critical Detachment." Gombrich contributed a review of Bing's edition of Warburg's *Gesammelte Schriften* to the institute's *A Bibliography on the Survival of the Classics*, vol. 2, published in 1938.

49 Gombrich's papers have been deposited at the Warburg Institute; also useful are the SPSL files (MS SPSL 187, fols. 234–388) and the Gombrich correspondence preserved among the Kris papers, housed in the Library of Congress. Saxl continued to find tasks and funds for the young Austrian. For Sir Percival David's support of Gombrich and Otto Kurz (engaged in writing textbooks for the Courtauld Institute), see Bing to Walter Adams, 16 March 1938, MS SPSL 187, fol. 242.

50 Klibansky and Paton, *Philosophy and History*, 339–46.

51 The Warburgians could offer little help. For Bing's frank letter to Edith Geheeb, composed 25 November 1936, in which she voiced her concerns about Solmitz, see Grolle, *Walter Solmitz*, 33–6.

52 WIA, GC: For the time in Nazi Germany and escape, see Grolle, *Walter Solmitz*, 27–42; Solmitz, *Piecing Scattered Souls*, 84–104. See also correspondence between Bing and Klibansky, 27 October–27 November 1938, WIA. Klibansky's telegram to the consulate, which he cited in a letter to Bing, read: "Please grant Walter and Elly Solmitz visa immediately stop guarantee for both during stay in England already given stop Klibansky Oriel College Oxford."

53 Solmitz submitted his general information to the SPSL in March 1939. In a grant proposal dated 6 June 1939, he spoke of his work on the *Corpus Platonicum* and his own research: "I should like at the same time to continue the work I was engaged upon in Germany, an analysis of different modes of logical and metaphysical thought by means of a combination of the methods of philology and psychology and philosophy – which should help to clarify certain philosophical and social questions and concepts. I have in preparation several special studies of the ways of thinking found in the works of Plato, Hegel and Goethe, which may, I hope, serve as some materials and 'experiments' towards a theory of consciousness," MS SPSL 320, fols. 325–6. Soon after his arrival, Solmitz wrote out a full account of his experiences at Dachau, printed in full in Grolle, *Walter Solmitz*, 89–126.

54 Ilse J. Ursell (SPSL) to Solmitz, 20 July 1949 (MS SPSL 320, fol. 406). For perspectives on Solmitz's American years, see Grolle, *Walter Solmitz*, 48–74; Solmitz, *Piecing Scattered Souls*, passim.

55 Klibanksy, *Le Philosophe et la mémoire du siècle*, 110–11 and 133–44.

56 Plato, *Meno, interprete Henrico Aristippo*, edited by Victor Kordeuter and Lotte Labowsky, was published by the Warburg Institute in 1940.

57 Warburg Institute, *Annual Report, June 1940–August 1941*, 4.

58 Klibansky edited the MARS volumes jointly with Richard Hunt and, later, Lotte Labowsky. See Southern, "Richard William Hunt (1908–79)," 383–4. Klibansky enlisted Hunt's aid in his wartime work for British Intelligence. See Klibansky, *Le Philosophe et la mémoire du siècle*, 141–2.

59 WIA: Extensive notes for the encyclopaedia project are preserved, uncatalogued.

60 Early on, Wind, as Saxl put it, had done "eminent service" on behalf of the Warburg Institute, to the point of securing an invitation from the National Gallery of Art and the Library of Congress for the library to transfer to Washington, DC, for the duration of the war should it prove necessary. Warburg Institute, *Annual Report, June 1940–August 1941*, 3–4.

61 Wind's resignation, announced in a letter to Bing composed on 15 and 30 June 1945, caught the Warburgians by surprise (Wind papers). See Sears, "Edgar Wind on Michelangelo," xxix.

62 WIA, GC: Bing to Walter and Elly Solmitz, 9 December 1945.

63 Klibansky would write to Bing from the Foreign Office on 15 January 1946 (DLA): "If I had remained in Government service, the chances of my being able

effectively to continue directing the edition of the *Corpus* and carrying on other scholarly work would have been very small indeed. I decided, therefore, to ask for my release and am now returning to my academic work in Oxford."

64 DLA, A, KLIBANSKY: Bing to Klibansky, 14 May 1946.

65 DLA, A, KLIBANSKY: Bing to Klibansky, 10 March 1947; see also 26 March 1947.

66 WIA, GC: It was at this point that Saxl asked another old ally, Richard Krautheimer, by then on the faculty at Vassar College, to become Director of Studies; Krautheimer politely declined. The exchange began with a cable from Saxl to Krautheimer, 13 January 1948.

67 DLA, A, KLIBANSKY: Solmitz to Klibansky, 15 October 1945. This was a birthday greeting.

68 DLA, A, KLIBANSKY: Klibansky-Solmitz correspondence, 1950–53. In 1934 the Geheebs had moved the Odenwaldschule to the Berner Oberland in Switzerland, renaming it the École d'Humanité.

69 DLA, A, KLIBANSKY: Klibansky to Solmitz, 10 May 1954, in which he indicated that Bing had written on Solmitz's behalf in Frankfort's name. Simultaneously, she and Frankfort were trying to get him a senior research fellowship at the Warburg Institute. Bing to Klibansky, 22 March 1954.

70 Solmitz, "Cassirer on Galileo," 750; Solmitz also co-contributed to the bibliography of Cassirer's writings, 883–910.

71 Taylor, "Henri Frankfort, Aby Warburg and 'Mythopoeic Thought'"; n.p. Panofsky had already declined an invitation to return as director; see his letter to Bing, 17 June 1948, in Panofsky, *Korrespondenz*, 2: 950–1: "I do consider myself as one of those who try to maintain what may be called the 'Hamburg tradition.'"

72 DLA, A, KLIBANSKY: Bing to Klibansky, 13 April 1949.

73 Solmitz to Ilse J. Ursell (SPSL), 29 March 1949 (SPSL 240, fol. 403).

74 Gombrich described his dilemma in a letter of 23 September 1945 to Kris, who by this time had emigrated to New York (Ernst Kris papers, Library of Congress).

75 Warburg Institute, *Annual Report, 1945–46*, 5.

76 Warburg Institute, *Annual Report, 1948–49*, 12. For the evolution of Gombrich's text, see Wedepohl, "Critical Detachment," 148–54.

77 Kris to John Marshall (Rockefeller Foundation), 21 March and 15 April 1949, Kris papers, Library of Congress.

78 The episode can be followed in correspondence between Gombrich and Meyer

Schapiro (26 November 1953, 29 June 1954; with a copy of the letter declining the post sent to the departmental chair, William Bell Dinsmoor, 19 March 1954), Meyer Schapiro Collection, Rare Book and Manuscript Library, Columbia University.

79 In any number of postwar letters to Kris, Gombrich described the situation at the institute and his personal hopes (Ernst Kris Papers, Library of Congress). DLA, A, KLIBANSKY: Bing wrote to Klibansky, 29 October 1954, that Gombrich had given "a very simple and dignified memorial speech to Frankfort" as he opened a lecture series.

80 DLA, A, KLIBANSKY: Bing to Klibansky, 5 February 1955.

81 DLA, A, KLIBANSKY: Solmitz to Klibansky, 12 and 28 January 1955; Klibansky to Solmitz, 1 February 1955.

82 DLA, A, KLIBANSKY: Solmitz to Klibansky, 5 December 1954. Gombrich and Karl Popper, philosopher of logic and science, a fellow Viennese émigré, kept up a constant correspondence during the war when Popper was in New Zealand; Popper would move to London in 1946. See Gombrich to Tess Simpson (SPSL), 18 October 1943, MS SPSL187, fol. 262. Popper advocated for a "critical rationalism" in which susceptibility to falsification became the criterion of genuine scientific theory.

83 Wedepohl, "Critical Detachment," 151, quoting Gombrich (1947): "with Warburg … there is *a vital difference between what he actually said and what he conveyed.*"

84 Solmitz factored in the force of personality in a memorial speech in honour of another mentor, delivered in New York on 16 April 1945: "I frankly admit that I was first attracted to the philosophy of Ernst Cassirer by the man Ernst Cassirer," but he justified his faith: "his personality was a living expression, representation, a symbol of his thought"; printed in Grolle, *Walter Solmitz*, 127–30.

85 In the Solmitz boxes, unsorted papers contain an array of thoughts. One heading, "Einleitungen zum Atlas (an Bing diktiert)" (Introductions to the "Atlas," dictated to Bing), suggests that Bing may have consulted him on Volume II of Warburg's *Gesammelte Schriften.*

86 Solmitz's son David, who as an eleven-year-old in 1954–55 had travelled with his parents to London, recalls that his father never fully recovered from the nervous breakdown he experienced there, for which he was briefly hospitalized. Communication with the author, 27 March 2016. See also Solmitz, *Piecing Scattered Souls*, 132–9.

87 DLA, A, KLIBANSKY: Solmitz to Klibansky, 5 February 1955: "Objectiv [sic! - ?]

gesehen, würde es dem Institute gut tun und gemäss sein, wenn ausser 'Wien' und 'England' auch 'Hamburg' (und nicht nur [durch] Bing) zu stärkerer Geltung käme)." Playing on the expression "Da liegt der Hase im Pfeffer," Solmitz went on to write: "Aber da liegt der Hase im Popper!" ("Popper is the rub!").

88 DLA, A, KLIBANSKY: Klibansky to Solmitz, 1 February 1955.

89 WIA: Solmitz to Bing, 25 May 1959; cited in Grolle, *Walter Solmitz*, 69.

90 WIA: Bing to Solmitz, 11 June 1959.

91 Solmitz, *Piecing Scattered Souls*, 1–16.

92 WIA: Gombrich to Klibansky, 27 January 1961.

93 In 1945, at war's end, it was found that the lead plates for the revised second edition (which had been typeset before the war and were at the printer's in Glückstadt near Hamburg) had been destroyed, requisitioned as war material, though the blocks for the illustrations had survived. Klibanksy, *Le Philosophe et la mémoire du siècle*, 150. For a rapid account, including the decision to publish in English and the problem with the order of authors' names on the title page, see Bing to Panofsky, 12 April 1949 (*Korrespondenz*, 2: 1071–3). For the entire halting history, see Weber, "Aktivitäten der Warburg-Bibliothek."

94 For family support of Bing's biography, see the letter of 5 December 1960 from Eric M. Warburg to Senatssyndicus Wilhelm Drexelius, asking for further funds from Hamburg (Hamburg Staatsarchiv, Bestandnr. 361–6, Sig. I, 126).

95 Bing, "A.M. Warburg." The Italian edition, with Bing's introduction, would appear as Warburg, *La rinascità del paganesimo antico: contributo alla storia della cultura*.

96 Wedepohl, "Critical Detachment," 133–4. Wind's review of Gombrich's book appeared in the *Times Literary Supplement*. Wind died of leukemia on 12 September 1971.

97 See Sears, "Warburg Institute Archive, General Correspondence."

98 Heckscher, "The Genesis of Iconology." Heckscher delivered the paper, treating Warburg's breakthroughs 1907–12, at the International Congress of the History of Art held in Bonn in 1964.

99 Bing to Heckscher, 25 May 1964, Warburg-Haus, Heckscher-Archiv.

TWO

The Warburg Library within German Judaism: Raymond Klibansky in His Letters to Fritz Saxl and Gertrud Bing

MARTIN TREML

In his 1977 autobiography, *From Berlin to Jerusalem*, his much anticipated *Alterswerk* (later work), Gershom Scholem, professor for the study of Jewish mysticism and Jewish thought at the Hebrew University of Jerusalem for almost fifty years, made a puzzling confession: "I used to define the three groups around the Warburg Library, Max Horkheimer's Institut für Sozialforschung (Institute for Social Research), and the metaphysical magicians around Oskar Goldberg, as the three most remarkable 'Jewish sects' that German Jewry produced. Not all of them liked to hear this."[1] Some lines before this passage, Scholem had already remarked about the KBW, the Kulturwissenschaftliche Bibliothek Warburg (the original name of the Warburg Library): "For about twenty-five years, it consisted almost entirely of Jews whose Jewish intensity ranged from moderate sympathy to the zero point and even below."[2]

A Jewish *hairesis*

As one might expect, Scholem, the founder of the academic study of the Kabbalah (or Jewish mysticism in its different forms since the late twelfth century), had nothing but twisted relations with both the KBW and the post-1933 Warburg Institute. How this situation emerged and why it lasted deserves a study of its own, so I will not discuss it here.[3] But let us return to Scholem's *aperçu* about the "sects" of German Jewry. The three sects are a hidden allusion to one of the most famous passages in Jewish historiography, drawn directly from the ancient historian of Judaism, Flavius Josephus, an apostate – a *Römling* (Heinrich Graetz), as he sympathized with Rome, then the "hegemonic empire" (Edward Luttwak). In most of his works, *The Jewish Antiquities*, *The Jewish War*, and his autobiographical *Life*, Josephus states that "Jewish philosophy, in fact, takes three forms. The followers of the first school are called Pharisees, of the second Saducees, of the third Essenes."[4] The Greek term for such a school (or "sect") is *hairesis*, in its original meaning of "party" and not "heresy."

Scholem's comparison of the situation in Roman Palestine with that of the Jews of the Weimar Republic is elucidating as well as amusing, insofar as both periods were ages of crisis. With respect to the ancient setting, we can refer, for example, to the insights of two contemporary historians. According to Pierre Vidal-Naquet, "The first century CE is the last great century of Jewish apocalyptic literature in which the 'Messiah' is an important figure."[5] Besides its apocalyptic fervour, Palestine was marked by "Jewish pluralism," provoked by what Tessa Rajak has described as "the compelling and at first challengingly different Greek culture which surrounded the Jews."[6] A time of *Angst* and of multiple traditions – be they Greek or German – was experienced in the first and in the twentieth centuries, at least by the not-so-orthodox or not-so-pious Jews.

From Josephus to Scholem, from the Flavian protégé to the *Yekke*, from Rome to Jerusalem, is a long way.[7] What historians of Aby Warburg and his legacy can learn from Scholem's *dictum* has a triple sense: first, that it is not always necessary to accurately define the Jewishness of a Jewish sect; second, that it is better not to assume that a so-called Jewish sect concerns itself with Jewish affairs and matters exclusively; and finally, that one can in fact look for and consider the KBW's place among the Jewish sects of Weimar Germany, if perhaps only as a *secte malgré elle*, or, to say it in Greek, a *hairesis*. The appositeness of such a term from the sociology of religion becomes clearer when we distinguish it from that of a "church," in Latin *ecclesia*, both in structure and in what I would like to call its working temperature (*Betriebstemperatur*).

In an *ecclesia*, the hierarchy is well structured, and the position of greatest authority is based on either election or bureaucratic procedure; in a *hairesis*, it is the charismatic personality who leads. As Philip Rieff observed almost fifty years ago, the charismatic, until recently replaced by the therapeutic, was the sacred root of culture.[8] By necessity, any cultural founder has to be a charismatic personality – and who would not describe Warburg as being one such? According to Peter Sloterdijk, the *ecclesia* possesses a "narrative scheme" that passes through three stages: *ecclesia oppressa*, *ecclesia militans*, *ecclesia triumphans*, "from the church under pressure to the fighting church, then from the fighting to the triumphant church," satisfied and saturated by its success and influence.[9]

In counterpoint to Sloterdijk's structure, I would say that a *hairesis* does not reach the end of this scheme. A *hairesis* never had its Constantinian shift, so forever moves from the first to the second phase and back again. A *hairesis* is necessarily on the move and so is very unstable, as it considers itself as put into danger especially by what one may call "orthodoxy" – this is what the KBW shares with other (and especially Jewish) sects of the first half of the twentieth century such as early Freudian psychoanalysis.[10]

A Long Parenthesis on Method

When one draws a portrait of Aby Warburg and his circle within the frame of German Judaism, one must follow what was begun by Carlo Ginzburg fifty years ago.[11] Warburg's legacy as such is a multiple one. It consists of an institution, the Warburg Institute. It possesses a method, hard to define, which is very interested in details and in processes of transmission, in *Nachleben*.[12] It certainly includes a body of people, a network as such. All of these people – famous, well known, almost unknown, even obscure, many of them more or less forgotten, who once assembled in Hamburg at the KBW and at the university where they studied under and worked with Ernst Cassirer, Fritz Saxl, Erwin Panofsky, and the late Warburg – deserve attention.[13] Many of them had to leave Germany later and were dispersed after the Nazi seizure of power; others could stay. Two stand in rather extreme contrast to each other.

The first is the historian Hans Liebeschütz (1893–1978), one of the very few representatives of *Wissenschaft des Judentums* (Judaic studies) in the Warburg circle. Liebeschütz was a *Privatdozent* in Middle Latin Philology at

Hamburg University from 1929, and instructor at a school of reform pedagogy, the Alfred-Lichtwark-Schule in Hamburg-Winterhude. Although an active soldier on the Western Front during the First World War, Liebeschütz was dismissed by the Nazis in 1934 and became active in the Jewish adult and higher education systems, both at the Hamburg Franz-Rosenzweig-Gedächtnisstiftung and the Berlin Lehranstalt (formerly Hochschule) für die Wissenschaft des Judentums.[14] These institutions were shut down in the summer and fall of 1938, respectively. During his last Berlin semester, Liebeschütz gave a course on the problem of religious autobiography in connection to Augustine's *Confessions*.[15] Far from being a pious Jew, in his German years he undertook research into Medieval Christian theology and philosophy, but had to "immigrate" to Jewish institutions after 1933. Before he could escape to England, where a brother already lived and to which his family had managed to flee, he was abducted to the concentration camp Sachsenhausen near Berlin. Fortunately, after some weeks he was released. In England, he underwent a new detention, now as an enemy alien, but he was soon able to start a new life and entered academic positions at the University of Liverpool. Immediately before receiving emeritus status he was granted an associate professorship at Hamburg University in 1957, part of the city's attempts to somehow "normalize" its relations to emigrants.[16]

The other example is the extreme opposite: Niels von Holst (1907–1993), a student of the KBW who became a Nazi (like Fritz Rougemont). He studied under Panofsky and later worked as a *Hilfskraft* (assistant) in the library. Traces of him can be found in the KBW annals; in 1929 for instance, Warburg jotted in the library's collective diary that at lunch von Holst had called Gertrude Bing, Warburg's assistant who completed her doctorate in philosophy under Cassirer, a "Pallas Athena, sprung from my head."[17] Soon after 1933, von Holst became an active Nazi. He worked in the *Außenamt* (foreign relations) of the Berlin museums, in the Reichsministerium für Wissenschaft, Erziehung und Volksbildung (Ministry of Science, Education, and Culture), and then, during the war, in the Einsatzstab Reichsleiter Rosenberg, an organization notorious for planning and participating in the Nazi plunder, especially in the Baltic region, from which von Holst originated.[18] After the war, he was the only one who failed to reinstate himself in the Berlin museums.[19] But he continued to work as an art expert, now on the free market, and even excelled in this capacity in relation to painters like Max

Beckmann, whose works had been condemned by his former Nazi masters as *entartete Kunst* (degenerate art). He was a productive and popular writer of art-historical city guides, for example to Rome, Naples, Paris, and Vienna, and only turned revisionist when he dealt with the German East, with Breslau or Danzig, now lost to Poland.[20] He authored handbooks and had also one bestseller, which was translated into English.[21] In 1968, when the young generation of art historians revolted against their fathers in Ulm at the eleventh *Deutsche Kunsthistorikertag* (German Art Historians Conference), von Holst of course sided with the reactionaries.[22] He was never pursued by the German authorities for his involvement in Nazi crimes.

Liebeschütz and von Holst followed extremely different careers indeed. To me, the Hamburg of the late 1920s and early 1930s resembles the setting of an Anton Chekhov play: while the bourgeoisie is enjoying its parties in the cherry orchard, the barbarians outside are on their march.

Fortuna blew into the sails of these men and women; she determined their courses. She was the great goddess and chief actor of any enterprise, as Warburg had once observed, when he found her adopted as the patron of bankers and businessmen like Francesco Sassetti in Renaissance Florence.[23] These fifteenth-century protagonists, with their hope and trust in "*Fortuna Audax*" (Bold Fortune), were kindred spirits, the peers of Warburg and his Hamburg family at the turn of the twentieth century.[24] This *Seelenverwandtschaft* is nicely illustrated by a comparison of the emergence of the Medici sons in the company of their tutors in Domenico Ghirlandaio's *The Confirmation of the Franciscan Rule* in Santa Trinità, with a photo of Warburg and his four brothers dating from around 1890.[25] Both groups seem to ascend from an underworld to bright light and good fortune.

From his mythological studies under Hermann Usener at Bonn University, Warburg knew about heroes returning from the other world, notably Orpheus, who twice lost his wife, Eurydice. The representation by Dürer in his *Death of Orpheus*, a drawing of 1494, now held by the Hamburger Kunsthalle, was one of Warburg's best *trouvailles*, and it became his male "pathos formula," springing from "the dark mystery play of Dionysian legend."[26] We may assume that the young men pictured in the Ghirlandaio and the Warburg family photograph were much happier than Orpheus, one of the most famous sufferers of ancient Greece.

But let us go back once more and start anew with a short description of sources and a digression on the art of reading them. For present purposes, I use a published obituary and have already used an institutional diary entry, but I am drawing mainly from unpublished letters scattered and kept in different archives. Letters are especially difficult and perilous stuff, by no means well accepted in academic studies, as they are, also in the case of professional letters and so-called *Gelehrtenbriefe* (letters by scholars), generally just by-products of more final and formally sanctioned outputs such as monographs, articles, essays, and the like. Second, they are regarded as private (which they are, in fact) and, dangerously enough, bordering on gossip (which is true, as well). Yet, it is exactly the ways of self-fashioning and styling that they reveal – and which bring them, as sources, into discredit – that give them an importance unmatched by other sources. They are less testimonies than trials and experiments, constituting a field of investigation that has also recently become part of the history of science.[27] And they approach one of Michel Foucault's epistemological figures, namely that of "practice."

Practice wants to historicize certain forms of rationality and, like discourse, is always oriented toward power and "truth-telling."[28] But to my understanding, practice not only renews sets of disciplines but is located beyond them. Through it, moments of freedom also become possible. A practice in this sense is more closely related to what Foucault calls *souci de soi*, "care of oneself," which lies somewhere between an ethics and an aesthetics of existence.[29] The care inherent in the concept of practice appears not so much as a normalizing form of taking care of oneself, but as a mode of self-fashioning that is not necessarily always fully conscious. It aims at different sets of subjectivity, not at one that is "normal" for everybody, even if it is established as a new norm for some. When applied to the study of Warburg and his legacy, the figure of practice is conceived not as a biographical element as such, but as one that becomes part of a "thought collective," as Ludwik Fleck has put it.[30] I am interested in an intellectual history, but with a Foucauldian turn. Nevertheless, there exists a proximity to Warburg's theory itself.

What I study here I would like to call *bewegtes Beiwerk*, Warburg's (and Darwin's) "accessories in motion," or "accessory forms in motion," a phrase that can be found on almost every page of his thesis on Botticelli's mythological paintings.[31] There he says that Alberti, in his *Libro della pittura*, "gives rein to his fancy, attributing organic life to inanimate accessory forms; at such moments he sees snakes tangling, flames licking, or the branches of a tree."[32]

I am doing much the same, as the letters that I read here become moving and animated objects, and I do not read them for "hard" information alone. Letters contain more than what their authors are writing about; they also convey the sound of the spoken, or heard. It is the tone, the expression, the phrase. From this perspective, letters resemble poems: when reproduced, nothing must be left aside. Like dreams, they give hints as to what they do not say, to what is actually missing from them, but in a most telling way. All this makes them quite untranslatable. Letters not only support us with information and supplement our knowledge through contextualization; they possess a charm and sometimes a charisma. Franz Kafka makes an elucidating remark about letters as such, especially those exchanged between lovers:

> The easy possibility of letter-writing must – seen merely theoretically – have brought into the world a terrible disintegration of souls. It is, in fact, an intercourse with ghosts, and not only with the ghost of the recipient but also with one's own ghost which develops between the lines of the letter one is writing and even more so in a series of letters where one letter corroborates the other and can refer to it as a witness. How on earth did anyone get the idea that people can communicate with one another by letter! … Written kisses don't reach their destination, rather they are drunk on the way by the ghosts.[33]

Letters are ghosts, *revenants*. Kafka, the maniacal writer of letters, asked Milena Jesenská, his beloved, a journalist who, as a Czech patriot and resistance fighter, was murdered in the concentration camp of Ravensbrück, if they might rather use a different art of writing, a *Flaschenpost* (message in a bottle). They never succeeded. Almost all her letters were drowned by the high tides of the European civil wars and her extinction by the Nazis (which did not succeed, as she is still much known and appreciated). At least Kafka's letters washed up onto the shores of our libraries.

Letters may thus turn into correspond*ences* rather than simply correspond*ence*. That this transformation is a charming (and even magical) one is best shown by Charles Baudelaire's poem of the same title, "Correspondances."[34] In the "forest of symbols" letters, which the poet evokes, as well as signs and links, are confusing; they are delivered by nature and history, *Nachleben* as such. Letters, which are correspondences, require a receiver, not necessarily the other correspondent, but a third or fourth person, a network of recipients. This network would need someone like a node, a person through whom correspondences are linked. In our case, Raymond Klibansky is just such a node.

Raymond Klibansky, Warburgian and Jew

In Gombrich's biography of Warburg, Klibansky is mentioned only in a footnote about Warburg's essay on Luther, in connection with the 1964 edition of *Saturn and Melancholy*.[35] This should not surprise us, as Gombrich appears to have judged Klibansky himself as being no more than a mere melancholic footnote to the Warburg Institute. But in Saxl's essay devoted to the history of the library at the end of Gombrich's biography, Klibansky finds a very nice, even prominent place:

> One of the memorable events of those days [meaning the seizing of power by the Nazis on 30 January 1933] was a visit from a young and active friend of the Institute, Dr. R. Klibansky. Filled with horror about what he saw going on at Heidelberg University, where he was a member of the teaching staff, he had conceived the idea of creating a centre of learning outside Germany where the old tradition of German humanism should be preserved. We decided on united action. The members of the Institute's staff – irrespective of race – and the Warburg family agreed on emigration. But emigrate to where?[36]

Both Klibansky and the KBW decided it would be England.

From Thomas Meyer's detailed intellectual biography of Cassirer, we learn that Klibansky came to the KBW as his student. Klibansky was introduced to the philosopher in 1926 by no other than Cassirer's son Heinrich, called "Heinz."[37] Although he was two years younger than Heinz, they were close schoolmates at the Odenwaldschule, a progressive school located in Heppenheim, a small town between Frankfurt and Heidelberg. The third in this relationship was Walter Solmitz, who also became part of the Warburg circle as a philosopher and was a life-long friend of Klibansky (and Bing).[38] Also Saxl's two children, Hedwig and Peter, nine and ten years Klibansky's junior, attended the institute.[39] Most former students of the Odenwaldschule felt a very strong connection to the school and their instructors, and there is a letter from Klibansky to Bing in which he enthusiastically proposes the nomination of Paul Geheeb, the school's founder, as a candidate for the Nobel Peace Prize.[40]

Cassirer was quite impressed by Klibansky. He invited him to Hamburg, where he joined the KBW and worked as a helping hand in structuring and cataloguing new books, as many students did.[41] In the already mentioned diary of the KBW, a collective enterprise of Warburg, Saxl, and Bing from 1926 to Warburg's death in October 1929, we find many remarks about Klibansky, usually by Bing.[42] One episode is very telling. In early 1927 Bing reported that Klibansky had made suggestions for the systematic acquisition (*systematische Anschaffungsvorschläge*) of, first, Aristotelian studies and, second, the works of Stefan George, whose writings he had described as the best examples of how the present stood in relation to antiquity.[43] The first suggestion was immediately followed, but it took several months for the second to be acted upon. On 4 April, Bing wrote that Klibansky would obtain books of and about George for a certain sum from Mario Uzielli, a book seller, antiquarian, and art dealer in Frankfurt.[44] The exchange shows what a strong position Klibansky had acquired just a few months after making contact with the library; illustrating at once how determined he was that the library should have these items, that his ideas were taken seriously at the KBW, and that he was entrusted to make purchases on its behalf.

Klibansky left Hamburg later the same year and returned to Heidelberg, where, together with his *Doktorvater*, the philosopher Ernst Hoffmann, he edited the *Opera omnia* of Nicholas of Cusa. Until his emigration in 1933, he was also working on the critical edition of the medieval theologian, mystic, and philosopher Meister Eckhart. By the early 1950s, however, Klibansky regarded his former cooperation with Hoffmann as a failed one. Again in a letter to Bing, he informed her that he had already written to Paul Oskar Kristeller (another former student of Hoffmann and *émigré*, now acting as a mediator).[45] There he stated: "[The] Cusanus Commission has all the materials which I left with them, the fruit of seven years work. They have the list of my MSS [manuscript] discoveries which, at Hoffmann's request, I gave him before leaving. They – or at least he – have the results of my research in London and other libraries which I sent him in many letters long after I ceased to be the Assistant of the Academy. These materials have been used, and are being used, by them."[46] The conflict was never resolved and ceased only with Hoffmann's death in January 1952. Tragically enough, Hoffmann, a partisan of the liberal-left Deutsche Demokratische Partei (DDP), was one of the few academic opponents to Hitler and thus resigned his Heidelberg professorship in 1935 only to return in 1945 and become emeritus three years later.

While Klibansky had a good, yet distant relationship with Cassirer, he had very little to do with Warburg himself. In his dialogue with Georges Leroux, he calls Warburg "un homme de génie" and "le grand Seigneur du labyrinthe."[47] Yet if for Warburg the labyrinth was the soul, for others it was Warburg's library. This was the case at least for Cassirer, one of the library's most passionate users, for whom it possessed the force of a magic spell. Saxl reported: "When Professor E. Cassirer first came to see the library he decided either to flee from it (which he did for some time) or to remain there a prisoner for years (which for a certain period he enjoyed doing in later years)."[48]

However, Klibansky himself was doubly vaccinated against too strong an influence from Warburg, first through his closeness to the George circle – namely to Friedrich Gundolf, whose studies on Caesar or Goethe, for example, exhibited more academically focused paths – and second through his own rabbinic ancestors. I will only dwell here on the latter point. In the very first pages of his memoirs, Klibansky proudly mentions that one of his maternal forebears was the famous Vilna Gaon.[49] Klibansky indeed possessed what, in Yiddish, is called a *yichus*, a distinguished ancestry or pedigree. Rabbi Elijah ben Shlomo Zalman (1720–1797), a rationalist teacher of law and well-known Kabbalist, was actually one of the great Jewish masters of the seventeenth century. He acted as an ardent opponent of Hasidism, the popular Jewish mystical movement of that time. Yet the Vilna Gaon was a mystic himself. In those years, "Kabbalah itself was never the subject of a comprehensive criticism, but only its 'heretical' interpretation, which was felt to have dangerous theological and social implications."[50] And Hasidism was but a much milder form of the wild heresy of Sabbatai Sevi, a Jewish child of Saturn (after whom he was also named, as "Sabbatai" is "Saturn" in

Hebrew). This messiah proved a melancholic in Klibansky's sense, as Moshe Idel has recently shown.[51] Since the 1660s his teaching had jolted the Jewish Diaspora as no *hairesis* had ever done before.[52]

Klibansky was descended from a family in which aspects of Halakhic life such as *kashrut* (preparing and eating kosher food), the observation of the Shabbat and the holidays, and daily prayer played an important role. He described his family's habits as observant of Jewish tradition, but "not in an obsessive way – especially not on my mother's part. It was more a way of life."[53] For Warburg, on the contrary, Jewish religion was definitely not such a mode; it was rather *un mode de ne pas vivre* – it would have been a kind of death for him. To cite only two examples of many, he decided to marry a Christian – whose parents had already converted to Protestantism – and not to let his son, Max Adolph, be circumcised.[54]

Regarding Judaism, Saxl proves to be a case of his own. He neither was raised in a religious way, nor ever left or broke with Judaism. The high school that he attended, the K.K. (Kaiserlich-Königliches) Maximilians-Gymnasium, was located in Vienna's ninth district, a quarter with a large and educated Jewish population. When Saxl entered first grade, out of 440 pupils, 133 were Catholic, 17 were Protestant, 3 were Greek-Orthodox, and 3 were without any confession, but 284 were Jewish.[55] One of his classmates was Martin, Freud's eldest son.[56]

In the obituary of Saxl by Hans Liebeschütz, one finds a very clear characterization of him that is the more important for its sharp contrast with Warburg, his master:

> Warburg, the eldest son of the well-known banker Moritz Warburg, had been brought up in a strong Jewish tradition, but for his own outlook on life it was more important that, during the nineteenth century, his family had obtained a standing in Hanseatic society. As a burgess of the city-republic on the Elbe he had an understanding of the great men of Florence. Saxl was not inclined to carry assimilation to such lengths. He was intensely aware of the fact that the independence in his European outlook, which he cherished as his most precious possession, was the outcome of his position as an outsider and a Jew, and he knew well that the impulse in him to find his own expression for the religious

> wisdom of the great masters was conditioned by the past of his own ancestors. In this way he stood as a guardian of a great tradition, of both the European and the Jewish legacy.[57]

In this respect, Saxl may have resembled Klibansky, who in any case was on excellent terms with him and Bing, as is proven by their correspondence. Most of their letters are now kept at the Warburg Institute Archive (WIA). But interesting *trouvailles* can also be made in Klibansky's literary estate at the Deutsches Literaturarchiv (DLA) in Marbach on the Neckar. There one finds many letters by Bing that do not exist in London, as they are hand-written.

In this correspondence, many traces emerge of the efforts of Saxl, Bing, and Klibansky, from 1923 to 1964, to complete and publish *Saturn and Melancholy*, shedding light on a continuous yet constantly interrupted enterprise that was, itself, a truly Saturnian and melancholic project if ever there was one. Different stages of this work, various fragments of it, and also its echo, can be found in the letters. Let me here mention one episode that includes a nice characterization of Panofsky, whom Klibansky met for the first time in the summer of 1929. He reported to Saxl:

> One evening until dawn, I spent with Panofsky, at first together with Mrs Panofsky and Miss Brauer, then alone with Dürer's Melencolia. Instantly Panofsky, being a true *chacham*, made some conjectures on some texts that I presented, but in general he seemed to agree with the development of the image of Saturn which I gave in outline; let us wait and see what you will say about it. I will write down all of my notes after my return to Heidelberg so that they will be readable for Panofsky, to whom I will send them; he wanted to work on the chapter on Dürer in the meantime.[58]

Most interesting in our context is that Klibansky describes Panofsky as "*chōchŏm*," which is the Ashkenazi ("German") pronunciation of the standard Hebrew *chacham*, designating a wise person and scholar, but also the honorary title that was given to a great and generally acknowledged Rabbinic authority. Klibansky's use here is typical of that of the Weimar Jews in general, who had dropped their Jewish tradition in behaviour, but kept it when, as here, making witty allusions to someone of the "family," or to another Weimar Jew.

In what follows, I present two episodes taken from the rich correspondence of Klibansky with Saxl and Bing centred around Warburg and his heritage.

Saxl and His *Nachfolge*

From the DLA material in Marbach we learn that Bing – and perhaps also Saxl – planned to install Klibansky as a possible successor to Saxl as director of the Warburg. Especially in 1947, a year after he had accepted the call to teach philosophy at Montreal's McGill University, the idea arose to give Klibansky a double position: a readership in classical philosophy at Oxford and the post of director of research (or of studies) at the Warburg Institute, a post similar to that occupied by Edgar Wind, who had acted as deputy director of the Warburg Institute from 1934 until 1942, when he left in bitter dispute with Saxl (and Bing). In 1947 almost every letter addressed by Bing to Klibansky deals with this plan. In March she wrote:

> Your readership is to have the added qualification "with Special Responsibilities" – a clause which finds expression in the increase of the salary by something like 200 £ above the normal Reader's salary. This, in addition to the post of Director of Studies at the W. I., raises your post anyhow above the usual rights and obligations of a Readership. As regards your proposal to return to London for 6 months during your second year of office at McGill it would be *excellent*, in fact nothing could be better, provided you would definitely decide to take over for good in August 1948. I think on that assumption our Committee would even be prepared to wait for you without your coming here until the session 1948/49. But I am afraid they would want a decision in the course of this summer term. When your cable was read at the last meeting the temper of the committee was obviously in favour of making all allowances provided the answer would be "yes" ultimately. If they could

count on that they might give you the time you want in order to leave McGill with all due considerations for them. And provided you were quite decided to take up the post here in August 1948, you might prefer to spend the intervening time either entirely at McGill or divide it between Canada and USA. But for us your offer would be admirable. Saxl would welcome your help enormously. Contacts might be made, plans laid, and curricula prepared to your liking in anticipation of better things to follow. There is one more thing which I feel I must add – at the risk of appearing to attempt a bit of blackmail. Saxl is – as Warburg used to say – alright from the collar upward; and his health is infinitely better than it was last year. He will carry gladly all the burdens imposed on him, and there is no danger of him breaking down under them. But some mysterious quality has gone out of his resilience. He is tired much more easily than he used to be, and with tiredness a kind of irritation comes over him at times which saps his energy, his convictions, and his will to achieve. In the long run this must affect his work. Up till now he always pulls himself together. But what I feel (or rather know) is that this would disappear the moment he would know that some date you would come to help *him*. He would feel the Institute was safe, in good strong hands; there would be someone to assist consolidating it, and he would not be alone to do everything singlehanded for an indefinite period of time. This should not decide you – no doubt he would be very angry with me for mentioning him at all – but if the balance is anyhow slightly in favour of your accepting the post here it might make it *a little* easier for you to do it *gladly*, knowing that a little bit of human relationship would be added to the scale in which the objective pros are being weighed.[59]

And a fortnight later, she continues:

Saxl is again very tired – and would need a break. Unfortunately we cannot at the moment afford it. But it is the more important that he should go away from London for two months in summer. That itself can be managed without your being here during that time although your presence would be most welcome. But your ultimate decision to

> accept the post of Dir. of Studies here and the Readership at the University would make all the difference in the world to him because it would relieve him of his greatest worry: the anxiety about the future and the present strain of carrying the burden alone. And in spite of my reluctance to put any pressure to bear upon you I cannot help saying that I know he looks to your joining the Institute as the one thing to aim at. There is a task here for you – something to build up which he feels too great and responsible to do alone. The "Warburg influence" is beginning to sink in deeply in this country now; and it happens time and again that people tell us "you have taught us something that we could not have had from anyone else" – a very British way of thinking, I feel – to realize something not when it is going to happen but only after it has happened. That is something in addition to what a Readership in Oxford could give you, I think. We have also made some progress in finding an answer to your misgivings as to your role in the Philosophy curriculum. Prof. Ayer was at the Institute the other day to attend a lecture given by Professor Meyer Shapiro of Columbia University. Time was too short then for Saxl to approach him properly. But he will soon have an opportunity for it, and from what we hear of Ayer's interests and personality there is no doubt that he would welcome your joining the Philosophy Board – as in fact you seem also to expect. We are anxiously expecting your next letter to hear of the result of your interview with the Principal. And it would be a great moment for Saxl and me if we could announce your favourable decision to our Board at their next meeting on 24th April. Particulars about the date, and about your presence here this summer are of minor importance compared with your ultimate "yes."[60]

It was agreed, then, that Klibansky could spend time both in Canada and the UK, and it looked promising. He wrote to Bing, "I am very glad indeed you think the proposal: this June–Christmas London; Christmas–end May Montreal may work."[61]

But in the end nothing came of it. Saxl died on 22 March 1948, and Henri Frankfort, a Dutch orientalist and friend of the Warburg Institute, became his successor in the autumn of the same year. Warburg's *hairesis* seemed to have been led back to Egypt, at least in its academic expertise, as the new director was working in Near Eastern Studies and as an excavator in several sites in Egypt and in Iraq. In a rabbinic perspective this "going back to Egypt" would have constituted a repetition of Israel's cardinal sin, on behalf of which the temple of King Solomon had been destroyed. After Frankfort's sudden death, Bing finally became director of the Warburg Institute from 1955 to 1959.[62] And though he opted to make Montreal his permanent home from 1948 as Frothingham Professor of Logic and Metaphysics at McGill, the charismatic Klibansky maintained strong ties with the Warburg Institute and a clear role in its projects. He became Honorary Fellow *in permanentia* and remained a frequent visitor to the institute.

After Catastrophe: Schramm's Case

The complexity of the structure that Warburg's *hairesis* possessed can perhaps best be observed in the person of Percy Ernst Schramm, historian of medieval political symbolism and ritual, one of the most highly regarded experts on the ideology of the German Middle Ages. A lot has been written about him and his connection to the KBW, on his friendship with Saxl, which finally broke in 1935, and on his commitment to Germany, which ended in collaboration with the Nazis, as he acted as the official staff diarist of the High Command of the German *Wehrmacht* from 1943 to 1945.[63] In 1935, Schramm joined the German protests against the first volume of the *Kulturwissenschaftliche Bibliographie zum Nachleben der Antike*, which culminated in a scathing review in the *Völkische Beobachter* in January 1935.[64] Saxl was alarmed by it and wrote to Klibansky, who then was away for research in Brussels: "The implications of the article in the *Völkische Beobachter* are rather considerable. We must talk about the matters calmly, when you are back."[65] Saxl's reaction was also influenced by a letter that Schramm had written two days earlier, in which he had expressed his discomfort that some member of the Warburg circle had declared to Ludwig Curtius, then the director at the Deutsches Archäologisches Institut (German Archaeological Institute) in Rome, that he would no longer enter the house of a German professor.[66] Touchiness of course plays a major role here and masks deeper conflicts connected to shame and guilt. In another letter, Schramm finally disclosed the identity of the anonymous author – who, in fact, was none other than Klibansky.[67]

I have found other traces of Schramm in the correspondence between Bing and Klibansky which were hitherto unknown. They deserve our interest and are contained in letters written twenty years after Schramm's break with Saxl.

At the end of a long letter dated May 1955, Klibansky posed the following question to Bing:

> I have been asked to join an international advisory board concerned with an interesting project. Requesting to see the names of the other members, I found that P. Schramm (Goettingen) is among them. Since you knew him well, you may perhaps be able to tell me whether he was a mere Mitlaeufer [follower] – *charakterlos* [unprincipled] as most of his colleagues – or more than a mere turncoat. In the latter case, I would make it clear that I do not wish to be associated with him and regretfully decline. If the more urgent matters mentioned above leave you time, I should much like to have your opinion of the man.[68]

A few days later, Bing replied:

> Your query about Schramm: "charakterlos" he certainly was, and I think more than a Mitläufer. The story goes that at one point he showed his students a photograph representing him with Hitler, and in any case during the latter part of the war he was historiographer to the Grosse Hauptquartier. You will also remember that before the outbreak of the war he behaved very cowardly towards Saxl when he was invited here for the Coronation and that Saxl in his goodness made him feel, I am glad to say, the shabbiness of his behaviour. After the war he tried to get straight with us, and I remember that Saxl wanted to write him a strong letter but in the end did not do it because he was sick of "Auseinandersetzungen" [quarrelling].
>
> After Saxl's death I had a very emotional letter from him (addressed to "Sehr geehrte Herren") to which I did not reply. Recently he wrote an impersonal letter asking our permission for a reprint of *Kaiser, Rom*

> *und Renovatio*. These are the facts as far as I know them. I do not know whether they warrant any action on your part with regard to the advisory board which you mention. As far as I can see, he now plays his old rôle as "pure" historian and I think he is better at that job than at politics. On the whole I feel that though I have no great mind for personal reasons to shake hands with the man ever again, he is no worse and no better than other German professors as far as character is concerned; and that it is hardly possible to avoid him if one agrees to co-operating with the Germans at all.[69]

Some days later, Klibansky closed the case and remarked, "Schramm. Thank you for your detailed information. This is exactly what I wanted to know. What a sorry fellow!"[70]

Such correspondences and related documents of the KBW, many viewed here through the "node" of Raymond Klibansky, reveal a Jewish dimension within the KBW – a *hairesis* – regardless of the fact that it was never an explicit aim of its founder. It is yet another way in which the Warburg Library transmitted traditions and transitions from the ancient world to the modern.

NOTES

1 Scholem, *From Berlin to Jerusalem*, 131. The initial 1977 publication was in German: *Von Berlin nach Jerusalem*.

2 Ibid., "deren jüdische Intensität von moderierter Sympathie bis zum Nullpunkt, ja darunter ging."

3 The only person, to my knowledge, who has written on the contacts between the Warburg group and the Jerusalem professors is Moshe Idel in *Saturn's Jews*, 88–97. Not being Scholem's student, Idel might have taken advantage of a certain distance from him, but he benefitted from contact with a younger faculty member of the Hebrew University, Shlomo Pines. I thank Menachem Lorberbaum (Jerusalem) for this information.

4 Josephus, *The Jewish War*, Bk. 2, Ch. 8, Par. 2 [= Bk. 2, Niese verse no. 119]. This is probably the oldest of Josephus's versions. See also Schäfer, *History of the Jews in Antiquity*, 71.

5 "Le premier siècle est le dernier grand siècle de la littérature apocalyptique juive,

dont le 'Messie' est un personage important." Vidal-Naquet, "Du bon usage de la trahison," 74 (my translation).

6 Rajak, *Josephus*, 112.

7 For a new reading of Josephus, see Treml, "Flavius Josephus im Jüdischen Krieg."

8 See, for example, Rieff, *Charisma.*

9 Sloterdijk, *God's Zeal*, 37, n. 23. For a further study of the narratives of feverishly changing institutions, see Huessy, *Out of Revolution.*

10 See Gay, *A Godless Jew*, 19.

11 See Ginzburg, "From Aby Warburg to E.H. Gombrich," in *Myths, Emblems, Clues* (1990). The original essay appeared in Italian in 1966.

12 See Treml, "Warburgs Nachleben." See also Treml, "Nachleben als Programm und Methode der Kulturwissenschaftlichen Bibliothek Warburg."

13 For a first, yet quite comprehensive attempt, see Schäfer, *Die Kulturwissenschaftliche Bibliothek Warburg.*

14 On Liebeschütz and the *Gedächtnisstiftung*, see Biester, *Der innere Beruf zur Wissenschaft: Paul Ruben (1866–1943)*, 132–8; on Liebeschütz and the *Lehranstalt*, see Simon, *Aufbau im Untergang*, 61–4.

15 Simon, *Aufbau*, 63, n. 14.

16 For a first overview on Liebeschütz, see Patschovsky's "Nachwort des Herausgebers," to Liebeschütz, *Synagoge und Ecclesia*, 237–9.

17 Warburg, *Tagebuch der Kulturwissenschaftlichen Bibliothek Warburg mit Einträgen von Gertrud Bing und Fritz Saxl*, 482.

18 See Petropoulos, *The Faustian Bargain*, 204–9. The so-called "Kümmel Report," a plan and inventory on how and what to plunder in occupied Europe and made upon Goebbel's orders, is supposed to have been authored by von Holst.

19 Saalmann, *Kunstpolitik der Berliner Museen 1919–1959*, 332.

20 Ibid., 236.

21 See von Holst, *Creators, Collectors, and Connoisseurs.*

22 See Mittig, "Ein Residuum der Unzufriedenheit," 53 and n. 3.

23 See Warburg, "Francesco Sassetti's Last Injunctions to His Sons," 241–5.

24 Ibid., 241.

25 This comparison was first made in Günther, "d'anima Fiorentino," 37. On the Ghirlandaio fresco, see Warburg, "The Art of Portraiture and the Florentine Bourgeoisie," 193–4 and fig. 25.

26 Warburg, "Dürer and Italian Antiquity," 555. For the Dionysian heritage of Warburg, see Treml, "Dionysos, Luther und der Teufel im Denkraum."

27 I thank Margarete Vöhringer, my former colleague at the Centre for Literary Culture and Research (ZfL) Berlin and now at Göttingen University, for having drawn my attention to this fact. For an application of the model, see Peter Galison, "Practice All the Way Down," in *Kuhn's "Structure of Scientific Revolutions" at Fifty: Reflections on a Science Classic*, edited by Robert J. Richards and Lorraine Daston (London: University of Chicago Press, 2016), 42–69.

28 Foucault, "The Order of Discourse," 52–3.

29 See Foucault, *The Care of the Self.*

30 See Fleck, *The Genesis and Development of a Scientific Fact.*

31 See Warburg, "Sandro Botticelli's *Birth of Venus* and *Spring*," 89, 93, 95, 96, 98, et passim.

32 Ibid., 96. Alberti's obsession was actually a contemporary one; see, for example, Spyros Papapetros, *On the Animation of the Inorganic. Art, Architecture, and the Extension of Life*, (Chicago: University of Chicago Press, 2012).

33 Kafka, *Letters to Milena*, 229 (translation slightly altered).

34 Baudelaire, "Correspondances." The poem begins: "La Nature est un temple où de vivants piliers [/] Laissent parfois sortir de confuses paroles; [/] L'homme y passe à travers des forêts de symboles [/] Qui l'observent avec des regards familiers." [Nature is a temple where living pillars [/] Let escape sometimes confused words; [/] Man traverses it through forests of symbols [/] That observe him with familiar glances.] The notion of "correspondence" was introduced by Karl Mannheim (I thank my colleague Falko Schmieder for this hint), but the theory of correspondence was established by no other than Walter Benjamin.

35 Gombrich, *Aby Warburg: An Intellectual Biography*, 190n.

36 Ibid., 336.

37 See Meyer, *Ernst Cassirer*, 125.

38 See Grolle, *Walter Solmitz*

39 Warburg Institute Archive (hereafter WIA), General Correspondence (hereafter GC): Fritz Saxl to Gertrud Bing, 14 June 1928. On the Saxl children, see McEwan, *Fritz Saxl: eine Biografie*, 17.

40 Deutsches Literaturarchiv Marbach, A: Raymond Klibansky (hereafter DLA, A, KLIBANSKY): Klibansky to Gertrude Bing, 28 January 1953. When rumours of pedophilic acts committed by former director Gerold Becker and others in the 1970s and 1980s arose in the late 1990s, they were quickly suppressed, but emerged again in 2010, leading to the closure of the Odenwaldschule five years later.

41 Leroux, *Raymond Klibansky 1905–2005. La Bibliothèque d'un philosophe*, 111–16.

42 Warburg, *Tagebuch*, 5–8, 10, 17, 20, 27–9, et passim.

43 Ibid., 54 ("die Stellung der Zeit zur Antike" [The relation of our time to antiquity]).

44 Ibid., 78 ("wird by Uzielli in Frankfurt für Mark 75, George-Literatur besorgen").

45 Klibansky and Kristeller in some sense shared a similar fate, but in one aspect also a very different one. While Hoffmann accepted to supervise Klibansky's *Habilitation* work, he told Kristeller that it would be impossible for him to do so with another Jew due to the anti-Semitism prevailing at German universities. I thank Philippe Despoix for this information.

46 WIA, GC: Klibansky to Bing, 27 February 1951.

47 Klibansky, *Le Philosophe et la mémoire du siècle*, 34 and 37.

48 Saxl, "The History of Warburg's Library," 331.

49 Klibansky, *Le Philosophe et la mémoire du siècle*, 2.

50 Idel, *Hasidism: Between Ecstasy and Magic*, 34.

51 Idel, *Saturn's Jews*, 47–83.

52 See Scholem, *Sabbatai Sevi*.

53 "Pas de façon obsessionnelle – surtout pas de la part de ma mère. C'était plutôt un mode de vie." Klibansky, *Le Philosophe et la mémoire du siècle*, 3.

54 McEwan, "Gegen die 'Pioniere der Diesseitigkeit.'"

55 Annual report 1900/1901 of the Kaiserlich-Königliches Maximilians-Gymnasium, now Bundesgymnasium Vienna 9, Wasagasse 10, archive.

56 Ibid., the annual reports from 1900/1901 to 1907/1908.

57 Liebeschütz, "Obituary" [of Fritz Saxl], 138. I found a copy of it in the Saxl-Klibansky correspondence folder of the DLA, A, KLIBANSKY files.

58 "Einen Abend bis zum Morgengrauen verbrachte ich bei Panofsky, zuerst zusammen mit Frau Panofsky u. Frl. Brauer, dann allein mit der Dürer'schen Melancholie. P. machte sogleich an einigen Texten, die ich vorlegte, ch ch m der er ist, einige Coniecturen, schien aber im Allgemeinen mit der Entwicklung des Saturn-Bildes, die ich im Umriß gab, einverstanden; bleibt noch abzuwarten, was Sie dazu sagen. Ich verzettele das Ganze nach meiner Rückkehr nach Heidelberg so, dass es für P. lesbar wird und schicke es ihm; er wollte inzwischen am Dürer-Kapitel arbeiten. " WIA, GC: Klibansky to Saxl, 10 August 1929.

59 DLA, A, KLIBANSKY: Bing to Klibansky, 10 March 1947.

60 DLA, A, KLIBANSKY: Bing to Klibansky, 26 March 1947.

64 WIA, GC: Klibansky to Bing, 23 March 1947.

62 Meyer and Treml, "Gertrud Bing – ein intellektuelles Porträt."

63 See: Grolle, *Der Hamburger Percy Ernst Schramm*; Grolle, "Percy Ernst Schramm – Fritz Saxl"; Thieme, *Percy Ernst Schramm und das Mittelalter*.

64 Meier, Newald, and Wind, *Kulturwissenschaftliche Bibliographie zum Nachleben der Antike*, vol.1, *Die Erscheinungen des Jahres 1931*; Rasch, "Juden und Emigranten machen deutsche Wissenschaft."

65 "Die Konsequenzen des Aufsatzes im 'Völkischen Beobachter' sind ziemlich erheblich. Wir müssen dann die Dinge in Ruhe besprechen, wenn Sie zurück sind." DLA, A, KLIBANSKY: Saxl to Klibansky, 22 January 1935.

66 Thieme, *Percy Ernst Schramm*, 379 (citing correspondence from Schramm to Saxl, 20 January 1935).

67 Ibid., (citing correspondence from Schramm to Saxl, 31 March 1935; the original letter is misdated). See also Grolle, "Schramm–Saxl," 104–5.

68 DLA, A, KLIBANSKY: Klibansky to Bing, 11 May 1955, carbon copy.

69 DLA, A, KLIBANSKY: Bing to Klibansky, 23 May 1955.

70 DLA, A, KLIBANSKY: Klibansky to Bing, 26 May 1955, carbon copy.

THREE

The Warburg Institute Reaches Out: Raymond Klibańsky and His British Contacts

GRAHAM WHITAKER

On a Foreign Shore: The Institute Sets Out Its Stall

Following the arrival of the Kulturwissenschaftliche Bibliothek Warburg (KBW) in London in December 1933, initially on loan from its home in Hamburg, Fritz Saxl, Edgar Wind, and others made strenuous efforts to acquaint British scholars and others who might have an interest in its collections with the newly established and renamed library. The Warburg Institute library was ready for re-opening in May 1934 within Thames House on Millbank, and Gertrud Bing and Wind both wrote descriptions of the library and its aims, which were published in the *Library Association Record*.[1] Saxl gave a paper ("The Origin and Survival of a Pictorial Type [the Mithras Reliefs]")[2] at the General Meeting of the Classical Association held at Southampton in April 1935, and a further paper ("The Revival of Late Antique Astrology")[3] also at Southampton in the following January.[4] In the *Annual Report* for 1934/35, he noted: "The Library is our first link with the public, the second is the series of our lectures … Our third link with the public consists in the series of publications for which we are responsible."[5]

The KBW publications had been initiated by Saxl in two series, the *Studien* (from 1922) and the *Vorträge* (first complete volume in 1923). These had been crucial in establishing the reputation of the KBW further afield, and in defining the research aims that Aby Warburg had hoped his library would promote. In particular, the *Studien* were contributed by a circle of scholars centred around the KBW, including Ernst Cassirer and Erwin Panofsky. In Saxl's report, however, he drew attention to more recent or planned publications through which the "link with the public," and indeed the purpose of the institute, might more usefully be demonstrated. These were the *Bibliography on the Survival of the Classics*, the *Festschrift* being prepared to honour Cassirer on reaching his sixtieth birthday in July 1934, and the proposed series of publications under the editorship of Raymond Klibansky, described as an *Organon* and designed to "comprise unpublished or rare texts, particularly those illustrating the relation of Mediaeval Christian, Jewish, and Arab writers to the Greek tradition." It is here that the first outline of the *Corpus Platonicum Medii Aevi* receives an official mention in the program of the institute. In this chapter, I discuss these three publications – the *Bibliography*, the *Festschrift*, and the *Corpus Platonicum*, together with its satellite, *Mediaeval and Renaissance Studies* – in relation to Klibansky and the contacts that he developed in the years from 1933 until the Second World War.

The *Bibliography* need only be briefly considered, as it was well underway before the KBW was transferred to London and Klibansky came to live in England. For its direct genesis we must go back to March 1929. In that month, the literary historian Richard Newald wrote to the KBW, having been commissioned to provide a contribution to the prestigious series of surveys of classical studies inaugurated in 1873 by Conrad Bursian as *Jahresbericht über die Fortschritte der classischen Altertumswissenschaft*. The format of these surveys provided for a detailed review of the literature within a specified period, often running to a hundred pages or more. Newald's survey of the classical tradition was the first to appear in the series, as volume 232 in 1931. He had begun work on it in 1924 or 1925, and gathered much of the material while he was in Munich, but was now finding it difficult to secure some of the references and literature he needed in Freiburg im Breisgau.[6] Newald therefore wrote to the KBW requesting details of that library's most recent publications and lectures.[7] In the following year he required more extensive assistance. Karl Münscher, the general editor of the *Jahresbericht*, wrote to the KBW in February 1930 on Newald's behalf to ask whether he could visit the library and use its resources; Bing replied, welcoming the idea and offering a small subvention to assist Newald.[8] His visit to Hamburg took place in April 1930, and it marked the beginning of a close working relationship in particular with the librarian Hans Meier, whose help was acknowledged in the preface to Newald's survey. A series of letters between the two throughout the remainder of 1930 documents Newald's queries on his survey and later the proofs of it that Meier was to check.

Shortly before its publication in 1931, Saxl approached Newald with the idea that the new collaboration between the KBW and himself might be extended by means of a subject bibliography, which could appear more regularly than the Bursian surveys allowed. His initial idea was to issue it as a supplement to the *Vorträge*.[9] The bibliography, while following the practice of Bursian in being annotated, would adopt a more critical approach, and this would be emphasized by its context. Newald was keen to retain the good working relationship he had established with the staff of the KBW, and with Meier in particular, and readily acquiesced to Saxl's proposal. There was also a practical consideration here, which soon became a necessity, in that the library, by means of promising a notice in the *Bibliography*, could hope to receive new acquisitions as review copies.[10] By July 1931, the forced discontinuation of the published lectures for reasons of economy meant that the *Bibliography* would be issued as a separate publication. Saxl also made it clear in a letter of January 1932 that the continuation of the project was directly owing to the support and interest of Max Warburg.[11]

Klibansky's involvement with the *Bibliography* began when he was approached by Edgar Wind, who wrote in September 1931 to ask if he would take on the subject area of the survival of antiquity in the history of philosophy.[12] In his reply, Klibansky agreed, but raised a number of questions in relation to the intended scope of the subject, which he felt was too general and raised problems of organization. Work on the *Bibliography* was soon to be disrupted in 1933, however, by the Nazis' rise to power and the consequent dismissal of "non-Aryan" professors. Klibansky was forced to give up his work on the editions of Nicholas of Cusa and Meister Eckhart, although he continued to visit libraries and examine manuscripts. At the same time he was concerned with the fate of the KBW and his own immediate family. It is not surprising, therefore, that he fell behind with his contributions, although his delay caused irritation to Meier and Saxl.[13] The first volume of the *Bibliography* was published in Germany in 1934,[14] with an introduction in

German by Wind that gave rise to a notorious anti-Semitic review by Martin Rasch.[15] It was reprinted in 1935, with a revised introduction in English, and a second volume for the years 1932–33 appeared in 1938. Klibansky contributed some eighty entries to the first volume, but his name is absent from the second, partly because he had reservations about the whole project and the time it consumed,[16] and partly because he was by then concentrating on the *Corpus Platonicum*.

Klibansky's Meeting with Clement Webb

It should not be forgotten that, well ahead of its transfer to London, members of the KBW staff and those associated with it, had been engaged in making contact with England. Cassirer, for example, had lectured at King's College London in 1927 and Saxl had worked briefly in London in 1928 on the third volume of his *Catalogue of Astrological and Mythological Illuminated Manuscripts*.[17] Even more significantly, four British academics were invited to the KBW in 1930–31, for a programme of lectures under the broad title of *England und die Antike*.[18] One of these, Sir Richard Winn Livingstone, would subsequently act as the conduit between Saxl and one of the earliest British scholars to befriend Klibansky, Clement Charles Julian Webb (1865–1954). Webb had been the first holder, from 1920 to 1930, of the Oriel (later, Nolloth) Chair in the Philosophy of the Christian Religion at Oriel College, Oxford, and the Gifford Lecturer in Natural Philosophy at Aberdeen during 1918–19. His two series of lectures there were published as *God and Personality* and *Divine Personality and Human Life*.[19] In addition, by the time he met Klibansky in 1933, Webb had published not only a further series of lectures given in Oxford in 1924, under the title *Kant's Philosophy of Religion*,[20] but also two editions of John of Salisbury, Bishop of Chartres,[21] and so had a direct interest in Klibansky's work on medieval philosophy.

Webb kept a series of detailed diaries for his entire adult life, from 1887 to 1954, the year of his death – they are preserved with the Webb family papers at the Bodleian Library – and these form a prime source for his initial meeting and later dealings with Klibansky.[22] On 3 October 1933, Webb's diary records the receipt of a letter "from Livingstone, enclosing one from Saxl, head of the Warburg Institute, wh. has been [turned] out of Germany, about a young man from Heidelberg who is editing Nicholas of Cusa & writing on the school of Chartres, & wants to be put into contact with others interested in these subjects." His initial reply to Livingstone, on the following day, in which he asked for further information about Klibansky, is preserved in the institute's archive.[23] Saxl evidently supplied this information and wrote to offer some volumes from the KBW's series of studies, thus demonstrating the "third link with the public" through the supply of publications, as was frequently to be the case during the early years in London.[24]

A further exchange of correspondence followed during which Webb invited Klibansky to stay overnight, and to lunch with him at Magdalen College the following day. His meeting with Klibansky at Oxford station on Tuesday, 24 October, is recorded as follows:

> I met young Klibansky at the station, whereat he arrived by the train getting in at 3.4. A very good looking, agreeable, & learned young man of 28 – keen and modest and scholarly. I took him up on top of bus[25] to Magdalen where he left his bag & then over the College, into the Botanic Garden, Ch. Ch. Meadow, into the cathedral, thro' Tom Quad, to the Union, into New College Cloisters & Garden & so back to Magdalen in time to catch the 5 oclock bus to Marston, wh. took us home to tea. E[leanor, Webb's wife] was delighted with our guest, whose talk was very interesting (tho' distressing, as regards the situation in Germany) & who retired by 10.[26]

At lunch the next day, Klibansky met Webb's other guests: Paul Benecke, Maurice Powicke, William Pantin, Richard Hunt, and C.S. Lewis.[27] With the exception, perhaps, of Benecke, whose published scholarship was limited by the services he rendered to Magdalen in teaching and administration over many years, these men represented an important cross-section of Oxford medievalists. From 1919, Powicke had been professor of mediaeval history at Manchester and, since 1928, Regius Professor of Modern History (as opposed to Ancient History) at Oxford. Pantin was one of his students at Manchester and followed Powicke to Oxford in 1933. Both were members of Oriel College, which was to be Klibansky's collegiate home from 1936. At that time the twenty-five-year-old Hunt was working on a doctoral thesis on Alexander

Neckam or Nequam (1157–1217), the English scholar and theologian; this was supervised by Powicke, and completed in 1936 after Hunt had moved to Liverpool University in 1934 as a lecturer in palaeography.[28] C.S. Lewis was working on his study of medieval literature and courtly love, published as *The Allegory of Love* in 1936. Webb reported that "they were all charmed by K.," while Powicke was sufficiently impressed by Klibansky to propose him for honorary membership of the Oriel Senior Common Room.[29]

This lunch was probably the occasion when Klibansky suggested to Webb that he might visit the Cassirers at their lodgings in Woodstock Road. Webb did so on 6 November; three months later, on 7 February 1934, the Cassirers dined at the Webbs' home, together with Livingstone, Sir David Ross, and their wives. Webb also attended the three lectures on Goethe that Cassirer gave at the Taylor Institution during February. On these occasions Cassirer spoke in German, and Webb noted that "I understood sometimes what he was talking about but did not follow what he said of it."[30] This may have been true of other members of the audience, as Cassirer was slow to learn English and this lack remained a difficulty during his time at Oxford. Klibansky, in contrast, had a fluency in languages and was able to claim, on his application form for a work permit in connection with his temporary lectureship at King's College London, that he could speak English "moderately well," but that in writing he was "not yet able to express philosophical thoughts in an adequate manner."

The document in which this is to be found is part of Klibansky's file in the Society for the Protection of Science and Learning (SPSL) collection at the Bodleian Library.[31] The general information that Klibansky supplied as part of his application is date-stamped 2 August 1934, and includes a list of eleven references; these include Cassirer, Saxl, and, of his British colleagues, both Webb and Powicke. The testimonial by Cassirer is dated "London, 8. Okt." – whether this is 1933 or 1934 is unclear; that by Saxl is dated 19 November 1934. It refers to to the planned Cassirer *Festschrift*, and to Klibansky's "idea that the Warburg Institute should serve abroad as a nucleus for studies into the history of civilisation in the same sense as before in Germany." A further important testimonial is offered by John Macmurray, Grote Professor of the Philosophy of Mind and Logic at University College London, who was asked by the Academic Assistance Council (forerunner of the SPSL) to interview Klibansky. Macmurray wrote as follows:

> Dr Klibansky seems to me to be a man of great natural philosophical ability, probably something of a "genius", in his own field. For the ordinary work of academic philosophy he is probably not well fitted. He is the embodiment of the "researcher"; also his field, which is mediaeval philosophy – but as a living issue for philosophy to-day, and not merely as of historical interest – is outside the scope of existing academic curricula in this country. At most there is a tendency towards a new interest in the Mediaevals showing itself in certain circles. Prof. A.E. [Alfred Edward] Taylor of Edinburgh, Prof. Webb of Oxford and perhaps Prof. [William George] de Burgh of Reading might be very interested. I should think that in his case the only thing to be done is to make arrangements that would permit of his carrying on his research work, and which would put him in touch with libraries – this is very essential and a little difficult in his case, but I understand that the library which is most essential is likely to come to London from Hamburg – and with persons who are moving in the direction of his own interests. That means that he should reside either in Oxford or in London, if he is to reside in this country.

The Cassirer *Festschrift*

The second conduit for Klibansky was the British Institute of Philosophy, founded in 1925, its purpose in part being to narrow the gap between academic philosophers and those with a more general interest in philosophical questions. The *Journal of Philosophical Studies* began publication in January 1926, shortening its title to *Philosophy* in 1931. It was to the tenth volume for 1935 that Webb, who was one of the editorial assistants, contributed a review of the first fascicule of Klibansky's edition of Meister Eckhart, the *Super oratione Dominica*.[32] His diary for 13 March 1934 records an occasion when, after a meeting of the institute that Webb was chairing at University College London, Klibansky had insisted on accompanying him back to Lancaster Gate tube station, to talk about the Cassirer *Festschrift*.[33] This seems to be the earliest such reference by Webb, and it is the *Festschrift* that now needs to be considered.[34]

Published under the title *Philosophy and History* on 23 April 1936 by Oxford University Press, the *Festschrift* was jointly edited by Klibansky and Herbert James (known as Hamish) Paton. Paton was at that time professor of logic and rhetoric in the University of Glasgow and one of the leading Kantian scholars in Britain.[35] Klibansky had conceived the idea of the *Festschrift* in 1933 to celebrate Cassirer's sixtieth birthday on 28 July 1934. A certain amount is known about its progress and production schedule from the project file (LB 7479) in the Oxford University Press Archive, although the file has been substantially weeded. The initial approach was made by Saxl and, following this, Klibansky met with Kenneth Sisam, later (from 1942) secretary to the Delegates of the Press. The first letter in the file is from Sisam to Klibansky and is dated 2 May 1934. It makes clear from the beginning Sisam's (and therefore the press's) view that, in order for the book to be marketable, all the contributions would need to be either in English or translated into English. It had evidently already been decided to offer the volume on subscription, but Sisam calculated the cost of production at £200, and suggested to Saxl that he should obtain a guarantee of 125 guineas (£131.25) toward this cost. The Delegates of the Press would not agree to publish honorary volumes at their own risk; the subscriptions were therefore an additional guarantee, and it would not matter if, as indeed happened, not all the subscriptions were taken up. Saxl was able to write on 30 May to confirm that the guaranteed sum could be made available from a Swiss source (Ledonia AG of Zürich); in fact, this was through Frau Toni Cassirer's brother-in-law, Max Waller, who had Swiss business interests.[36] He had also written to Paton in Glasgow to ask whether he would act as joint editor, in view of the obligation to publish in English, and it was Paton who arranged for the necessary translations, several of which were carried out by staff of the university at Glasgow.

One point in the history of the *Festschrift* has been unclear, and the accounts of Toni Cassirer and John Michael Krois (editor of Cassirer's selected letters) might seem to conflict to some extent. By the time of Cassirer's actual birthday, the volume later published as *Philosophy and History* was nowhere near ready, and Klibansky decided hurriedly to assemble as an alternative a *Festgabe*, to which Cassirer's students and younger colleagues might contribute.[37] Evidence for this has now come to light in the Klibansky *Nachlass*, in the Deutsches Literaturarchiv at Marbach. During June and July 1934, Klibansky was concurrently enlisting contributors for the *Festgabe* and the *Festschrift*. For the former, these included Ernst Zinn (1910–1990), to whom he wrote on 16 June; Zinn, however, declined as he was preparing for his *Promotion*.[38] The letter confirms that the *Festgabe* was to be a private publication to honour Cassirer and to avoid any suggestion of partisanship. He also wrote among others to Conradine Lück (1885–1959), the educationalist and author, and to Eric(h) Weil (1904–1977), a student of Cassirer's.[39]

In the preparation of the *Festschrift* Klibansky requested Paton's help in securing a contribution from the elderly Samuel Alexander (1859–1938), of the University of Manchester. His essay, "The Historicity of Things,"[40] proved to be his swansong as a philosopher. In part it returns to the themes of his Gifford Lectures at Glasgow during 1916–18, published as *Space, Time, and Deity* (1920). Alexander had also contributed the first article, "Art and Science," to the initial volume of the *Journal of Philosophical Studies*; like Webb and the third British contributor to the *Festschrift*, Susan Stebbing,[41] Alexander was one of the assistant editors of the *Journal*. There is a sympathetic portrait of him in Naomi Mitchison's memoir, *You May Well Ask*.[42] Stebbing (1885–1943), professor at Bedford College, a college for women, was the first woman in Britain to hold a chair of philosophy. Cassirer had been elected to the staff association at the college in 1934 with the support of the principal, Geraldine Jebb.[43] In January and February 1935, he gave a series of lectures on Goethe at the college, similar to those he presented at the Taylor Institution the previous year. Stebbing's contribution, "Some Ambiguities in Discussions Concerning Time,"[44] is essentially a critique of John McTaggart's *The Unreality of Time* (1908);[45] before writing this critique, Stebbing had asked to borrow the third volume of Cassirer's *Philosophy of Symbolic Forms* (*The Phenomenology of Knowledge*) from the institute library, although her single Cassirer quotation is from *On Einstein's Theory of Relativity*.[46] Klibansky approached a number of other potential British contributors who declined for various reasons, including Ross (1877–1971), who was preparing his 1935 Gifford Lectures at Aberdeen on "Foundations of Ethics"; Gilbert Murray (1866–1957), who at the time chaired the International Committee on Intellectual Cooperation in Geneva; and Bertrand Russell (1872–1970), who was too busy.[47]

Saxl, Edgar Wind, Erwin Panofsky, and Klibansky represented the KBW tradition in the *Festschrift*. Other contributors included Ernst Hoffmann, who had invited Klibansky to contribute to the edition of the works of Nicholas of Cusa, and was also a close friend of Cassirer. Hoffmann at first demurred from contributing; in a letter to Klibansky he pointed to the boycott by German academics of those publications that would not accept contributions in German and offered to withdraw from the project or to substitute another publication in honour of Cassirer's birthday.[48] He also required to be satisfied that none of the contributors was ill-disposed to Germany (*aggressiv gegen Deutschland*). Saxl wrote an emollient letter, explaining that the decision to publish the work in English was due solely to financial considerations and to the press's advice on the difficulty of selling a multilingual volume.

Publication of the *Festschrift* in April 1936, by which time Cassirer had moved from Oxford to Gothenburg, was of particular importance to Saxl and the institute. It came at a time when there were still distinct uncertainties over whether the institute would remain in London, and when these uncertainties had caused British and other sponsors to be cautious about committing funds to it. These concerns are set out in an important letter from Bing to Toni Cassirer, dated 24 March, less than a month earlier.[49] Aside from the *Festschrift* being one of the publications that would help to make the institute's work more familiar in its London home in the period before it had established its own *Journal*, Saxl viewed the inclusion of British contributors – and its overall high quality – as providing continuity between London and the former KBW in Hamburg. At the same time, it was a portrait of Cassirer and the breadth of his philosophical concerns – as its epigraph, a fragment attributed to the *Antiope* of Euripides,[50] suggests – and it would serve to make him better known in the English-speaking world through reviews.[51]

The critical reception of the *Festschrift* was mixed. It was not reviewed in any periodical published in Germany. This is scarcely surprising, in view of the blatantly anti-Semitic review of the *Bibliography* by Rasch.[52] Copies were, however, sent to German periodicals, and Paton queried the lack of any result in a letter written to the press in June 1938.[53] Sisam replied on this point as follows: "I shall consult our review department in London about the possibility of enquiring their reasons for not reviewing, but I need hardly say that the subject is delicate: a well-wisher of Professor Cassirer might be unwilling to publish an unfavourable review, and unable to publish a favourable review; and if I were a German publisher in that case, I should not like to give reasons."[54]

One review, at least, did appear in German; this was the notice by Theodor Wiesengrund-Adorno, in the 1937 volume of the *Zeitschrift für Sozialforschung*, edited by Max Horkheimer in Frankfurt, but which by that time was being published by the Parisian firm of Félix Alcan.[55] Adorno took issue with the *Festschrift* on several counts; in particular, he disliked the fact that all the contents were in English and drew attention to the disparate and indeed conflicting nature of the separate essays: "The authors included are not simply of disparate historical academic opinions, but also of actual conflicting political positions, as if their differences were merely those of academic debate."[56] The *Festschrift* did, in fact, receive a number of favourable and often detailed reviews, such as the one by William de Burgh in *Mind*. In this the word "fresh" occurs as a description of the approach taken in many of the essays, as it does in the letter that Sisam wrote to Cassirer after publication.[57]

Other Oxford Contacts and the Early Years of the *Corpus Platonicum*

In the same year, 1936, Klibansky moved to Oriel College, Oxford, at the invitation of Sir David Ross, provost of the college; with the British Academy, this proved to be a third conduit for contacts. Oriel was then a centre of medieval studies in Oxford, with the presence of Powicke and Pantin. In his memorial notice of Powicke, (Sir) Richard Southern noted that:

> his individual genius as a teacher ensured that he made a greater contribution to the study of history at the university than any professor since [William] Stubbs [1825–1901], and that Oxford replaced Manchester as the leading centre for medieval studies. Illuminating and suggesting rather than explaining, and encouraging graduate students to follow their own way while remaining the most important single influence in

their work, he produced a generation of distinguished medievalists often very different in style from himself.[58]

Like Ross and Webb, Powicke was a Fellow of the British Academy. He acted with Ross on the advisory committee that the academy was to establish to oversee the *Corpus Platonicum*, their names being printed on the title page verso of the first three volumes of the *Plato Latinus* and all three of the *Plato Arabus*. Saxl also served on this committee as the representative of the institute.

Ross was the pre-eminent Aristotelian in Britain during much of the twentieth century, not least because of his long life. He inaugurated the series of Aristotle translations with his *Metaphysics* in 1908, while his Oxford Classical Text of the *Analytica*, one of six and a half that he edited in that series, was issued in 1964 only seven years before his death. Born in Thurso in the north of Scotland, he was also an administrator of distinction, serving for example as president of the British Academy for four years; he was also a British representative on the Union Académique Internationale (UAI) and, after the war, its president. Ross had played a central part in the development of the *Corpus Aristotelicum*, which was financed and published under the auspices of the union.

This is not the place to discuss the *Corpus Platonicum* in detail, in view of the other essays in this book, but from documents in the Warburg Institute Archive I can sketch some of the administrative background that might not otherwise be known. In a memorandum that he prepared sometime after Saxl's death in 1948 – a likely hypothesis is that it was prepared for Sir Mortimer Wheeler (1890–1976), honorary secretary of the British Academy – Klibansky reviewed the history of the *Corpus*,[59] noting that his initial plan had been submitted to Saxl in 1933, and "frequently discussed with him in 1934"; and that it was first mentioned in print in Saxl's annual report of the institute for 1934/35, which also contained the justification for undertaking it:

> The extent and importance of the Platonic tradition from the end of the classical to the Renaissance period – which Dr. Klibansky tries to demonstrate in its continuity – can only be realised by a survey in its

> entirety of the manuscript material which has remained practically unknown to our day. A "Corpus Platonicum," that is, a complete collection of these documents, is therefore essential as a counterpart of the "Corpus Aristotelicum" … The Institute can undertake the Corpus Platonicum only in collaboration with other bodies and also hopes to secure the help of English scholars.[60]

Klibansky's report records the adoption and sponsorship of the *Corpus Platonicum* by the British Academy in April 1936 through the active support of Ross, who had just assumed the presidency. In May of the following year the program was submitted to the UAI as part of what was to appear two years later as *The Continuity of the Platonic Tradition during the Middle Ages.*[61] The text of this work, with its designation of the component parts of the *Plato Latinus* and *Arabus*, would therefore have been substantially complete at this time. It was also circulated to various British scholars, who, Klibansky hoped, might be persuaded to participate. He mentioned that the UAI decided to sponsor the project, although Ross in his president's reports made it clear that, unlike the *Corpus Aristotelicum,* it remained in the ownership and responsibility of the academy and the institute.[62] There is also a section on the *Plato Arabus* in which Klibansky refers to an initial adjustment of the editorship. It had been decided that Paul Kraus (1904–1944) and Richard Walzer (1900–1975) should have joint responsibility, but in November 1936 Walzer wrote to Klibansky suggesting that he should be sole editor, on the grounds of simplifying procedures (Kraus was at the time living in Paris but moved to Cairo in 1937) and "the fact that the Corpus was meant … to promote the understanding of the history of European philosophy as a whole, and only in a secondary way Arabic studies as such." Klibansky agreed to this and Walzer thereafter received a grant from the Academic Assistance Council.[63]

The question of a separate *Plato Byzantinus* also occupied Klibansky at an early stage. This was flagged up in *The Continuity* … but not in detail.[64] In October 1936, however, on the advice of Jacques Pirenne, he wrote to Henri Grégoire setting out a scheme for the possible contents of this part of the *Corpus*; in this letter he made it clear that he considered the *Byzantinus* an essential part to enable an understanding of the whole process of the Platonic tradition, even though it was not part of any direct approach to the British Academy for funds.[65] I have not so far traced a reply from Grégoire, but

Klibansky continued to mention the possibility of a *Plato Byzantinus* in letters to other potential contributors, including Paul Henry (1906–1984), the editor with Hans-Rudolf Schwyzer (1908–1993) of Plotinus.[66]

Finance in the early years of the *Corpus* was a recurrent problem. Grants were made by the British Academy, initially from the Henriette Hertz Fund during the period from 1936 to 1940. From 1941 onward, the Academy grants came from its General Fund and, although this fund was much reduced during the war, it was at this time that larger and regular grants were given to the *Corpus* project, up until the mid-1950s. Saxl was also able to find money from the institute's publication fund toward the costs of printing and, occasionally, obtaining photostats. The problem lay, however, in the funding of individual collaborators (Klibansky's usual word for contributors to the *Corpus*), in order to cover their research expenses. He had hoped to secure funding from humanities endowments in other countries, but this was not always forthcoming. One example must suffice. In October 1936 Klibansky wrote to another Oxford resident, Roberto Weiss (1906–1969), the historian of humanism in England and Italy, and later professor of Italian at University College London, who at that time had connections in Canada through the Hudson's Bay Company.[67] He contacted Weiss, asking him to write to John Buchan (1875–1940), Lord Tweedsmuir, governor general of Canada:

> The trouble is that the economic foundation of the whole is only partly secured. As the Academy can c[o]ntribute only a part of the expen[s]es it is necessary to appeal to other learned bodies and influential individuals. Every contribution will be welcome. If you write to Lord Tweedsmuir you can of course refer to the President of the British Academy (i.e. the Provost of Oriel, W.D. Ross). I told him already that you were probably going to write to Lord T. – As a sign of good will, we received a sum of L 5. - from a now empoverished [*sic*] lady. It would be nice if there were more such paupers. Should Lord T. not succeed in inducing some Canadian Institute, learned society or University to contribute he might perhaps some wealthy Canadians.[68]

This appeal fell on stony ground. Weiss reported Buchan's view: "I wish I could do something about your friend Dr. Klibansky's most excellent scheme, to which I wish all success. But I fear there is no interest in Canada in classical studies and no institutions in the least likely to consider the scheme. The most that can be done would be to get one or two public libraries to subscribe to the volumes when you have got the prospectus out."[69] This may have been a rather sweeping generalization – and this at a time when Buchan was concerned with the fall-out from Edward VIII's involvement with Wallis Simpson[70] – but it should be remembered that the Ontario Classical Association, forerunner of the Classical Association of Canada, was formed only in 1944 and its periodical, *The Phoenix*, commenced publication in 1946.

An Offshoot of the *Corpus Platonicum*, and Other Later Developments

The documentation relating to the periodical *Mediaeval and Renaissance Studies* or MARS, edited jointly by Klibansky and Richard Hunt and published between April 1941 and November 1968, makes it clear that various difficulties had to be overcome in both finance and organization. I mentioned earlier that Hunt met Klibansky as early as 1933. They corresponded while Hunt was at the University of Liverpool, and in December 1936 Hunt suggested that he would like to work for the *Corpus Platonicum* on one of the twelfth-century commentaries on the *Timaeus*. He went on to say, however: "What makes me hesitate is that I have started so many things and none of them are finished."[71] The "so many things" likely included the idea of a *Corpus catalogorum* which the Balliol classical scholar Roger Mynors had suggested to him, following the successful submission of his DPhil thesis.[72] Hunt's thesis was not published in his lifetime; nor was much of his work to be found in library catalogues. His biographer, Richard Southern, suggests that, once Hunt moved to Oxford in 1945 to take up the post of Keeper of Western Manuscripts at the Bodleian Library, his emphasis shifted to enhancing the library's manuscript collections and its internal records, and to answering reader enquiries and correspondence.[73] This, coupled with Klibansky's move to McGill University a year later, ensured that the intermittent publication of MARS during the war years, for reasons of paper rationing and lack of manpower at the Trinity Press, was continued during the post-war years.[74] As Regina Weber has suggested, it was largely thanks to Lotte

Labowsky, who had been officially engaged on the *Corpus Platonicum* project in February 1937, that the periodical was kept going in those years.[75]

During the period from 1937 to 1943, however, Hunt seems to have committed a substantial amount of time to MARS. The first, more general announcement of the new title was made in the *Proceedings of the British Academy* for 1938 (published in 1939). As Ross referred to it in his presidential report, "The Warburg Institute has decided to establish a new periodical, *Mediaeval and Renaissance Studies*, or in short MARS, for the publication of by-products of these researches; let us hope that its short name does not prove appropriate to the year of its establishment."[76] In an annex to the *1940/41* institute annual report, Klibansky noted: "The periodical comes into the compass of the *Corpus Platonicum Medii Aevi*, for, besides its wider purposes, it is intended to serve as a repository for discoveries made and results obtained in the course of research connected with the editions. It is hoped to publish here all that information which would unduly burden the prefaces to the texts."

Klibansky and Hunt started discussions in 1937, and Hunt had begun to seek funding locally in Liverpool, without much success, as he wrote to Klibansky in August: "I got no further in Liverpool, and just before I came away received a homily on the changed times. The 'rich families' there are no longer so wealthy, and the new rich will only give money for buildings."[77] Funding was eventually obtained however from the University of Liverpool and the Jowett Trustees at Balliol College, as well as in the form of a small grant from the institute. Another problem was raised by the editors of the institute's own *Journal*, founded in 1937, at the time when a prospectus for MARS was being prepared early in 1939. Rudolf Wittkower, the first head of the institute's photographic collection, wrote to Hunt to suggest that, unless the wording of the prospectus was modified, there would be an insufficient distinction between the purpose of the two periodicals. He thought it should be made clear that, while the *Journal of the Warburg Institute* was concerned with the humanities in the broadest sense, MARS was supposed to concentrate in particular on philosophy and theology.[78] Hunt was initially unconvinced by this distinction, and it was left to further discussion – and to the ever-diplomatic Saxl – to sort out.

In fact, the range of the articles in MARS was wider than that of a merely ancillary publication to the *Corpus Platonicum*, particularly in respect of manuscript studies. The first issue was delayed by the need to reprint it; communication with the original printers in Bruges was lost after the invasion of Belgium and a substitute was found in the Trinity Press, Worcester. The editorial preface is dated January 1941. In addition to several articles by the editors, the first volume (two issues, the second in 1943) contained articles by Father Daniel Callus, Labowsky, Eleanor Rathbone, Beryl Smalley, and Webb.[79] It was extensively reviewed, including by Roberto Weiss in the *Modern Language Review*.[80]

One further aspect of the *Corpus* concerns work that was initially designed to be part of it, but was eventually published elsewhere or not at all. In the case of Dorothea Singer (1882–1964), historian of science, and the first president of the British Society for the History of Science, Klibansky wrote to her on 6 February 1936, in a letter setting out how he saw the *Plato Latinus* section developing, and asking whether she would be interested in that part of the *pseudepigrapha* that dealt with alchemical manuscripts, to cover those relevant to the *Latinus* or *Arabus* sections. At that time, the scheme for the *Corpus Platonicum* had not been formally adopted by the British Academy and Klibansky asked Singer to treat the matter as confidential. Singer and her husband, Charles, a historian of medicine, were known to Saxl well before the KBW moved to London, and Charles Singer had contributed a review of the first two volumes of Saxl's catalogue of astrological manuscripts to the *Times Literary Supplement*.[81]

Dorothea Singer was ideally suited to this work, having published in 1924 her catalogue of Greek alchemical manuscripts in the series sponsored by the UAI, followed by the Latin and vernacular manuscripts in 1928–31.[82] Klibansky specified that:

> [It would mean] selecting the most important passages from works and the most characteristic sayings ascribed to Plato, which we know thanks to your excellent catalogue. You will, of course, know of much other material in manuscripts outside Great Britain and Ireland. Should you be interested in the plan, the question of which material should be included could be easily settled in accordance with your wishes. In my opinion, the aim of this section should be to give a comprehensive survey of the kind of alchemy ascribed to Plato rather than to publish this material in full.[83]

Singer accepted this offer and in the following year received a copy of the draft version of *The Continuity of the Platonic Tradition* that Klibansky had prepared for the UAI. As the Singers lived at Par in Cornwall, in a house later owned by Daphne Du Maurier, Dorothea Singer enlisted the help of Annie Anderson (dates uncertain), who lived in Highgate, North London, and had assisted in preparing her previous catalogues. There are letters from Lotte Labowsky during 1938 enquiring about progress, and, in reply to one of these, Singer mentioned that, since the *Anschluss* in March, she had been engaged in helping refugees from Vienna to resettle and train as nurses.[84] Her humanitarian work seems to have taken up an increasing amount of time, and nothing further happened until after the end of the war. In 1946 Singer published her summary of the relevant manuscripts not as part of the *Corpus Platonicum*, but in *Ambix*, the *Journal of the Society for the Study of Alchemy and Early Chemistry*.[85]

This was not the only example of a publication originally intended to be part of the *Corpus* that ended up elsewhere. The edition by Erwin Rosenthal of Averroes's commentary on Plato's *Republic*, originally planned for publication as part of *Plato Arabus*, was issued instead by Cambridge University Press in 1956.

Although Klibansky and Labowsky's close collaboration on the *Corpus Platonicum* might be said to have finished with the publication of the third volume of *Plato Latinus* in 1953,[86] they planned a more ambitious project to produce a full edition of the Greek text of the Proclus commentary. This was submitted as a proposal to Oxford University Press in 1959, and the full submission, preserved in a copy in the press archive,[87] details the reasoning behind it, including the need to replace the unsatisfactory nineteenth-century edition of Victor Cousin, the discovery of new manuscripts, and the relation of the Greek text to the Latin translation of William of Moerbeke (1215–1286). The press asked E.R. Dodds, Regius Professor of Greek at Oxford and an expert on Proclus, for his opinion on the initial proposal, which he gave in a letter to the press dated 21 July 1959:

> I warmly commend Klibansky's project for an edition of *Proclus in Parmenidem*. This is the only one of Proclus' Plato-commentaries which is not yet available in a critical modern edition, although it is particularly important for the light it throws both on the history of Platonism and

> on the text of Plato, as well as for its influence on various medieval and renaissance thinkers. The old Cousin editions are not only unreliable but unobtainable (I never succeeded in buying a copy myself). The need for a new one has been strongly urged by H. Langerbeck in his review of the partial edition of the Latin version (*Plato Latinus* vol. 3) by Klibansky and Labowsky (*Gnomon* 1955, p.102; worth looking at). Klibansky … is a good scholar and palaeographer, with an excellent knowledge of Proclus (on whom he has worked for many years); and his assistant, Miss Labowsky, is also a very accurate and capable person.[88]

Bing also showed an interest in the project, and expressed the hope that it might somehow be linked to the *Corpus Platonicum*.[89] Klibansky and Colin Roberts, secretary to the Delegates of the Oxford University Press, met in London on 23 September to discuss the matter further. A report from Roberts details their meeting:

> I saw Klibansky in London yesterday. He told me that he realized it would hardly be practicable to print the Latin as well as the Greek text; the memorandum, which suggested the contrary, came from his collaborator Dr. Labowsky. Even so, 200,000 words in Greek is a pretty formidable proposition; K. realizes this and would keep his introduction as brief as possible and also his apparatus. He has shown to his own satisfaction that most MSS. can be ignored for textual purposes, as they are merely copies of others; hence his apparatus (which will of course draw on the Latin version) will be brief and "elegant."
>
> There is one important MS. in Paris which ought to be collated afresh; he hopes to persuade Father (?) [Henri Dominique] Saffrey [1921–] to join the team with the object of making a new collation of this MS. The work will take some time to do; he estimates about five years … K. said an additional reason for producing an edition of Proclus' Commentary on the Parmenides – apart from the fact that no good critical edition existed – was that it was a fundamental text of German philosophy; it had greatly influenced Meis[t]er Eckhart and subsequent German philosophers down to Hegel, being largely responsible for the German dislike of formal logic.[90]

On 30 October the proposal went before the Delegates, who approved it despite the length and estimated cost (between £4,000 and £5,000).[91] In July 1964 and again in April 1966 Klibansky reported that he and Labowsky were still working on the text, but there is nothing further in the archive file before it was closed in January 1975. The likely explanation is that the size of the undertaking conflicted with Klibansky's expanding international interests and Labowsky's preoccupation with her work on the library of Cardinal Bessarion, which resulted in her important 1979 book.[92]

This portrait of Klibansky in his late twenties and early thirties has, I hope, shown him arriving in Britain and more specifically in the milieu of Oxford, eager to establish new contacts; eager also to develop projects that would demonstrate his expertise, particularly in the area of manuscripts and medieval thought, and which were at the same time of great importance to advancing recognition of the Warburg Institute. The fact that he was able to engage with such a wide range of contacts justifies my title. I never knew Klibansky, but he seems to have been someone who had the good fortune to encounter the people he most needed to meet, and when he most needed to meet them. Perhaps this is as true of his time in Oxford as anywhere else.

ACKNOWLEDGMENTS

For access to and help on archival sources, I am grateful to the following: Colin Harris and the staff of the Special Collections Reading Room, Bodleian Libraries, University of Oxford; the staff of the Manuscripts Reading Room, Deutsches Literaturarchiv Marbach; Martin Maw, archivist, Oxford University Press; Claudia Wedepohl, archivist, Warburg Institute. Permission to quote from individual letters has kindly been granted by the Warburg Institute (Gertrud Bing, Fritz Saxl); United Agents LLP on behalf of Jean, Lady Tweedsmuir, the Lord Tweedsmuir, and Sally, Lady Tweedsmuir (John Buchan); Professor Donald Russell and the secretary to the Delegates of Oxford University Press (E.R. Dodds); Sir Timothy Hunt (Richard Hunt); Professor Ethel Groffier (Raymond Klibansky); Stephen Wordsworth on behalf of CARA (the Council for At-Risk Academics), and the Bodleian Libraries, University of Oxford (John Macmurray); the secretary to the Delegates of Oxford University Press (C.H. Roberts and Kenneth Sisam); the Bodleian Libraries, University of Oxford (Clement Webb). Except where noted, translations are by the author.

NOTES

1 Bing's article "The Warburg Institute," in the August 1934 *LAR*, includes a diagram and photograph of the Reading Room and shelves in Thames House: the following May, *LAR* published Wind's "The Warburg Institute Classification Scheme." The institute also helped to compile a supplementary list of modern German literature and books on history and art, which was published in *LAR*, 4 series 4:3, [vol. 38] (February 1936): 60–4.

2 Summarized in Classical Association, *Proceedings,* vol. 32 (1935), 32–5.

3 Reprinted in Saxl, *Lectures*, 73–84, specifically pl. 43–8; also in Saxl, *A Heritage of Images*, 27–41, pl. 37–53.

4 A third pre-war link with the association was a one-day meeting held at the institute on 6 January 1939, in conjunction with a photographic exhibition on "The Visual Approach to the Classics," Classical Association, *Proceedings,* vol. 36 (1939), 42.

5 Warburg Institute, *Annual Report, 1934/35*, 5, 7–10.

6 Richard Newald studied in Munich (*Promotion*, 1921) and Freiburg im Breisgau (*Habilitation*, 1926). He was appointed as an assistant professor at the University of Fribourg (Switzerland) in 1930.

7 Warburg Institute Archive (hereafter WIA), General Correspondence (hereafter GC): Richard Newald to KBW, 9 March 1929.

8 WIA, GC: Karl Münscher to KBW, 10 February 1930; also Gertrud Bing to Münscher, 20 February 1920; Münscher was the general editor of the *Jahresbericht.*

9 WIA, I,11,1 (*Bibliography on the Survival of the Classics* [BSC] 1932–36 (K–N)): Fritz Saxl to Newald, 22 February 1931.

10 WIA, GC: Bing to Walter Paatz, 4 March 1932: "Durch die Rezensionsexemplare hoffen wir auch, unserer Buchanschaffung aufzuhelfen"; quoted in Panofsky, *Korrespondenz 1910–1968*, 1: 466 (letter 296B4).

11 WIA, I.11.1 (BSC 1932–36 (K–N) file): Saxl to Newald, 20 January 1932: "Herr Max Warburg, who is very interested in this, and I remain robustly steadfast that, in spite of all the curbs on salaries and acquisitions, we definitely wish to maintain this project. I can assure you that in Herr Max Warburg you have gained a true friend." ["Herr Max Warburg, der sich sehr dafür interessiert, und ich halten

eisern daran fest, dass wir diese Sache trotz aller Streichungen von Gehältern und Anschaffungen unbedingt aufrecht erhalten wollen. Ich kann Sie versichern, dass Sie an Herrn Max Warburg einen warmen Freund gewonnen haben."]

12 WIA, I.11.1 (BSC 1931–33 file): Edgar Wind to Raymond Klibansky, 3 September 1931.

13 WIA, GC: This is clear from a letter to Saxl (Klibansky to Saxl, 12 January 1933), which Meier annotated. Aside from his work on Nicholas of Cusa and Meister Eckhart, Klibansky was also involved, during November and December 1932, in reading and correcting *Aristoteles im Mittelalter und Vergilius im Mittelalter*, a bibliography prepared by Marie Luise Bulst (1906–1992). It was such digressions that Bing perhaps had in mind when she wrote of "Raymond's 23 simultaneous projects": "und seine Zersplitterung zwischen den 23 Arbeiten, die er laufend hat, lässt seine ganzen Lebensumstände weiter sehr schwierig erscheinen," Bing to Toni Cassirer, 24 March 1936.

14 *Kulturwissenschaftliche Bibliographie zum Nachleben der Antike*, in Gemeinschafte mit Fachgenossen bearbeitet von Hans Meier, Richard Newald, Edgar Wind; herausgegeban von der Bibliothek Warburg. Erster Band: *Die Erscheinungen des Jahres 1931* (Leipzig: Teubner, 1934) xxviii, 333 pp. 18 M.

15 In the Nazi newspaper *Völkischer Beobachter* (North German edition) of 5 January 1935 (p. 5), under the title "Juden und Emigranten machen deutsche Wissenschaft" [Jews and Emigrants Manufacture German Scholarship]; reprinted in Wuttke (ed.), *Kosmopolis der Wissenchaft*, 295–9. Three days later this article was republished in the South German edition under the title "Das alte listige Spiel" [The old sly trick].

16 WIA, KBW Internal Correspondence (Bing/Saxl): Klibansky was not alone in this. Bing had misgivings from the outset: "I had the feeling that, with such a scheme, the Bibliography is either a stillborn child, because it is much too complicated to function even halfway by itself, or that it necessitates for the Library an expenditure of effort by the staff that we shall not have at our disposal." ["Ich hatte das Gefühl, dass bei einem solchen Apparat die Bibliographie entweder ein totgeborenes Kind ist, weil er viel zu kompliziert ist, um auch nur halbwegs von selbst funktionieren zu können, oder aber, er bedingt für die Bibliothek einen Aufwand an Arbeitskräft, den wir nicht zur Verfügung haben werden."] Bing to Saxl, 14 September 1931. Edgar Wind also came to disapprove of it; see Wind Papers, File IV.6A.i/3.

17 McEwan, *Fritz Saxl: eine Biografie*, 125.

18 The lectures were published as *Vorträge der Bibliothek Warburg, 1930/1931*, ed. Fritz Saxl. The four speakers were: Ernest Fraser Jacob (1894–1971), "Some aspects of classical influence in mediaeval England" (*Vorträge*, 1–27); James Alexander Kerr Thomson (1879–1959), "Erasmus in England" (64–82); Ernest De Sélincourt (1870–1943), "Classicism and romanticism in the poetry of Walter Savage Landor" (230–50); and Sir Richard Livingstone: "The position and function of classical studies in modern English education" (251–77). The other contributors were Hans Liebeschütz (1893–1978), Walter Schirmer (1888–1984), Oskar Fischel (1870–1939), Ernst Cassirer, and Edgar Wind. Cassirer's paper (136–55) was entitled "Shaftesbury und die Renaissance des Platonismus in England."

19 London: Allen & Unwin, 1919–20.

20 Oxford: Clarendon Press, 1926.

21 John of Salisbury, *Ioannis Saresberiensis episcopi Carnotensis Policratici … libri VIII* and *Ioannis Saresberiensis episcopi Carnotensis Metalogicon … libri IIII.*

22 The diaries are written in an unusual manner, in that Webb wrote only on the recto of a leaf until he reached the end of the book; he then turned this over and wrote on the verso (which therefore became the "recto") back to the beginning. The actual verso numbering accordingly has the odd effect of declining as the dates proceed.

23 WIA, GC 1933–36: C.C.J. Webb to R.W. Livingstone, 4 October 1933: "Of course I will gladly do anything for the young man that I can. I am always glad to meet people who are interested in the School of Chartres! I will write to him at once and, as soon as I can fix dates, will ask him to stay here … I don't know much about the Warburg Institute: but I think it was from it that I received some time ago the present of an interesting book by Cassirer on the Cambridge Platonists."

24 Webb wrote subsequently to Saxl (Webb to Saxl, 9 October 1933, WIA, GC 1933–36,) noting that he had previously received a copy of Cassirer's *Die platonische Renaissance in England und die Schule von Cambridge*, and asking for Eduard Norden's (1868–1941) *Die Geburt des Kindes*. Webb's diary records that he began to read Norden on 8 February 1934 (Webb Diaries, Bodleian Library, MSS. Eng. misc. d.1125, 61^{v}).

25 Webb means on the top deck of a double-decker bus.

26 Webb Diaries, Bodleian Library, MSS. Eng. misc. d.1125, 147^{v}.

27 Paul Benecke (1868–1944), Maurice Powicke (1879–1963), William Pantin (1902–1973), Richard Hunt (1908–1979) and C.S. Lewis (1898–1963).

28 The thesis remained unpublished during Hunt's lifetime and was edited by Margaret Gibson and published as *The Schools and the Cloister: The Life and Writings of Alexander Nequam, 1157–1217*.

29 Webb Diaries, Bodleian Library, MSS. Eng. misc. d.1125, 147^{v} & 76^{v}.

30 Webb Diaries, Bodleian Library, MSS. Eng. misc. d.1125, 46^{v}. Hermann George Fiedler (1862–1945), Taylor Professor of the German Language and Literature, chaired the lectures, which were given on 12, 19, and 26 February 1934. Cassirer's notes for these are printed in Barbara Naumann's edition of his *Kleinere Schriften zu Goethe und zur Geistesgeschichte, 1925–1944*, 15–21.

31 SPSL, Bodleian Library, 316/3, fol. 284–435. The Cassirer testimonial is fol. 321 with a copy at fol. 295. Saxl's testimonial is fol. 296–98 and Macmurray's at fol. 295. On the SPSL more generally, see: Zimmerman, "The Society for the Protection of Science and Learning and the politicization of British science in the 1930s."

32 *Philosophy* vol. 10 (1935): 228–9.

33 Webb Diaries, Bodleian Library, MSS. Eng. misc. d.1125, 35^{v}.

34 Webb's diary for 11 February 1935 records that he was correcting the proofs of his *Festschrift* article (Webb Diaries, Bodleian Library, MSS. Eng. misc. d.1127, 79^{v}).

35 Paton moved to Oxford in 1937 to be White's Professor of Moral Philosophy and Fellow of Corpus Christi College. He played an important role in the affairs of the Cassirers, by arranging for Heinz Cassirer (1903–1979) to be taken on as a research student and assistant lecturer at Glasgow in 1934, and to complete his 1938 PhD, "A Commentary on Kant's Critique of Judgment" (Glasgow University Library, Special Collections, Thesis 487); this was published the same year by Methuen, and reviewed by G.C. Stead in *Mind*.

36 Frau Toni Cassirer (1883–1961), Max Waller (1886–1969). WIA, GC: T. Cassirer to Saxl, 10 May 1934; a letter from Ledonia to Frau Cassirer, 8 May 1934 (Deutsches Literaturarchiv Marbach, A: Raymond Klibansky [hereafter DLA, A, KLIBANSKY], XXIII.1) confirms the source.

37 Toni Cassirer, *Mein Leben mit Ernst Cassirer*, 223–4; Ernst Cassirer, *Ausgewählter wissenschaftlicher Briefwechsel* (edited by J.M. Krois), 270–1. Frau Cassirer notes a kind of *tabula gratulatoria*, produced by the press, detailing the contents of the *Festschrift*, and paying homage to Cassirer on his birthday. Krois mentions the *Festgabe*, but notes that there is no trace of it in Cassirer's books or preserved papers.

38 Later published as *Der Wortakzent in den lyrischen Versen des Horaz*. Zinn's supervisor was Rudolf Pfeiffer (1889–1979).

39 DLA, A, KLIBANSKY, XXIII.1: Klibansky to E. Zinn, 16 June 1934; Zinn to Klibansky, 28 June 1934; Conradine Lück to Klibansky 26 June 1934; E. Weil to Klibansky, 24 June 1934, where Weil offered to revise an earlier essay on Plotinus.

40 Klibansky and Paton, *Philosophy and History*, 11–25.

41 In a letter from Klibansky to Paton, 18 January 1961, Oxford University Press (hereafter OUP) Archive, LB 7479, Klibansky claimed to have secured Stebbing's contribution.

42 Mitchison, *You May Well Ask*, in the chapter "Beauty and the Bicycle," 87–94.

43 Ernst Cassirer Papers. Addition. General Collection, Beinecke Rare Book and Manuscript Library, Yale University, Geraldine Jebb to Ernst Cassirer, 27 June 1934. Cassirer's notes for these are printed in his *Kleinere Schriften* (ed. Naumann), 22–55.

44 Klibansky and Paton, *Philosophy and History*, 107–23.

45 *Mind* 17 (1908): 456–73.

46 Cassirer, *Philosophie der symbolischen Formen*. vol. 3; Cassirer, *Zur Einstein'schen Relativitätstheorie*.

47 DLA, A, KLIBANSKY, XXIII.1: W.D. Ross to Klibansky, 3 July 1932 [i.e. 1934]; Lady Mary Murray to Klibansky, 18 July 1934; M.P. Spence to W.J. [*sic*] Paton, 14 July 1934. Marjorie Patricia Spence, known as "Peter," was to become Russell's third wife in 1936.

48 WIA GC: Ernst Hoffmann to Klibansky, 30 May 1934. Saxl's reply to Hoffmann is dated 2 June. The alternative publication offered by Hoffmann was his *Platonismus und Mystik im Altertum*.

49 WIA GC: Bing to T. Cassirer, 24 March 1936. The letter goes into details about the financial situation of the institute at that time, and the question of whether a more secure home might have been found in America. Felix Warburg (1871–1937), Aby Warburg's brother in New York, had wished to see the institute established in America, but by the time of this letter he had been persuaded by the members of the Warburg family in Hamburg to accept the *status quo* in London. He had, however, withdrawn his allowance of £2,000, which represented about a quarter of the institute's finances.

50 Kannicht, *Tragicorum Graecorum fragmenta*, vol. 5, *Euripides*, 917–18. It is also included in vol. 7 of the Loeb edition of Euripides, *Fragments I*, 226–7, as an uncertain fragment from *Antiope*. The translation given there is as follows: "Happy

the man who has gained knowledge through inquiry, not aiming to trouble his fellow citizens, nor to act unjustly, but observing eternal nature's ageless order, the way it was formed, and whence and how. Such men are never inclined to practise shameful deeds."

51 WIA GC, WF 34/36: Saxl wrote to Felix Warburg to this effect, 1 June 1934.

52 See note 15, above.

53 Herbert James Paton to Robert William Chapman, 15 June 1938, OUP Archive, LB 7479.

54 Kenneth Sisam to Paton, 17 June 1938, OUP Archive, LB 7479.

55 Adorno, *Zeitschrift für Sozialforschung*, vol. 6, 657–61 (=Adorno, *Gesammelte Schriften*, vol. 20, no. 1, 221–8).

56 Ibid., 657 and 221: "Autoren nicht bloss disparater historischer Lehrmeinungen, sondern auch real widersprechender politischer Haltung sind aufgenommen, als seien ihre Differenzen bloss solche der akademischen Diskussion." It might be worth noting that the disparity of which Adorno complained is not unknown in other *Festschriften*.

57 De Burgh, Review of *Philosophy and History;* Sisam wrote: "So many of the essays are fresh, and not merely a slightly altered presentation of matter already familiar in books." (OUP Archive LB 7479, Sisam to Cassirer, 29 April 1936.)

58 Southern, "Powicke, Sir (Frederick) Maurice (1879–1963)"

59 WIA, IV.20.2: Undated memorandum by Klibansky (*Corpus Platonicum* 1940–53).

60 Annual Report, Warburg Institute, 1934/35: 10.

61 Klibansky, *The Continuity of the Platonic Tradition*. (London: Warburg Institute, 1939).

62 *Proceedings of the British Academy* (hereafter PBA) 23 (1939), 8: "The general direction of the *Corpus Platonicum* remains with the British Academy, which initiated the project and has made itself responsible for the greater part of the cost." Presidential Address, PBA 24 (1938), 24; PBA 25 (1939), 26.

63 For citation, see note 59, above.

64 Klibansky, *The Continuity of the Platonic Tradition*, 19–21.

65 WIA, IV.19.1: Klibansky to Henri Grégoire, 10 October 1936.

66 WIA, IV.19.1: Klibansky to Paul Henry, S.J., 13 October 1936. Henry was asked by Klibansky whether he would contribute to the section on the Latin tradition of Plotinus. He replied on 13 November that he was interested, although he thought that Porphyry had a stronger claim than Plotinus.

67 Weiss was officially employed by the Hudson's Bay Company in its Records (Archives) Department from 1 January 1937 until 31 March 1938 (Hudson's Bay Company Archives of Manitoba, Winnipeg, London staff salary books and records of service. HB2007/180). Information kindly supplied by Bronwen Quarry, archivist, Hudson's Bay Company Archives. He subsequently obtained a lectureship in Italian at University College London, eventually becoming professor there in 1946.

68 WIA, IV.19.1: Klibansky to Roberto Weiss, 16 October [1936].

69 WIA, IV.19.1: Weiss to Klibansky, undated letter [end of October 1936].

70 Although Edward VIII did not abdicate until 11 December 1936, Wallis Simpson had filed for divorce from her second husband, Ernest Simpson (1897–1958), a decree *nisi* being granted on 27 October.

71 WIA, IV.19.1: Richard Hunt to Klibansky, 4 December 1936.

72 On this, see Southern, "Richard William Hunt (1908–1979)," PBA 67 (1981), 371–97 at 376, 380–4.

73 Ibid., 390–2.

74 On the delays at the Press, see WIA, IV.20.1: Gertrud Bing to Lotte Labowsky, 26 July 1943.

75 Weber, *Lotte Labowsky (1905–1991), Schülerin Aby Warburgs, Kollegin Raymond Klibanskys*, 126–8. A draft letter offering Labowsky employment on the *Corpus* is in [Klibansky] to Lotte Labowsky, 9 February 1937 (WIA, IV.19.1), with an additional letter dated 25 February, answering questions that Labowsky had raised. She had arrived in Britain in October 1934 and worked unofficially on the *Corpus* since at least October 1936.

76 *Proceedings of the British Academy* 25 (1939), 27.

77 WIA, IV.19.1: Hunt to Klibansky, 23 August 1937.

78 WIA Correspondence, *Mediaeval and Renaissance Studies* (*MARS*) Collaborators/Editors 1938–1964 box: Rudolf Wittkower to Hunt, 11 January 1939.

79 Rathbone (dates uncertain) completed a PhD thesis at King's College London, under the title "The Influence of Bishops and of Members of Cathedral Bodies in the Intellectual Life of England, 1066–1216." This was supervised from 1934 by Claude Jenkins (1877–1959), Regius Professor of Ecclesiastical History, Oxford. Rathbone is not to be confused with Eleanor Florence Rathbone (1872–1946), the campaigner for women's rights and social reform.

80 Weiss reviewed *MARS* 1.1 in *Modern Language Review* 36:4 (1941): 520–2, and 1.2 in *MLR* 36:2 (1944): 136–88.

81 Saxl, *Verzeichnis astrologischer und mythologischer illustrierter Handschriften des lateinischen Mittelalters* was reviewed with other works on astrology by Charles Singer in the *Times Literary Supplement*, 139. See McEwan, *Fritz Saxl: eine Biografie*, 125.

82 Singer, *Les Manuscrits des Îles Britanniques*; and *Catalogue of Latin and Vernacular Alchemical Manuscripts*.

83 WIA, IV.19.1: Klibansky to Dorothea W. Singer, 6 February 1936.

84 WIA, IV.19.1: Singer to Labowsky, 20 September 1938.

85 Singer, "Alchemical Texts bearing the Name of Plato."

86 *Parmenides usque ad finem primae hypothesis nec non Procli commentarium in Parmenidem*.

87 OUP Archive, PP. 10631 [undated, but between late July and 23 September 1959]. As Klibansky was abroad during much of this period, the typed proposal probably devolved largely upon Labowsky.

88 Eric R. Dodds to P.J. Spicer, 21 July 1959, OUP Archive, PP. 10631.

89 Bing to Spicer, 31 July 1959, OUP Archive, PP. 10631: "I am wondering whether this edition, if it comes off, might be shown to be connected with our *Corpus Platonicum*. The work for it arose, as you know, from Professor Klibansky's and Dr. Labowsky's work on the Latin translation of Proclus's Commentary but surely this is a detail which can be discussed much later, and I do not want to suggest anything which might militate against your edition."

90 Colin H. Roberts, internal memorandum, 24 September 1959, OUP Archive, P. 19047.

91 Spicer to Cecil Maurice Bowra, 28 October 1959, OUP Archive, P. 19047.

92 Labowsky, *Bessarion's Library and the Biblioteca Marciana*. Since 1975 there has been a substantial amount of scholarship on the Proclus Commentary, including a full edition of the Greek text in the Oxford Classical Text series by Carlos Steel.

FOUR

Tracing an Intellectual Afterlife in Library and Archival Sources: Raymond Klibansky and His Warburg Library Networks

JILLIAN TOMM

Reconstructions of intellectual transmission and networks are a messy business. As the research in this volume illustrates so well, historians routinely navigate published attributions and references that are by no means innocent of personal vanity or preference, just as correspondence or diaries can be rife with bias or obfuscation. For historians, such aspects can be obstacles, but they are also information; these elements too are part of the true story, and help to better understand the agency of individuals and the dynamics of exchange.

Research on networks around the Kulturwissenschaftliche Bibliothek Warburg (KBW) and the early Warburg Institute of London (essentially the period from the beginning of the KBW in the mid-1920s to the last issue of the Warburg Institute periodical *Mediaeval and Renaissance Studies* in 1968) is supported by a generous quantity and range of both published and archival documents. Copies of KBW and early Warburg Institute publications are preserved in several institutions, as are a wealth of archival materials pertaining to these publications and related exchanges among various participants, as well as to other institutional operations, activities, and projects. Adopting Klibansky as a nexus for exploring networks around early collaborative Warburg Library projects leads us to three primary source document repositories: the Warburg Institute Archive (WIA) in London; the Deutsches Literaturarchiv Marbach (DLA); and the McGill University Library in Montreal. Additional bulk sources include records of institutions such as the Society for the Protection of Science and Learning (SPSL) held at at the Bodleian Library, the Heidelberg University archives, or the Hamburg state archives, as well as various scattered personal *fonds*.[1]

The Warburg Institute Archive remains the primary holder of source documents for research on the Warburg Library network, including Klibansky's interactions with it. Preserved there, in addition to individual project files and documents pertaining to daily functioning, is incoming correspondence as well as systematically gathered copies of outgoing correspondence. Hundreds of letters to, from, and about Klibansky are found in WIA General Correspondence (WIA GC) files from 1926 forward. These are rich in information about Warburg Library projects and publications since, while engaged in many KBW and Warburg Institute activities, Klibansky was often away from its offices, first in Germany and then in England.[2] A first estimate suggests that more than seven hundred letters are preserved here from Klibansky's exchanges with Fritz Saxl and Gertrud Bing, the pair at the core of Warburg Library functioning from the KBW's opening in the 1920s, through the transition to the Warburg Institute in England in 1933, and until Saxl's death in 1948 and Bing's retirement as director in 1959.[3] A full exploration and listing of Klibansky's correspondence has yet to be undertaken, but these documents have informed several of the essays in this volume.

The holder of Klibansky's personal *fonds* is the Deutsches Literaturarchiv Marbach (DLA). The DLA's *Nachlass Raymond Klibansky* (DLA, A, KLIBANSKY) holds approximately thirty boxes of working papers and another thirty boxes of correspondence, each set covering Klibansky's entire career. This material also has yet to be fully listed and explored, but a provisional listing created by Ethel Groffier and Regina Weber shows that it contains substantial holdings from Klibansky's early life in Germany and from his life-long involvement with Warburg Library projects.[4] Acquired shortly after Klibansky's death in 2005, this *fonds* has already supplied essential material for a monograph titled *Lotte Labowsky (1905–1991) – Schülerin Aby Warburgs, Kollegin Raymond Klibanskys* by Regina Weber, which draws from more than two hundred letters between Labowsky and Klibansky, written between 1927 and 1991.[5] More than four hundred and fifty additional letters connected with the Warburg Library network have been noted, over half of which are identified as being to or from Saxl or – most especially – Bing.[6]

The third major holding of materials on Klibansky is the Raymond Klibansky Collection (RKC) acquired by the McGill University Library in 2005. This collection consists of Klibansky's personal library, built over his lifetime, as well as several boxes of archival material and offprints found among his office contents at the end of his life (Klibansky's final McGill office was in fact within the McGill Library, and housed his collection). His library proper has been catalogued as a special collection within McGill's Rare Books and Special Collections.[7] The archival materials have yet to be formally listed, but preliminary explorations by Sophie Trolliet-Martial have revealed well over a hundred and thirty letters to or from Warburg Library intimates – dozens each from Fritz Saxl and Klibansky's doctoral director and colleague Ernst Hoffmann, with smaller groups from Gertrud Bing and contemporaries Walter Solmitz, Lotte Labowsky, and Edgar Wind.[8] Much of this correspondence dates from the 1930s, shortly after the KBW relocated from Hamburg to London. Among this material was located the only known copy of Klibansky's *Antrittsvorlesung* (fig. 4.1).[9]

The sources held at these primary holding institutions – newly held in the case of the DLA and the McGill Library – and which include published and archival documents of all formats, form an abundant source base for new research and reflection. The recent surfacing of many of these sources and the access provided by the holding institutions to all, through description, preservation, and digitization has made much of the research for this volume possible and will sustain much further enquiry.[10]

The most thoroughly described of the three major Klibansky holdings to date is McGill's Raymond Klibansky Collection. The following examples from it give an idea of how these holdings can add to, nuance, or simply bring to life various details and our overall understanding of Klibansky's Warburg Library relationships.

The Raymond Klibansky Collection of McGill: Traces of a Weimar *Bildung*

Consisting primarily of published documents, the Raymond Klibansky Collection of McGill's Rare Books and Special Collections offers an incomplete but particular and very personal record of the Warburg Library world as he

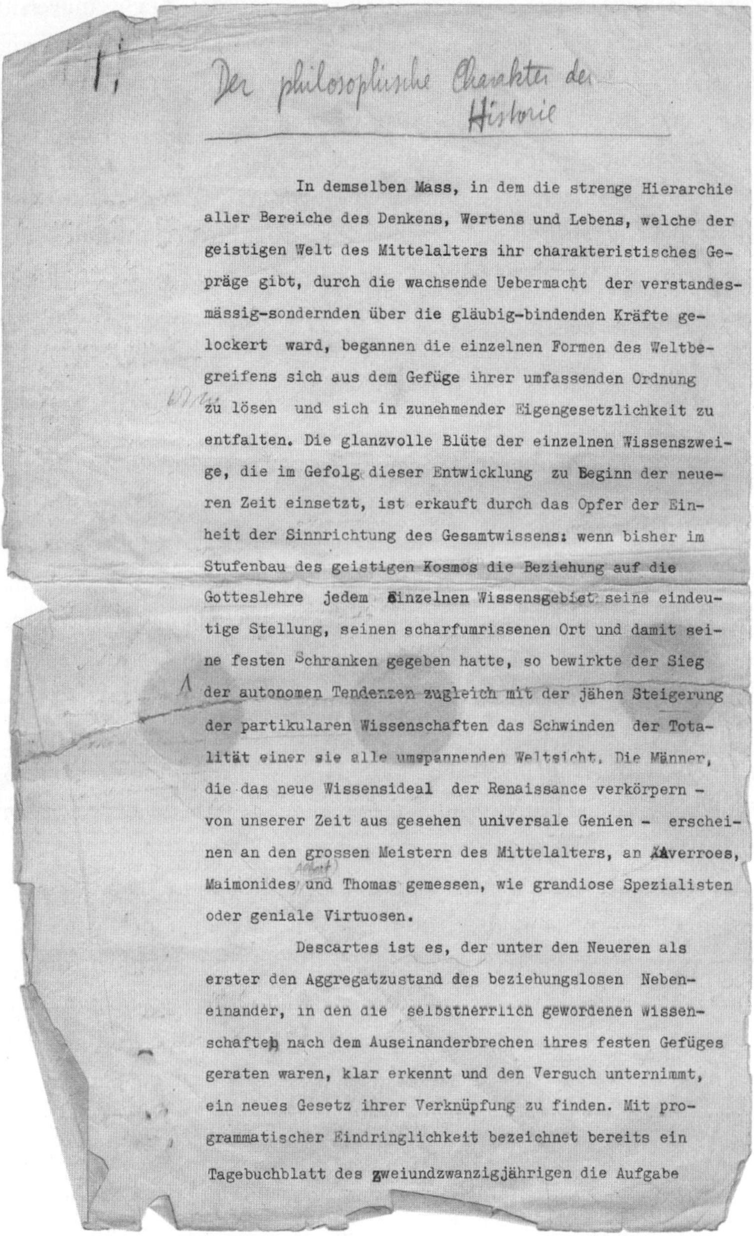

1. Der philosophische Charakter der Historie

In demselben Mass, in dem die strenge Hierarchie aller Bereiche des Denkens, Wertens und Lebens, welche der geistigen Welt des Mittelalters ihr charakteristisches Gepräge gibt, durch die wachsende Uebermacht der verstandesmässig-sondernden über die gläubig-bindenden Kräfte gelockert ward, begannen die einzelnen Formen des Weltbegreifens sich aus dem Gefüge ihrer umfassenden Ordnung zu lösen und sich in zunehmender Eigengesetzlichkeit zu entfalten. Die glanzvolle Blüte der einzelnen Wissenszweige, die im Gefolg dieser Entwicklung zu Beginn der neueren Zeit einsetzt, ist erkauft durch das Opfer der Einheit der Sinnrichtung des Gesamtwissens: wenn bisher im Stufenbau des geistigen Kosmos die Beziehung auf die Gotteslehre jedem einzelnen Wissensgebiet seine eindeutige Stellung, seinen scharfumrissenen Ort und damit seine festen Schranken gegeben hatte, so bewirkte der Sieg der autonomen Tendenzen zugleich mit der jähen Steigerung der partikularen Wissenschaften das Schwinden der Totalität einer sie alle umspannenden Weltsicht. Die Männer, die das neue Wissensideal der Renaissance verkörpern – von unserer Zeit aus gesehen universale Genien – erscheinen an den grossen Meistern des Mittelalters, an Averroes, Maimonides und Thomas gemessen, wie grandiose Spezialisten oder geniale Virtuosen.

Descartes ist es, der unter den Neueren als erster den Aggregatzustand des beziehungslosen Nebeneinander, in den die selbstherrlich gewordenen Wissenschaften nach dem Auseinanderbrechen ihres festen Gefüges geraten waren, klar erkennt und den Versuch unternimmt, ein neues Gesetz ihrer Verknüpfung zu finden. Mit programmatischer Eindringlichkeit bezeichnet bereits ein Tagebuchblatt des zweiundzwanzigjährigen die Aufgabe

Fig. 4.1 Klibansky's "Antrittsvorlesung" lecture for his *Habilitation*, 1932: "Der philosophische Charakter der Historie," later revised in English for the 1936 Cassirer *Festschrift*.

preserved it.[11] Klibansky's education, or *Bildung*, was rooted in his university experience with professors such as archaeologist Ludwig Curtius and philosophers Karl Jaspers, Ernst Cassirer, and Ernst Hoffmann. But it is also more broadly based in his friendships with contemporaries Walter Solmitz and Lotte Labowsky, who alike developed into Warburg Library intimates; with mentors outside the university, including Marianne Weber, wife of sociologist Max Weber, and literary scholar and poet Friedrich Gundolf; and with the KBW and Warburg Institute, especially with Fritz Saxl, Gertrud Bing, and art historians Erwin Panofsky and Edgar Wind. This world – Klibansky's Weimar and the many intellectual paths that began there – is strongly reflected both in the books held in the collection and in its many instances of provenance evidence.

The collection is an impressive personal library in the humanities, counting over seven thousand titles, mainly in philosophy, religion, literature, and history. It covers more than five centuries of printing, with hundreds of volumes predating the nineteenth century – many of them beautiful volumes for book-historical study – and includes substantial content in English, German, French, Italian, Latin, and Greek. As a connection to Klibansky's intellectual landscape, these books reflect the entire sweep of his productive life, from his earliest interests in medieval thinkers and the Platonic tradition to his later efforts disseminating contemporary thought and promoting the notions of tolerance and liberty. Hundreds carry traces of friends and colleagues in inscriptions and other signs of provenance.

Klibansky inscribed his ownership in only a little more than 250 of his books, and the ownership inscriptions that are dated stem mostly from his Weimar years. Several books contain his markings or annotations, though relatively few are heavily commented. Some are more simply reminders of different stages of life – his changing signature styles, for instance. Klibansky's earlier signatures tend to be larger, heavier, and more detailed, and become – especially in the Second World War years – more restrained. Among the more complete inscriptions, "Raymundus Klibansky, stud. phil. Heidelbergae 1927" is written in Adolf Trendelenburg's *Erläuterungen zu den Elementen der aristotelischen Logik*.[12] Trendelenburg had been a teacher of Wilhelm Dilthey, Franz Brentano, and Hermann Cohen, all recent giants in Klibansky's intellectual environment, and he collected many editions of Trendelenburg's work, one of which is among the heavily annotated volumes.[13]

The sheer amount of German humanistic scholarship in the Klibansky Collection makes it valuable for the study of this heritage. The more than fourteen hundred pre-1934 titles produced in Germany (mostly in German but with about 15 percent in Latin, Greek, or other languages) cover a broad range of topics and include early editions of leading figures in this tradition, among them Leopold von Ranke and Wilhelm von Humboldt, as well as contemporary scholars. German literature also holds a particularly special place here. From his early school days, Klibansky signals Schiller, Goethe, Kleist, Lessing, Herder, and "above all" Hölderlin as having made a deep impression,[14] and nineteenth- and especially several early twentieth-century editions of these writers contribute much to the strength of this part of the collection.

But poets closer to Klibansky's own time – personal friends such as Karl Wolfskehl and also luminaries like Rilke or more especially Stefan George – are particularly numerous. George has been described as the "melancholy prince,"[15] a literary manifestation of the period's broader fascination or engagement with melancholy that also forms a backdrop to Klibansky's scholarly interest in the area. The followers (many say disciples) of George in some cases form a bridge between the literary world and the more strictly scholarly realm, and this too we can see here in works by "Georgians" such as economist Edgar Salin, historian Ernst Kantorowicz, philosopher and psychologist Ludwig Klages, and psychiatrist Oskar Kohnstamm.[16] Through these and other authors, the Klibansky Collection offers an interesting selection of creative activity from this time, both in terms of texts and as representatives of the aesthetics of the period (fig. 4.2). The collection serves, furthermore, as something of a material manifestation of his stated methods of cross-disciplinary and situated approaches to understanding philosophical texts.[17]

The two anchors within Klibansky's contemporary German books are, on the one hand, the Hamburg world of philosopher Ernst Cassirer and the KBW and, on the other, the Heidelberg world of the university and the literary world around Friedrich Gundolf. We'll concentrate here on these, but a broader view of the interlacing networks of Klibansky's youth is reflected in the collection. For example, two volumes, including a posthumous edition of Max Weber's *Economy and Society (Wirtschaft und Gesellschaft)* that Klibansky recalls having helped to prepare, are inscribed by Marianne Weber, in whose home Klibansky lived for a time.[18] Heinrich Zimmer, who taught Indian

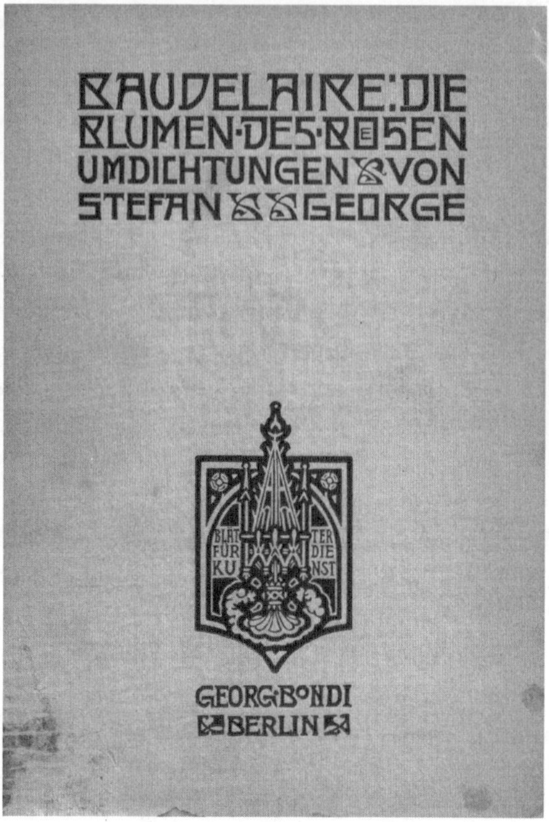

Fig. 4.2 Stefan George's translation of Baudelaire's *Fleurs du mal.* Above the publisher information is the device of George's literary periodical *Blätter für die Kunst.*

philology at Heidelberg and who Klibansky considered part of the soul of the city, inscribed a handful of books on Hindu philosophy, religion, and mythology.[19] Inscribed gifts from student friends like the philosophers Guido Calogero and Jeanne Hersch (with both of whom he remained in contact for the greater part of his life), add to the richness of the collection as a source on Klibansky's social book world. In these books – their authors, their subjects, and their inscriptions – we find a deep impression of this extraordinary youth, and of the Warburg Library network. And it is worth remembering that Klibansky brought this presence both physically and in spirit to Montreal at the end of the 1940s, during the still early decades of the

Warburg Institute, and that the traditions and thinkers of – and behind – this group now stand implicitly in the development of the many scholars that Klibansky taught and mentored over his long career in North America.

Cassirer, and Klibansky's Early Decades with the KBW

Klibansky singled out his 1926 introduction to Ernst Cassirer, Aby Warburg, and the Warburg circle of researchers as key to his development.[20] We see this in several ways in his library.

Ernst Cassirer

Cassirer is the most frequently appearing contemporary author in the RKC. Klibansky had many reasons to be attracted to Cassirer, who had such a vast range of interest and expertise – his knowledge has been described as "stupendous."[21] Along with the likes of John Dewey, Bertrand Russell, and Albert Einstein, he was selected in the 1940s for the *Library of Living Philosophers* series, for which Walter Solmitz provided the bibliography. Rooted in humanism, interested in science, philosophy and the problem of knowledge, and history, "more than any other German philosopher since Kant, Cassirer aimed to devote equal philosophical attention to the (mathematical and) natural sciences (*Naturwissenschaften*) and to the more humanistic disciplines (*Geisteswissenschaften*)."[22] Books by Cassirer in the RKC cover philosophical topics, physics, myths, and some of Klibansky's favourite poets, as in *Idee und Gestalt: Goethe/Schiller/Hölderlin/Kleist*, of which there are two copies.[23]

The library provides no evidence, however, of any warm exchange between Cassirer and Klibansky in inscribed books, perhaps reflecting a relationship more formal than those that sprung up between the young man and other more senior scholars such as Ernst Hoffmann or Fritz Saxl. The few brief inscriptions from Cassirer – one "with many thanks and best wishes, E.C." (*Mit vielen Dank u. herzlichen Grüßen, E.C.*) – are found in offprints published the year after the appearance of Cassirer's 1936 *Festschrift* co-edited by Klibansky in England with the support of the Warburg Institute.[24] A more personal note appears in Cassirer's *Die Begriffsform im mythischen Denken*

(Conceptual form in mythical thought), published in 1922 as the first of the Warburg *Studien*. It is inscribed by Cassirer's son Heinrich (Heinz) to his friend in 1926, the year of Klibansky's introduction to the elder Cassirer, which triggered so many other important encounters: "My dear Raymond Klibansky, dedicated by his Heinz Cassirer" (*Meinem lieber Raymond Klibansky, Zugeeignet von seinem Heinz Cassirer*).

A book from Cassirer's own library, which Klibansky described as "magnificent," is also preserved here: Cassirer's copy of Max Dessoir's 1929 *Beiträge zur allgemeinen Kunstwissenschaft*, inscribed to the philosopher by the author, is but one of several items in the collection through which the larger intellectual networks of Klibansky's close circle are materially evident.[25] (figs. 4.3a and 4.3b).[26] Direct traces of Klibansky's own thought can be sought in his copy of Cassirer's 1927 *Individuum und Kosmos*. This copy of the book that stimulated fresh interest in Nicholas of Cusa, a lifelong topic for Klibansky, and which includes in appendix Klibansky's own first publication (an edition of Charles de Bovelles's early sixteenth-century *Liber de sapiente*), is among the small group of Klibansky's books that are marked by him throughout.

The KBW in the Klibansky Collection

From 1926 forward, Klibansky entered into a wide range of KBW activities, starting off as a student assistant in the library organizing sections in philosophy, classics, and encyclopaedias. His long experience with that library raises questions about the extent to which he was influenced by the Warburg Library system in establishing his own book order; that is, his own way of structuring the intellectual universe. We are able to reproduce only a small portion of Klibansky's book order,[27] and it is clear that while he did not reproduce the Warburg system, he did follow the method of mixing very early editions (for example a 1514 edition of Nicholas of Cusa, with pencil annotation in Klibansky's hand) alongside contemporary editions and commentary, and of freely mixing languages, both ancient and modern. Unlike the Warburg system of group-level identification whereby several different titles carry an identical shelving code, Klibansky gave his shelf-marked books a specific code representing a bookcase (upper-case letter), a shelf (lower-case letter), and the book sequence (number), giving for example "D.a.1." So each book has a specific place within its group. This specific order does not, how-

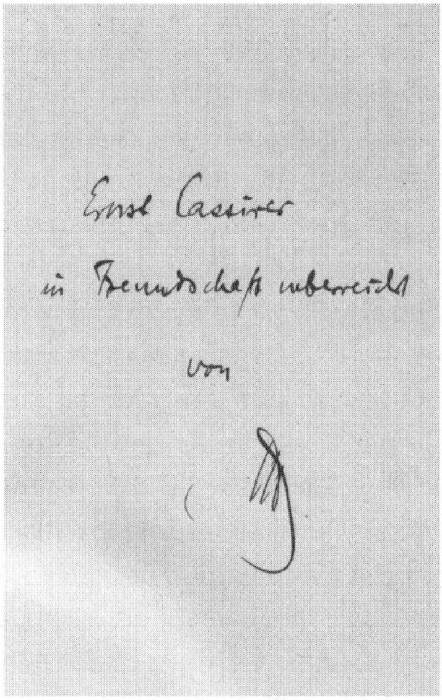

Fig. 4.3a *Left* Max Dessoir's presentation copy to Ernst Cassirer of *Beiträge zur allgemeinen Kunstwissenschaft.*

Fig. 4.3.b *Right* Max Dessoir's inscription to Cassirer.

ever, always appear to follow a system, while the book groups and their order are clearly fundamental to the library's semantic structure. This attention to group coherence over specific sequence makes his system of book organization resemble in practice, more than in form, that of the Warburg Library. What is certain is that the dynamic juxtaposition that existed in the Warburg Library imprinted itself on Klibansky's memory to his last years, and that the world around that library is materially very present in his own collection.

A great many early KBW publications are preserved in Klibansky's library, as we shall see, and this not only makes the collection a useful source for those in or near Montreal who are interested in the KBW and the Warburg Institute, but acts as an introduction or mode of discovery for a North American audience less familiar with the institution and its circle of researchers. They include those Klibansky was personally involved with – the *Bibliography on the Survival of the Classics*, the *Corpus Platonicum Medii Aevi*, the many editions of *Saturn and Melancholy*, MARS, and many others also. The *Bibliography*, in particular, with its entry summaries by contributor, offers an excellent window into sources known to various contributors.

Interestingly, while most of the *Studien der Bibliothek Warburg* – monograph-length studies published by the KBW published before the 1933 move to London – are in the RKC (they number around two dozen), there is a notable absence of the second of the series, Panofsky and Saxl's 1923 work on Albrecht Dürer's Renaissance masterpiece, *Melencolia I*. Did Klibansky not wish to keep a copy of this piece, which he studied in such detail for the purpose of continuing the work he co-authored with these two in *Saturn and Melancholy*? Did he remove a copy that was marked or annotated in a way he did not wish the public to see? Perhaps he simply never kept a copy in his collection, or perhaps it strayed from his shelves; one way or the other, the absence of this work upon which he built so much contrasts with his apparently more habitual pattern of preserving texts pertinent to his own publications.

A perusal of the *Studien* and of the published lectures given at the KBW from 1921–31, titled *Vorträge der Bibliothek Warburg*, brings to light several topics that became central to his research: lectures of Gustav Pauli on Dürer (*Dürer, Italien und die Antike*, 1921–22), of Ernst Hoffmann on Platonism in the Middle Ages (*Platonismus und Mittelalter*, 1923–24), of Hans Liebeschütz on cosmology in twelfth-century education (*Kosmologische Motive in der Bildungswelt der Frühscholastik*, 1923–24); or the 1927 study by Paul Lehmann on pseudo-antique medieval literature (*Pseudo-Antike Literatur des Mittelalters; Studien der Bibliothek Warburg, XIII*). Some of these carry occasional markings that seem likely to be his, but, as also for the *Studien* and the *Bibliography*, the pages of most sections remain uncut, and there seems to be a deliberate desire simply to preserve them. They highlight the extent to which Klibansky's interests were rooted in a tradition and in this specific environment. (In a more ephemeral complement to these printed traces, we can see which KBW lectures Klibansky attended – those by, for instance, Cassirer, Ferdinand Noack, or Otto Franke, during the 1926–27 year – as attested by his signature on the attendance lists preserved at the Warburg Institute Archive in London.[28])

A different aspect of the Warburg world can be seen through provenance evidence. Indications of previous Warburg Library ownership in inscriptions, stamps, bookplates, and labels remain in around twenty of Klibansky's books, covering topics such as philosophy, religion, Greek and Latin literature, bibliography, and occultism.[29] Some reflect the breadth of the library's geographical reach, with volumes inscribed from researchers outside Germany or England. Just one example is the 1914 Loeb Classical Library bilingual Greek-English edition of Plato, which is historically interesting.[30] Klibansky's copy of the first volume bears an inscription to Aby Warburg from the collection's founder, James Loeb, dated 1924 (figs. 4.4a and 4.4b). Loeb was the American-born banker and philanthropist who founded the series, and the Loeb and Warburg families had connections through marriage.[31] According to Warburg's 1927 notes in the KBW daily journal, the *Tagebuch*, it appears that discussions took place at that time regarding a possible joint venture, perhaps a German Loeb series (ancient texts in Latin or Greek with modern translations). The venture never materialized, and Klibansky was among those with reservations, as Warburg notes Klibansky's concern about finding an editor and capital.[32]

Items from the personal library of philologist and historian of astrology Franz Boll, friend and colleague to Aby Warburg and mentor to Fritz Saxl, also made their way into Klibansky's library via the KBW. They offer further material evidence of early KBW intellectual networks.[33] After Boll's death the KBW took a leading role in the dispersal of his library (a handwritten catalogue of that library remains at the WIA). Klibansky was involved in sorting and organizing the books,[34] and inscriptions to Boll (most from authors and editors), as well as the commemorative Boll bookplate commissioned by the KBW, appear in several of Klibansky's books.[35] Warburgian themes abound in these volumes – the history of the ancient world, symbols, myths, astrology, religion, the occult, and philology – and the books, with their combination of topics and signs of personal exchange through provenance evidence, again underscore both the extent to which Klibansky's interests were embedded in this community, and the simple fact that there was a *community* sharing these interests.

The Pillars of the KBW: Saxl and Bing

Fritz Saxl and Gertrud Bing, who were at the core of KBW and early Warburg Institute functioning, figure individually in Klibansky's collection through

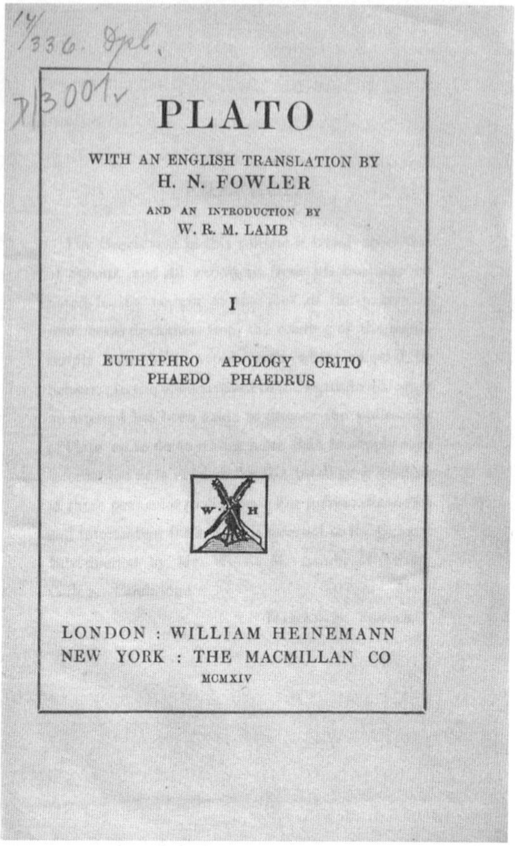
PLATO

WITH AN ENGLISH TRANSLATION BY
H. N. FOWLER

AND AN INTRODUCTION BY
W. R. M. LAMB

I

EUTHYPHRO APOLOGY CRITO
PHAEDO PHAEDRUS

LONDON : WILLIAM HEINEMANN
NEW YORK : THE MACMILLAN CO
MCMXIV

Fig. 4.4.a Title page from the first volume of Plato in the Loeb Classical Library series, given by James Loeb to Aby Warburg.

their own published works as well as through more personal traces. Saxl was Klibansky's closest colleague within the Warburg circle, and evidence of their early cooperation can be noted in presentation copies. The tone of a 1927 inscription to Klibansky in an offprint of "Aller Tugenden und Laster Abbildung," on allegory in medieval book illumination, "with many thanks for all the help,"[36] is friendly enough if pretty standard.[37] But if an unfinished note (laid in a 1929 essay by Martin Grabmann) can be taken as a possible communication from Klibansky, still a student, to Saxl, as director of the KBW, a more casual character seems already to be established: "Dear Mr. Saxl, Since arriving in Rome, no, since arriving in Florence, not a day has passed that I did not mean to write; and it never happened. Why?"[38]

The extent to which the physical spaces in books were, for this group, natural vehicles through which to commemorate, record, and remember the

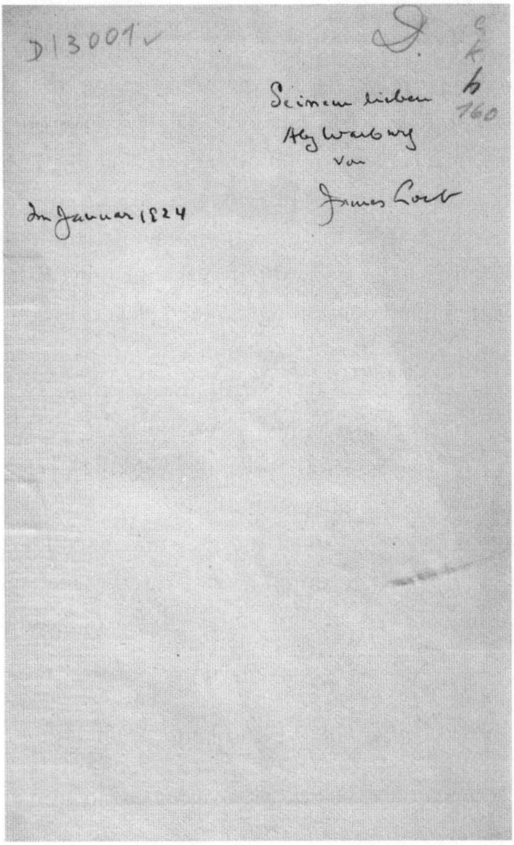

Fig. 4.4.b Inscription from Loeb to Warburg, dated January 1924. Also visible in pencil in the top right corner is a Warburg Library shelf mark.

events and people of these years is visible through this collection. The collective displacement to London in 1933 and efforts to adapt in England are marked, for instance, by a book gift: providing an orientation to the anglophone research universe, William Rose's *An Outline of Modern Knowledge* (in bright Gollancz yellow) is inscribed – in what appears to be Saxl's hand – to "*Raymond Klibansky | herzlichst; v.d.* KBW|*29/9 1933*" a month after Klibansky's arrival in London.[39] Bing's 1957 memorial essay offprint on Saxl is inscribed by Bing to Klibansky, "For Raymond | in memory of old times | G.B. | July 1957."[40] Repetition itself is a mode of preservation, and a number of titles by or about Saxl and Bing are collected in more than one copy or in more than one language.

Saxl and Bing were also Klibansky's main Warburg Library correspondents, and although by far the bulk of that correspondence is held at either or both the WIA and the DLA, a few dozen letters from Saxl, and around twenty from Bing, can be consulted at McGill. It remains to be seen what is in fact unique. Much of what is preserved at McGill is official, typed Warburg Institute correspondence for which copies would normally exist at the WIA, yet occasional handwritten additions may not be preserved in official sets, and for these and for manuscript notes, this collection may offer unique sources. Just one example is a typed letter from Saxl in 1935 touching on the *Plato Latinus*, with a handwritten note mentioning the Rockefellers in connection to funding efforts (fig. 4.5).

Fully handwritten letters, of which there are a small number from each of Saxl and Bing in this collection, deal also with Warburg business, mostly in the mid-1930s, referring to Walter (Solmitz), to Panofsky, to the *Corpus Platonicum*, to Klibansky's colleagues from his Eckhart edition project, and so forth. Their tone is sometimes more personal and they may be unique, but it will take further exploration to determine the value of these letters for understanding the workings of the Warburg Library network and its projects (fig. 4.6).

Klibansky's Contemporaries: Walter Solmitz and Lotte Labowsky

Born all in 1905, Walter, Lotte, and Raymond formed a trio of brilliant students who joined the Warburg circle in the mid-1920s and stayed within or near it in one way or another throughout their lives. (Richard Hunt, a few years younger, was an early UK addition to this new Warburg generation. With Klibansky, and later Labowsky also, he edited the journal *Mediaeval and Renaissance Studies* [*MARS*].) Raymond and Walter had been friends for years, from the Odenwaldschule, before they both became students of Cassirer and got involved with the KBW. Solmitz published relatively little, and so is not very present in the collection – a reminder of the limitations of libraries in assessing intellectual networks, and their often more complementary value alongside other kinds of archival and published source types. What there is by Solmitz, however, is telling of his intimacy with two giants of the Hamburg Warburg circle: as one of the authors on the 1929 eulogies for Aby Warburg upon his death; and as author of "Cassirer on Galileo: An Example of Cassirer's Way of Thought," reprinted from the Library of Living Philosophers edition of *The Philosophy of Ernst Cassirer* (1949). In Klibansky's

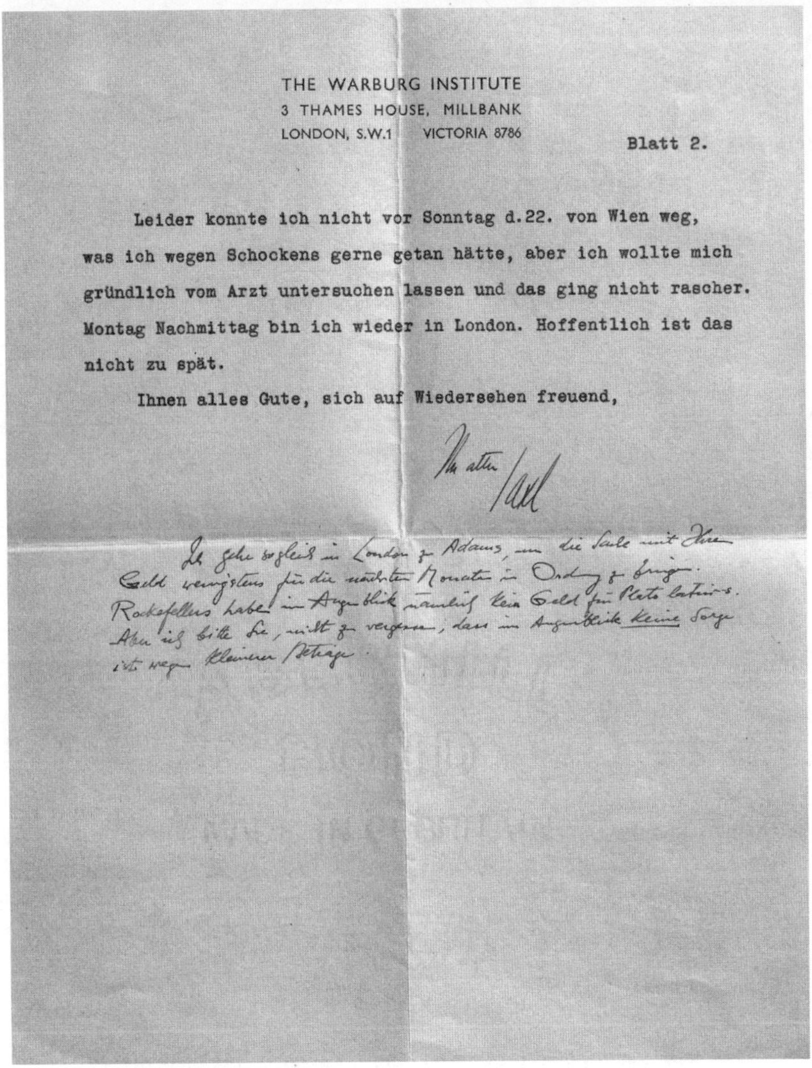

THE WARBURG INSTITUTE
3 THAMES HOUSE, MILLBANK
LONDON, S.W.1 VICTORIA 8786

Blatt 2.

Leider konnte ich nicht vor Sonntag d.22. von Wien weg, was ich wegen Schockens gerne getan hätte, aber ich wollte mich gründlich vom Arzt untersuchen lassen und das ging nicht rascher. Montag Nachmittag bin ich wieder in London. Hoffentlich ist das nicht zu spät.

Ihnen alles Gute, sich auf Wiedersehen freuend,

Ihr alter Saxl

Ich gehe sogleich in London zu Adams, um die Sache mit Ihrem Geld wenigstens für die nächsten Monate in Ordnung zu bringen. Rockefellers haben im Augenblick nämlich kein Geld für Plato latinus. Aber ich bitte Sie, nicht zu vergessen, dass im Augenblick keine Sorge ist wegen kleinerer Beträge.

Fig. 4.5 Saxl's handwritten note after his typed letter to Klibansky from Vienna, 20 September 1935, refers to the Rockefeller family in connection with funding for the *Plato Latinus* project.

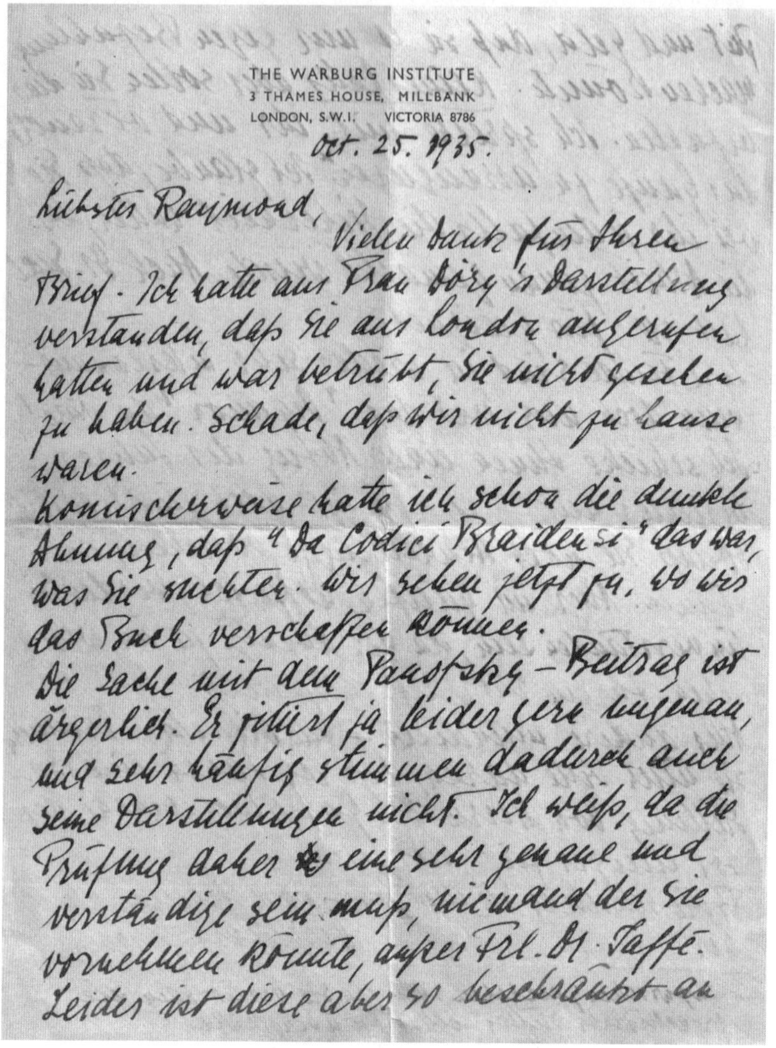

THE WARBURG INSTITUTE
3 THAMES HOUSE, MILLBANK
LONDON, S.W.1. VICTORIA 8786

Oct. 25. 1935.

Liebster Raymond,

Vielen Dank für Ihren Brief. Ich hatte aus Frau Börg's Darstellung verstanden, daß Sie aus London angerufen hatten und war betrübt, Sie nicht gesehen zu haben. Schade, daß wir nicht zu Hause waren.

Komischerweise hatte ich schon die dunkle Ahnung, daß "De Codici Braidensi" das war, was Sie suchten. Wir sehen jetzt zu, wo wir das Buch verschaffen können.

Die Sache mit dem Panofsky-Beitrag ist ärgerlich. Er zitiert ja leider gern ungenau, und sehr häufig stimmen dadurch auch seine Darstellungen nicht. Ich weiß, da die Prüfung daher eine sehr genaue und verständige sein muß, niemand der sie vornehmen könnte, außer Frl. Dr. Jaffé. Leider ist diese aber so beschränkt an

Fig. 4.6 *Above and opposite* Letter from Bing to Klibansky, 25 October 1935 (2 pp.), typical in the variety of subjects touched on. This note includes mention of Panofsky.

Zeit und Geld, daß sie es nur gegen Bezahlung machen könnte. <u>Keinesfalls</u> aber sollen <u>Sie</u> dies bezahlen. Ich spreche mit ihr und versuche das Ganze zu arrangieren.* Ich glaube, daß Sie bei ihr jedenfalls die Sicherheit hätten, daß die Arbeit genau gemacht würde. Auch Dr. Saxl hält sie für geeignet.

Ihre Funde sind ja wieder sehr interessant – wenn doch nur erst das "Organon" da wäre!

Ich schicke Ihnen einen Abzug des Jahresberichtes mit – es kommt noch eine Revision, sodaß Sie noch Aenderungen vorschlagen können. Aber im Ganzen, hoffe ich, werden Sie einverstanden sein, da der Absatz ja im wesentlichen Ihrem Entwurf entspricht.

Alles andere mündlich – am Dienstag. Erinnern Sie mich bitte daran, daß ich Ihnen eine Bestellung von Herrn Dr. Gurwitsch mache, der vor einiger Zeit hier war.

Bitte schicken Sie die Pan.-Korrekturen gleich her!

Herzlichst Ihre

Gertrud Bing.

* Inzwischen geschehen. Würden Sie bereit sein, die griechischen Stellen selbst zu überprüfen?

copy of this last, is Solmitz's undated handwritten note, circling the word "printed" and adding, "Thanks to you! Walter" (fig. 4.7). This kind of informal agency, or personal dynamic, may not be recorded in more official ways.

Handwritten letters to Klibansky add to the sense of Solmitz's self-effacing character ("I am so glad that you didn't mind to come to London last Wednesday and even to attend my talk. Let us meet again soon! ... Don't forget me"), and the closeness he felt with Klibansky ("this afternoon I felt you sitting beside me").[41]

If Solmitz was Klibansky's earliest friend, Lotte Labowsky was the most long-lasting of his Warburg ties. Labowsky's books mark the longevity of their connection and their shared links to the Warburg, and with over forty titles either by her or with her provenance signs, they constitute the second-largest group of books connected with one individual from the Warburg circle, after Cassirer. Her copy of the 1929 eulogies for Aby Warburg and her author-inscribed copy of Gombrich's 1970 intellectual biography of Warburg, both of which now sit beside Klibansky's own copies, testify to some of their shared experience. She too preserved an early aid to British life, signing her 1930s copy of *The Little Londoner: A Concise Account of the New Life and Ways of the English with Special Reference to London*. The presence of her doctoral dissertation, with the handwritten note of its acceptance by her supervisor, "Imprimatur Regenbogen, 23. M. 34," and many of her other titles, makes Klibansky's library a useful repository on her work and intellectual trajectory.[42] More important as evidence of unofficial Labowsky-Klibansky collaborations is her hand-corrected copy of Klibansky's 1961 Latin edition of Locke's *A Letter on Toleration*, which also sits now beside his own hand-corrected copy. These volumes offer a complement to the extensive correspondence between the two preserved at the DLA, of which there is little trace here (fig. 4.8).[43]

The Art Historians: Erwin Panofsky and Edgar Wind

I have found no great store of warm inscriptions or correspondence in the collection on the part of Panofsky to Klibansky. Panofsky is a topic more than a source, and appears as such in a smattering of correspondence from Saxl and Bing in particular. The one inscribed offprint on art interpretation

Thanks to you! Walter.

Reprinted from
THE LIBRARY OF LIVING PHILOSOPHERS
THE PHILOSOPHY OF ERNST CASSIRER
1949

21

CASSIRER ON GALILEO: AN EXAMPLE OF CASSIRER'S WAY OF THOUGHT

"Als wie der Tag die Menschen hell umscheinet
Und mit dem Lichte, das den Höhn entspringet,
Die dämmernden Erscheinungen vereinet,
Ist Wissen, welches tief der Geistigkeit gelinget."
—Hölderlin.*

I

THE following passage may be regarded as a typical "Cassirer" text. It can call to mind a few characteristics of Cassirer's philosophical style.

> Galileo emphasized unceasingly that the law which rules the phenomena, and their underlying reasons *(ragioni)*, cannot immediately be read off of the phenomena by sensory perception. What is required for the discovery of those laws is rather the spontaneity of mathematical reasoning. For we learn to know the eternal and necessary in things not by means of mere piling up and comparison of sense experiences; rather the mind must have grasped it "from within itself" in order to be able to find it again in the phenomena. Each intellect knows from itself *(da per sè)* the true and necessary things, i.e., those which could not possibly be [or act] otherwise;—or else it is impossible for the mind ever to know them.[1]

There is nothing very extraordinary about this passage. It is an historical passage from an historical book, written in a rather

* "Bright is broad day that beams around the man,
Uniting with the light that comes forth from the heights
The various things appearing in the dusk.
Thus too beams knowledge that has blessed the spirit's depth."

[1] *Individuum und Kosmos in der Philosophie der Renaissance.* Studien der Bibliothek Warburg, vol. X, (Leipzig, 1927), 173.

731

Fig. 4.7 Solmitz's offprint of "Cassirer on Galileo: An Example of Cassirer's Way of Thought," from *The Philosophy of Ernst Cassirer*, with his note of thanks.

Der Begriff des Πρέπον in der Ethik des Panaitios

Mit Analysen von
Cicero De officiis I 93—149 und Horaz Ars poetica

Inaugural-Dissertation
zur Erlangung der Doktorwürde
der Hohen Philosophischen Fakultät
der Badischen Ruprecht-Karls-Universität zu Heidelberg

eingereicht von

Lotte Labowsky
aus Hamburg

Druck von Robert Noske in Borna-Leipzig

Fig. 4.8 Lotte Labowsky's dissertation, with the handwritten note of her supervisor's approval: "Imprimatur Regenbogen, 23. M. 34."

(1932) dates from before the attribution wars began with respect to authorship on *Saturn and Melancholy*, for which Panofsky long maintained that Klibansky should not hold full authorship status.[44]

Edgar Wind, author of *Art and Anarchy* and *Pagan Mysteries in the Renaissance* (of which Klibansky had several copies) was a few years senior to Solmitz, Labowsky, and Klibansky, but followed a similar path, studying with Panofsky and Cassirer, and working as a research assistant at the Warburg in the late 1920s. Two of Wind's publications in particular bridge the Hamburg-Heidelberg realms of Klibansky's Weimar experience: he co-edited the Warburg *Bibliography on the Survival of the Classics*, and he also helped compile a posthumous volume of writings by Klibansky's great friend from Heidelberg, Friedrich Gundolf (figs. 4.9a and 4.9b).[45] Klibansky's copies attest to their shared interests and common network, but on a more personal level his shelves are silent.

Heidelberg: The University and Its Literary Universe

Ernst Hoffmann

A friend of Cassirer's, Ernst Hoffmann was no stranger to the Warburg circle.[46] But Klibansky's relationship with him developed through his studies at the University of Heidelberg. Klibansky says little about Hoffmann in his published memoirs and interviews despite Hoffmann's having been his doctoral supervisor, *Habilitation* sponsor, and co-editor on the Heidelberg Cusa edition. Yet following Hoffmann's death in 1952, Klibansky took pains to secure his library for the Université de Montréal, where Klibansky taught in the Institut d'études médiévales as a visiting professor. In fact, following Klibansky's move to England, a rift opened between them, and part of the circumstances of these cooler relations was noticed in Klibansky's library. In the collection is a copy of a book that provides the continuation of Klibansky's first work with Hoffmann (and supported by the KBW) on Nicholas of Cusa, the *Cusanus-Texte. I, Predigten.1*. The continuation, *Cusanus-Texte. I, Predigten. 2./5* came out in 1937, and carries the subtitle *Vier Predigten im Geiste Eckharts. Lateinisch und Deutsch mit einer*

ANFÄNGE DEUTSCHER GESCHICHTSCHREIBUNG

von

FRIEDRICH GUNDOLF

HERAUSGEGEBEN VON
ELISABETH GUNDOLF
UND EDGAR WIND

„ELSEVIER" AMSTERDAM

Fig. 4.9a Posthumous volume of Gundolf's writings.

literarhistorischen Einleitung und Erläuterungen (*Four sermons in the spirit of Eckhart. Latin and German with a literary-historical introduction and explanatory notes*). The work had Hoffmann's collaboration again, using, Klibansky believed, his own notes, and furthermore, was edited by Josef Koch, whose presence could have constituted an acute wound to Klibansky: Koch was a member of a team producing a full edition of the works of Meister Eckhart – often referred to as "the Stuttgart edition," and still the standard modern critical edition. The Stuttgart team – supported by the Nazi government – was in direct competition with Klibansky's own edition project of the medieval thinker, and in fact Klibansky felt that his work had been used by this other group after he had been locked out of his Heidelberg office in 1933.[47] A copy of a typescript document held at the

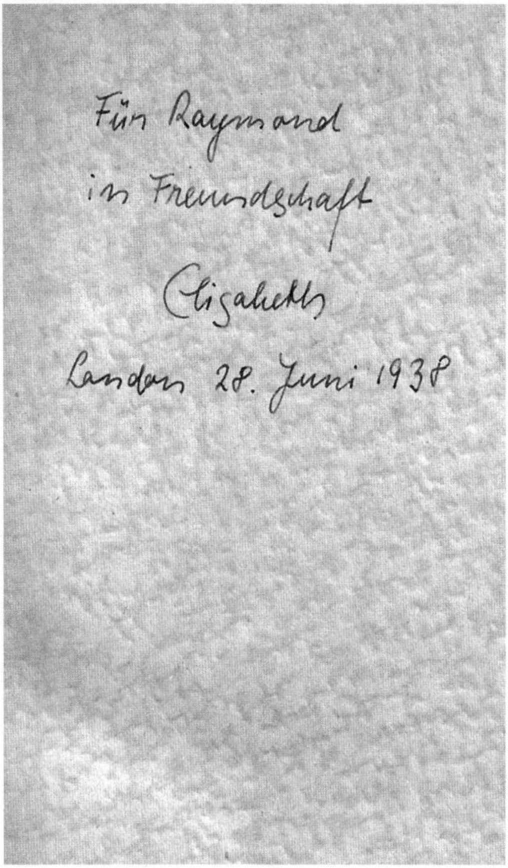

Fig. 4.9b Inscription to Klibansky from Elisabeth Salomon-Gundolf.

Warburg Institute Archive details several specific complaints about the edition published out of Stuttgart, and in it Koch is specifically named.[48] Hoffmann's acceptance of Koch's participation in the project may have been quite a blow, regardless of his qualifications. An extraordinary example of Klibansky's annotation, sometimes clearly indignant in direct response to the edition, is preserved in the collection.[49]

Earlier book inscriptions speak to a warm relationship, however, and of affection on the part of Hoffmann, and casting a light quite different from what one can discern in Klibansky's own autobiographical statements. The earliest trace of Klibansky recording for himself the source of a gift is, in fact, in the text co-authored by Hoffmann and Ernst Cassirer on the history of ancient philosophy; the inscription reads: "Geschenk von Prof. E. Hoffmann,

Heidelberg 1926." Hoffmann appears again in gift inscriptions, in a book on aesthetics by Kuno Fischer that he gave Klibansky for Christmas, 1928, and in an edition of writings and lectures of German philosopher Paul Hensel, co-edited by Hoffmann with Heinrich Rickert, in 1930. Around three dozen letters to or from Hoffmann, yet to be studied, are held at McGill, many dating from the time at which Hoffmann would likely have been working on projects Klibansky considered his own.

Gundolf

Klibansky's most personal link to Heidelberg's literary milieu was the literary scholar Friedrich Gundolf, who had famously shifted away from an early intimacy with the figure and world of Stefan George. He is the single most visible figure in the collection with respect to Klibansky's social book world. When he died, in 1931, Klibansky said that it marked the end of Heidelberg.[50] A recent monograph on Gundolf's library emphasizes Klibansky's role in helping to catalogue the library after Gundolf's death in 1931, and in aiding its transfer out of the country with the crates destined for the Warburg Insitute in 1933.[51]

Like Cassirer, Gundolf is one of the very few main authors who appear frequently in the collection catalogue who are contemporary with Klibansky, and he is the only one appearing so often whose titles are not primarily in philosophy or religion. The many volumes by him on, for instance, Shakespeare, Julius Caesar, Goethe, or Stefan George, reflect the broad intellectual scope of this friend who, with Cassirer, Warburg, and others, provided Klibansky with a formidable set of mentors. More specifically with respect to method, Klibansky describes Gundolf's work on Caesar as an exploration of how he had been viewed and represented through history, an approach that has clear resonances with Warburgian and, specifically, Klibansky's own methods.[52]

Several of the collection's more interesting inscriptions – messages that document bookstore adventures and a more playful attitude toward books – are those in volumes given to the young Klibansky by Gundolf. Just one example is found in a book by Gustav Pfizer (on the fifteenth-century poetry of Pope Pius II, among others) inscribed by Gundolf with a poem, excusing the book's author for his weakness on Nicholas of Cusa on account of Klibansky's not having yet been born.[53]

As a collector, Gundolf has been described as one of the last great models of this European tradition.[54] His own library has been studied, and a small part of that legacy has lain quietly here, now publicly accessible, in Klibansky's collection. Over a dozen books from Gundolf's highly-prized collection have been noticed here, among them a volume containing several early seventeenth-century titles by theologian and mystic Valentin Weigel, who was singled out by Klibansky as a clear precursor to Kant.[55] In his study of Gundolf's library, Michael Thimann quotes Gundolf's excitement, in a 1930 letter to Karl Wolfskehl, at finding a "rarissima" volume of Weigel with several titles bound together (nine titles of Weigel and one by Andreas Rudolf Karlstadt) – a description that fits precisely a volume now in Klibansky's collection with Gundolf's signature (dated Hamburg, 1930), in which the first of the several bound-together publications is the *Theologia Weigelii*.[56]

But Gundolf was not simply a bibliophile who shared Klibansky's love of books; as a historian who was close to Cassirer, Karl Jaspers, Marianne Weber, and other mentors of Klibansky, whose work was selected for inclusion in the Cassirer *Festschrift*, and whose library was protected in part by the Warburg Institute in its move to England, Gundolf represented yet another – and a richly creative – intersection of Klibansky's Heidelberg and Hamburg worlds. Like that of the intimate Warburg circle, Gundolf's own legacy is somewhat scattered across a number of institutions.[57] If the treasures from Gundolf's library constitute something of a tributary that helped form Klibansky's library, Gundolf's education and traditions were likewise, along with other Heidelberg and Hamburg mentors, intellectual tributaries to Klibansky's *Bildung* and his lifework. And just as the value of those volumes, passed from hand to hand among these circles, is heightened by being situated among so many others that together provide a strong intellectual and cultural backdrop, so the library and archival materials of Klibansky and each member of the Warburg Library circle acquire value as they are increasingly available to be brought together to illuminate agencies at play in this unique twentieth-century group.

These have been just a few examples of what the RKC has to offer to its users. As a sub-collection connected to Klibansky's early years, preserved through periods of geographic, professional, and cultural shifting, it has an air of a personal monument to *his* Weimar. Complementing materials preserved at London, Marbach, and elsewhere, this collection is among the sources that help to understand the network of scholars touched by the immense project of the Warburg Library. As Klibansky forms a nexus through which the Warburg Library Network can be viewed, so his library constitutes a nexus of its central figures, their precursors, and their wider circles and environments.

Klibansky's library and papers in their various holding institutions constitute a new intersection at which the legacies of Heidelberg's Weimar and the Warburg's Hamburg connect and overlap; where books previously owned by Friedrich Gundolf or Franz Boll are shelved alongside heavily marked-up Aristotelean studies for German high school students, rare volumes of Nicholas of Cusa, highly stylized exemplars of the art nouveau of Stefan George, or the sober volumes of the KBW. Hundreds of such volumes help tell the story of an extraordinary period and of a group that influenced developments in humanities scholarship in both Europe and North America. It is, finally, among the core material that remains as a testament to an education and a philosophy of education that strove for tolerance and self-discipline in historical approaches, a worldview from which there is perhaps yet much more to learn.

NOTES

1 For example, Ernst Cassirer's papers are at Yale University's Beinecke Rare Book and Manuscript Library.

2 At the time of writing, the WIA online database had indexed General Correspondence up to and including 1930. Klibansky, active with the group from 1926, is the sender, receiver, or a subject in nearly 150 of these records.

3 Elisabeth Otto made an assessment of these materials in 2016; I thank her for sharing her results and providing the following supplementary estimation of the Warburg projects led by Klibansky: more than fifteen hundred in- and outgoing letters for the *Corpus Platonicum Medii Aevi* project; and more than four hundred letters in the correspondence for the editing of the journal *Mediaeval*

and Renaissance Studies (including letters to and from Lotte Labowsky and Richard Hunt).

4 Many thanks to Ethel Groffier and Regina Weber for providing copies of this list as it developed.

5 See Weber, *Lotte Labowsky (1905–1991). Schülerin Aby Warburgs, Kollegin Raymond Klibanskys.*

6 Thanks to Regina Weber for sharing this information.

7 A more detailed study of the catalogued portions of this library can be found in Jillian Tomm, "The Imprint of the Scholar: An Analysis of the Printed Books of McGill University's Raymond Klibansky Collection" (PhD diss. McGill University 2012). Individual catalogue records of the Raymond Klibansky Collection can be searched through the McGill Library Classic Catalogue (http://catalogue.mcgill.ca/F/).

8 Sophie Trolliet-Martial of the McGill University Library identified and documented the WLN-related archival materials held in complement to the Raymond Klibansky Collection (RKC) at McGill University Rare Books and Special Collections. Examples used here from that group were signalled and listed by her (not available online at time of writing).

9 The document was located in 2015 as a result of a specific search thanks to the determination of Philippe Despoix and Georges Leroux, who used it toward a new French edition of the text – based on Klibansky's 1936 published English version, "The Philosophical Character of History" – in their recent volume of texts selected and presented by them: *Raymond Klibansky: Tradition antique et tolérance moderne*, 47–67.

10 Many thanks to Roland Kamzelak of the Deutsches Literaturarchiv Marbach (DLA) for his creation of a common database, initiated in 2015 and populated by holdings at the DLA, the WIA, and McGill University. McGill University's holdings from the RKC archival materials were submitted by Sophie Trolliet-Martial, and were the most completely represented of the three institutions at the time of writing.

11 A selection of the volumes was presented in the exhibition curated by Georges Leroux, *Raymond Klibansky (1905–2005) – La bibliothèque d'un philosophe/A Philosopher's Library*, at the Grande Bibliothèque, Montréal (BANQ), 13 November 2012–25 August 2013; an essay catalogue with the same title was published by the BANQ in 2013.

12 Trendelenburg, *Erläuterungen zu den Elementen der aristotelischen Logik*; McGill

University Library Rare Books and Special Collections (hereafter McGill RBSC), Raymond Klibansky Collection (RKC) no. B491 L8 T7 1861.

13 Aristotle, *Selecta ex Organo Aristoteleo capitula* (ed. by Trendelenburg); McGill RBSC, RKC no. PA3893 O8 1897.

14 Klibansky, *Le Philosophe et la mémoire du siècle*, 11.

15 See for example: Norton, *Secret Germany*, 166.

16 Edgar Salin (1892–1974), Ernst Kantorowicz (1895–1963), Ludwig Klages (1872–1956), Oskar Kohnstamm (1871–1917).

17 "To understand the problem of man ... it was necessary to know philosophy, starting with the Greeks. But to access Greek philosophy – and this was my firm conviction – it didn't suffice to read the works of philosophers; it was necessary to really know *la langue* of the philosopher, the Greek *langue.* It was necessary also to study Greek Poetry ... I thought furthermore that it is incomplete to want to approach philosophy and civilization in general simply by what is written; one must also know art." Klibansky, *Le Philosophe et la mémoire du siècle*, 16 (my translation).

18 Ibid., 48.

19 Klibansky met Zimmer, who was also one of the frequent visitors to Gundolf's home, in 1927. For more on this, see Thimann, *Caesars Schatten,* 29. In 1938, Klibansky arranged for Zimmer, who was married to Christiane von Hofmannsthal, daughter of poet Hugo von Hofmannsthal and of Jewish descent, to come to Oxford. Zimmer moved to the United States in 1940 to teach at Columbia University, and passed away just three years later.

20 Klibansky, *Le Philosophe et la mémoire du siècle*, 32–4.

21 Gawronsky, "Ernst Cassirer: His Life and Work," 9.

22 Friedman, "Ernst Cassirer," n.p.

23 Both published in Berlin by Ernst Cassirer's cousin Bruno Cassirer, in different formats, 1921 and 1924; McGill RBSC, RKC no. PT351 C3 1921; PT351 C3 1924.

24 Inscription is from an offprint of Ernst Cassirer, "Descartes et l'idée de l'unité de la science."

25 Klibansky, *Le Philosophe et la mémoire du siècle*, 32.

26 Max Dessoir's presentation copy to Ernst Cassirer of *Beiträge zur allgemeinen Kunstwissenschaft*; McGill RBSC, RKC no. BH203 F29 1929. Dessoir edited the 1925 volume that included Cassirer and Hoffman's "Die Geschichte der antiken Philosophie."

27 Some six hundred volumes carry Klibansky's shelf marks, each recorded in the notes of individual McGill Library catalogue records. A complete list or summary of the content of the shelf-marked group are available from the author.

28 WIA, I.9.18: "Besucherlisten," lecture attendance lists: Vorträge and other events in the KBW. [1921–31].

29 These books can best be identified in the McGill Library Classic Catalogue by searching the term "Warburg" in the Notes field (advanced search).

30 Plato, *Euthyphro, Apology, Crito, Phaedo, Phaedrus*; McGill RBSC, RKC no. PA3612 P6 1914.

31 James Loeb's sister Nina was married to Warburg's brother, Paul.

32 Warburg, *Tagebuch der kulturwissenschaftlichen Bibliothek Warburg*, 71.

33 Boll provenance is documented in the "Notes" field of McGill Library catalogue records.

34 Warburg, *Tagebuch*, 20 and 43.

35 The Boll bookplate designed by the KBW, with the motto "per mostra ad sphaeram" around the image of an astronomer from Johannes Angelus's *Astrolabium*, has been reproduced in Gombrich's *Aby Warburg* (191 plate 39c) and elsewhere. It is the plate noticed in the RKC. A different Boll bookplate, with Egyptian figures carrying books, can be seen in McEwan, "Saxl and Boll," 12.

36 "S./l. Klibansky mit vielen Dank für alle Hilfe 2/2 27 d. Verf."

37 Saxl, "Aller Tugenden und Laster Abbildung." McGill RBSC, RKC no. fol. N7710 S29 1927.

38 "Lieber Herr Saxl, Seit ich in Rom bin, nein, seit ich in Florenz war, verging kein Tag, an dem ich Ihnen nicht schreiben wollte; und nie kam es dazu. Warum?" Manuscript note laid in Grabmann, *Mittelalterliche lateinische Ubersetzungen von Schriften der Aristoteles*. McGill RBSC, RKC no. AS182 M823 1929 Heft 7 (my translation).

39 Rose, *An Outline of Modern Knowledge*. McGill University Library, RBSC, RKC no. AG105 R755 1932.

40 Bing, "Fritz Saxl 1890–1948: A Memoir" (offprint); McGill RBSC, RKC no. N7483 S286 B5 1986 (a second copy, bearing an almost identical inscription, is preserved in the RKC offprint cabinet file for Saxl).

41 Solmitz to Klibansky, undated but likely from the 1954–55 year that Solmitz spent in London (see Elizabeth Sears in this volume on Solmitz's interactions with the WIA), McGill RBSC, RKC, archival materials, container 9 (S/47.d.); the

second quotation is from a note written by Solmitz to Klibansky from Cambridge, Massachusetts, 23 July 1940, McGill RBSC, RKC, archival materials, container 9 (S/47a).

42 Labowsky, "Der Begriff des Prepon in der Ethik des Panaitios"; McGill RBSC, RKC no. B595 Z7 L2 1932.

43 A letter from Labowsky to Klibansky dated 1975 and tipped into a volume of dialogues of Plato, for example, comments on publication proofs recently arrived from Rome (her *Bessarion's Library and the Biblioteca Marciana* was published in Rome by the Edizioni di storia e letteratura, 1979).

44 The inscription ("S.l. Raymond Klibansky d. Verf. 31/2.32.") is written in Panofsky's "Zum Problem der Beschreibung und Inhaltsdeutung von Werken der bildenden Kunst"; McGill RBSC, RKC, offprint filing cabinet: Panofsky. On the topic of the disagreement over attribution in *Saturn and Melancholy*, see Part 3 of this volume.

45 Gundolf, *Anfänge deutscher Geschichtschreibung*; McGill RBSC, RKC no. D13 G9 1938.

46 As noted above, Hoffmann was among the early contributors to the *Vorträge der Bibliothek Warburg* with his "Platonismus und Mittelalter."

47 Klibansky, "Raymond Klibansky, philosophe et historien," 140. See Klibansky's comments regarding Hoffmann's use of this material in chapter 2 of this volume; Treml (66–7).

48 WIA, GC, 1934–36: Klibansky. Eckhart edition. "Remarques sur la méthode employée par l'édition des œuvres de Maître Eckhart sous le patronage de la 'Forschungsgemeinschaft.'" The text is signed "les auteurs de l'édition de Sainte Sabine" and appears to have been written in or near 1936. Regina Weber has informed me that copies of the document can also be found in Klibansky's *fonds* at the DLA.

49 A brief description of this case and some images of Klibansky's copy can be viewed on the Rare Books and Special Collections blog on the McGill University website: https://blogs.library.mcgill.ca/rbsc/politics-and-scholarly-publishing-in-1930s-germany-the-eckhart-latin-edition/, accessed 5 October 5 2015.

50 Klibansky, *Le Philosophe et la mémoire du siècle*, 58.

51 See Thimann, *Caesars Schatten,* on Klibansky esp. 33–9. Klibansky's catalogue does not seem to have survived, and Gundolf's library is now dispersed after a number of sales; the largest groups of Gundolf's books survive at the Institute

for Germanic and Romance Studies at the University of London, and at Duke University in North Carolina. See: Bock, "First Report on the Gundolf Papers at the Institute of Germanic Languages and Literatures in the University of London"; and Thimann, *Caesars Schatten,* esp. 37–42; 105–6; 161. Thimann's work includes a partial reconstruction and study of the library and of Gundolf as a collector. The reconstruction does not take into account volumes in Klibansky's library with Gundolf provenance, as it predates public access to Klibansky's collection. Gundolf provenance in the RKC is noted in the McGill Library catalogue records.

52 Klibansky, *Le Philosophe et la mémoire du siècle,* 54.

53 Pfizer, *Der Welsche und der Deutsche*; McGill RBSC, RKC no. PT2445 P57 W4 1844.

54 Thimann, *Caesars Schatten*, 9.

55 Klibansky, *Le Philosophe et la mémoire du siècle,* 72.

56 Thimann, *Caesars Schatten*, 228. The first title in this volume containing multiple publications, *Theologia Weigelii: das ist, Offentliche Glaubens Bekändtnüsz desz Weyland Ehrwürdigen* ... ("Gedruckt zu der Newstatt: Bey Johan Knuber, anno 1618") [i.e., Halle an der Saale: J. Krusicke], is the primary record in the McGill Library catalogue (McGill RBSC, RKC no. BV5080 W45 1618). The subsequent titles in the volume are listed in this first record but are also catalogued individually with fuller publication information. All share the call number BV5080 W45 1618.

57 Large groups of Gundolf's papers are held at the Institute of Modern Languages of the School of Advanced Study of the University of London, at the DLA, and at the Württembergische Landesbibliothek Stuttgart.

PART TWO

The Continuity of the Platonic Tradition

FIVE

From the Cusanus Edition to the *Corpus Platonicum Medii Aevi*: Klibansky's Collaborations with Ernst Hoffmann, Ernst Cassirer, and Fritz Saxl

REGINA WEBER

Influences on Raymond Klibansky's general working procedures and his intellectual approach to philosophy during his early academic career are the focus of this chapter. The period in question begins in 1927, with the initiation of the Cusa edition of the Heidelberger Akademie der Wissenschaften, and ends in 1938, with the launch of the *Corpus Platonicum Medii Aevi* project of the Warburg Institute London, described in the 1939 publication *The Continuity of the Platonic Tradition during the Middle Ages.*[1] Following his German-Jewish academic teachers, Klibansky contributed to a history of a tradition that constructed a narrative of the survival of the classics during the Middle Ages and the Renaissance in competition with the dominant Western history of Christianity and of the Church – a narrative in whose development Judaism played an integral part.

The Intellectual Individuality of the Outsider and Early Methodological Influences

The generation of German-Jewish scholars who mentored Klibansky were molded by the Whilhelmine Reich, the First World War, and the Weimar Republic. In the 1920s, they found themselves in an academic environment dominated by nationalism, racism, and anti-Semitism. They carried the status of "outsider"; as Hans Liebeschütz put it *positively* in 1948 in his obituary of Fritz Saxl: "The independence in his European outlook, which he cherished as his most precious possession, was the outcome of his position as an outsider and a Jew."[2] The Catholic Church especially, whose theology and tradition Klibansky himself confronted as a historian of the Middle Ages and Renaissance, had not yet embraced modern developments. And the exclusion of Jewish scholars by the dominant academic society at the time may be compared structurally with the assumed privilege of groups often described in North American society as WASPS (White Anglo-Saxon Protestants), who do not want their identity questioned by people of colour, women, or Jews.

If Klibansky's fundamental intellectual influences dated from his university days, his belonging to the "outsiders" did not. Already in his high school years, he opted for an alternative route and, in choosing an experimental school – the Odenwaldschule – over the excellent but traditional Goethe-Gymnasium, Klibansky was unfettered by concerns of fitting in. The Odenwaldschule, too, was set apart from established educational institutes: the *Reformpädagogische Landschulheim* was not bound by religious affiliation and – like the more prestigious Schloss Salem School founded ten years later – was subsidized by Jewish donations. From this period also originates the question that motivated Klibansky's philosophical studies generally, and which led him to the beginning of his philosophical inquiry into antiquity: what is man? Not the Christian, nor the Jew, but the man – and this question found its first answer at the Odenwaldschule, whose curriculum was directed by the humanistic ideals of German classicism and the motto of Pindar: Become the person who you are.

In 1927, at the age of twenty-two, Klibansky became integrated into a social academic network consisting mainly of German-Jewish scholars a generation older than himself, and often outside his primary areas of study. At Heidelberg University, where he studied classic philology and philosophy, he more often found his place, for example, outside the university schools of Neo-Kantianism, which was represented by Heinrich Rickert, or the movement of Existentialism led by Karl Jaspers (who nonetheless influenced Klibansky's views on human exchange and communication[3]). Both, in his opinion, neglected history ("*Ils négligeaient l'histoire*").[4] A "receptivity to history"[5] Klibansky found instead in Friedrich Gundolf, professor of German literature and one-time intimate of Stefan George, with whom he became friends in the late twenties; and in Indologist Heinrich Zimmer. The works of both Gundolf and Zimmer during these years represent approaches that find clear echoes in Klibansky's later historical work: Gundolf's publication *Caesar: Geschichte seines Ruhms* (1924), traces transformations in representations of the Roman hero through the centuries; and Zimmer's work on the image of the elephant from antiquity to the Renaissance, which Klibansky mentions enthusiastically in a 1927 letter to Fritz Saxl, concerns no less than "the history of the development of a symbol."[6]

This discovery of intellectual (and human) resonance did not take place in a void; a year earlier, in 1926, Klibansky had studied for a term at the University of Hamburg, where he had stayed at the home of the philosopher Ernst Cassirer, whose son Heinz had been a friend since their school days at the Odenwaldschule. Already before meeting him personally, Klibansky was one of Cassirer's most enthusiastic readers. In 1916, during the First World War, Cassirer's book *Freiheit und Form: Studien zur deutschen Geistesgeschichte*[7] (Freedom and Form: Studies in German Intellectual History) was published. This work, Klibansky's earliest reading of Cassirer, touched him "still more than his systematical writings … The way he looked at the German past and described Lessing and Kant, Schiller and Goethe; even in his interpretation of Fichte he emphasized the Fichte who did not jump on the nationalist bandwagon."[8] Also in 1916, Gundolf's *Goethe* appeared, a work that motivated Cassirer to make contact with Gundolf, and their ensuing friendship came to include Klibansky.

Both the weight and the liberty of the "outsider role" can be seen in many of Klibansky's influences at the time. Although Cassirer, a German-Jewish intellectual who saw himself as deeply rooted in the history of German thought, was named rector of the new Hamburg University, he nevertheless met with hostility within the German university scene, just as his supervisor, Hermann Cohen, had before him. Cohen was the founder of the Marburg lineage of Neo-Kantianism, but again, in the year 1916, anti-Semitic journalistic attacks were directed against Cohen as an interpreter of Kant: "Herman Cohen was not able to understand Kant, for as a Jew he was a foreigner."[9] Early in the 1930s, Klibansky would be similarly attacked as the editor of the Latin texts of Meister Eckhart for the Heidelberg Academy; a Jew would not be able to understand the great German mystic Meister Eckhart who, at that time, had been appropriated by the ideologist of the Nazi Party, Alfred

Rosenberg. In his *Mythos des 20. Jahrhunderts* (*The Myth of the Twentieth Century*), Rosenberg claimed Eckhart as the founder of the national-socialist worldview, the "creator of a new religion, our religion."[10] Confronted with such argumentation, as well as by concrete obstacles to his work, Klibansky withdrew his editorship.

It was an opportune moment for these "outsiders" to find common interests, and at the same time explore their various areas of interest with greater intellectual individuality than they might otherwise have sought. In 1926, when Klibansky came to Hamburg, Cassirer, who had been teaching at the University of Hamburg since 1920, had already long been connected with the Kulturwissenschaftliche Bibliothek Warburg (KBW), first through the Austrian art historian Fritz Saxl, then vice-director of the KBW, and then through Aby Warburg himself, after the latter's return from the Binswanger Clinic in Kreuzlingen in 1924. Warburg's methods fell outside the academic mainstream, and Cassirer was fascinated by the man and the resources he had accumulated. Contacts between art historians and philosophers at the University of Hamburg, founded in 1919, and at the KBW (whose staff counted philosopher Gertrud Bing in addition to Fritz Saxl) led to close and frequent cooperation. Just one example is the 1926 book by Cassirer, presented to Aby Warburg on his sixtieth birthday, *Individuum und Kosmos in der Philosophie der Renaissance*,[11] in which he praises, in the dedication, this unique "freundschaftliche Zusammenarbeit" (friendly cooperation).[12] In a letter dated from 1927 and addressed to Saxl, Klibansky designated the book the "new Cassirer-Bible," as his Heidelberg friends called it.[13] The book's extensive appendix includes Klibansky's first publication, an edition of a Latin text by French Platonist Charles de Bovelles, and he would have had every reason to be pleased with his association with both the author and the dedicatee.

The Hamburg circle around Warburg and Cassirer, like the research program of the KBW itself, was outstanding. As Claudia Naber describes the community, it was "a circle unique in its way, more of a private scholarship than of academic character, of mostly Jewish philosophers and art historians, which had arisen in Hamburg in the 1920s around Cassirer and the culture-historian Aby Warburg."[14] About the group and the library, Naber continues: "They looked at the problem of the meaning of the survival of antiquity as an intellectual center, around which, so to speak, these books were arranged, something which still constitutes the fundamental difference between the Warburg Library and every other book collection on cultural history."[15]

Orientations and Pathways in the History of Philosophy

The unacknowledged model for the Warburg circle was the fifteenth-century Platonic Academy in Florence, as the Early Florentine Renaissance formed the centre of the research on the history of art and culture of Aby Warburg. As late as in his 1945 essay "Ficino's Place in Intellectual History,"[16] which was composed during his exile in New York City, Cassirer characterized the Quattrocento Platonic Academy in Florence, headed by philosophers Ficino and Pico della Mirandola, as an ideal intellectual space which, barely obscured, reflected the lost paradise for the KBW. He writes: "What the Platonic Academy created was a new atmosphere of philosophical and literary life … even if all the results of the Platonic Academy have been forgotten, the idea of the Academy still survives. Here was no corporation of scholars or clerics obliged to fulfill certain official duties and bound to maintain a fixed tradition. The Academy was a circle of friends who freely discussed their philosophical problems."[17] In the philosophy of the Early Italian Renaissance, Cassirer found "a rebirth of Platonism. For in his Academy Plato had furnished the first great example of an entirely free organization of philosophical and scientific thought."[18] In the context in which Cassirer writes, these ideas are far from esoteric; they were essential to the methods explored by the researchers that built the KBW and by those, like Klibansky, who developed within it.

For Klibansky, exiled in England, research on Platonism, and the confrontation of the *Corpus Platonicum Medii Aevi* project with the much more well-known Latin corpus of Aristotle, was likewise a very special enterprise, moving beyond established academic mainstreams both present and past. In his 1939 plan for the project, he wrote:

> The dominating position of Aristotelianism in later mediaeval speculation and learning is a commonplace. The influence of Plato is not so easily recognized. It is less apparent in the official teaching of schools and faculties than in the esoteric doctrine of small circles and single

outstanding thinkers. For this reason very shadowy notions are still prevalent concerning the nature and meaning of mediaeval Platonism.[19]

But let us return once more to the year 1927, which marked the beginning of Klibansky's academic career. Thanks to his contribution to Cassirer's *Individuum und Kosmos* and his connections with the Warburg Library in general, he was well prepared for involvement in the long-planned editorial project of the Latin works of Renaissance philosopher Nicholas of Cusa (or Nicolaus Cusanus), which was finally initiated in 1927. The Leipzig publisher Felix Meiner, who since 1911 had included the project in his program of forthcoming publications, had first approached Herman Cohen as editor. Due to the outbreak of the First World War and the death of Cohen in 1919, this plan could not be realized. Now, however, Meiner had gained the support of Cassirer, whose *Individuum und Kosmos* was heavily focused on Cusa, and especially on the *De docta ignorantia* and its relations with the Italian humanists. Cassirer had in fact studied Cusa for a long time and had found an ardent collaborator in the Heidelberg professor of philosophy Ernst Hoffmann. Cassirer and Hoffmann first met in Berlin when Hoffmann, at that time a high school instructor, attended Cassirer's lectures on Cusa, and in 1925 they published a book together on the philosophy of antiquity, *Die Geschichte der antiken Philosophie*.[20] Hoffmann, too, was involved with the KBW, and thus it was natural that in 1927 Felix Meiner, Cassirer, and Hoffmann resolved to edit the *Opera omnia* of Cusa under the auspices of the Heidelberg Academy. There is a photograph in the Klibansky *fonds* in Marbach showing the student Klibansky flanked by Ernst Cassirer and Ernst Hoffmann, who embraces him. Hoffmann became Klibansky's mentor at Heidelberg University, and also examined his *Habilitation* (qualification for the position of university lecturer) in 1932. Together, they edited the first publications of the *Opera omnia*.

Although the Warburg Library was not an official sponsor of the project, the Warburg orientation was in the background of several of those involved in the project. Warburg's interest as an art historian focused on the Early Italian Renaissance, when the rebirth of pagan antiquity in the Latin occident promoted the modern concept of freedom as well as the development of the mind. As an example, Warburg referred to the symptomatic figure of the *Ninfa fiorentina*, the graceful handmaid in Ghirlandaio's *Birth of John the*

Baptist who, as Georges Didi-Huberman noted, intrudes upon the territory of the Church – "the Church as a sacred area just as a community of believers with their values and taboos."[21] Warburg followed the transformations of the pagan deities "in exile," by which he meant "under the world domination of Christianity, from antiquity to the Renaissance." In the final comment of his Roman lecture in 1912 he explained:

> The new great style which the artistic genius of Italy has brought us, had its roots in the effort of social will to free Greek humanity from Oriental-Latin "practice." With this desire for restitution of Antiquity "the good European" – to cite Nietzsche herewith – began his fight for enlightenment in that epoch of international migration of pictorial images, which we call – somewhat too mystically – the epoch of the Renaissance.[22]

Subsequently, it was Cassirer who in the *Individuum und Kosmos* volume dedicated to Aby Warburg would portray Cusa in the light of the Italian Quattrocento. Cassirer maintained that it was only in Italy that the German cleric took the decisive turn from entrenchment in German medieval dogmatism to the bright and lucid clarity of mind that in turn exercised its influence on the Italian humanists. Cassirer's portrayal of Cusa, which up until the present has drawn repeated criticism from the scientific community – he really could not adequately substantiate his references[23] – can only be understood by paying attention to Aby Warburg's interpretation of the Renaissance as the decisive turn to the consciousness of freedom of modern times. Cassirer completed the cultural-historical view of Warburg by trying to underpin it with observations drawn from the history of philosophy and the history of culture.

As late as 1945, in his essay on Ficino, Cassirer persisted in his interpretation of the philosophers of the Renaissance: "To them it was impossible to think or speak of philosophy as an *ancilla theologiae* [maidservant of theology]. An attitude of passive obedience, of complete submission to an external authority, was no longer intelligible to the religious thinkers of the Renaissance."[24] Cassirer referred to Cusa as the first philosopher to anticipate Kant and Hegel. He looked upon Cusa as the founder and champion of modern philosophy who, as the Cusa specialist Hans Georg Senger stated, "marked the turn from mediaeval ontology to modern philosophy of mental consciousness, which he considered the focus of Renaissance thought, from which the philosophy of the Renaissance has to be viewed."[25]

In contrast to the more revealing Christian religion, with its pretension to absolutism, Warburgian research on the "survival of the classics" aimed to showcase the history of the development of human *Ratio*, the human Mind, by looking at the individual and the cosmos in a scientific way. Even Herman Cohen and Ernst Cassirer – both, in addition to their training in philosophy and philology, well versed in mathematics – were especially interested in the scientific aspects of Cusa's philosophy. Accordingly, the books of the Warburg Library, with their interdisciplinary arrangement, consistently provided scholars with a complement of cosmological, astrological, and scientific documents. Such was the nature of one of Klibansky's primary grounds of exploration and development as a thinker: at once open to new forms of research, and highly conducive to a reflection on the cross-pollination among types and forms of thought and creativity.

From Orientation to Action: Transforming Education into Method and Results

Steeped for years in this intellectual universe, Klibansky saw as his task, from his earliest years as a professional scholar, the knotting together of the varied and dispersed links of the Platonic tradition in Western philosophy. In a *curriculum vitae* written in 1940 on the occasion of an application for a professorship of philosophy at the University of Durham, Klibansky stated:

> From 1927, I travelled extensively, at first on behalf of the Heidelberg Academy, later on behalf of the British Academy, visiting the principal European libraries and examining the smaller libraries of monasteries and towns in Italy, Austria, France, and the Low Countries. The aim of my research was to study the various ways and forms in which ancient philosophy has been transmitted to modern times.[26]

The early travels for the Heidelberg Cusa edition were necessary in order to establish the manuscript tradition of the text, and were used to construct a nearly complete registration of known Cusa manuscripts. Hans Gerhard Senger, who in 1982 edited with Klibansky one of the Meiner edition volumes,[27] called him a migrating, travelling philosopher: "A *peripatetikós* of the 20th century? … In terms of *motus mentis*, because his occupation with Platonism is closer to the academies – the old-, middle-, Neo-Platonic and Florentine academies – he is therefore an *akademikòs*."[28]

Aby Warburg himself gave his blessing to Klibansky's first journey to Italy, in the autumn of 1929, in the form of a letter of recommendation whose purpose was to open the doors of famous European libraries for its carrier:

> Herr Dr. Raymond Klibansky, who is starting off on an *Iter Italicum* to look for manuscripts of Nicolaus Cusanus for the Heidelberg Academy, has already for a number of years proved himself to be an excellent and competent collaborator on the publications of the Warburg Library. Every support which the directors of libraries and book collections might give to him will be gratefully appreciated as an essential contribution to the sciences by the director of the K.B.W. (Aby Warburg).[29]

A personal note from Gertrud Bing illustrates both Klibansky's status as an intimate of the Warburg circle and the personal as well as intellectual attachments that members felt toward their Italy: "I'll be thinking of you very much, with my particular preference for Italy, hoping that you'll love the country just as much as I do."[30]

That Klibansky's work had developed in directions resonant with KBW ideals was expressed in other concrete ways. The correspondence of Klibansky and Saxl further illuminates the close relationship between Klibansky and the KBW, as well as shedding light on the financial support Klibansky's research received from the library, which, for example, covered various library costs or the purchase costs of new books. Because of budgetary shortfalls, the KBW could not sponsor the printing of Klibansky's *Habilitationsschrift* in 1932, but Saxl assessed that "the work belongs absolutely to our circle."[31] From the outset of research on Cusa, Saxl assisted Klibansky continuously as a mentor and friend. In fact, as Klibansky writes in 1927, it was Saxl who "had given me an idea of the cosmological problems and the thought processes in that period."[32]

Beyond the great edition itself, Klibansky's involvement in the Cusa project was a cornerstone of his career. In the course of investigations in Cusa's library in Bernkastel-Kues, Klibansky made a sensational discovery: in a manuscript with the commentary on the *Parmenides* of Proclus (fifth century), written in a Latin translation of the thirteenth century, he found the previously unknown end of the seventh book. Thus the end of the text, which was missing in the existing Greek versions, could for the first time be evaluated for its significance to the history of Platonism. In 1995 Kurt Flasch honoured Klibansky's find as a unique scientific event: "This discovery provides a concrete link connecting the philosophy of late antiquity with Cusanus and the dialectics of Hegel."[33] Presenting his thesis on the topic in "Ein Proklos-Fund und seine Bedeutung," Klibansky received his doctoral degree from the University of Heidelberg in 1929. This document offered an extraordinary basis for development of the *Corpus Platonicum* project to come. That he discovered the document was a matter of chance and alertness; but that he recognized its full significance shows a strong sensitivity to the careful tracing of traditions fully embedded in his thinking.

In terms of the specific methods that Klibansky developed out of this environment, one clear example is his provision, in the first volumes of the Cusa *Opera omnia* edition, of indices added to the texts, documenting the continuity of the Platonic tradition. Indeed, they attracted attention in reviews of the first two publications. Thus, historian of philosophy Martin Grabmann in 1932 stated that Klibansky "added not only an index of sources (*fontes*), indicating passages cited by Cusanus from earlier authors, but also an index of references (*testimonia*), indicating passages in Cusanus's texts that have been quoted by later authors."[34] This apparatus enormously facilitates research on Cusa, and new and ongoing assessments of Cusa's position in the history of thought. Saxl articulated the significance of the method as follows: "I don't need to tell you how much I admire the apparatus as a scientific work. The quoted names clearly show how the historical scene now turns out very differently."[35]

Furthermore, Klibansky tried to make use of the indices of names to confirm Cassirer's concept of the influence of Cusa on the Italian humanists. And he directly links his ability to do so to his experience at the KBW: "If the success of the proof, that the Italians of the XVth century, and especially Bruno, made use of the writings of Cusanus, should be endorsed, it is due to the very rich material of the KBW, at which I could only uncover the tip of the iceberg, so brief was my stay there,"[36] he writes in a letter to Saxl.

But unlike Cassirer, Klibansky was interested also in medieval Platonism, and from the beginning of his participation in the Cusa edition he cultivated contacts with clerical scholars throughout Europe to better understand this aspect. With the help of these networks he was able to demonstrate that the medieval Platonism of the School of Chartres in the twelfth century offered an additional Platonic source for Cusa – this became the subject of his 1932 *Habilitationsschrift*, titled "Bernhard und Thierry von Chartres,"[37] which to this day remains unpublished. Klibansky maintained – contrary to the popular assumption held at the time – that even before Greek scholars emigrated from the decaying Byzantine Empire to Italy in the fifteenth century, Platonic ideas had reached the Latin Western world during the Middle Ages at the cathedral school of Chartres, where they dominated the curriculum and informed Cusa's reception of Platonism. As Klibansky explained to Saxl: "If for example Cusanus says: 'Now I'll show the doctrine of Pythagoras,' then in fact he deals with the teachings of the twelfth century."[38] In his *Habilitationsschrift* Klibansky writes:

> For Cusanus it was most important that, in taking up the curriculum of the School of Chartres, he became rooted in the Platonic tradition. If so far the image of Renaissance Platonism had been determined by the conviction that there was no connection between it and the Platonic heritage of the Middle Ages, we can see now the continuity of the development of Occidental thought and the close affiliation of the period we call the Renaissance with the Christian Middle Ages.[39]

As to the curriculum at Chartres, the sciences, or *artes liberales*, were of foremost interest. Carved in stone on the western portal of the Cathedral, the *artes liberales* were portrayed as the philosophers of antiquity, represented thus, as Klibansky stressed, for the first time in the context of a Christian iconographic program.[40] In his reflections on the School of Chartres, Klibansky puts the focus – just as Aby Warburg and Cassirer would have done – on the development of *Ratio* which, newly breaking into the territory of the medieval Church, strove for self-representation. Klibansky writes to Saxl: "In the context of philosophy – and I believe that I can state that without exaggeration and prove it in detail – the results of the School of Chartres form the basis of the emancipation of human thought on the visible world from the supremacy of theology … That is exactly what has happened here and not only in 16th century Paris."[41]

During his exile in England, Klibansky attempted to prove some of the assertions made in his *Habilitationsschrift* by publishing the Latin Plato dialogues that were already well known in the Middle Ages. These constituted the *Plato Latinus* component of the *Corpus Platonicum Medii Aevi* series, published under his editorship and in collaboration with Lotte Labowsky. The most important source of the direct Platonic tradition during the Middle Ages was the *Timaeus*, a text mostly read in the translations of Calcidius (fourth century) and of Cicero, and included in the curriculum at Chartres. While he was drafting the introductory publication to the *Corpus Platonicum: The Continuity of the Platonic Tradition during the Middle Ages*, Klibansky wrote to Cassirer: "I am making here an effort to show, among other things, that in the Platonic literature of the Middle Ages – especially in the commentaries on the *Timaeus*, which I discovered myself, as well as in the writings of Thierry of Chartres – we can recognize the first approaches leading to the modern concept of sciences."[42] In the final publication of *The Continuity*, Klibansky even goes one step further by setting the affirmative Platonic worldview against the rejection of the world by the Church of Early Christianity: "But apart from their value for the development of science, the *Timaeus* and the literature to which it gave rise preserved, through the centuries in which an attitude of contempt towards the visible world was prevalent in the accepted church doctrine, the memory of the Hellenic appreciation of the rational beauty of the universe."[43]

Klibansky and his colleagues may themselves well have been searching for a "rational beauty of the universe" in the 1930s; thus, let us return once more to the year 1934, when Klibansky, already exiled in England, was nevertheless still occupied with research on Cusa, whose *De pace fidei* of 1453 became most important to the Jewish scholars who had escaped Nazi Germany. Klibansky, now in Oxford, and Ernst Hoffmann, who was still in Heidelberg, made a common plan to publish as soon as possible this so-called *Friedensschrift* of Cusa in the *Opera omnia* of the Heidelberg Academy. Composed when Cusa was a Roman cardinal, the text was inspired by the fall of Constantinople and the perceived Islamic threat to the Western World.[44] Cusa's *De pace fidei* presents, in reply to the threatening outbreak of war, a vision of peace among the different religious confessions as a symbol of the sole but diverse truth, the sole God: "Una veritas in variis signis varie resplendet."[45] While planning the edition, a deeply affected Klibansky wrote to Ernst Hoffman that he had found documents showing a connection between *De pace fidei* and Lessing's play on tolerance, *Nathan der Weise* (1779): "To put it plainly, one work stands as godfather to the other one." He tells Hoffmann that he will write a short note about it to send him, adding a handwritten title to the typed letter: "On the history of the German idea of humanity" (*Zur Geschichte des deutschen Humanitätsgedankens*).[46] Hoffmann's immediate letter of thanks ended with the words: "You *will* bring this find in the *Cassirer-Festschrift*, won't you? No other contribution could be more fitting for it."[47]

A few years later, in his essay on Ficino, Cassirer revisited once more Cusa's idea on tolerance, which he believed was transmitted to the philosophers of the Renaissance. Making a clear break from Christian doctrine, Cusa presented a visionary image of a new religion, which in the course of time would include the manifold monotheistic religious denominations of Judaism, Christianity, and Islam. Cassirer writes:

> [Ficino] strove for a universal religion, not for a universal church. Everyone who worshipped and loved God was welcome. There were no heretics in this new religion. For what is essential in religious life is not any dogmatic formula. According to Ficino the difference between formulae, between external signs and symbols, does not endanger the unity of faith; on the contrary, it confirms this unity. This was the common conviction of the religious thinkers of the Renaissance. We find it – almost in the same terms – in Nicholas of Cusa's *De pace fidei*, in Ficino's *De christiana religione*, in Pico della Mirandola's defense of the *libertas credendi*. "*Una veritas in variis signis varie resplendeat*" ... Thus the principle, *Extra ecclesiam nulla salus*, is abandoned.[48]

When, in 1956, Klibansky was finally about to publish Cusa's *De pace fidei*[49] in the *Mediaeval and Renaissance Studies* of the Warburg Institute London, Cassirer's reflections found themselves echoed – almost in the same terms – in the prospectus announcing the publication: "The diversity of rites should not be abolished but tolerated and even valued as being conducive to greater devotion."[50] It was an idea that was not only appreciated intellectually but was manifest in Klibansky's 1939 publication of *The Continuity of the Platonic*

Tradition, in which Klibansky integrated the Arabic, Byzantine, and Latin traditions. The thus-outlined project of the *Corpus Platonicum Medii Aevi*, which was also to include a "Plato Syrus and a Plato Hebraeus in an appendix,"[51] was never fully realized, but even into the 1960s Klibansky strove to complete the historical record through this pluralistic base.

During the postwar decades, having outlived most of his early companions, Klibansky, "as a representative of the next generation," made it his business to "carry the torch of German-Jewish intellectual life,"[52] as defined by Aby Warburg in 1928. As a "travelling philosopher" – or playing the part of Ahasver, the wandering Jew? – with a command of many languages, Klibansky moved between the scientific communities of the Old and the New World, the Western and the Eastern hemispheres, and disseminated the concepts of tolerance and international understanding. As an initiator and editor of philosophical publications – from Cusa's *De pace fidei* to John Locke's *Letter Concerning Toleration* – he contributed to the survival of the spirit and ideals of the Kulturwissenschaftliche Bibliothek Warburg.

NOTES

1 Klibansky, *The Continuity of the Platonic Tradition during the Middle Ages.*

2 Liebeschütz, "Obituary [for Fritz Saxl]," 138.

3 See, for example, Eric Méchoulan's chapter (7) in this volume.

4 Klibansky, "Raymond Klibansky, philosophe et historien," 137.

5 Klibansky, *Erinnerung an ein Jahrhundert*, 61.

6 Warburg Institute Archive, General Correspondence (hereafter WIA, GC), Raymond Klibansky to Fritz Saxl, 10 May 1927.

7 Cassirer, *Freiheit und Form.*

8 Klibansky, "Die Grenzen des akademischen Lebens sprengen," 274. Translations from the original German are mine, unless otherwise specified.

9 Klibansky, "Erinnerungen an Ernst Cassirer," 282.

10 Rosenberg, *Der Mythos des 20. Jahrhunderts*, 246.

11 Cassirer, *Individuum und Kosmos in der Philosophie der Renaissance.*

12 Cassirer, "Widmung," [to Aby Warburg] (signed Hamburg, 13 June 1926) in *Individuum und Kosmos*, xiii.

13 WIA, GC: Klibansky to Saxl, 11 November 1927.

14 Naber: "'… die Fackel deutsch-jüdischer Geistigkeit weitertragen,'" 395.

15 Ibid.

16 Cassirer, "Ficino's Place in Intellectual History."

17 Ibid., 488.

18 Ibid.

19 Klibansky, *The Continuity of the Platonic Tradition*, 13.

20 Cassirer and Hoffmann, *Die Geschichte der antiken Philosophie*. Pt. 1 is by Ernst Cassirer and is titled: "Die Philosophie der Griechen von den Anfängen bis Platon"; pt. 2, titled: "Die antike Philosophie von Aristoteles bis zum Ausgang des Altertums," is by Ernst Hoffmann.

21 Didi-Huberman, "Die leichtfüßige Dienerin," 265.

22 Warburg, "Italienische Kunst und internationale Astrologie im Palazzo Schifanoja zu Ferrara [1912–22]," 397.

23 Cassirer's theory of Cusa's influence on the Italian Platonists, made in his *Individuum und Kosmos*, met again and again with partly stiff opposition. As John Herman Randall had already stated in 1949, Cassirer "undoubtedly overestimated that of his favorite Cusanus, as he came reluctantly to admit" (Randall, "Cassirer's Theory of History as Illustrated in his Treatment of Renaissance Thought," 714n47). Randall here cites the corresponding passage in Cassirer's essay of 1945 "Ficino's Place in Intellectual History" (492n27): "I avail myself of this opportunity to revise a former statement made in my *Individuum und Kosmos.* In the second chapter I tried to show that Nicholas of Cusa's philosophy exerted a strong influence on the general development of Italian thought in the Quattrocento. I still think this to be highly probable, but I should perhaps have spoken with more caution. I quite agree that, on the strength of new historical evidence we cannot give a direct and definite proof of this thesis. It is possible that Ficino conceived his general theory independently of Nicholas of Cusa. In this case the close relationship between the two thinkers would be all the more important and interesting from the point of view of the general history of ideas. For it would show us the common background of the philosophy of the 15th century – the general intellectual and religious atmosphere of the Renaissance."

24 Cassirer, "Ficino's Place in Intellectual History," 493.

25 Senger, "Zur Geschichte der Edition der *Opera omnia* des Nicolaus Cusanus," 49.

26 Deutsches Literaturarchiv Marbach, A: Raymond Klibansky (hereafter DLA, A, KLIBANSKY): Klibansky, "Curriculum Vitae," (typed document, 5 pages), appended to Klibansky's application for a professorship of philosophy at the University of Durham, 13 June 1940.

27 Nicholas of Cusa, *Opera omnia*, vol. 12.

28 Senger: "In memoriam Raymond Klibansky," XI.

29 DLA, A, KLIBANSKY, XX–XXI: Aby Warburg to Klibansky, 25 September 1929.

30 WIA, GC: Gertrud Bing to Klibansky, 8 October 1929.

31 WIA, GC: Saxl to Klibansky, 10 November 1931.

32 WIA, GC: Klibansky to Saxl, 11 November 1927.

33 Flasch, "Der Hüter des Erbes," 31.

34 Grabmann, review of *Nicolai de Cusa Opera omnia*, vol. 1, 688.

35 WIA, GC: Saxl to Klibansky, 23 December 1931.

36 WIA, GC: Klibansky to Saxl, 11 April 1932.

37 Klibansky, "Bernhard und Thierry von Chartres." Parts of this were published much later, and in different form, as "The School of Chartres," in *Twelfth-Century Europe and the Foundations of Modern Society*.

38 WIA, GC: Klibansky to Saxl, 11 February 1929.

39 Klibansky: "Bernhard und Thierry von Chartres," 100.

40 Ibid., 101: "If in the Cathedral of Chartres the representatives of the sciences of antiquity appeared for the first time in sculptural portraits integrated into the architecture of the Church – if Aristotle, Cicero, Euclid, Ptolemäus, Donat and Pythagoras appear on the west facade – then we may not look upon them as more or less unimportant decoration but have to accept the very new fact that pagans are included in prominently visible places in the building of the Church; the representatives of the pagan *Ratio*, admitted as indispensable links within the system of the (Christian) Fides – this synthesis was the foremost goal of the two great chancellors of Chartres."

41 WIA, GC: Klibansky to Saxl, 1 October 1931.

42 DLA, A, KLIBANSKY: Klibansky to Cassirer, 26 January 1938. The letter is published in: Ernst Cassirer, *Ausgewählter wissenschaftlicher Briefwechsel*, 357.

43 Klibansky, *The Continuity of the Platonic Tradition*, 28.

44 DLA, A, KLIBANSKY: Ernst Hoffmann to Klibansky, 10 February 1934. Hoffmann here agrees to Klibansky's proposal to publish Cusa's *De pace fidei* as soon as

possible, and expresses his hopes of "having a direct effect with this '*Friedensschrift*' on human minds.")

45 Klibansky and Paton, Preface to *Philosophy and History*, VIII.

46 DLA, A, KLIBANSKY: Klibansky to Hoffmann, 5 February 1934.

47 DLA, A, KLIBANSKY: Hoffmann to Klibansky, 26 February 1934.

48 Cassirer, "Ficino's Place in Intellectual History," 490–1.

49 Nicholas of Cusa, *De pace fidei* (=*Mediaeval and Renaissance Studies supp.* 3).

50 DLA, A, KLIBANSKY: quotation from the prospectus of the the Warburg Institute London, June 1956: "'Just out': *Nicolai de Cusa. De pace fidei*" (Leaflet).

51 DLA, A, KLIBANSKY: quotation from the prospectus of the Warburg Institute London: "Forthcoming publications of the Warburg Institute 1939" (Leaflet).

52 Naber, "'... *die Fackel deutsch-jüdischer Geistigkeit weitertragen*,'" 399.

SIX

Raymond Klibansky and the *Corpus Platonicum Medii Aevi*: A Discussion of the *Plato Latinus* Series

GEORGES LEROUX

The importance of the *Corpus Platonicum Medii Aevi* project was first recognized by Raymond Klibansky's Warburg Institute colleagues, who encouraged his research and, as his numerous reports to the British Academy over many years testify, provided steadfast support for the series that was inaugurated by the publication, in 1939, of the text of his research program.[1] When the first volumes came into print, they were acknowledged with enthusiastic reviews in most scholarly journals. The project was to be published in different series, among which the *Plato Latinus* was to be the most important, if only because the main thrust of the research was to demonstrate the continuity of the Platonic tradition within Western thought. A second series, the *Plato Arabus*, charts an indirect eventual transmission back to the Latin world. A third series, the *Plato Byzantinus*, although carefully planned, was never completed.

As series editor, Klibansky invited a range of specialists to act as volume editors of a particular text or group of texts for the *Plato Latinus* (four volumes) and for the *Plato Arabus* (three volumes). Together with Lotte Labowsky, he edited volume three of the *Parmenides* and Proclus's *Commentary* on the dialogue. Among the reviews that appeared during the first years, one of the most important was signed by Paul Oskar Kristeller,[2] who discusses in particular this third volume and the philosophical importance of Proclus's *Commentary* of the *Parmenides*. During the Middle Ages, the works of Proclus that had been translated into Latin were considered to be almost as important as those of Aristotle and, according to Kristeller, as constituting "the most extensive source of Greek Platonism available."[3] This statement refers, of course, not only to the *Commentary* but also to the *Elements of Theology*, a text that was circulated under its Latin title, *Elementatio theologica*, and fully commented in the first half of the fourteenth century by the German Dominican theologian Berthold of Moosburg in his *Expositio super Elementationem theologicam Procli*. It further refers to the set of three philosophical *Opuscula* that have been preserved only in this medieval Latin translation. The importance of Proclus derived from his influence not only on thirteenth-century philosophy and theology but also, and in Klibansky's view most certainly, on later German thinkers such as Meister Eckhart and Nicholas of Cusa.[4] Klibansky recognized this link at a very early stage in his research program. As early as 1929, in his doctoral dissertation, he had demonstrated that the Latin version of the Proclus commentary on the *Parmenides* included a final section of the manuscripts of the Platonic work that had not been transmitted in the Greek tradition and had now, for the first time, become available in Latin. Moreover, as we shall see, this section also offered, as part of the commentary itself, a complete Latin version of the first part of Plato's *Parmenides*. Klibansky had come to this important discovery while he was studying the copies of Proclus's works owned by Cardinal Nicholas of Cusa and found in his personal library.[5]

In this chapter I discuss the program devised by Klibansky for the *Plato Latinus* series of the *Corpus Platonicum Medii Aevi* in light of subsequent research on the Latin tradition that he worked to reconstruct. As illustrated by the symmetrical example of the Aristotelian tradition, which led to the *Aristoteles Latinus* editorial program, this tradition was thought to be continuous and to pervade the whole of medieval thought, thus complementing the Aristotelian tradition. The main texts afferent to this tradition were first and foremost the aforementioned Proclus commentary on the *Parmenides*, and Calcidius's Latin translation of and commentary on the great cosmological dialogue, the *Timaeus*. Klibansky commissioned J.H. Waszink to oversee this formidable edition, which appeared in the fourth and last volume published in the *Plato Latinus* series in 1962. The series also included translations of the *Meno* and the *Phaedo* made in the twelfth century by Henricus Aristippus. Although these dialogues are of great importance, they did not circulate as widely within the tradition as did the *Parmenides* and the *Timaeus*; thus, for the purpose of the present study, I mention them only briefly.[6]

After giving an outline of the genesis of these editions and commenting on their contribution to the main thesis of the program, I conclude with some brief remarks on the discovery of an unknown *Summarium Platonis librorum atque placitorum* – a summary of Plato's dialogues that Klibansky identified in a manuscript of the Vatican Library and which he wished to edit in the *Plato Latinus* series but would not be able to complete before his death in 2005. A recent edition of this text will constitute a welcome indirect addition to the *Corpus Platonicum* editions even if, as we shall see, the edition planned and nearly completed by Klibansky was never altogether superseded.

Background to the *Plato Latinus*: Nicholas of Cusa

A document found in Klibansky's personal archives gives us a first glance at his research perspective, which dates back to as early as 1931. It is the text of a *Lebenslauf* (a textually extended form of résumé,) that Klibansky presented to the Faculty of Philosophy of Heidelberg in order to obtain his *Habilitation* and thus be authorized to teach in the faculty.[7] In this *Curriculum Vitae*, which includes a page outlining his education, Klibansky first recalls his 1929 doctoral research on Proclus and his edition of the *Liber de sapiente*, by Charles de Bovelles,[8] published in 1927 as an appendix to the volume of Ernst Cassirer, offered to honour Aby Warburg's sixtieth birthday, *Individuum und Kosmos in der Philosophie der Renaissance*. Both are linked to his interest in the works of Nicholas of Cusa, which he was already engaged in editing by the time of his *Habilitation*. Indeed, Klibansky's first publication on the subject had been the 1929 edition of Cusa's sermon *Dies sanctificatus*, prepared in collaboration with Ernst Hoffmann, who had supervised his thesis on Proclus.[9] The main perspective in this *Lebenslauf* is evidently the scholarly work on Nicholas of Cusa. When we note that the dissertation on Proclus was published as part of a series titled *Cusanus Studien*, we are led to understand that the Platonic tradition is considered above all as the background to the study of late medieval and early Renaissance Platonism. This observation, of course, can be linked not only to the larger project that Klibansky shared with Ernst Hoffmann – namely that of the Heidelberg edition of the works of Nicholas – but also to his discussions with Ernst Cassirer while he was the latter's student in Hamburg in 1926–27.

In his 1931 *Lebenslauf*, Klibansky mentions this Hamburg period as the time when he first met with the staff and scholars associated with the Kulturwissenschaftliche Bibliothek Warburg, which was then directed by Fritz Saxl. Klibansky seems to have taken great pride in his collaboration with the library, as he makes clear in the following passage: "It is from their presentation of the problems and under the direction of its leaders, professors Warburg and Saxl, that I found the most inspiring motivation." At the time when he wrote his *Lebenslauf*, however, the project of the *Corpus Platonicum* had not yet been clearly articulated; rather, the main thrust of the research planned at that date by Klibansky was his contribution to the Heidelberg edition of the works of Nicholas of Cusa. As we shall see, the *Corpus Platonicum* appears only later, in a series of notes presented to the Warburg Institute in October 1935.[10]

To cast further light on the genesis of Klibansky's great project, it is worthwhile returning to the discovery, published in 1929, that he had made during his doctoral research.[11] Already involved in studying the thought of Nicholas of Cusa, he had found in Cusa's personal library the Latin translation of one of the most important philosophical texts of late antiquity: the monumental commentary elaborated by Proclus, one of the last leaders of the Athenian Academy, on the *Parmenides* of Plato. Before this discovery, there had been little awareness that, already during the Middle Ages, this commentary had been known in full Latin translation. Transmitted by way of a fifteenth-century manuscript, this Latin translation had been the work of Wilhelm of Moerbeke in the thirteenth century and it offers a complete text, testifying to a more complete tradition than the surviving Greek manuscripts suggested.[12] We should note that this Latin translation offers the complete text of the conclusion of the commentary – the last part of Book VII – which was until then considered lost. The Greek tradition of the commentary stops at *Parmenides* 141E, an interruption that marked the definitive end of the text in Victor Cousin's first modern edition.[13] In Cousin's version, Proclus comments on Plato's negative dialectics as referring to the transcendent One, and he extends this dialectics to the doctrine of the negation of negation and the act by which thought annihilates itself.

In his dialogue, Plato had distinguished between the affirmation of the One and the negation of the One, thereby generating a double set of hypotheses submitted to dialectical reflection. What, for example, are the consequences of the negation of the One, both for itself and for all that is other than One?

These themes were of utmost importance to the history of dialectics, as we can see in the thought of Nicholas of Cusa, who in his treatise *De visione Dei* reflects on the concept of *remotio negationis.* This concept is based on the method of negative theology, inherited from the pseudo-Dionysius: can the human mind reach a knowledge of God that would not depend on the "negation" of limitations and imperfections? In this tradition, the *Parmenides* was read as a method that applied to the divine, and not only as a dialectical exercise of unity and multiplicity.[14] The cardinal had studied the text of Proclus very closely, as Klibansky remarks while examining his *marginalia*, and had identified in Proclus's arguments the doctrine of the Infinite One: "We find in the doctrine of Proclus about the One the real dialectical origin of Nicholas of Cusa's thought."[15] All of this contributed to Klibansky's assessment, in his doctoral thesis, of the significance of the discovery of this copy of Proclus's text. If we leave aside the codicological considerations that occupy the first section of the 1929 thesis, we can concentrate on the four conclusions put forward by Klibansky.

The first conclusion concerns the identity of the translator, Wilhelm von Moerbeke, and the quality of his work on the text. Based on the full lemmas of the text, the second conclusion emphasizes the importance of the Latin translation for the edition of Plato's text. The third conclusion is the most important for my discussion, and one we return to shortly: it concerns the importance of this translation for the way Plato was perceived during the Middle Ages.[16] The fourth conclusion of the 1929 thesis concerns Klibansky's research program on Nicholas of Cusa, which is an aspect that does not require further attention within the present context.

Assessments of Continuity

With respect to the third conclusion, Klibansky refers at this point to the work of his master, Ernst Hoffmann, who had written in his 1926 essay "Platonismus und Mittelalter,"[17] published in the *Vorträge der Bibliothek Warburg* series, that there exists, from the standpoint of the historical study of the formation of concepts (*Begriffsbildung*), no sharp difference between ancient Platonism and Medieval Platonism. If this difference does not lie in the ontological structure of metaphysics, the task of the historian is now to give a more precise description of the representation of Plato's doctrine in the Middle Ages. How was it interpreted? Was it read as a metaphysics of separation, resulting in setting up a hierarchy of the intelligible world and the sensible world, or did it include the later scheme of monism put forward by Plotinus? From John Scotus Eriugena to Nicholas of Cusa, this structure had been stable, but what exactly were the features that medieval thinkers attributed to Plato?

A possible answer to this question begins to emerge if we consider Plato's philosophical personality as it is revealed within the works of these philosophers as well as the dynamics of the literary tradition that they illustrate. This page of Klibansky's thesis includes, *in nuce*, the full program of the *Corpus Platonicum*: it begins with the Calcidius translation of the *Timaeus*, and then goes on to present Norman cleric Henricus Aristippus's twelfth-century translations of the *Meno* and the *Phaedo*.[18] Proclus stood at the centre of this tradition, since his translation of the *Parmenides* made the text available up to the end of the first Hypothesis, as well as his *Elementatio theologica* and the three *opuscula*: *On Providence*, *On Destiny and Freewill*, and *On Evil*. In his appraisal of the importance of Proclus, Klibansky writes:

> Through the late antique system, in which the theological speculation of oriental mysticism meets the strict architecture of the Greek *logos* and brings about a new synthesis, Proclus appears as one of the great intermediaries between the thought of antiquity and the medieval. And this is true for the West as well as for Byzantium, and also, if in a lesser measure, for the Arabic world.[19]

Here we find the first specific mention of Klibansky's idea of a research project leading to an edition of the direct tradition of Plato during the Middle Ages that would encompass all surviving texts.[20] When, years later, Klibansky and Labowsky edited the new Proclus text portion for the *Plato Latinus*, they did not aim to edit the entire extant Latin text of the commentary. Their edition contains the following two elements: the version of Plato's *Parmenides* as incorporated in Proclus's commentary (126a–142a) and the concluding section of Proclus's commentary that was absent from the surviving Greek text. The texts of Proclus are accompanied by an English translation by Labowsky and philosopher Elizabeth Anscombe. Plato's text is accompanied by an apparatus that identifies the more important readings of the Greek manuscripts that seem to have been used by Moerbeke. The edition also includes the text of Cusa's marginal notes.

In his review, Kristeller reminds the reader that the Klibansky-Labowsky edition is based on the small number of five manuscripts and one fragmentary copy, and that only one of these manuscripts is older than the fifteenth century, his argument being that this translation might not have had an influence of quite the magnitude that Klibansky imagined. Although Kristeller is the first proponent of this critique, we shall in fact encounter this criticism again in others. At the same time, however, Kristeller acknowledges that some of these early editions belonged to scholars such as Cusa, who were to have a profound effect on their time in terms of the dissemination of thought. But the criticism based on the number of manuscripts appears again in the arguments of a recent editor of both the Latin and the Greek versions of the text, Carlos Steel, at the University of Louvain.

Steel notes that the discussion presented in the 1929 thesis is not reproduced in full in the *Plato Latinus* edition, and yet he remarks that its conclusions are taken for granted. In fact, the relation of the Latin version to the original Greek text is discussed in the Klibansky-Labowsky edition, although at that time the Greek manuscripts of this work had not yet been compiled and studied for a modern critical edition. It is worth noting that the Greek text of Proclus's commentary on the *Parmenides* was not edited during the Renaissance, a situation that is surprising if we consider the importance of commentaries on the *Timaeus* and the *Republic*, some of which were published as early as 1534 in Basel. The edition of the Greek text is now being completed by two competing teams of scholars who disagree on the manuscript tradition – a word about them will prove illuminating, even if we need not here enter into the details of that sophisticated discussion.

The first team, headed by Steel in Louvain, began by publishing the Latin text in a way that took into account Klibansky's discovery, and then proceeded – on the basis of that text – to reconstruct the lost Greek text.[21] The second team, headed by the late Alain-Philippe Segonds and Concetta Luna, had first embarked on a common project with the Louvain team, but due to deep disagreements over the text,[22] this joint venture was abandoned and each team proceeded with its own edition. Both teams acknowledged their debt to the Klibansky edition in the *Plato Latinus* series.

One important reason for this debt is that Moerbeke is now recognized as a much better translator than Aristippus, as we can observe when we study the translations of the *Phaedo* and of the *Meno* realized by Aristippus. Moerbeke's knowledge of Greek was far superior and his philosophical lexicon more adequate. This had been noted by Kristeller, who also signalled the introduction of new words by Moerbeke, and his tendency "to retain in his version some of the original Greek terms in transliteration."[23] This led Kristeller to argue, following Klibansky, that "this translation stands for a lost Greek original, and consequently adds to our knowledge of ancient philosophy."[24] He praised the edition as an admirable accomplishment and expressed his wish for a rapid achievement of the whole *Plato Latinus*. This admiration is shared by the French editors Segonds and Luna, who consider the Klibansky-Labowsky edition as the "foundation of the modern critical edition."[25] Klibansky and Labowsky discuss the five Latin manuscripts (*Ambrosianus*, A 167; *Cusanus Hospitalis s. Nicolai*, 186; *Lipsiensis*, 27; *Oxoniensis Bodleianus Digbeianus*, 236; and *Vaticanus latinus*, 3074), which they classify into two families, both deriving from a common model. A minute discussion of the philological analysis they propose is not possible here, but the modern editors recognized the importance of the critical contribution of the *Plato Latinus* edition, most notably due to the analysis put forward by Klibansky and Labowsky of the role of the Latin translation in the establishment of the Greek text. This text is edited by its modern editors on the basis of a tradition of thirty-five Greek manuscripts.

The *Corpus Platonicum* Program: The Direct and Indirect Traditions

With respect to the place of the *Parmenides* in the larger picture of the tradition, we can turn to Klibansky's program, which he submitted to the Warburg Institute and published in 1939 as *The Continuity of the Platonic Tradition during the Middle Ages: Outlines of a Corpus Platonicum Medii Aevi*. This program, circulated as early as 1935, is based on the early Proclus discovery of 1929, and proposes two parts: first, an overview of the Platonic tradition in the Middle Ages, divided into different streams (Arabic, Byzantine, and Latin, of which the Proclus is a part), with important appendices on the Arabic tradition, and on Ficino and his relation to the Platonic tradition; second, the conspectus of the projected editions for the Warburg Institute. Details of the plan and the inevitable changes made to it can be followed in the second edition of *The Continuity of the Platonic Tradition*, in which Klibansky refers to his reports on the progress of this work and presents the editions that had already been completed by 1980.[26]

In this second edition he also mentions his discovery of the text of a *Summarium Platonis librorum atque placitorum*, found in a Vatican manuscript of the mid-thirteenth century (*Reginensis lat.* 1572). Klibansky presents this summary of Plato's works as a "Latin translation, dating from late Antiquity, of a hitherto unknown Greek work of the second century A.D."[27] He states here that he plans to publish this text as the fifth volume of the *Plato Latinus* series.[28] The research program was developed by Klibansky to reconstruct an image of the Platonic tradition, since the existing image of the tradition held it to be far less important for medieval thought than was the Aristotelian tradition, the understanding of which was built on the critical work of the *Aristoteles Latinus* realized, from 1929, by the team directed at the University of Louvain[29] by Auguste Mansion. A new image was needed, in order to counter the idea of "the very shadowy notions ... still prevalent concerning the nature and meaning of mediaeval Platonism."[30] What were these "shadowy notions" if not the Neoplatonic framework imposed by the indirect tradition on the knowledge of Plato's doctrine? The distinction between the direct tradition, based on translations, and the indirect tradition, based on commentaries and doxography, plays a crucial role here. (We must note here that the Latin translations of the important commentaries – mainly the commentaries of Proclus, but also the commentaries on Aristotle written by Neoplatonic scholars such as Simplicius and Philoponus, all translated into Latin in the thirteenth century – were part of the original *Plato latinus* project, but most were realized by others.)[31]

It is altogether startling, given Klibansky's previous work on Proclus's Latin commentary, that the program should open with a description of the importance of the indirect Arabic tradition in the work of, for instance, such great philosophers as al-Kindi and al-Farabi. Among the works cited, the

Synopsis dialogorum Platonicorum by Galen, which included his paraphrase of the *Timaeus*, seems, according to Klibansky, to have represented a most important thread that ran through the whole tradition. This Arabic stream offers no direct testimony to the importance of the *Parmenides*, and the synopsis of Galen, which offers an indirect summary of the dialogue, is therefore a very significant element. By comparison, the Byzantine tradition "never entirely lapsed from the closing of the Academy in Athens by Justinian until the time when a new Academy was opened in Florence."[32] The important element here seems to be the permanent exchange of Byzantine ideas and materials with Western schools. It is not insignificant that Proclus's texts, which were translated into Latin by Wilhelm of Moerbeke, were found in a Byzantine monastery.

The project of the *Plato Byzantinus* was part of the original research program and detailed in the 1939 publication, but as already mentioned it was never realized. As for the *Plato Latinus* the better understanding of this stream was of course Klibansky's main objective. Thus, in his program, he discusses the relative extension of the indirect tradition, apparently more important according to the number of texts testifying to the knowledge of Plato, and the direct tradition, made up of translations of Plato's works. Klibansky refers here to his previous work in Proclus's commentary on the *Parmenides*: "Through this work, furthermore, philosophers became acquainted, from about 1280, with the *Parmenides* itself, known earlier only through casual references in Aulus Gellius and Chalcidius [Calcidius]."[33] Let us pay attention at this point to an important comment that Klibansky made about the consequences of this tradition on its readers:

> As Proclus' work, however, and with it the Latin text of the dialogue which is embedded in the commentary, extended only as far as the end of the first hypothesis, they were led from the beginning to view this work in the orthodox Neoplatonic interpretation. The Latinised Proclus was thus of marked influence on the conception of Platonism and gave rise to some fundamental concepts of modern philosophy, such as Cusanus' and Brunos' doctrine of the "coincidentia oppositorum."[34]

In an important study, published in 1943 in the Warburg journal *Mediaeval and Renaissance Studies*, which he had pioneered with his friend Richard

Hunt, Klibansky gave a full historical sketch of the interpretation of the *Parmenides* during the Middle Ages and up to Ficino and Pico. This study focuses on the prevalence of the Neoplatonic interpretation, which proposed that the medieval scholar would understand as having been built on the antithesis between the *Parmenides* and the *Timaeus* – an opposition we will explore further – notwithstanding the fact that the tradition of the *Parmenides* was not comparable before the end of the thirteenth century to the eminence of the *Timaeus*, demonstrated by a wealth of surviving manuscripts. But this situation changed radically – and this is the main point of Klibansky's argument – after the translation of the *Parmenides* into Latin by Moerbeke.

Klibansky's article addresses the basis of the opposition between a mystical interpretation of Plato, derived from the *Parmenides*, and a more physical doctrine, derived from the knowledge of the world exposed in the *Timaeus*: "The newly translated writings of Proclus soon gained a wide circulation, for the Western world was not unprepared for the message they contained. Philosophers and theologians were quick to observe the affinity of his doctrines with those of one of the most eminent Fathers of the Church, Dionysius of Areopagitica."[35] In his study, Klibansky insists on the convergence between the indirect and the direct tradition of the *Parmenides*, and he refers to the number of extant manuscripts that bear witness "to the study of the text in fourteenth century England and Italy."[36] This formulation of his interpretation of the tradition has drawn some critical remarks to which I return later.[37] First, however, I want to return to Klibansky's statement from his 1939 program: the Platonic tradition remained continuous, and there is no such thing as a "definite break between mediaeval and Renaissance Platonism."[38] The research that his conspectus of editions embodied was meant to document in full that thesis: "The mediaeval Platonic Tradition as a whole is much too complex to be described indiscriminately as either Platonism, as was formerly, or Neoplatonism, as is now, the rule."[39] Does this statement apply correctly to such a long tradition? In his review of the 1939 program, Kristeller, who monitored the project from the beginning, expressed some doubts: "The continuity of the Platonic tradition should be proved not only by the presence of certain translations and quotations from Plato, but also through the influence of Platonic theories upon medieval thinkers."[40]

This remark can be read as an invitation to complete the edition program with a more philosophical discussion of the tradition – a perspective that no one would of course deem unimportant – but it was clearly not the goal of Klibansky's program for the critical edition. Kristeller's call for a discussion of the concept of tradition, although pertinent, cannot eclipse the importance of the *Corpus Platonicum*, since it is certainly from the firm philological standpoint of the history of texts that the history of interpretation and the reconstruction of philosophical traditions can be achieved.

Kristeller recognized the importance of the program and hoped that the new editions would lead to a new history of the Platonic tradition. A discussion of the essential traits that the historian of ideas must consider as truly Platonic would be at the core of this new history. If, according to Klibansky, a Neoplatonic reading cannot be a priori a truly Platonic reading, then one is obliged to discuss all the pertinent elements of an authentic Platonic interpretation in the tradition. Thus, it is worth looking in some detail at the tradition viewed through the *Timaeus* to get a sense of Klibansky's work.

Aspects of the Medieval Interpretation: The *Timaeus*

The *Timaeus* represents the most important Platonic text of both the direct and indirect traditions in the Middle Ages, and it constitutes an essential link between the scholars from Chartres and Nicholas of Cusa. Klibansky had already pointed to that fact in his edition of Cusa's *De docta ignorantia*, published in 1932 with Ernst Hoffmann. The great edition of the Latin translation of Calcidius and of his commentary, realized by J.H. Waszink for the *Plato Latinus*, can be considered a masterpiece and is of utmost importance in the series.

Part of Klibansky's 1932 *Habilitation* from the University of Heidelberg had consisted of the presentation of his research on Thierry and Bernard de Chartres. This work, which comprises a collection of the main texts of the twelfth-century masters from the School of Chartres, remains unedited.[41] It illustrates Klibansky's early interest in the tradition of the *Timaeus* and demonstrates his knowledge of the scholarly work on Plato that was being done within these schools. This study formed an important part of the preliminary work leading to the research program, since it contributed to an understanding that the Neoplatonic ontological structure of late antiquity, ranging from Plotinus to Proclus, had been built upon a rigorous knowledge of the *Timaeus*. Indeed, on the basis of philological demonstration of the presence of Latin translations of this dialogue during this very long period, a strong hypothesis of philosophical continuity emerges.

If only for the impressive number of extant manuscripts, this edition bears witness to the uninterrupted circulation of the *Timaeus* from Calcidius to the School of Chartres, and later to Petrarch and Ficino.[42] According to scholars, this number varies from 138 to 189 manuscripts, depending on whether one includes the Latin translation of the dialogue, the commentary, or both.[43] There is no monastic library that would not have counted at least one copy of the text among its possessions. Thus, Klibansky was prompt to recall that Petrarch owned a copy of Calcidius's translation of the *Timaeus* (Ms, Bib. Nat. lat, c. 6280), which he had meticulously studied and annotated. Ficino himself had copied this manuscript in 1454, when he was twenty years old. In comparison, the *Meno* was known through only five manuscripts, and the *Phaedo* through nine manuscripts. None are anterior to 1300, a fact that imposes serious limits on the central and general thesis of a widespread circulation of Plato's dialogues during the Middle Ages. One massive fact remains, then: the supreme importance of the *Timaeus*.

It is therefore not surprising that Klibansky would place at the centre of his 1929 program the commentary of Calcidius, a text which, in the West, would function as the main historical gateway to the knowledge of Platonic philosophy. "The *Timaeus*," writes Klibansky, "with its attempted synthesis of the religious teleological justification of the world and the rational exposition of creation, was, throughout the earlier Middle Ages, the starting point and guide for the first groping efforts towards a scientific cosmology."[44] Indeed, most thinkers who were connected to the doctrinal exposition of the *Timaeus* and active within the tradition of its commentary can be looked upon as "cosmologists." In fact, Klibansky himself would later present a synthesis of the School of Chartres,[45] even though his initial interest in the text dated back to his *Habilitationsschrift*.

The roots of this exposition, the scholarly milieu of Calcidius, and the date of his commentary are discussed by Waszink in the *Plato Latinus* edition and are still being examined by scholars today.[46] In the Platonic circles of Milan, the date accepted as most probable is around 380 CE. This would signal the proximity to Ambrosius and one cannot exclude that Saint Augustine would have known the work when he stayed in Milan. This rich commentary belongs to a vast tradition of commentaries of the *Timaeus*, containing up to twenty different texts, most of which are known to us only indirectly. The commentary of Calcidius is part of this tradition, which leads at a later date to the Greek commentary of Proclus. The *Timaeus* was read in Latin circles by scholars who knew Greek, but it was translated into Latin by Cicero himself and much later by Calcidius. Recent scholarship concentrates on a comparison of these classical translations. Despite the fact that these concern different sections, this comparison tends to credit Cicero with a better reading of Plato's philosophical doctrine than the one offered by Calcidius. Cicero translated the section comprising pages 27d5 and 47b2, with two lacunae (37c2–38c3 and 43b3–46a2), while Calcidius translated Part I of the dialogue in full, from 17a1 to 53c3. This illustrates their shared interest in the cosmological doctrine, and in particular in section 27d–47d.[47] There is, however, no agreement on the question of the influence of Cicero's translation on the work of Calcidius.

Calcidius's philosophical sources remain opaque: what, for example, is the role of Posidonian stoicism in his thought? This discussion was, during the youth of Klibansky, a standard example of the method of *Quellengeschichte*.[48] Was he a so-called middle Platonist? From the beginning, Klibansky criticized all these categories and, as Kristeller noted disapprovingly, he went so far as to refuse to refer to the medieval tradition as a "Neoplatonic" interpretation. He preferred to present it as an original synthesis of metaphysical speculation, in which the doctrine of the providential will of God had replaced the rational principle of the *Timaeus*. The commentary of Calcidius contributed to this tradition by offering a first metaphysical standpoint, the doctrine of matter being a case in point.

We need not enter here into the details of its influence, on Boethius, for example, in his *Consolatio philosophiæ*. The main point is the following: modern scholarship confirms that as early as the Carolingian period (for example in Alcuin's circle), the commentary of Calcidius was the main source for the transmission of Plato's doctrine. The full story of the School of Chartres bears testimony to this growing influence in the twelfth century, most notably through the writing of *Glosae*, of which Wilhelm of Conches is a most illustrious representative. Thus, it is the richness of this history that had been anticipated in Klibansky's research program.[49]

The first volume of the *Plato Arabus* stands as a complement to Waszink's Latin *Timaeus*: the *Compendium Timaei Platonis*, an Arabic version of Galen's *Synopsis*, was edited by Paul Kraus and Richard Walzer and published before the Waszink edition had been released.[50] The Greek original, comprising eight books, is now lost; the Arab translators knew only four of these, of which only the summary of the *Timaeus* has survived. The first translation, from Greek to Syriac, had been the work of the famous Hunaïn ibn Ishaq and, sometime around 876, this translation was retranslated into Arabic by a disciple.

A Late Discovery in the Tradition: The *Summarium*

While studying the Latin tradition of the *Timaeus*, Klibansky embarked upon a study of the manuscripts of Apuleius, the author of an *expositio* of Plato's doctrines published under the title *De Platone et dogmate ejus*. This work is at the core of the so-called middle-Platonic tradition, which led Klibansky to do a full study of the tradition that he published in 1993 with Frank Regen. One manuscript in particular pertaining to this tradition, namely the *Vaticanus Regin. Lat.* 1572, turned out to be of great interest in Klibansky's research, and he examined it while staying in Rome sometime after the war. It contains a hitherto undescribed and unidentified *Summarium Platonis librorum atque placitorum*, copied on folios 77ra to 86rb. Klibansky reported his find in one of his first reports to the Warburg Institute[51] and he included the edition of this text in his 1939 program as part of the *Plato Latinus* series. In his opinion, this text was a late Latin translation of a summary of Plato's dialogues, most probably deriving from the Platonic circles of the second century. This summary opens with the middle of the third book of the *Republic*, and offers short notes on the *Euthyphro*, the *Menexenus*, the *Apology*, the *Crito*, and the *Phaedo*, followed by general considerations and notes on some books of the *Laws*, the *Epistles*, the *Parmenides*, the *Sophist*, the *Politicus*, the *Timaeus*, and the *Critias*. In 1993 Klibansky dedicated a short study to the history of the manuscript and continued to work on this edition until his death in 2005. According to Klibansky's hypothesis, this summary was a Latin translation of a lost Greek original, and thus it was "closely linked with the Plato interpretation of the Second Century."[52] In his surviving papers, he left his edition of the Vatican manuscript, including a complete apparatus, an *index fontium*, and all the material pertaining to the annotation and commentary that he planned for the *Plato Latinus* edition. In his draft for the introduction, Klibansky also discussed the relation of this text to the tradition of Apuleius. The text of this manuscript, in a different edition and unconnected with Klibansky's work, was recently published by Justin A. Stover, who privileges the hypothesis of Apuleian authorship and considers the text to be the lost portion of the *De Platone*.[53]

I would like to conclude with some remarks on the scholarly appraisal of this research program. From the time his first editions came out up until the present moment, the work of Raymond Klibansky has met with enthusiastic approval; from a scholarly perspective, the editions were considered important contributions to the study of the medieval Platonic tradition. However, starting with Kristeller's reviews and building up to a more recent critical overview by Carlos Steel, Klibansky's main argument has been criticized as "exaggerated." Not only do these critics tend to regard the circulation of the translations as limited – with the notable exception of the *Timaeus* – but they argue that the translations, including those of the *Parmenides*, had no actual influence on the medieval period's conception of Platonism.

According to Steel, if one searches for a Proclian influence, one should look first to the *Elementatio theologica*, a text transmitted in a tradition of twenty-seven manuscripts and quoted by Aquinas, Albertus Magnus, and many others. In his opinion, Proclus's other texts "were almost not circulated."[54] There is indeed only one quotation from Proclus's commentary on the *Parmenides* before Nicholas of Cusa, and Steel speaks of a "minimal influence on medieval thought."[55] His conclusion regarding the main thesis of the *Corpus Platonicum* is therefore rather clear: the *Plato Latinus* series cannot be considered as contributing a counter-image to the classical Aristotelian image, drawn from the *Aristoteles Latinus* series. If the influence of Plato must be re-evaluated, this should be done through the indirect tradition, and not on the basis of the circulation of the translations themselves. Christian authors, Arab intermediaries and their influence on scholastic thought, pagan authors from Cicero to Apuleius, and minor late authors such as Macrobius, Martianus Capella, Calcidius himself, and Boethius: all these play an important role in the spread of Platonic doctrines during the Middle Ages.[56]

What conclusion, then, can we draw from this discussion? We can only agree with Klibansky's main interpretation of medieval Platonism as resulting from a continuous and rigorous "spiritual" evolution of thought. But one must also agree with Steel that this "continuity" is the result of a long tradition maintained and transformed by different schools, where the distinction between the contribution of Neoplatonism (or Middle-Platonism, or even stoicism) has become blurred and indistinguishable from original Platonism. This conclusion requires a philosophical discussion of the main axioms of Platonism, of the type introduced by Luc Brisson in 1974. In Brisson's very important study, the French scholar proposed to read the *Timaeus* as the exposition of an ontological structure whose variations were exemplified at various stages of its tradition.[57] One example of these variations is the interpretation by different authors of the concept of the Demiurge, understood, for example, by Plotinus as the Intellect and by others as the World-Soul. Without a doubt, Klibansky would have considered that this philosophical history would be possible once all the texts were available in modern editions, and for this, as everyone likely agrees, he must be thanked.

As to the question of why, beginning with the schools of the twelfth century, the Middle Ages never sought to produce a complete translation of Plato, it might indeed be possible to provide a simple answer. For what reasons did the translation of Aristotle supersede the translation of the *Timaeus* as the essential text for the knowledge of the world, leaving only a "marginal place" for Plato's translations? Steel aptly recalls that Plato was the admired master of the twelfth century, a *princeps philosophorum*, according to John of Salisbury. The answer lies in an interpretation of a deep mutation in the nature of philosophical inquiry after the twelfth century. Since the metaphysics of Aristotle were easier to reconcile with his physics, he appeared to be the philosopher most capable of producing a systematic vision of the world. By comparison, Plato remained a religious philosopher, following the declaration of Ficino:

Plato noster utramque viam mirabiliter conjunxit in unum et ubique religiosus est pariter atque philosophus, disputator subtilis, pius sacerdos, facundus orator.[58] / In a marvellous fashion, Plato united each way of knowledge into one for us, and everywhere he stands equally as philosopher and religious man, fine dialectician, pious priest and eloquent orator.

NOTES

1 Klibansky, *The Continuity of the Platonic Tradition during the Middle Ages: Outlines of a Corpus Platonicum Medii Aevi*. A new edition was published in 1981, adding to the title, "… *with a new Preface and Four Supplementary Chapters, together with Plato's* Parmenides *in the Middle Ages and the Renaissance*." In the notes that follow, when not indicated otherwise, I refer to the original 1939 edition.

2 Kristeller, "Review of the *Corpus Platonicum Medii Aevi*, vols. 2 and 3," 196–201. Kristeller also studied under Ernst Hoffmann at Heidelberg University before making his career in the United States, becoming recognized as one of the foremost twentieth-century scholars of the Renaissance. His *Iter Italicum* series was published by the Warburg Institute and Brill (1963–1992)

3 Ibid., 201.

4 See Watanabe, "The Origins of Modern Cusanus Research in Germany and the Establishment of the Heidelberg *Opera omnia*," 25.

5 Klibansky, *Ein Proklos-Fund und seine Bedeutung*.

6 See Kristeller, "Review of *Corpus Platonicum*, vols. 2 and 3," 196–8. This translation was owned and read by scholars like Petrarch and Salutati. In his review, Kristeller points to some difficulties with L. Minio's edition of the text, and he discusses the work of Aristippus, a translator of philosophical terms, which he describes as lacking in clarity.

7 Klibansky, *Lebenslauf*. This document is a handwritten submission to the Faculty of Philosophy of Heidelberg, and is composed of nine pages, recto/verso. It is signed by Raymond Klibansky and dated 4.XI.1931. It is now in the Klibansky Archive in the Deutsches Literaturarchiv in Marbach (hereafter DLA, A, KLIBANSKY). An earlier two-page *Lebenslauf* submitted for the doctoral examination at the University of Heidelberg remains in their archives (UAH, Promotionsverfahren 1928/1929).

8 Carolus Bovillus [Charles de Bovelles] (ed. Klibansky), *Liber de sapiente.*

9 Klibansky and Hoffmann, *Cusanus-Texte. I.*

10 One of these notes, dated October 1935, mentions the inclusion of a *Corpus Dionysiacum*, for which Klibansky acknowledges the anticipated collaboration of Father Gabriel Théry. On these matters, one can consult Klibansky, *Report[s] on the progress of the* Corpus Platonicum Medii Aevi.

11 See Klibansky, *Ein Proklos-Fund und seine Bedeutung.*

12 Manuscript from Cusa, *Codex cusanus hospitalis S. Nicolai,* 186.

13 Proclus, *Procli Opera Inedita*. The text of the *Parmenides* runs from pages 126a to 166c in the Stephanus edition.

14 Klibansky has commented on this influence in his preface to the edition of the Proclus Commentary; see *Plato Latinus III: Platonis* Parmenides *usque ad finem primae hypothesis nec non Procli Commentarium in Parmenidem*, XI.

15 Klibansky, *Ein Proklos-Fund*, 13 (my translation).

16 Ibid., 18–25.

17 Hoffmann's lecture on "Platonism und Mittelalter," though published in 1926, was given during the 1923–24 year.

18 These translations were published as volumes I and II in the *Plato Latinus* series.

19 Klibansky, *Ein Proklos-Fund*, 22.

20 Ibid., 20.

21 Proclus, *Commentaire sur le* Parménide *de Platon*. The Greek text is found here: Steel, Macé, and d'Hoine (eds.), *Procli in Parmenidem Commentaria. Tomus I, Libros I–III continens*. It was followed by Steel, Gribomont, and d'Hoine (eds.), *Procli in Platonis Parmenidem commentaria. Tomus II. Libros IV–V continens*, and Steel and Van Campe (eds.), *Procli In Platonis Parmenidem commentaria. Tomus III Libros VI–VII et indices*. The Greek text, accompanied by a French translation of the commentary, is now being edited in the Budé series: Luna and Segonds (eds.), *Proclus, Commentaire sur le* Parménide *de Platon*. In their general introduction, published as the first volume to their edition, Segonds and Luna have noted the importance of Klibansky for their research; ibid., VIII and CDLX–CDLXIII. They discuss the analysis of the tradition as reconstructed by Klibansky and Labowsky and they recognize the importance of the Latin translation in the edition of the Greek text. They criticize what they present as an exaggerated importance given to the interventions of Bessarion, a fact that has prevented them from arriving at a clear stemma for the Greek tradition.

22 On this issue, see Luna and Segonds, "Introduction générale"; ibid., CCLXI–CCCLXIII.

23 Kristeller, "Review of *Corpus Platonicum*, vols. 2 and 3," 196–8.

24 Ibid.

25 Luna and Segonds, *Proclus, Commentaire sur le* Parménide, VIII and CDLX–CDLXIII.

26 Klibansky, *Continuity of the Platonic Tradition* [1981], 5. The reports mentioned by Klibansky are the following: *Proceedings of the British Academy*, 1941–59; the *Rapports annuels sur le progrès du Corpus platonicum*, and the *Annual Reports* of the Warburg Institute, University of London, 1943–59.

27 Klibansky, *Continuity of the Platonic Tradition* [1981], 7.

28 Klibansky presented a full analysis of the history of the codex; see "La découverte d'un texte platonicien inconnu de l'Antiquité classique."

29 Klibansky was well aware of this research. The pertinent literature on this great project is enormous; one can recall the numerous reports such as Mansion, "Les progrès de l'*Aristoteles Latinus*," 90–111. The whole corpus is now available online under the title *Aristoteles Latinus Database*, a project sponsored by the Union Académique Internationale and available from Brepols Publishers.

30 Klibansky, *Continuity of the Platonic Tradition*, 13.

31 On this tradition, see Gerson, *The Cambridge History of Philosophy in Late Antiquity*.

32 Klibansky, *Continuity of the Platonic Tradition*, 19.

33 Ibid., 26.

34 Ibid.

35 Klibansky, "Plato's *Parmenides* in the Middle Ages and the Renaissance: A Chapter in the History of Platonic Studies," 4. Reprinted as a supplement to the 1981 edition of *Continuity of the Platonic Tradition*, 284–5.

36 Ibid., 7 and 287.

37 The tradition of the *Parmenides* was the topic for a symposium edited by John D. Turner and Kevin Corrigan, *Plato's Parmenides and Its Heritage*.

38 Klibansky, *Continuity of the Platonic Tradition*, 35.

39 Ibid., 36.

40 Kristeller, "Review of *The Continuity of the Platonitc Tradition During the Middle Ages*," 411.

41 A copy of the dissertation, in the form of a typescript, is present in the Klibansky

archive in Marbach (DLA, A, KLIBANSKY), under the title *Bernard und Thierry von Chartres.*

42 *Plato Latinus IV:* Timaeus, *a Calcidio translatus commentarioque instructus* (edition of J.H. Waszink).

43 See the discussion in the recent French edition and translation, presenting a complete discussion of the critical issues and full indexes: Bakhouche (ed.), *Calcidius, Commentaire au* Timée *de Platon.*

44 Klibansky, *Continuity of the Platonic Tradition*, 28.

45 Klibansky, "The School of Chartres." For a recent presentation, see Dronke, *A History of Twelfth-Century Western Philosophy.*

46 See Bakhouche (ed.), *Calcidius, Commentaire au* Timée *de Platon*, 68–98, including a discussion of all the diagrams. There is also an Italian translation by Claudio Moreschini, based on the *Plato Latinus* edition by Waszink: Calcidius, *Commentario al Timeo di Platone.*

47 The history of the reception of the *Timaeus* has been discussed in Neschke-Hentschke, *Le* Timée *de Platon.*

48 Raymond Klibansky had read the works of Karl Reinhardt, both his study on Posidonius and his more general study on stoicism. See Reinhardt, *Poseidonios* and also *Kosmos und Sympathie.*

49 See the detailed story in Bakhouche (ed.), *Calcidius, Commentaire au* Timée *de Platon*, 53–67.

50 Kraus and Walzer, *Plato Arabus I.* The two subsequent volumes in the series were prepared by Franz Rosenthal and Richard Walzer (Al-Farabi, *Alfarabius, De Platonis philosophia*) and Francesco Gabrieli (Al-Farabi, *Alfarabius, Compendium Legum Platonis*), respectively.

51 See Klibansky and Regen, *Die Handschriften der philosophischen Werke des Apuleius,* 110, in which one finds all references to the reports mentioning this manuscript.

52 Klibansky, "La découverte d'un texte platonicien inconnu de l'Antiquité classique," 41.

53 See Stover, *A New Work by Apuleius.* It is of course very sad that this author did not try to contact the heirs of Raymond Klibansky, who would have gladly discussed the matter with him. In his study, Justin Stover does not mention the 1993 study that Klibansky devoted to the history and interpretation of the manuscript. I cannot present here a discussion of Mr Stover's research, but, since it explores a totally different hypothesis than the one put forward by Ray-

mond Klibansky, it will be interesting to come back to it on some other occasion. The material left by Raymond Klibansky was transmitted after his death for an edition in the Budé Series, where it should be completed by Luna, to whom it was entrusted by the late Segonds, director of the Belles-Lettres series, before his untimely death in 2009. Should this edition proceed, one would hope that it will take into account the research offered by this new edition, but this presents a problem for the editors. Should the material left by Raymond Klibansky be published as a posthumous work, and thus left untouched, or should it be presented as a pioneering contribution to be completed by younger scholars?

54 Steel, "Plato Latinus (1939–1989)," in Hamesse and Fattori, *Rencontres de cultures dans la philosophie médiévale*, 306.

55 Ibid., 307.

56 Steel refers to the important work of Stephen Gersh, *Middle Platonism and Neoplatonism*. Steel presents this work as realizing one of the objectives of Klibansky's research program, by putting together all the materials available in the indirect sources to medieval thinkers curious about Platonic doctrines. Ibid., 309.

57 Brisson, *Le même et l'autre dans la structure ontologique du Timée de Platon*. A second edition, which included corrigenda and a new bibliography, was published by Sankt Augustin Academia Verlag in 1994.

58 Ficino, "Letter to Martin Preninger," in Klibansky, *Continuity of the Platonic Tradition*, 45.

SEVEN

Raymond Klibansky's Ethics of Transmission

ERIC MÉCHOULAN

The editorial project of the *Corpus Platonicum Medii Aevi* was intended to measure the historical effects of cultural transmission and evaluate Plato's influence. Here, mirroring Aby Warburg's interest in transmission and afterlife, Klibansky shows the importance of thinking about intellectual legacies through the historical study of material editions. Emphasizing the materiality of transmission is not only a matter of historical research, however; it is also an ethical and political position. That is why I would like to connect these editorial and archival practices to Klibansky's work on tolerance. Understanding ancient authors is a way to try to understand others.

In May 1937, Klibansky, then based in Oxford after having fled Nazi Germany, presented to the Union Académique Internationale his manuscript entitled *The Continuity of the Platonic Tradition during the Middle Ages: Outlines of a Corpus Platonicum Medii Aevi*. It was accepted by the British Academy and was to be published in Germany. For obvious reasons, that was not an option; it was finally published in the fall of 1939 by the Warburg Institute in London. The text outlines a large-scale editorial project that was subsequently completed, albeit only in part, during and after the war. It consisted of a reflection on how Platonic thought had fuelled philosophical thinking as it had fuelled artistic and literary creation; and heralded the creation of an edition of the medieval Latin translations of Plato's works. This project is typical of Klibansky's intellectual activity. For him, there was manifestly no hermetic separation between a palaeographic examination of a reader's marginal comment in a manuscript of the *Phaedo* and an attentive exegesis of Socratic morality. Klibansky shows the greatest respect for authors. But this deserved respect is conjoined with a respect for the readers, copyists, printers, and editors whose contributions make it possible that a work conceived two thousand and five hundred years ago can be not only readable but also rewarding to us in the world today – a world the author would be stunned, if not aghast, to gaze upon. A double principle of continuity reigns in Klibansky: a continuity from the material to the ideal in social space; a continuity of works in human time.

Let us acknowledge the originality of Klibansky's intellectual position among his contemporaries, both philosophers and historians. The modern historiographic process is founded on a double temporal alterity or a double alteration of time: for history, such as we still know it, to come into existence, the past must first be rendered strange (or even foreign) to the present. Thus Marc Bloch insists on "the abyss that separates two mentalities (ours and that of the medieval world)."[1] More generally, it is a matter of understanding the movement of time under the authority of the cut in that flow. As Michel de Certeau writes, "Modern Western History essentially begins with the differentiation between the *present* and the *past*. In this way it is unlike tradition."[2] Each time we make a radical cut between two timeframes, we render a retrospective gaze necessary. This differs from tradition – a constant "updating" of the past – which catapults the ancient into the recent. Briefly, while tradition maintains the living past in the present, taking on new forms, historiography is the present writing of a dead past. As Marc Bloch affirms, "the good historian resembles the ogre of legends: where he smells human flesh, there he finds his prey."[3] We could put this conflict in terms of fairy tales: tradition is the princess's kiss that transforms the toad of the present into the Prince Charming of the past; history is Sleeping Beauty, untouched in the bed of time, who awaits the kiss of the historian to awake her (but we know that, in this fairy tale, the mother of the historian–Prince Charming is no other than an ogress who dreams of devouring the wonderfully fresh flesh of the past).

In our modern age, it is no longer the past that renders the present intelligible: the present invents models of intelligibility for the past. History has even become *a survival instinct*:

> An instinct that tells us that forgetting is necessary for groups, for societies that wish to live, for them to be able to live, to not let themselves be crushed by this formidable heap, by this inhuman accumulation of inherited facts. To not be crushed by this irresistible pressure of the dead on the living – laminating the thin layer of the present under their weight, to the point of taking away all of the present's power to resist.[4]

The past does not uphold the living; it crushes them. After the First World War, which immediately preceded Bloch's writing, just as after the Second, one cannot help but be struck by this obsessive reference to the weight of the cadavers of the past on the starved body of the present.

This thinness of the latest moment in time also affects the meaning of each present. Indeed, on top of this first temporal alterity – rendering the past and present irreducibly strangers and foreign to each other – a second alterity must be produced from it to legitimize the historiographic gaze: modern history also supposes that each present proves to be a stranger to itself, blind to what it is, just as soon dissipated in immediacy, unable to lift itself outside its fugitive moment to glimpse the landscape it is composing; it lacks the historical lever of mediation. There is knowledge only of long ago, never of today.

Fernand Braudel writes: "An era must be sufficiently detached from us and from all ties to the living present, it must have toppled over and dwelt for enough time in the morgue, just as for certain anatomical preparations, for its deep structure to be revealed."[5] In Braudel's methodological reflections one senses the stage that must be set for the past in itself to finally appear. In fact, we find ourselves within a hair's breadth of a very beautiful paradox: in order for the historian to say what happened, he must show it such as it never actually existed. (Indeed, neither Cervantès nor Philip II saw a century, a demographic curve, a growth cycle, a series of testaments, a Baroque age, or even the Mediterranean, which serves as context for Braudel.)

Is it so surprising to find the fundamental establishment of this same movement in the great philosopher of history, Hegel? Knowledge of one's self fatally escapes he who resides in the immediacy of the appearances of the sensible world: "Certainly there is no knowledge to be had of this inner world, as we have it here … on account simply of the nature of the case, because in the void there is nothing known."[6] To fill this void of sensible immediacy, one must pass through the supersensible, wherein the being of immediacy acts like a blind man in the middle of wealth or like the seeing man in pure light. But the supersensible cannot live only in this world cut from its anchoring in the sensible; it returns to immediacy, laden at once with appearances and their interiority: "The supersensible is the established truth of the sensible and perceptual. The truth of the sensible and the perceptual lies, however, in being appearance. The supersensible is then *appearance qua appearance*. We distort the proper meaning of this, if we take it to mean that the supersensible is therefore the sensible world, or the world as it is for immediate sense-certainty and perception."[7]

The Hegelian inversion that makes the immediate unknowable, except for becoming full of its own interiority thanks to mediation by the supersensible, repudiates the idea of finding immediately intelligible the world expressed through sensible immediacy, under the pretext that it would truly be a *distortion* (*the world inverted*). The immediate is decipherable only through the mediation of the intelligible, which alone can render perceivable the inner truth of appearances.

Resistant to the dominant conceptions of his era, Klibansky shows trust in sensible phenomena (even those of a quill scratching the surface of a parchment) and in the human ability to understand, if not the totality of each present, at least its most important parts. It is perhaps this *trust* that gives him an exemplary lucidity in a historic moment in which so many eminently excellent people hesitated or wandered, if they were not completely led astray. The quickness with which he realized the need to flee Nazi-governed Germany, for people but also for an institution like the KBW, indicates that it was entirely possible to predict this very imminent event.

Thus, faced with the principles of a double discontinuity in the historical process, he affirms a double continuity: from material effects to forms of thought, on the one hand, and from vestiges of the past to the present moment, on the other. This is not to say that he succumbs to the charms of tradition; rather, he knows how to find, beneath the anachronisms of traditions, the meaning of what is an authentic transmission. Again, I would like to make it clear that this does not imply the attribution of authenticity – or truth – to what is, will be, or "should be" transmitted. Authenticity resides more in transmission than in the objects of transmission thus conveyed through time.

We see this thinking at work in an exemplary way when Klibansky writes a text in homage to Ernst Cassirer titled "The Philosophic Character of History." In this essay, he underscores the gap between the past and the present, the restricted condition of each present, almost closed on its universe of a more or less short duration, to the point that the historian himself cannot escape from the magic circle of his own culture and particular moment in history: "It would be easy ... to show how our given forms of history are conditioned by the specific time-aspect of their civilization, and even how in differentiated periods the particular time-illusion of the individual historian makes itself felt."[8] But he proposes a critique of historical reason (all the more astute and detailed for a text in homage to the Neo-Kantian that Cassirer was) that does not limit itself to contesting the objectivity of historical science in the name of this inevitability – that is, the inscription of historians in a time and place that are necessarily subjective. It is, rather, the very meaning of objectivity that must change:

> Though the objectivity of history only grows from a subjective basis, this cannot imperil its value as a form of knowledge. To say that the attempt to reach an absolute *Always* must forever start from a relative *Now* and *Here*, can betoken a depreciation only in the eyes of one who fancies himself standing, like a dogmatist of the old learning, in a space without time; or to an intelligence suspended *in vacuo* ... We notice in all creations of the human mind, in the most primitive stages of language, in magic and religious myth as well as in all branches of art, the spontaneous tendency to force into stable shapes the flux of things that come and go ... the transcending of time which we observe in history amounts to an ever deeper immersion in the time of past destiny, and to an ever new condensation of its changing appearances into lasting pictures.[9]

Let us then take an example of this "deep immersion" in time to grasp how these "lasting pictures" are composed: the case of Plato.

Historians of medieval philosophy have long underscored the pre-eminence of Aristotle, more discussed and more popular in schools of theology than his "master," Plato, who would have to wait until the Renaissance to return to the forefront of philosophy. Put differently, in the Middle Ages there was a caesura in the transmission of Platonism. Yet, through his vast editorial project, the *Corpus Platonicum Medii Aevi*, Klibansky seeks, among other things, to show the contrary. Without limiting himself to the common tradition that indeed makes Aristotle *the* philosopher, he discerns the profound continuity, on the one hand, of Platonic and Neoplatonic legacies and, on the other, of Plato's strong presence, at least with respect to certain points as fundamental for medieval theologians as the relationship between faith and reason, or the creation of the world by one God alone. As Klibansky notes, in the fourteenth and fifteenth centuries, "the main historical significance of the *Timaeus* becomes evident. The mediaeval scholar could read into this work his own conception of a divine being, and, at the same time, learn the postulate of a strict rational thought":[10] "No Christian can deny, Petrarch exclaims, that of all philosophers Plato came nearest to Christianity ... In contrast with Aristotle, Plato shares the Christian view of creation."[11]

To make this long presence understood, Klibansky has to open up Platonic texts to the history of their editions, as well as to their geographic, linguistic, and cultural courses of distribution. When we attempt to grasp transmission over time, we of course begin by following specific transmissions in particular places and by way of defined cultural objects. He therefore reconstitutes the three channels through which Platonic texts were transmitted: by the Arabs, the Byzantines, and the Romans. There exists, then, according to Klibansky, "no definite break between mediaeval and Renaissance Platonism."[12] And even from an institutional perspective, which proves to be equally important for Klibansky, Platonism has been constantly reinvigorated: first with the Academy Plato created, which lasted until Justinian (up to the fourth century CE) but also in Byzantium, where the baton was subsequently taken up. "The tradition of Byzantine Platonism never entirely lapsed from the closing of the Academy in Athens by Justinian until the time when a new Academy was opened in Florence."[13] Whether it was through the texts regularly copied from one library to another, the commentaries on or appreciations of these texts, or the institutions that ensured their preservation and use, Platonism in its deep continuity was systematically studied.

One can even say that this analysis of modes of transmission not only touches on languages, countries, translations, and the organization of works but it also takes into account forms of knowledge other than the philosophy taught at universities. Klibansky emphasizes, in the 1982 (second and augmented) edition of his pre-war text, that: "the change in the valuation of Plato was not due to the universities. It seems in fact a characteristic feature in the development of Platonism that the impulse leading to a new phase of its history does not come from the school philosophers but from men outside their traditional orbit."[14] He thus alludes to Jean de Meung (c. 1240–c. 1305) as much as to his near contemporary Petrarch (1304–1374). Yet, as early as the first version of the text, Klibansky also opened the corpus to images: "The different forms assumed by the mediaeval Plato found expression in contemporary miniatures, sculpture, and painting. A complete iconography would therefore serve as the shortest and best commentary on the many trends in mediaeval tradition."[15] Plato is represented, for instance, as a naturalist and healer, or as the philosopher who has foreshadowed the Christian Trinity; very often, Plato deals with the divine sphere, while Aristotle deals with the human sphere (fig. 7.1).

The modalities of an author's presence are to be studied in all their variety. It is not because our subject is a creator of philosophical texts that we should restrict ourselves to university philosophy or even to texts. Anecdotes or satires can show forms of either appreciation or opposition. Thus, Klibansky reports the frequent satires of Aristotle submissive before a woman, or an anecdote about Plato that shows him to have been rather modest in admitting his lack of knowledge. There is not then, *a priori*, a hierarchy of noble texts *vs* secondary texts, nor of eloquent texts *vs* mute images. As Klibansky – who has perfectly grasped Warburg's lessons – emphasizes: iconography can be the best commentary.

This diversity of sources doubles the work of the philologist philosopher: on the one hand, he is tasked with establishing the most faithful original text possible; on the other hand, knowing that a text is also the product of its various transmissions, he must be able to highlight these effects of reading. For example, from the twelfth to the thirteenth century, the conception of Platonism begins to be governed by Plotinus, or rather, Klibansky says, "by a strange combination of the Latin, Greek, Arabic, and Jewish heirs of [Plotinus's] thought ... fused in a universal system of emanation."[16] And this – being submitted to the vagaries of reading, of re-composition, of different uses – is just part of the life and also the means of survival of a text.

Fig. 7.1 Detail from Raphael's *School of Athens*.

We should not draw the conclusion that the work of establishing a text no longer has any importance. On the contrary, it is all the more essential that we do not fetishize this "first" text but that we unfold its significant materialities. This allows us to better read others' ways of reading. Klibansky recalls having heard Heidegger's lecture on metaphysics in 1929: "I was struck by the mix of true and apparent depth … and by the insouciance with which, at the end of his speech, he abused the Greek text of Plato's *Phaedrus* to support his thesis."[17] It is important to take care of texts and to do them justice as scrupulously as possible. This is part of what we could call an "ethics of reading." This respectful attention to textual or iconic traces left by human beings responds to the search for truth against fanaticism. It is not coincidental that, when he wants to highlight this heterogeneity, Klibansky takes up an author whose tremendous work, with all its subtleties, became a lifelong focus: "the maxim proclaimed by Nicholas of Cusa in his struggle against the fanatical imposition of uniformity: *Una veritas in variis signis varie resplendet*" ("one truth, in various signs, shines variously").[18]

The question of transmission does not, then, raise only technical or epistemological considerations. If we agree that a possible synonym of transmission could be "inheritance," perhaps we will better understand the ethical stakes. Hannah Arendt, in her preface to *Between Past and Future*, cites René Char's aphorism from the end of the Second World War: "Notre héritage n'est précédé d'aucun testament" ("our inheritance was left to us by no testament").[19] She likens it to Toqueville's famous phrase, upon returning from his exploration of the New World: "When the past no longer illuminates the future, the spirit walks in darkness."[20] We have seen that the historians of the Annales school drew epistemological resources from the break between past and the present: to write history was to recognize this alterity of the past; history would no longer be *magistra vitae* (life's master or life's teacher), as Cicero had written. However, it may still be a teacher of survival. The task of the philologist philosopher is, then, to update the multiple testaments that have formed our inheritance.

The stakes of these testaments and this inheritance are nowhere more central than in another of Klibansky's major interests: the question of tolerance. Again, this concept comes to us through critical editions of earlier authors. As he acknowledged in an interview with Georges Leroux,[21] Klibansky intended, after the war, to make what he believed to be important texts on tolerance more widely available, and therefore founded the monograph series "Philosophy and World Community." The series consists in published translations of modern works by, for example, Spinoza on liberty and Locke on tolerance, but it also includes earlier texts such as a declaration by Asoka, Indian emperor in the third century BCE, who reconquered territories that had been taken by Alexander and who was the first to declare that one must not kill for a religion or even impose a religion. Klibansky himself edited the Latin version of Locke's *Letter on Toleration* for several bilingual editions. His intention, with this series, was that these texts would thereby more easily reach the young people of the world and that they would "transmit a certain tradition. Let's say that of toleration."[22]

We can also see that Klibansky's investment in the International Institute of Philosophy relates both to questions of historicity and to a concern for tolerance. The institute was created in 1937 to inform philosophers of the world about who was working on what and with what results. It was a way of taking stock of the different facets of philosophy at regular intervals. Notably, if the subtitle in English is "Survey," it is "Chroniques" ("Chronicles") in French; in that terminology lies the necessary historicity for the impetus of philosophical thinking, even when it claims to be ontology. But it is also a question of an indispensable opening to several questionings and many schools of thought – in short, of intellectual tolerance. One senses Klibansky's worry when he writes:

> The situation of philosophy to-day may well give rise to perplexity ... the present state of philosophical discussion is characterized not only by an unusually large variety of approaches and divergent positions, but above all by sharp disagreement as to the very nature and purpose of philosophy ... To the adherents of some of the most influential schools, their own conception is the only admissible one; whoever does not share it, will no longer be taxed with faulty argument and erroneous conclusions: his very questions will be ruled out of court; worse still, his activity may be deemed devoid of meaning.[23]

In other words, a variety of approaches does not present a problem – until, that is, it seems to summon forms of intolerance that no longer aim for discussion or dispute but, rather, seem to call for the radical denial that this or that style of philosophical thought would be recognized as thought or philosophy at all.

For a philologist, an error is never without interest, but for some of these new philosophers it is a question of not even recognizing the other camp's discourse as a discourse as such. It is not a matter of pointing out a possible error, because what the other says is not even heard. This is how the intolerant acts: when the other speaks, he is neither right nor wrong because in fact he is not speaking at all; at most he makes noises as enigmatic as they are useless. Even if Klibansky contents himself with expressing – with great tolerance – his (as he says) "perplexity," it is clear that it is a highly problematic situation for whoever claims to be philosopher, and even whoever claims to be human.

One could contrast this with some older *mores* that Klibansky points to (again, very lightly) in his edition of David Hume's letters. In their introduction, the editors highlight Hume's very courteous and tolerant manner of entering into an intellectual conversation. Thus, Hume wrote to Montesquieu, his fierce but nevertheless respectful opponent: "Why cannot all the World entertain different Opinions about any Subject, as amicably as we do?"[24] They recall also that: "It was the *manner* of this controversy which led Montesquieu to express his admiration for the participants" (my italics).[25] That is what an ethics of discussion or reading of others is, whether they belong to our present or to a more distant past.

When Klibansky brings up the importance, to him, of Karl Jaspers's teachings in the 1920s, he recalls a crucial element: "The human being, [Jaspers] said, only finds himself with another being and never by knowledge alone. From whence the importance he accorded to *Kommunikation*. This term for him did not designate information, but the possibility of entering the mind of the other, of participating in his intellectual life … as the basis for all understanding."[26] But alongside Jaspers, there is another fundamental influence that is likewise an opening to another cultural space: the influence of Aby Warburg. Klibansky likes to recall, in French, a particular phrase: "Je suis juif de sang, Hambourgeois d'esprit et Florentin de cœur"[27] ("I am by blood a Hebrew, in spirit a Hamburger, and by heart a Florentine"). It is funny that in English, according to the Warburg Library Website, there is a slight philological variation: "[I am] by heart a native of Hamburg, by blood a Hebrew, in spirit a Florentine." ("Ebreo di sangue, Amburghese di cuore, d'anima Fiorentino.")[28] Thanks to transmission errors – and traditional tolerance – spirit and heart after all are themselves translatable.

Klibansky thus comments on Warburg's sentence: "It is this vision that made an indelible impression when he brought me in, in 1926, when I was a young student in Hamburg and he offered me a position in his library."[29] The intellectual curiosity that draws together images, texts, and people in geography and history also depends on an ethics of reading that expands its thought through that of others as an example of tolerance.

NOTES

1 Bloch, *Les Rois thaumaturges*, 17.

2 Certeau, *The Writing of History*, 2.

3 Bloch, *Apologie pour l'histoire ou le métier d'historien*, 51. Unless otherwise specified, translations from the French originals are my own.

4 Febvre, *Combats pour l'histoire*, 436.

5 Braudel, "L'histoire, mesure du monde," 48–9.

6 Hegel, *The Phenomenology of Mind*, 83.

7 Ibid.

8 Klibansky, "The Philosophical Character of History," 332.

9 Ibid., 336–7.

10 Klibansky, *The Continuity of the Platonic Tradition … with a new preface* (1982), 76.

11 Ibid., 69.

12 Raymond Klibansky, *The Continuity of the Platonic Tradition* (1939), 35.

13 Ibid., 19.

14 Klibansky, *The Continuity of the Platonic Tradition … with a new preface* (1982), 69.

15 Klibansky, *Continuity of the Platonic Tradition* (1939), 34–5.

16 Klibansky, *The Continuity of the Platonic Tradition … with a new preface* (1982), 62.

17 Klibansky, "L'Université allemande dans les années trente: notes autobiographiques," 152.

18 Klibansky and Paton, "Preface," in *Philosophy and History*, vii.

19 Arendt, *Between Past and Future*, 3; and Char, "Feuillets d'Hypnos," 102.

20 Ibid. and Tocqueville, *Democracy in America*, Vol. 2, Bk. 4, Ch. 7.

21 See Klibansky, *Le Philosophe et la mémoire du siècle.*

22 Klibansky, *Le Philosophe et la mémoire du siècle*, 224.

23 Klibansky, "Introduction," in *Philosophy in the Mid-Century*, 1: vii.

24 Hume, *New Letters of David Hume*, xiv and 30.

25 Ibid., xiv.

26 Klibansky, *Le Philosophe et la mémoire du siècle*, 21.

27 Raymond Klibansky, "La notion de *Kulturwissenschaft*" (RACAR) 145 / (*Tradition antique et tolérance moderne*) 345.

28 Original quotation by Gertrud Bing: "*Ebreo di sangue, Amburghese di cuore, d'anima Fiorentino (Jude von Geburt, Hamburger im Herzen, im Geiste ein*

Florentiner)" in her "Aby Warburg. Vortrag von Frau Professor Dr. Gertrud Bing," 464.

29 Klibansky, "La notion de *Kulturwissenschaft*," (RACAR) 145 / (*Tradition antique et tolérance moderne*), 345.

PART THREE

The Saturn and Melancholy Project

Fig. 8.1 Albrecht Dürer, *Melencolia I* (1514). Engraving on laid paper (24.2 × 19 cm).

EIGHT

Editing the "Melancholy Project": A Schematic Overview

ELISABETH OTTO

The history of the "Melancholy Project" is not only complex; it is also long. Starting decades earlier than the actual publication of *Saturn and Melancholy* in 1964,[1] the project shifted from a monographic study on Albrecht Dürer's *Melencolia I* (fig. 8.1) by the Austrian art historian Karl Giehlow,[2] to a collective project of the Warburg Library undertaken by Fritz Saxl, Erwin Panofsky, and Raymond Klibansky. As early as 1923, Panofsky and Saxl had collaborated on *Dürers 'Melencolia I'. Eine quellen- und typengeschichtliche Untersuchung*,[3] the second volume in the series *Studien der Bibliothek Warburg*. Based on Giehlow's 1903 ground-breaking reinterpretation of Dürer's famous print, Aby Warburg – who had become interested in Dürer's oeuvre some time earlier[4] – picked up where Giehlow left off at his early death in 1913, and hoped to complete the latter's work. After becoming ill in the aftermath of the war, Warburg in turn was unable to contribute to its publication himself and left its execution to Saxl.

Following Klibansky's entry into the Warburg circle in 1926, Saxl and Panofsky invited the young PhD student to collaborate with them on what was planned as a new edition of *Dürer's 'Melencolia I,'* but would ultimately turn into the monumental study *Melancholie und Saturn. Studien zur Geschichte der Naturphilosophie, Charakterlehre und bildenden Kunst*,[5] the unpublished German edition of 1939. In 1990, fifty-one years after the first German text was established, *Saturn und Melancholie*[6] would finally be published – but translated into German from the 1964 English edition of the now canonical *Saturn and Melancholy* – under the direction of Klibansky, its only remaining living co-author. Like no other Warburg project, *Saturn and Melancholy* reflects the transitions, challenges, and adaptations of the Warburg Library circle through key events of the twentieth century, through language translation, and through shifts in the culture of editing (fig. 8.2).

Significant changes took place over time in terms of content and overall layout, most notably with respect to illustrations and appendices. A brief material summary of the numerous editions and translations that constitute this publication history reveals the skeletal structure behind the various transitions analyzed in the contributions that follow.

Editing *Saturn and Melancholy*, 1923–90: Summary of Major Changes by Edition

Erwin Panofsky, Fritz Saxl, Dürers 'Melencolia I.' Eine quellen- und typengeschichtliche Untersuchung (Leipzig-Berlin: B.G. Teubner, 1923).

This comprehensive treatise on the problematic of Saturn and the concept of melancholy as represented in Dürer's *Melencolia I* is structured in four parts, tracing these topics from antiquity through to the Middle Ages and the Florentine Renaissance, and closing with a chapter on Albrecht Dürer. In the preface, Giehlow's literary executor, Arpád Weixlgärtner, tells the prehistory of the project that originated in Vienna years earlier and was finalized at the Kulturwissenschaftliche Bibliothek Warburg (KBW) in Hamburg.[7]

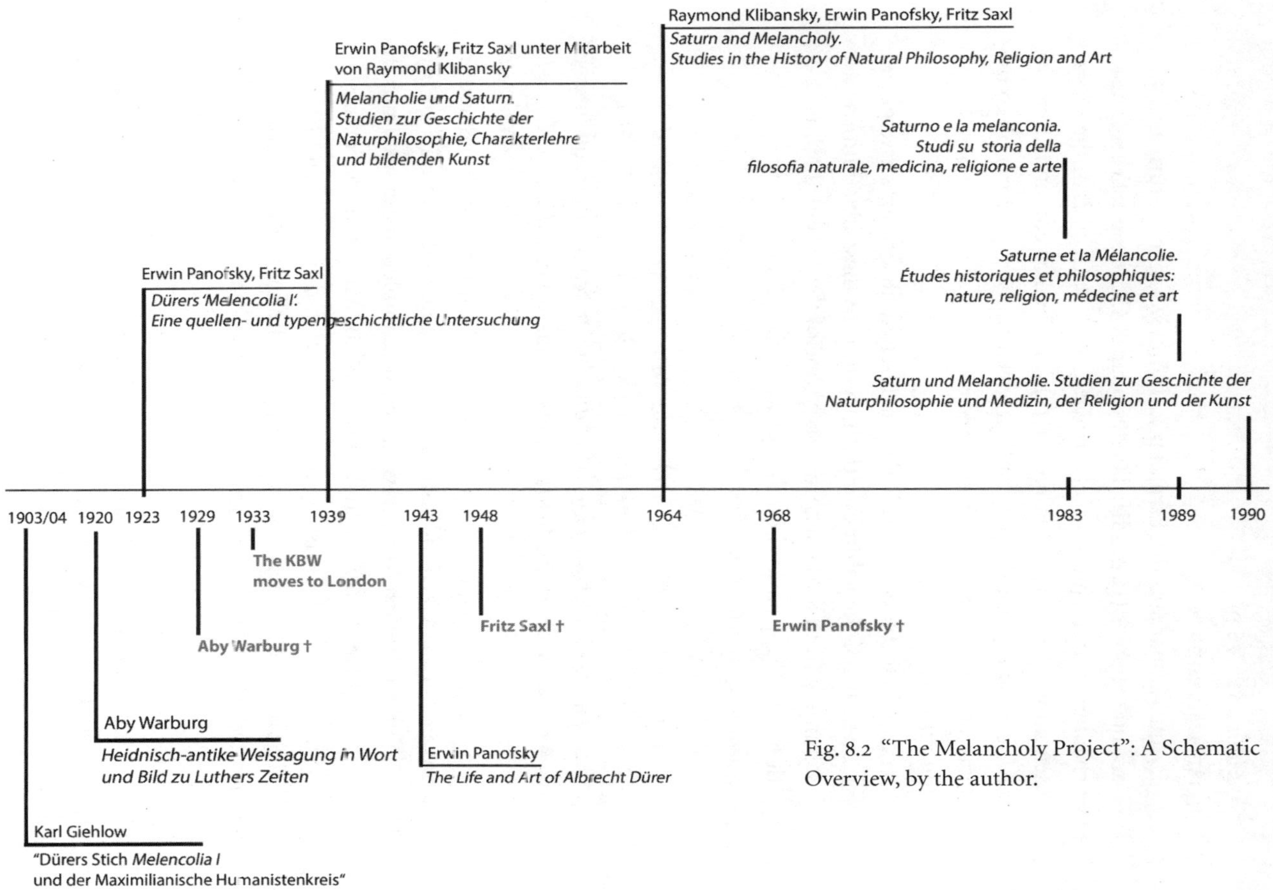

Fig. 8.2 "The Melancholy Project": A Schematic Overview, by the author.

Anhang I–VII / p. 77
Abbildungen / p. 161

Main text: 76 p.
Appendices: 78 p.
I: Abu Ma'shar and Ibn Esra (4 p.); II: Abu Ma'shar's Saturn and its antique Sources (12 p.); III: The Problem XXX.1 (12 p.); IV: Selected chapters from Ficino's *De vita triplici* (16 p.); V: Genesis of the representation of Saturn's Children (16 p.); VI: The Polyeder in Dürer's *Melencolia I* (3 p.); VII: Portraits of Melancholy after Dürer up to the 17th century (16 p.).
Illustrations: 68
The main text is accompanied by sixty-eight illustrations assembled at the back of the volume, with thirty-nine of these illustrations stemming from Karl Giehlow. (Sixty-one of the sixty-eight illustrations will reappear in the subsequent editions.)
Format: 19.5 x 26.5 cm

Erwin Panofsky, Fritz Saxl, unter Mitarbeit von Raymond Klibansky, Melancholie und Saturn Studien zur Geschichte der Naturphilosophie, Charakterlehre und bildenden Kunst, (London: The Warburg Institute, 1939) [not published].[8]

Surviving proofs from the German printer, J.J. Augustin, in Glückstadt recently discovered at the Warburg Institute Archive date to the summer of 1939. They include a title page of the volume, the complete main text, and the plates. Missing are an introduction, a table of contents, and appendices.

Having criticized the missing philosophical and theological history of melancholy since antiquity as presented in the 1923 edition, Klibansky was invited by Saxl to contribute to a second edition of the work in 1926. The preparation of this volume was interrupted by the KBW's move from Hamburg to London and the authors' emigration to England and the United States. While Klibansky and Saxl continued working on the book and the proofs until the outbreak of war in the fall of 1939, Panofsky had little involvement in this project after his permanent move to the United States and his recruitment at Princeton in 1935.[9]

The main text is divided into five parts that deal, in turn, with the notion of melancholy and the influence of Saturn, followed by one chapter on poetic melancholy after the Middle Ages, one on Dürer, and another on his successors. This treatise follows a chronology from antiquity to late medieval times, crossing the fields of medicine, philosophy, religion studies, literature, cosmology, and astrology, as well as the visual arts.

Main text: 426 p.
Illustrations: 147
Assembled in the back, sixty-one of the 147 illustrations are identical with those of the 1923 edition. The remaining plates were prepared by the Warburg Institute.[10] Not taken over from the 1923 edition are seven illustrations of the "melancholics."[11]
Format: 21 x 28.5 cm

Raymond Klibansky, Erwin Panofsky, Fritz Saxl, Saturn and Melancholy. Studies in the History of Natural Philosophy, Religion and Art (London: Nelson, 1964).[12]

Klibansky's efforts to publish *Melancholie und Saturn* immediately after the end of the war remained for a long time unsuccessful. Indeed, after having published *The Life and Art of Albrecht Dürer* in 1943, Panofsky was not very keen on publishing another book dealing with Dürer's *Melencolia I*.[13]

As Panofsky mentions in the foreword to the first edition of *The Life and Art of Albrecht Dürer*, he had developed his monography during his Norman Wait Harris Lecture delivered at Northwestern University in 1938. This lecture was complemented by material that was already published but remained, until then, inaccessible to the American reader: a 1923 book on the engraving *Melencolia I* as well as the unpublished collaboration with "Dr. Saxl and his associates."[14]

The English version – translated by Frances Lobb – of the 1939 unpublished German edition was launched only in 1964 as *Saturn and Melancholy: Studies in the History of Natural Philosophy, Religion and Art* with Klibansky, Panofsky, and Saxl as co-authors.[15] The 1964 edition is highly structured with a variety of illustrative, textual, and paratextual elements. These include, in order: an illustrated cover, a frontispiece, a title page, a preface by Klibansky and Panofsky, a contents page, a list of acknowledgments, a list of illustrations, a list of abbreviations, the main text, appendices, index of manuscripts, and a general index, as well as the illustrations themselves.

Preface / p. v

—

Part I.	The Notion of Melancholy and Its Historical Development / p. 1
Part II.	Saturn, Star of Melancholy / p. 125
Part III.	"Poetic Melancholy" and "Melancholia Generosa" / p. 215
Part IV.	Dürer / p. 275

—

Appendices / p. 400
Illustrations / p. 431

Main text: 399 p.
Appendices: 6 p.
I. The Polyhedron in "Melencolia I" (3 p.); II. The Meaning of the Engraving B70 (3 p.)
Illustrations: 146 plus 5 figures in text.
The 146 illustrations were mostly reproduced from the blocks made for the projected German book in 1939 and differ from this unpublished edition only in their sequence and in two cases.[16]
Format: 18 x 27.2 cm

Raymond Klibansky, Erwin Panofsky, Fritz Saxl, Saturno e la melanconia. Studi su storia della filosofia naturale, medicina, religione e arte (Torino: G. Einaudi editore, 1983)[17]

Even though Italian editor Einaudi was, as early as 1949, the first one to show interest in a translation of the unpublished *Melancholie und Saturn*, it would take another forty years to launch an Italian edition.[18]

In a letter to Gerda Panofsky, Klibansky recounts the "prehistory of the Italian edition" and reports on two failed attempts to produce a satisfactory translation from the unpublished German text right after the war.[19] Only after the great success of the 1964 English edition, which was soon out of print (and reprinted only once in a 1979 facsimile published in Liechtenstein), was an Italian translation from the English edition commissioned. In its overall structure, the 1983 Italian edition follows its 1964 predecessor without any additions in the main text or changes in the illustrations or the appendices.

Prefazione / p. xix

—

Parte prima. La nozione di melanconia e le sue trasformazioni storiche / p. 3

Parte seconda. Saturno, astro della melanconia / p. 117

Parte terza. "Melanconia poetica" and "Melancholia generosa" / p. 203

Parte quarta. Dürer / p. 259

—

Appendices / p. 375

Illustrations / grouped together in the middle of the volume (84 p.)

Main text: 374 p.

Appendices: 8 p.

I. Il poliedro nella *Melencolia I* (3 p.); II. Il significato dell'incisione B70 (5 p.)

Illustrations: 151 plus 5 figures in text.

The blocks of illustrations having been destroyed by the English

publishers after 1964, it was Enrica Melossi who recreated the original plates with their 151 illustrations.
Format: 15 x 20.8 cm

Raymond Klibansky, Erwin Panofsky, Fritz Saxl, Saturne et la Mélancolie. Etudes historiques et philosophiques: nature, religion, médecine et art (Paris: Gallimard, 1989)

The French translation of the 1964 edition, by Fabienne Durand-Bogaert and Louis Évrard, is preceded by a foreword written by Klibansky in December 1988. This new general introduction, absent from the English edition, provides an overview of the genesis and the further history of the notion of "melancholy."[20]

Main text: 653 p.
Appendices: Increased from the 1964 edition to five appendices (29 p.)
I: "Le Polyèdre dans *Melencolia I*" (4 p.); II: "La signification de la gravure B 70" (5 p.); III. Illustrations (1989): Appendix discussing the illustrations that were added to the 1964 edition (9 p.); IV. "Additions et corrections diverses (1989)": Appendix referring to the updates on secondary literature that had been published on the subject between

1964 and 1989 (12 p.); V. "Génie (Note du traducteur)": Appendix by the French translator discussing the challenges to translate the English "genius" into the French "génie" via the Latin "ingenium" and "genius" (8 p.).
Illustrations: 179
The structure of image inclusion has changed. The now 179 illustrations are grouped together within individual chapters on the visual tradition of Saturn, Dürer's *Melencolia I*, and the respective appendices. Of these illustrations, the 151 that are identical with those of the 1983 Italian edition were provided by the editing house Einaudi.
Format: 16 x 21.5 cm

Raymond Klibansky, Erwin Panofsky, Fritz Saxl, Saturn und Melancholie. Studien zur Geschichte der Naturphilosophie und Medizin, der Religion und der Kunst (Franfkurt am Main: Suhrkamp Verlag, 1990), (reprint: Frankfurt am Main: Suhrkamp Taschenbuch Wissenschaft, 1992)

The German edition was published not from the 1939 German original text but as *Saturn und Melancholie* in a translation by Christa Buschendorf from the 1964 English edition. This new German version combines aspects of the preceding editions by keeping the main text from the English version and the new foreword from the 1989 French edition by Klibansky, and by adding new literature on the subject in the form of footnotes and a selected bibliography.

Auswahlbibliographie / p. 573
Verzeichnisse und Register/ p. 571

Main text: 556 p.
Appendices: 12 p.
I. Der Polyeder der "Melencolia I" (3 p.) II. Die Bedeutung der Radierung B70 (3 p.) III. Lukas Cranachs Melancholiedarstellungen (6 p.)
Illustrations: 155 plus 5 figures in text.
As for the Italian edition, the illustrations are grouped together in the middle of the volume. The first 151 are identical with those of the 1983 Italian edition, augmented with 4 new illustrations for a total of 155.[21]
Format: 16 x 21.5 cm

Three appendices, different from both the 1964 and the augmented 1989 French edition, follow the main text. Instead of adding further appendices explaining the additions in illustrations and literature, this edition integrates new literature and new translations into English and German, with respect to the 1964 edition, by way of footnotes. In particular, these notes include new aspects on Babylonian Astrology, the pseudo-Aristotelian Problem XXX,1 (which the authors attribute to Theophrastus), and Saturn as a planet. Also new here is a selected bibliography of recent research on the subject, which is presented at the very end of the volume.

Due to the success of the Italian, French, and German editions, *Saturn and Melancholy* was translated in the following years into Spanish (1991), Japanese (1991), Romanian (2002), Polish (2009), and Slovenian (2013).[22]

NOTES

1 Klibansky, Panofsky, and Saxl, *Saturn and Melancholy*.
2 Giehlow, "Dürers Stich Melencolia I und der maximilianische Humanistenkreis."
3 Panofsky and Saxl, *Dürers 'Melencolia I.'*

4 Warburg, *Heidnisch-antike Weissagung in Wort und Bild zu Luthers Zeiten.*

5 Warburg Institute Archive (hereafter WIA), Fritz Saxl Papers, boxes "Saturn und Melancholie."

6 Klibansky, Panofsky, and Saxl, *Saturn und Melancholie.*

7 See Claudia Wedepohl's chapter (9) in this volume.

8 WIA, Saxl Papers, boxes "Saturn und Melancholie."

9 Deutsches Literaturarchiv Marbach, A: Raymond Klibansky (hereafter DLA, A, KLIBANSKY) VI, 1, Saturn and Melancholy, "Das Verfasserproblem": Klibansky recalls the "Saga du livre" in his own words: "ils [Saxl and Panofsky] avaient écrit un livre en 23 sur la Mélancolie de Dürer, un très beau livre, très intéressant et j'ai pris la liberté de la critique parce qu'il ne tenait pas assez compte des racines philosophiques et théologiques. Ils ont reconnu que mes critiques n'étaient pas dépourvues de fondement et m'ont invité à les formuler et de là est né le désir d'écrire un nouveau livre. Dans les années 28–29 … le travail sur le nouveau livre sur la mélancolie a procédé assez lentement parce qu'il fallait traiter de tout, commencer à partir des origines de l'Antiquité … En 33, on était déjà arrivé à une première composition mais arrivait le nazisme et M. Panofsky avait perdu sa place à Hambourg et devait émigrer. A partir de 33, il n'a plus pu s'en occuper, il déclarait qu'il ne pouvait plus parce qu'il devait se créer une nouvelle existence aux États-Unis."

10 In the 1936 proofs held in the WI Archives, I found the following note: "N.B. It should be stated somehow that the plates were not made by us but supplied by the kindness of the Whg. Inst." (WIA, Saxl Papers, boxes "Saturn und Melancholie.")

11 *Der Melancholiker*, unidentified drawing, 15th century; *Der Melancholiker*, Brunsvick, Nüw Distillierbuch, Straßburg 1508; *Kronos,* antique bronze, Museo Gregoriano; (Craftsmen), Kusejr 'Amra (in: Alois Musil, *Kusejr 'Amra*, Vienna 1907); *Luna*, Florentiner Kupferstecher, 15th century; (Hellenistic Relief), Capitol, Rome; *The Melancholic in Eobanus Hessus, De conservanda bona valetudine*, Frankfurt, 1551.

12 Reprint: Nendeln (Liechtenstein), Kraus, 1979.

13 Panofsky, *The Life and Art of Albrecht Dürer.*

14 Quoted from Panofsky, "Preface to the First Edition," in the 4th edition of *The Life and Art of Albrecht Dürer,* xi. See also Philippe Despoix's chapter (10) in this volume.

15 See Davide Stimilli's chapter (11) in this volume.

16 The 1964 edition reproduces Matthias Gerung's *Melancholy* (1558) as one image rather than two. Where the 1939 edition supposedly includes the frontispiece to Peter de Jode, "Varie figure academiche" (1600), the 1964 edition proposes the page "Honore, disegno, labore" from a 1639 edition of De Jode's treatise (see DLA, A, KLIBANSKY: VI, 1, Saturn and Melancholy). As mentioned in the acknowledgments, the Warburg Institute, University of London, procured the photographs for the illustrations.

17 The Italian edition, translated by Renzo Frederici and published for the first time in 1983, turns out to be the highest-selling edition, running to a third edition in 2010. The editor points out that the Italian translation was based on the 1964 English edition and reworked in 2002 based on both the 1990 German edition and the 1989 French edition.

18 DLA, A, KLIBANSKY: XX–XXI, 1, Warburg Institute: Giulio Einaudi confirmed in a telegram sent to Klibansky on 11 February 1949: "Grato proposta accolta con entusiasmo mandi manoscritto."

19 From the copy of Klibansky's letter to Gerda Panofsky from 1974: "In 1949, an agreement was reached with the Turin publisher, Giulio Einaudi, who undertook to produce a translation based on the proofs of the unpublished German text. The translation was examined by Dr. Gertrud Bing of the Warburg Institute, and by myself. We found it unsatisfactory. A revised translation, made some time later, was also found unacceptable. As a result, the matter was allowed to drop. Another publisher – La Nuova Italia with whom I was in touch, then approached me, to obtain his consent, and heard from him that, though he could not promise any cooperation, he would not object. However, financial difficulties prevented La Nuova Italia from carrying out their plan.

"Prompted by Italian scholars, who admired the book, Einaudi wrote that he was still anxious to publish an Italian translation. Instead of being based on the proofs of the rather complicated German text of 1938, the new translation is to be made from the English text, published in 1964. This will be a much easier task, and I have obtained the assurance that the work will be entrusted to a competent translator, familiar with the subject, and in particular, with your late husband's writings ... The English book has been out of print for a long time. Since it is obviously much in demand – as appears from the many enquiries that have reached me during the last 4 or 5 years – the Italian translation, which is sure to be well produced, will go some way to fill the gap." (DLA, A, KLIBANSKY: XX–XXI, 2, Warburg Institute)

20 See Jean-Philippe Uzel's chapter (12) in this volume.

21 There are four new images in this edition: Lucas Cranach, *Melancholie*, 1532; Lucas Cranach, *Melancholie*, 1524; *Formae Saturni*, *Picatrix*, Biblioteka Jagiellonsky, Krakau; *Correspondence between Microcosmos and Macrocosmos*, Isidore of Seville, *De natura rerum*, Augsburg, 1472.

22 The translated titles are: *Dosei to merankorī: shizen tetsugaku shūkyō geijutsu no rekishi no okeru kenkyū* (Tokyo: Shōbunsha, 1991); *Saturno y la melancolía: estudios de historia de la filosofía de la naturaleza, la religión y el arte* (Madrid: Alianza, 1991); *Saturn si melancolia: studii de filosofie a naturii, religie si arta* (Bucharest: Polirom, 2002); *Saturn i melancholia: studia z historii, filozofii, przyrody, medycyny, religii oraz sztuki* (Krakow: Towarzystwo Autorow i Wydawcow Prac Naukowych Universitas, 2009); *Saturn in melanholija: studije o zgodovini filozofije narave, medicine, religije in umetnosti* (Ljubljana: Studentska zalozba, 2013).

NINE

The Genesis, Writing, and Re-Writing of Erwin Panofsky and Fritz Saxl's *Dürers 'Melencolia I'*

CLAUDIA WEDEPOHL

In a letter to his wife Mary, dated 18 February 1923, Aby Warburg mentioned that he had "skimmed over the proofs of Saxl and Panofsky's Saturn study" and that he found it to be "an admirable scholium on an old text."[1] Evidently Fritz Saxl had made available the first proofs of *Dürers 'Melencolia I'. Eine quellen- und typengeschichtliche Untersuchung*, which consisted of the main text, written up by Erwin Panofsky.[2] The two authors were still at work on the extensive appendices and tables, which would ultimately take up more pages than the main text itself. By March 1923 the entire manuscript, with the exception of Arpád Weixlgärtner's preface and the forty-five plates, was with the printers (B.G. Teubner in Leipzig),[3] and in January 1924 *Dürers 'Melencolia I,'* the second volume in the series *Studien der Bibliothek Warburg*, was released.

In these years Warburg was undergoing psychiatric treatment in Ludwig Binswanger's clinic in Swiss Kreuzlingen. Saxl, in regular contact with him, tried to keep him abreast of events at the library. Warburg, for his part, wanted to have a say in all that went on, and he had a particular interest in this project, which represented a continuation and expansion of his own work on Dürer's enigmatic print. It is not surprising that he read through the proofs with critical attention; although he wanted to discuss various possibilities for expansion with Saxl,[4] he was impressed overall and called the study "simply astonishing" (*einfach staunenswert*).[5]

The "old text" that Warburg referred to in his letter to Mary was Chapter XXX.1 of the pseudo-Aristotelian *Problemata*, a free-standing text usually today ascribed to Theophrastus.[6] In it the ancient author investigated the relation between melancholy (literally "black bile") and genius – a relation that would become a *topos* in the Romantic period. At the beginning of the twentieth century the art historian Karl Giehlow had discovered that this ancient theory – which had been reintroduced into the doctrine of the temperaments by the Florentine Neoplatonist and physician Marsilio Ficino – was the basis of the iconography of Dürer's *Melencolia I*.[7] Warburg was well acquainted with Giehlow's interpretation, which, published as a three-part essay in 1903 and 1904, is today regarded as one of the first examples of an "iconological" analysis – if not the very first.[8]

In his own studies Warburg frequently made reference to Giehlow's work, both its content and its method. Learning that Giehlow had embarked on a monographic study of *Melencolia I*, left unfinished at his sudden death in 1913, he tried for years, without success, to gain access to Giehlow's papers so as to help in the completion of this particular work. In this sense, the study undertaken by his two young colleagues represented the fulfillment of a longstanding desire he himself had been unable to satisfy. Still, Panofsky and Saxl's 1923 study was possible only because of the connection Warburg had forged with Giehlow's literary executors. In the introduction to their text, Panofsky and Saxl defined their task; it was not to arrive at a more or less astute solution to a challenging visual puzzle but rather to offer an explanation of the print based on a developmental history so as to bring to light the premises of Dürer's conception. The authors respectfully suggested that they had done no more than to proceed along paths charted by two great scholars – Giehlow and Warburg – and to go a bit further than had seemed necessary or possible to the pathfinders themselves.[9] In letters to Warburg, Saxl repeatedly described their work in similar terms.

Warburg, Giehlow, and the Interpretation of Dürer's *Melencolia I*

In a certain sense, the origin of Panofsky and Saxl's text predated its publication by a good twenty years. As early as 1897, Warburg had begun to focus on the exchange of forms, motives, and ideas between northern and southern

Europe – a phenomenon that he famously examined through the example of Dürer's oeuvre in 1905. Just two years earlier, in 1903, Giehlow had published the first part of his fundamental reinterpretation of *Melencolia I* – an undertaking that seems to have been a by-product of his research into the iconography of Dürer's design for the Triumphal Arch of Emperor Maximilian I. On the basis of his study of literary sources, Giehlow posited a connection between Dürer's *Melencolia I* and Ficino's three-part treatise *De vita*, written between 1482 and 1489. He believed that the iconography in the print could be attributed to Emperor Maximilian's circle of humanist advisers, who were demonstrably familiar with Ficino's writings. Giehlow's starting point was Maximilian's interest in the "type" of the so-called Hercules Aegypticus, known from an ancient silver coin that had been found in Hungary. He could show that the Augsburg-based humanist Conrad Peutinger, in a report compiled for Maximilian in February or March 1514, had subsequently linked this type of the ancient hero with Ficino's *topos* of the melancholy genius.[10]

In his *De vita*, Ficino discussed the different effects of black bile on the body and the mind as observed by the author of *Problem* XXX.1: black bile was said on the one hand to lead, in extreme cases, to madness and, on the other hand, in favourable cases, to foster genius. Basing himself on the ancient text, Ficino described the causal connection between the two forms of melancholy and explained how, under certain conditions, a warming and thinning of harmful black bile became possible; this triggered the positive effect.[11] For Giehlow, Ficino's treatise was the key to understanding the iconography of Dürer's print. He believed that Dürer was making reference to two modes of influence of this bodily fluid – direct and indirect. Ficino's specific dietary recommendations, as well as remedies and astrological magic (in particular, an invocation of the planet Jupiter, which has the power to appease the malignant planet Saturn), seem to find parallels in elements depicted in the print: the wreath of braided medicinal herbs, the enema syringe, and the magic square, composed of four rows of four numbers each adding up to thirty-four. Giehlow was thus convinced, on the basis of Peutinger's report for the emperor (who, like his supposed ancestor Hercules Aegypticus, suffered from outbursts of anger) that the reception of Ficino generally altered "popular conceptions of melancholy in the first quarter of the 16th century in Germany."[12]

Not only was Warburg persuaded by Giehlow's thesis but he also found the latter's investigation into the afterlife of ancient learning in a north-

European court to be of methodological significance. Working in Vienna, Giehlow had offered a prototype for investigating the interplay between text and image that Warburg would propagate throughout his scholarly life. From this perspective, Giehlow's approach anticipated Warburg's much heralded "iconology," that is, an approach to objects that is at once philologically precise and grounded in an interdisciplinary cultural science. Martin Warnke, in a critical essay on methodology, noted that Giehlow had grounds to dispute Warburg's position as founder of this method,[13] even if Giehlow's iconographic-iconological studies led to an engagement with the emblematic, while Warburg would be concerned with the symbolic content of images. Methodological parallels had already been recognized in Warburg's lifetime. In an obituary for Giehlow, Ernst Schwedeler-Meyer, director of the Nordböhmisches Gewerbemuseum in Reichenberg, referred, without naming him, to a scholar who was seeking solutions to "similar art historical problems" – surely thinking of Warburg.[14] The significance of his observation must be measured against the response to Giehlow's work by the main representative of formalism in art history, Heinrich Wölfflin. In the second edition of his popular monograph on Dürer, reprinted in 1908, Wölfflin briefly referred to Giehlow's thesis but nonetheless stood by his own interpretation of the print: Dürer's engraving, he believed, was a representation of the traditional characteristics of the melancholic, a symbol of sloth, of sluggishness in performing mental or physical activities.[15]

Just how important Dürer's *Melencolia I* was for Warburg's study of the transformation and migration of the ancient planetary deities is evident in a shift in the focus of his research: beginning in 1908 his study of the afterlife of ancient mythology was increasingly linked to the investigation of astrology. Following the one attested encounter between Warburg and Giehlow, at a meeting of the Kunsthistorische Gesellschaft in Berlin on 8 May 1908 (at which Giehlow presented), Warburg wrote to his wife and expressed his regret that he had not been able to discuss shared interests with him. Obviously much interested in the question of the reception of Ficino, soon afterward he got in touch with Giehlow by letter and asked for more information on Peutinger's letter to Maximilian.[16] Although the subject of migration of the planetary gods was still new to Warburg at the time,[17] only a few months later he delivered his first lecture on the topic, "Die antike Götterwelt und die Frührenaissance im Norden und Süden" (The ancient Pantheon and the early

Renaissance in the North and South).[18] *Melencolia I*, he argued in this text, was the result of an affinity (*Wesensgemeinschaft*) between Ficino's "new theories of the more positive destiny of the saturnine man" and "Dürer's typical Northern European internal capacity to depict man [menschenschildernde Kraft]." The print, for Warburg, became a transitional product between the "traditional horoscopic practices of late antiquity" and the new need to "use the compass so as to recreate the world order on the basis of natural laws."[19]

As Warburg initially took note of Giehlow's reinterpretation of *Melencolia I*, he was less interested in the negative influence exerted by Saturn on those born under his sign than in Dürer's appropriation of so-called pathos formulas (*Pathosformeln*) from the visual language of his Italian contemporaries. Warburg had defined the concept of the pathos formula to designate ancient forms and formulas of lively movement; he believed that these made their way from Italy to the North in prints, notably the so-called pathos sheets (*Pathosblätter*). These prints "announced," as Warburg put it, "the haute école of stylized passion" in the spirit of ancient tragedy as it was reanimated by humanists.[20] When, in October 1905, Warburg delivered his lecture entitled "Dürer und die italienische Antike" before an audience of philologists and archaeologists in Hamburg, he differentiated among the types of images of the temperaments within Dürer's oeuvre.[21] He was thinking here of distinctions, gestural and physiognomic, in the expression of the condition of madness, whether in a state of ecstasy or of complete spiritual immersion. Warburg found these represented on the one hand in the avenging maenads in Dürer's drawing *The Death of Orpheus* (1494) and figures such as the raging Hercules, and on the other hand in the personified Melancholy. This insight, too, can be traced back to Giehlow, who drew the connection between Hercules's rage and the supposed effects of black bile. But Warburg had additionally recognized that Dürer's pictorial inventions rested on ancient formulas,[23] namely on a tradition that Panofsky and Saxl would later call the "history of types" (*Typengeschichte*). He then went on to differentiate "ancient pathos-laden images of the temperaments" such as *Hercules* and *Effects of Jealousy*, from *Melencolia I*, for which the just-mentioned earlier works constituted a kind of "organic preparatory step." *Melencolia I* was thus, for Warburg, the "*Temperamentsbild* of Dürer's maturity," which, in contrast to the early images, carried within itself the "mark of a passionately introverted [*zusammengefasste*] melancholy." As such, the print testified to Dürer's "organic reshaping" (*organische Umformung*) of a conception of antiquity widespread in Italy.[23]

Warburg developed these ideas further in 1909 when he opened the final segment of a comprehensive seven-part lecture series entitled "Einführung in die Kultur der Renaissance" (Introduction to the Civilization of the Renaissance) with representations of the planets.[24] Here he described in even greater detail transformations in the iconography of images of the gods, ending with the recovery of the original ancient forms in the fifteenth century. Subsequently he set out the "migration" of these images from Italian centres of humanistic learning to the North. Dürer's *Melencolia I*, as Warburg noted, was not only the "most important monument of Dürer's German style freed from Italian muscle rhetoric [*Muskelrhetorik*]"[25] but it was also the first image of a planet that does not include a "symbol of the deity." Saturn, the "cannibal," had been replaced by an "inward-turned, humane symbol of the ruminating, self-focused human subject" – a symbol of *Contemplation*.[26]

On one other occasion Warburg broached the topic of Dürer's print – namely, in a lecture with the title "Die Planetenbilder auf der Wanderung von Süd nach Nord und ihre Rückkehr nach Italien" (The Images of the Planets and Their Migration from South to North and Their Return to Italy). He delivered this lecture in 1913 within the framework of a summer course sponsored by the Oberschulbehörde in Hamburg.[27] Here Warburg described in detail the characteristics of the planetary god Saturn, as well as their origins and afterlife.[28] He spoke of the "reformation of the medieval doctrine of Saturnian man" on the part of the "enlightened spirits of humanism [*erleuchtete Geister des Humanismus*] in the North and South," and he introduced Dürer's *Melencolia I* as witness.[29] Warburg's summary of Giehlow's work allowed him to arrive at the thesis that Ficino, by virtue of remaining rooted in natural philosophy, took only the first step toward a revaluation of "inner concentration," which he sought to attain by means of a "cosmophysical" method. According to Warburg, then, "the discovery of the modern subject, who, self-reliant, seeks natural laws in order to interrogate the future scientifically" was to be ascribed to Dürer.[30]

Only a few months earlier, Giehlow had unexpectedly died at the age of forty-nine. He had only just completed his magnum opus, *Die Hieroglyphenkunde des Humanismus in der Allegorie der Renaissance, besonders der Ehrenpforte Kaiser Maximilians I. Ein Versuch.* In this work, he developed the thesis, based on Horapollo's *Hieroglyphica* (which he himself had discovered) that hieroglyphs had a significant influence on sixteenth-century art. Keenly interested in Giehlow's works, Warburg enquired immediately after his death about the fate of his unfinished research. Schwedeler-Meyer informed him that Giehlow's *Nachlass* was to be published in the *Jahrbuch der kunsthistorischen Sammlungen des allerhöchsten Kaiserhauses*[31] – yet ultimately only the *Hieroglyphenkunde* would be published there.[32] Two years later, in 1915, Warburg received an inquiry from art historian Friedrich Dörnhöffer, asking if he might help with the publication of the unpublished *Melencolia* study. Giehlow had set aside the study as early as 1904, but 144 pages of text as well as the illustrations had already been printed. Beyond this, there existed drafted pages as well as a collection of data on index cards.[33] Warburg immediately declared his willingness to help, but then heard nothing back from Vienna – neither from Dörnhöffer nor from Giehlow's literary executor and curator at the Kunsthistorisches Museum in Vienna, Arpád Weixlgärtner, to whom Warburg had also offered his services.[34]

Warburg was determined to see that Giehlow's research became better known. He felt a pressing need to "protect the legacy" and to secure the method and the results of Giehlow's study which, like a "handbook," could serve as an alternative to the "formalism" that dominated research at the time.[35] In 1917 Warburg wrote a letter to the ethnologist Johannes Bolte in which he summarized the contributions of Giehlow to art- and cultural-historical scholarship; there he also indicated his own, new, now politicized reading of the *Melencolia I*:

> I see in Giehlow's work, in its far-reaching and transforming significance, a hitherto insufficiently acknowledged attempt to lead art history back from formalism to a historical positivism, and indeed from a point that makes graspable the otherwise elusive astrocratic [*astrokratisch*] understanding of a history of the European Renaissance permeated by a fear of Saturn. This fear is the core of the doctrine of catastrophe, based on planetary conjunction, whose significance was disseminated from Padua to the rest of Europe (even up to the present day) on the basis of practices and teachings, Hellenistic in origin, transmitted through Arabic learning. The teaching of the coming Reformation was, in part, a doctrine of revolution; that is, revolution taken in the strictest

astrological sense, a teaching concerning the periodic return of the great conjunction. The essence of the danger of these "conjunctions" lies in the struggle between Jupiter, Saturn, and Mars, and depends, too, on the astrological sign in which their struggle takes place. Indeed, we are here dealing with living mythical forces that confront their believers with continuously renewed forces to carry out their Homeric fights (though Hector and Achilles are here replaced by Saturn and Jupiter). The main question in all prognostications is whether the benign Jupiter is subdued by the malign Saturn. Dürer's melancholy genius is precisely the individual who tries to fight his Saturnian fate and does so in a twofold manner: through rational self-reflection and activity, on the one hand, and by using the help of magic, in this case Jupiter's magic square, on the other. According to Ficino's spiritual doctrine of healing, the black bile of manic melancholy is converted into benevolent white bile, which transforms itself from the Saturnian sin of acedia into the modern genius of discovery. Dürer's print is thus for me one of the chief monuments of German Reformation inasmuch as here ancient fatalism was reshaped into an ideal of free labor. I am here only indicating in general terms what I would soon like to demonstrate in a broader context, taking as my starting point the body of evidence analyzed by Giehlow.[36]

In January 1916 Weixlgärtner had announced that he himself was now planning to prepare Giehlow's study for publication via the Gesellschaft für vervielfältigende Kunst.[37] When nothing had materialized by July 1918, he tried to calm an impatient Warburg, saying that only after the war could he devote himself to the task. But Warburg then fell ill and, beginning in November 1918, had to undergo psychiatric treatment for the aforementioned mental breakdown; at this time, with great effort and Saxl's intensive support, he just succeeded in completing *Heidnisch-antike Weissagung in Wort und Bild zu Luthers Zeiten* ("Pagan-Antique Prophecy in Words and Images in the Age of Luther") for publication. In this lengthy study he praised Dürer's *Melencolia I* in a few pointed sentences: "The truly creative act – that which gives Dürer's *Melencolia I* its consoling humanistic message of liberation from the fear of Saturn – can be understood only if we recognize that the artist has taken a magical and mythical logic and made it spiritual and intellectual." As Warburg put it: "the malignant, child-devouring planetary god" was "humanized and metamorphosed by Dürer into the image of the thinking, working human being." He had found confirmation of this interpretation in the works of Luther's ally, the humanist Melanchthon who, in his *De anima*, characterized Dürer's genius as "the highest type of true melancholy, spiritualized by favorable planetary configuration."[38] At its most basic, however, Warburg had already developed this thesis in 1909, when he characterized the print as a witness to "the transition from medieval to modern man." Finally, he had concluded, "thinking had been liberated from the influence of the stars," and a mathematical understanding of the laws of the cosmos had become possible.[39] According to Warburg, Dürer had found a new form of concentration – the keyword "sophrosyne" (*Besonnenheit*) surfaces in his notes – out of which the "inventor of the technical-mechanical world" would emerge.[40] Even if he had not yet coined the term, Warburg clearly already understood *Melencolia I* as an allegory for the *Denkraum der Besonnenheit* – a space for reflection.

Saxl, Panofsky, Giehlow's *Nachlass*, and Dürer's *Melencolia I*

Saxl first made contact with Weixlgärtner in September 1920, when the final phase of the joint work on Warburg's Luther text was still ongoing. He informed his Viennese colleague that Warburg's interpretation of Dürer's *Melencolia I* was in fact extending Giehlow's results and would allow the placement of Dürer's print within a larger developmental history. Since he, Saxl, was now himself familiar with the material, he would be happy, he said, to contribute, insofar as it was in his power, to the final preparation of Giehlow's manuscript for print. The following November, Saxl reiterated his offer to edit Giehlow's research.[41] Warburg at this point was undergoing therapy as a patient at a clinic in Jena; in 1921 he would be transferred to Kreuzlingen.

In Jena, Warburg learned that Saxl had given a lecture on *Melencolia I* at the Warburg Library on 17 January 1921 as part of Erwin Panofsky's introductory seminar (*Übungen*) on Dürer – one of the joint projects Saxl was seeking to establish with the newly appointed representative of the discipline in Hamburg.[42] "Against my expectations," Saxl wrote, "I actually spoke for an hour on the topic." He had developed his argument on the basis of the concept of "temperament" and had made his way to Empedocles and then to Aristotle and Plato's idea of the "melancholia generosa"; he had gone on to discuss the Nergal-Chronos-Saturn problem and thus showed both how features of Babylonian religion were absorbed into Greek mythology and how the Babylonian deity had taken on features of a Greek philosopher god. Having treated calendar literature, Abu Ma'shar, the decoration of the Palazzo della Ragione in Padua, and the filiation with Saturn, he finally arrived at Dürer's print, where all the lines of interpretation came together:

> [T]ogether with the magically conjured Jupiter, we have now arrived at the amazing insight that lets us see melancholia as "generosa," as the representation of "mens" which, in the Middle Ages, was derived etymologically from measuring – mens mensurando. Taken together with your discovery of Melanchthon's statement on Dürer, the print can thus be viewed as a self-portrait of Dürer's thinking. As you will see, we … have in essence been expanding upon your thoughts throughout. Once the filiation with Saturn had been so clearly set out, as you had done, it became easy to interpret the individual elements and, once the "compass of the genius" had been identified, it was no longer difficult to connect it all back to Dürer's art. Nothing more can be done with the relationship to Maximilian, I'm sure, and we were very cautious in that respect. The connection to Marsilio Ficino, on the other hand, has stood up wonderfully.[43]

Here for the first time, Saxl indicated the direction the interpretation of the print would take in the future. It became obvious that he and Panofsky would distance themselves from Giehlow's central thesis that the genesis of the print was dependent on Emperor Maximilian. In July 1921, Saxl had still not heard back from Weixlgärtner,[44] and yet it had rapidly become clear to them that the reflections resulting from his and Panofsky's collaborative work had to be recorded and published. Their first plan was to submit the piece to the *Wiener Jahrbuch für Kunstgeschichte*.[45]

Only in November could Saxl report to Warburg that he had received Giehlow's unfinished study from Vienna. With no small astonishment, he described the immense collection of material. He noted that the incomplete printed text overlapped substantially, in one part, with Giehlow's previously published essay; however, in another part, Giehlow had put forward the new idea that Dürer's *Melencolia I* was to be construed as hieroglyphic – an approach that Saxl found wholly unpersuasive. He added: "I do, for better or worse, somehow want to bring the whole thing to completion, naturally with the reservation that I cannot pursue the hieroglyphic route." In the same letter, he made clear his intention to complete the book with Panofsky and, addressing Warburg directly, wrote: "I hope I can, with this work, bring you some pleasure, since you've always very much wanted to see Giehlow's research published. Indeed, what you deem to be right has again and again served me as a guideline."[46]

In early January 1922, Saxl first informed Giehlow's executor of the progress of his and Panofsky's work, saying it would likely be completed by February. Diplomatically he explained that, if Giehlow had been unable to complete his study, this was because it had proved impossible to sustain a hieroglyphic interpretation of the print. Nonetheless, the two Hamburg scholars had first pursued the plan to publish Giehlow's already printed text in full and to provide an additional text, putting forward their own interpretation, which would complement Giehlow's.[47] In late January, however, they received the news that Giehlow's printed chapters had mistakenly been pulped by the Austrian Hof- und Staatsdruckerei. Shortly afterward Panofsky and Saxl suggested that the idea of a reprint be abandoned; the expense, they said, could not be justified by the content of the work.

The debacle in Vienna was in fact, for the two scholars, a welcome turn of events. They proposed to Weixlgärtner that they would publish in the series *Studien der Bibliothek Warburg* "everything new that Giehlow added to his old essay" and supplement this with their own appendix. They reminded Weixlgärtner that Giehlow himself had never quite found the courage to publish his work.[48] About this time it seems to have been decided that Panofsky's newly prepared "manuscript" would become the main text of the book. This text was completed by 5 October 1922. Shortly thereafter, Weixlgärtner reached an agreement with the Austrian Staatsdruckerei whereby the press would take over the preparation of the plates as compensation for having destroyed the existing text.[49] Not least because of the distribution of tasks between the printer in Vienna and the publisher in Leipzig, which needed to be coordinated, as well as many other delays originating in Vienna, the production of the volume took a further fourteen months. At the very end there came a discussion over Weixlgärtner's account of the genesis of the text as put forward in his preface. Panofsky made the point that the Hamburg text had already been conceived by the time the scholars gained access to Giehlow's printed chapters, manuscript pages, and notes. Panofsky and Saxl wanted this to be noted.[50] This insistence may be seen as their attempt to dissociate themselves from Giehlow's central thesis without in any way damaging the reputation of the scholar. His preparatory work would ultimately find its way into their book principally in the form of footnotes.

Toward a Second Edition

Probably because their book took shape as the result of compromise and was rapidly written, but also because it was quickly sold out, Saxl and Panofsky began to consider preparing a revised and expanded edition as early as October 1926 – just two and a half years after its initial appearance. At this time, the young historian of philosophy Raymond Klibansky, who was studying for two semesters with Ernst Cassirer in Hamburg, had become a regular at the Kulturwissenschaftliche Bibliothek Warburg (KBW).[51] Saxl immediately recognized Klibansky's extraordinary learning and talent. Though, in 1927, just embarking on his doctoral dissertation,[52] he was already becoming involved in the preparation of a complete edition of Nicholas of Cusa's works, sponsored by the Heidelberger Akademie der Wissenschaften. At the KBW, where he was helping the staff decide on acquisitions and establish the order of books on the shelves, he was apparently asked to comment on the KBW's policies and initiatives. In one of these discussions, as Klibansky later recalled, he criticized Panofsky and Saxl's volume, suggesting that it did not sufficiently take into account the philosophical and theological roots of the concepts treated within.[53] The authors agreed and invited him to collaborate with them on the new edition, particularly on the chapters he had found in need of improvement. As it turned out, their decision to involve Klibansky had major consequences: it effectively relocated the emphasis of the study. Originally conceived by Panofsky, the specialist on Dürer, as an interpretation of the print *Melencolia I*, the book would eventually become a seminal study on the concept of melancholy within the history of ideas.

On 30 November 1927, several months after Klibansky's return to the University of Heidelberg, his home university, Panofsky and Saxl discussed the outline of the revised book. They decided to add an entirely new chapter on melancholy in ancient Greek tragedy, philosophy, and medicine before Aristotle, feeling that the philosopher's approach to the concept could only be defined in relation to this tradition. More emphasis would also be laid on the different medieval currents: the reception of a secular-Greek tradition, a distinctively spiritual-Christian tradition, and a scholastic-medical tradition that was independent from the ancient Greek roots of the concept. Finally, the two authors decided to rewrite the chapter on Ficino, treating three different aspects of his notion of melancholia separately: his thinking in relation to the writings of Arnaldus de Villanova; the role of *Problema* XXX.1 in his thought; and the content of Ficino's own commentaries on Plotinus. Moreover, a large number of new illustrations had meanwhile come to light, awaiting interpretation.[54] The distribution of tasks remained the same as before: Saxl was responsible for collecting sources, especially on the so far slim corpus relating to the astrological aspects of the topic; Panofsky, to ensure coherence, would turn everything into running text. In addition, the two authors asked Klibansky to sketch passages relating to his field of expertise, but, above all, to supply references to ancient and medieval sources on the phenomenon of melancholy.[55] Apparently another of Klibansky's tasks was to search the authors mentioned in the first edition for possible references to Saturn. They wanted to give this aspect more prominence in the reworked version of the study.

Initially the collaboration was intense and the production quick; 1928 was the most prolific year in the process of rewriting the study. Already on 12 January Saxl was able to report to Klibansky that, with the help of the latter's notes, Panofsky had written "the whole prehistory up to Aristotle" from scratch. Confident of rapid progress, Saxl promised Klibansky the opportunity to check the results before they went into print. At the same time he lamented the lack of material regarding the prehistory of astrology.[56] The book had at this stage become a proper collaborative venture. Keen to involve Walter Solmitz, Cassirer's doctoral student who, too, was closely associated with the KBW, Panofsky had asked his help with a thorny issue, the attribution of the idea of an association between melancholy and genius (as explained in *Problema* XXX.1) to Aristotle, and its relation to Plato's doctrine of *mania*.[57] Panofsky finally settled on assigning the concept to Aristotle's closest circle.

Four months later the first chapter of seventy pages (from the Pythagoreans to Bede) was close to completion. In a letter of 25 April 1928, sent to Saxl in London, Panofsky summarized those results that reached beyond the 1923 study, mainly the attribution of *Problema* XXX, 1, and a discussion of the ancient origin of the doctrine of the Four Temperaments. By then the chapter on Saturn was in progress, but was proving difficult. Evidence for the moment when melancholy was first associated with Saturn (and the temperaments with the planets) remained impossible to find.[58]

In June 1928 Saxl finally received from Panofsky the first chapter, together with apologies for the lengthy excursus on the history of medicine; Panofsky believed it was essential to the interpretation of Dürer's print. He had by then moved on to the Middle Ages. After some research, he became convinced that it was possible to identify four types of sources that existed before the renewal of the concept in the fourteenth and fifteenth century: texts written by medical doctors; by scholars who interpreted the doctrine of the Four Temperaments, whether in terms of physiognomy, or of character and morals; and finally by theologians. A related question was that of the date of the first traceable illustration of these temperaments. Panofsky, to Saxl, ventured the new idea that Dürer's *Four Apostles* (Alte Pinakothek, Munich) represented the Four Temperaments, and he added some "wild ideas" about the meaning of the "I" in *Melencolia I*.[59] Saxl replied with praise for their collaborative gathering of knowledge to answer "a really central cultural-historical question" (*eine kulturgeschichtlich doch wirklich zentrale Frage*). He, in turn, discussed a possible iconographical relation between the Four Temperaments and the Virtues and Vices.[60] Later the same month Panofsky commended Saxl for finding a twelfth-century manuscript that seemed to mark the beginning of the history of pictorial types of the Four Temperaments. Clearly, the ancient depiction of both the seasons and the ages of man played a role, in combination with the iconography of the vices, but it was necessary to find more examples.[61] Klibansky's help was requested once again, and Saxl pushed him gently to produce notes similar to those relating to melancholy in antiquity. When these notes finally arrived by mid-December, Saxl thanked him and reported that Panofsky was as touched as he was by Klibansky's "friendship" for the project (and for them). Saxl had, at this stage, become more involved in the writing process. Commenting on the second part, about which he knew more, he said he thought it a commendable achievement on Panofsky's part; the result, he acknowledged, was dry and rather lacking in terms of style, but he did not wish to press Panofsky too much, for that might again result in "too many constructions" (*zuviele Konstruktionen*), that is, too many hypotheses. This comment, addressed to Klibansky, offers a remarkable insight into the existing discrepancy between Panofsky's and Saxl's approach to the subject (and their discipline in general) compared with the affinity between the latter's and Klibansky's.[62] Along the same lines Saxl reiterated the problems he was encountering when trying to produce the central chapter on Saturn, impossible for either of the authors to write without Klibansky's help.[63] The only solution seemed to be to meet in Heidelberg (where Klibansky was involved in finishing up his doctorate) and to work together on this chapter:

> May I tell you how things stand with Saturn? As you know, Panofsky has now written the chapter, which you know, on the history of melancholy in antiquity, and, as a counterpart, we should provide a history of the ideas relating to Saturn. Yet we are struggling to find material. We are in fact only interested in that part of the documentation that leads to the astrological concept, and that material is extraordinarily late and sparse. It seems, now, that the decisive turn toward the good in the character of the god can be followed in the works of both Orphic and Neoplatonic thinkers. But all these are so far only very indefinite ideas, and we want to develop them into a proper history which identifies the key moments, not a sketch that intentionally leaves matters vague (as has been the case). Beyond this we have no proper collection of materials for the Middle Ages. For both we would be glad of your help. I enclose what we already have on Saturn.[64]

The proposed meeting between Saxl and Klibansky did indeed take place – in mid-June 1929 – and the collaboration turned out to be decisive for the mutual esteem and friendship the two scholars shared and (presumably) even for Klibansky's future affiliation with the Warburg Institute. A few weeks later, upon his return from a long trip following his stay in Heidelberg, a most grateful, deeply touched Saxl wrote: "Raymond, I hope wholeheartedly that in our future lives we can be and work together. And I shall hope that in this connection some uncertainties in your life might be settled and that you may be spared some unnecessary difficulties."[65] After this the working relationship between Saxl and Klibansky grew closer. Their scholarly interests, namely their encyclopaedic engagement with cultural history and the afterlife of ancient thought in the Middle Ages, had always overlapped; yet through intense collaboration Saxl recognized Klibansky's extraordinary aptitude to "pursue philosophical and historical trains of thought," and his talent as an editor.[66]

In August and September 1929, after Klibansky had delivered his broadly sketched "image of Saturn" (*Saturn-Bild*)," and this image had been further developed in direct exchange with Panofsky, the chapter began to take proper shape.[67] Still it was far from finished at the end of the year, and Warburg's death on 26 October 1929 greatly slowed progress. In May 1930, over dinner in Panofsky's home, Panofsky and Klibansky believed they had finally solved the riddle of the original conjuncture of Saturn and melancholy. Klibansky soon summarized the results of their conversation for Saxl, namely the three "sequences of causes (*Ursachen-Reihen*)" they had identified – one relating to physics, another to physiognomy, and a third to the presumed ethical qualities of Saturn. Apparently, at some point in history these various qualities of Saturn were believed to be shared by human beings under the planet's influence and, quintessentially, to correspond to the characteristics of a melancholic personality. They had recognized Ptolemy, in the first century CE, as the first thinker to discern similarities between saturnine men and melancholics.[68]

After this discussion Panofsky went on to finish his chapter on Dürer. Saturn remained pending,[69] and in time completion of this difficult chapter caused significant delays in the preparation and printing of the volume. Other factors contributed to the deferment of its completion: first, the need to incorporate additions that Klibansky sent sporadically to Hamburg; second, the demands of a new project, the *Bibliographie zum Nachleben der Antike* (a project designed to maintain the supply of new publications after painful budget cuts by Aby's brothers in America, Paul and Felix Warburg, in response to the Great Depression);[70] and, third, the temporary departure of Panofsky to teach at New York University in the winter semester of 1931–32. Just before Panofsky left Hamburg, Klibansky wrote to Saxl lamenting that the manuscript remained incomplete despite the amount of time and effort that had been invested in the new edition.[71] A year after Panofsky's return, with the break-up of the Hamburg circle in 1933, Panofsky's permanent move to the United States, and the Warburg Library's transfer to London, the problems multiplied. The last effort before the various departures, made by Panofsky in May and June 1933, involved on the one hand making cuts to the text in response to the approaching deadline – the end of 1933 – and to the meagre funds available for printing; and, on the other hand, revising the chapter on Ficino. By then Panofsky called the project a never-ending incubus.[72]

By the time war broke out, all the corrections and the typesetting of a second German edition had finally been completed in London in the summer of 1939. As described by Klibansky, the typeset plates, produced by J.J. Augustin in Glückstadt, were subsequently confiscated and destroyed during the war, leaving only the galley proofs.[73]

When Saxl died, only three years after the end of the war, Klibansky took over the responsibility for a project that now held little interest for Panofsky. Ultimately the original plan to move swiftly to the revised edition went fully unrealized. Only in 1964, thirty-eight years later, would the constantly expanding volume, which steadily moved further and further away from Dürer's print, be published in English, under the new title *Saturn and Melancholy: Studies in the History of Natural Philosophy, Religion, and Art*. This study, significant in its own right, had, after all, fairly little relation to Panofsky and Saxl's *Dürers 'Melencolia I'. Eine quellen-und typengeschichtliche Untersuchung*. Yet the original continued and continues to hold a place in the history of art history. In both content and method, the study did much to further the reorientation of the discipline, initiated by Giehlow and decisively influenced by Warburg. Not only with respect to the interpretation of Dürer's *Melencolia I* did the latter follow Giehlow, but also in his greatest scholarly success: the reinterpretation of the cosmological program of the *Sala dei Mesi* in Ferrara's Palazzo Schifanoia. The idea of "unveiling" (*Entschälen*) an ancient archetype through his new analytical method,[74] and, in particular, the introduction of the idea of the humanist adviser at Renaissance courts having an impact on imagery, hark back in spirit to Giehlow.[75]

From these beginnings, Panofsky and Saxl developed the idea of combining a morphological and historical approach, expressed in their use of the term *typengeschichtlich* in the subtitle of their original study.[76] Indeed, Panofsky's analysis of Dürer's master print can be considered the first of its kind in the history of the discipline – an analysis whose method soon would come to be described as "iconographic-iconological."[77]

ACKNOWELDGMENTS

A slightly different, shorter version of this essay is published in Italian as an introduction to Panofsky and Saxl, *La 'Melencolia I' di Dürer*, 9–25. Sincere thanks to Elizabeth Sears for her attentive reading, which substantially improved this essay, and her revisions of the translation. I am also most grateful to Caroline Bem for translating the larger part of this text. Unless otherwise marked, translations of quotations by Warburg, Panofsky, Saxl, and Klibansky are our own.

NOTES

1 Warburg Institute Archive (hereafter WIA), Family Correspondence (hereafter FC): Aby Warburg to Mary Warburg, 18 February 1923.

2 WIA, General Correspondence (hereafter GC): Fritz Saxl to Aby Warburg, 23 February 1923.

3 WIA, GC: Erwin Panofsky to Arpád Weixlgärtner, 28 March 1928.

4 WIA, FC: Aby Warburg to Mary Warburg, 4 February 1924; Aby Warburg to Erwin Panofsky and Fritz Saxl, 19 February 1923; Warburg to Saxl, 24 February 1923; 18 February 1924. Cf. Wedepohl, "Warburg, Saxl, Panofsky and Dürer's *Melencolia I*."

5 WIA, GC: Warburg to Panofsky and Saxl, 19 February 1923 (published in Panofsky, *Korrespondenz 1910 bis 1968*, 1: 122–3).

6 Panofsky and Saxl, *Dürers 'Melencolia I,'* 93–104; Klibansky, Panofsky, and Saxl, *Saturn and Melancholy*, 15–41; Flashar, *Melancholie und Melancholiker in den medizinischen Theorien der Antike*, 60–72; van der Eijk, *Aristoteles über die Melancholie*, 55–61; van der Eijk, *Medicine and Philosophy in Classical Antiquity*, 155–60.

7 Johann Carl Friedrich Giehlow (1863–1913), who published under the name Karl Giehlow, was a trained lawyer who gave up a position as *Regierungsassessor* in Berlin to study philosophy and art history. From 1898 he worked as an independent scholar in Vienna. Cf. Schwedeler-Meyer, "Karl Giehlow †"; Weixlgärtner, "Zum Geleit"; Mrazek, s.v. "Giehlow, Johann Carl Friedrich"; Susanne Müller, "Introduzione," in Giehlow, *Hieroglyphica – La conoscenza umanistica*.

8 Giehlow, "Dürers Stich Melencolia I und der maximilianische Humanistenkreis," published in three parts, 2: 29–41 (an appraisal by Conrad Peutinger pertaining to the melancholia of Hercules Aegypticus); 4: 6–18 (treating Konrad Celtis's attitude toward Ficino's study of the melancholic temperament) and 57–78 (dealing with Maximilian's position in relation to the new theories on the nature of melancholia); Schuster, *Melencolia I. Dürers Denkbild*, 1: 32.

9 Panofsky and Saxl, *Dürers 'Melencolia I'*, 1. The accuracy of this statement is questioned by Davide Stimilli. See chapter 11 in this volume.

10 Austrian National Library, Vienna, Cvp 3344, fols. 1r–9r; Giehlow, "Dürers Stich Melencolia I," 2: 29–41; Peutinger, *Briefwechsel*, 240–2; Ott, *Die Entdeckung des Altertums*, 75.

11 Panofsky and Saxl, *Dürers 'Melencolia I'*, 32–48; Klibansky, Panofsky, and Saxl, *Saturn and Melancholy*, 254–74.

12 Giehlow, "Dürers Stich Melencolia I," 2: 41.

13 Warnke, "Aby Warburg (1866–1929)," 122. However, Warnke writes of a "modern iconography" (my translation).

14 Schwedeler-Meyer, "Karl Giehlow †": "He wanted to establish which artistic and literary influences were at work here [in Dürer's drawings] and so he searched through the art of the Renaissance and the literature of humanism, often arriving at important and surprising discoveries, a part of which, however, is unfortunately still waiting to be published … Among his peers, there is only one who, in a similar fashion, sought to solve a problem pertaining to the Italian Renaissance in the same way Giehlow sought to do for the German Renaissance" (my translation).

15 Wölfflin, *Die Kunst Albrecht Dürers*, 237–42.

16 WIA, FC: Mary Warburg to Aby Warburg, 8 May 1908; Aby Warburg to Mary Warburg, 9 May 1908; WIA, GC: Karl Giehlow to Warburg, 22 June 1908.

17 WIA, FC: Aby Warburg to Mary Warburg, 9 May 1908.

18 WIA, III.73.1.1.2: The summary of this presentation, which is largely composed of key words, can be found in Warburg's *Gesammelte Schriften* (hereafter GS), 2: 454. See also the images on Panel 59 in Warburg, *Der Bilderatlas Mnemosyne*, 108–9.

19 WIA, III.73.1.2.3, fols. 4, 6. Cf. GS II, 526–29.

20 WIA, III.75.6.1, fol. 40.

21 Warburg delivered the lecture "Dürer und die italienische Antike" on 5 October 1905 at the annual meeting of German philologists and teachers. The text (WIA, III.61.6) has so far remained unpublished and will appear in vol. III.2 (*Kleine Schriften und Vorträge*) of the *Studienausgabe* of Warburg's collected writings. GS 2: 443–9 contains a summary with same title, written by Warburg and first published in the *Verhandlungen der 48. Versammlung deutscher Philologen und Schulmänner*, 1906, 55ss.

22 WIA, III.61.6, fol. 39.

23 Ibid., fols. 36v, 44, 46.

24 WIA, III.75.7.2 (published in Warburg, *Il primo Rinascimento italiano*, 367–437).

25 GS 2: 454. See also: WIA, III.75.7.2, fol. 56.

26 WIA, III.75.7.2, fols. 50–1.

27 WIA, III.87.1.2, delivered on 6 August 1913.

28 Ibid., fols. 33–47 (published in Treml, Weigel, Ladwig, *Werke in einem Band*, 359–65).

29 WIA, III.87.1.2, fol. 48 (published in Treml, Weigel, Ladwig, *Werke in einem Band*, 366).

30 WIA, III.87.1.2, fol. 51, 57 (published in Treml, Weigel, Ladwig, *Werke in einem Band*, 367, 369).

31 WIA, GC: Ernst Schwedeler-Meyer to Warburg, 10 April and 17 December 1913.

32 Published as Vol. 32 (1915), ed. Weixlgärtner.

33 Weixlgärtner, "Zum Geleite," IX.

34 WIA, GC: Warburg to Arpád Weixlgärtner, 23 March 1915.

35 WIA, GC: Warburg to Friedrich Dörnhöffer, 4 October 1915; Warburg to Schwedeler-Meyer, 18 October 1915.

36 WIA, GC: Warburg to Johannes Bolte, 29 May 1917: "Ich halte Giehlows Arbeit überhaupt für einen bisher in seiner einschneidenden und umformenden Bedeutung nicht genug gewürdigten Versuch, die Kunstgeschichte aus dem

Formalismus zu geschichtlichem Positivismus zurückzuführen und zwar von einem Punkte, von dem aus die sich so schwer begreifbare astrokratische Geschichtsauffassung der europäischen Renaissance in ihrer Saturnfürchtigkeit erfassen lässt. Diese ist das eigentliche Kernstück der Katastrophenlehre durch Gestirnkonjunktion, deren Bedeutung von Padua aus auf Grund der hellenisierende Praktiken und Lehren vermittelnden arabischen Gelehrsamkeit Europa (bis auf den heutigen Tag) vermittelt wurde. Die Lehre von der kommenden Reformation ist z.T. eine Revolutionslehre, d.h. Revolution auch im wirklichen astrologischen Sinne genommen, eine Lehre vom periodischen Umlauf der gefährlichen grossen Gestirnskonjunktion. Das Wesen der Gefahr in diesen ‚Zusammenfügungen' besteht in einem Kampfe zwischen Jupiter, Saturn und Mars, wobei es auch darauf ankommt, in welchem Tierkreiszeichen sie ihre Kämpfe ausführen. Wir haben es tatsächlich mit lebendigen mythischen Gewalten zu tun, die in immer neuer Lebenskraft den Gläubigen vor Augen stehen und am Himmel ihre homerischen Kräfte ausfechten, Hector und Achill sind freilich an dieser Stelle Saturn und Jupiter. In allen Prognostiken finden Sie ja als Hauptfrage, ob der gütige Jupiter durch den bösen Saturn ‚unterdrückt wird', und Dürers Genius der Melancholie ist eben der Mensch, der gegen sein saturnisches Schicksal auf zweierlei Weise anzukämpfen versucht, einerseits durch vernunftgemässe Selbstbesinnung und Betätigung und andererseits durch magische Mithilfe, d.h. durch das Planetenzahlenamulett des Jupiter. Die schwarze Galle der manischen Melancholie wird, der geistigen Heilslehre Ficinos entsprechend, in die wohltätige weisse verwandelt, die aus der saturnischen Sünde der Accedia zum modernen Erfindergenie sich umformt. Dürers Kupferstich scheint mir deshalb eines der Hauptdenkmäler deutscher Reformation; der antike Fatalismus formt sich um zum Ideal der freien Arbeit. Ich deute Ihnen hier nur in allgemeinen Zügen an, was ich auf Grund von Giehlows erforschtem Beweismaterial in grösserem Zusammenhang in absehbarer Zeit vorlegen möchte."

37 WIA, GC: Weixlgärtner to Warburg, 12 January 1916; III.2.1, ZK 31, no 031/017213.

38 GS 2: 528–9; trans. by David Britt in Warburg, "Pagan-Antique Prophecy in Words and Images in the Age of Luther," 644.

39 WIA, III.75.7.2, fols. 52, 56.

40 Ibid., fol. 62.

41 WIA, GC: Saxl to Weixlgärtner, 30 September and 23 November 1920.

42 When transforming the KBW from a *Privatbibliothek* to a proper research institute, subsequent to the foundation of the University of Hamburg in 1919, Saxl had envisaged a close collaboration with the new art history department; this was provisionally established in the basement of the Hamburger Kunsthalle. Assuming that the KBW would be the department's main resource, Saxl was convinced that any future Chair should be familiar with Warburg's approach. Supported by Gustav Pauli, director of the Kunsthalle, on 31 December 1919, Erwin Panofsky was appointed to fill the post of *Privatdozent* without salary but with the promise of a professorship after a successful *Habilitation*; in January 1926 he was finally granted a full professorship. As a member of Adolph Goldschmidt's *Seminar* in Berlin, Panofsky had been introduced to Warburg's method during a visit on 27 December 1915. See WIA, I.8.2, fol. 7 (Saxls "Bericht über die Bibliothek Warburg und ihre Entwicklung zu einem öffentlichen Forschungsinstitut") and III.88.7.1–2; Bredekamp, "Ex nihilo. Panofskys Habilitation," 31–47; Wuttke, "Einleitung," in Panofsky, *Korrespondenz 1910 bis 1968*, 1: XIX.

43 WIA, GC: Saxl to Warburg, 21 January 1921: "[N]un kommt die wunderbare Erkenntnis mit dem magisch herangerufenen Jupiter, die uns die Melancholie als die ‚generosa' erkennen lässt, als die Repräsentation der *mens*, die ja im Mittelalter etymologisch von Messen – mens mensurando – hergeleitet wird. Und so zusammengehalten mit Ihrem Fundstück, der Äußerung Melanchthons über Dürer, lässt sich in dem Blatt ein Selbstporträt von Dürers Denken erblicken. Sie sehen, dass wir ... überall eigentlich Ihre Gedanken weitergesponnen haben. War einmal die Saturnkindschaft so klar dargestellt, wie dies bei Ihnen der Fall war, dann war es ein Leichtes, die einzelnen Dinge zu deuten, und war einmal der ‚Zirkel des Genies' erkannt, so war es nicht mehr schwer, das Ganze auf Dürers Kunst zu beziehen. Dass mit der Beziehung zu Maximilian nichts mehr zu machen sein wird, halte ich für sicher. Wir waren ja auch diesbezüglich sehr vorsichtig. Ausgezeichnet bewährt sich dagegen die Beziehung auf Marsiglio Ficino."

44 Warburg also attempted to establish contacts with other colleagues, see WIA, GC: Saxl to Hans Tietze, 22 June 1921; Erich Petzet to Saxl, 28 July 1922.

45 Weixlgärtner, "Zum Geleite," IX–X.

46 WIA, GC: Saxl to Warburg, 21 November 1921; Saxl to Ludwig Volkmann, 31 October 1922.

47 WIA, GC: Saxl to Weixlgärtner, 7 January 1922.

48 WIA, GC: Weixlgärtner to Saxl, 29 January 1922; Saxl to Weixlgärtner, 7 March 1922.

49 WIA, GC: Saxl to Weixlgärtner, 5 October 1922; Weixlgärtner to Panofsky, 20 November 1922; Panofsky to Weixlgärtner, 12 March 1923.

50 WIA, GC: Panofsky to Weixlgärtner, 18 May 1923 (published in Panofsky, *Korrespondenz 1910 bis 1968*, 1: 124–5).

51 See entries between 25 August 1926 and 4 April 1927 in Warburg, *Tagebuch*, 5, 8, 10, 27–9, 43, 54, 57, 62, 63, 68, 71, 77; WIA, GC: Saxl to Raymond Klibansky, 28 September 1929 (containing a reference, written a few days earlier and sent to Marianne Weber: "Dr. Klibansky hat während seiner Studienzeit für die Bibliothek Warburg gearbeitet und zwar als Mitarbeiter am systematischen Katalog. Bei dieser Arbeit, die ja über die Kräfte eines gewöhnlichen Studenten bei weitem hinausgeht, konnte ich einmal wahrnehmen, welche besondere Gabe in ihm ist, sich aufs Rascheste in weite wissenschaftliche Gebiete, die ihm unbekannt waren, einzuarbeiten und ferner welchen erstaunlichen Umfang schon das Wissen des Studenten sowohl auf dem Gebiet der Philosophie-Geschichte, als der Philologie hatte. Dazu kam, dass er dabei eine mehr als durchschnittliche Fähigkeit bewies, schwierige Systemisierungsprobleme, die sich bei der Klassifizierung von Büchern doch regelmässig ergeben, scharf und rasch durchzudenken.") Klibansky's proper integration into the Hamburg circle began with the publication of Cassirer's study *Individuum und Kosmos*. Cassirer dedicated the work, based on his inaugural lecture for the opening of the new library building on 1 May 1926 (titled "Freiheit und Notwendigkeit in der Philosophie der Renaissance"), to Warburg on his sixtieth birthday (13 June 1926). The volume later appeared in print with an appendix containing an edition of the *Liber de sapiente* by the sixteenth-century French humanist and mathematician Carolus Bovillus (Charles de Bovelles); the twenty-year-old Klibansky had prepared both text and index.

52 Klibansky handed in his doctoral dissertation (entitled "Ein Proklos-Fund und seine Bedeutung") in 1929. Klibansky's *Doktorvater*, Ernst Hoffmann, was a friend of both Ernst Cassirer and Aby Warburg.

53 "I took the liberty of criticizing the volume since I felt it did not take sufficient account of the philosophical and theological roots of the various concepts of melancholy. I was surprised to see that they found my objections justified and

asked me to phrase them. This led to the idea to write a new book" (my translation) Klibansky, *Le Philosophe et la mémoire du siècle,* 35. Cf. Weber, "Aktivitäten der Warburg-Bibliothek," 104. For a critical evaluation of the work see also Heidt, *Erwin Panofsky: Kunsttheorie und Einzelwerk,* 200–26.

54 Warburg, *Tagebuch*, 152.

55 Some of Klibansky's notes, *Noten*, and slips of paper, *Zettel*, are extant in the Warburg Institute Archive in the collection of papers and proofs relating to the project.

56 Warburg, *Tagebuch*, 176, 178; WIA, GC: Saxl to Klibansky, 12 January 1928. Cf. Saxl's entry of 2 January in the journal of the Warburg Library, Warburg, *Tagebuch*, 176. Klibansky, in turn, suggested a meeting to discuss this problem in person, see WIA, GC: Klibansky to Saxl, 8 February 1928.

57 WIA, GC: Panofsky to Saxl, 12 and 20 March 1928 (Panofsky, *Korrespondenz 1910 bis 1968*, 1: 260–1); Warburg, *Tagebuch*, 227. For Walter Solmitz's contribution see Elizabeth Sears's essay, chapter 1, in this volume.

58 WIA, GC: Saxl to Klibansky, 7 February 1928; Panofsky to Saxl, 25 April 1928 (Panofsky, *Korrespondenz 1910 bis 1968*, 1: 270).

59 WIA, GC: Panofsky to Saxl, 5 May 1928 (Ibid., 273–5) and 6 June 1928.

60 WIA, GC: Saxl to Panofsky, 17 June 1928 (Ibid., 283–5).

61 WIA, GC: Panofsky to Saxl, 21 June 1928 (Ibid., 289–93).

62 Cf. note 65.

63 WIA, GC: Saxl to Klibansky, 5 and 13 December 1928.

64 Deutsches Literaturarchiv Marbach, A: Klibansky (hereafter DLA, A, KLIBANSKY), XX–XXI, 3: Saxl to Klibansky, 23 and 31 May 1929: "Darf ich Ihnen sagen, worum es sich mit Saturn handelt. Panofsky hat nun das Kapitel, das Sie ja kennen, über die Geschichte der Melancholie im Altertum geschrieben und als Parallel dazu sollte eine Geschichte der Saturn-Vorstellungen geschrieben werden. Aber wir finden dazu nur sehr schwer das Material. Uns geht ja doch nur jener Ausschnitt aus dem Material an, der zur astrologischen Vorstellung hinführt und das Material hierfür ist ausserordentlich spät und spärlich. Nun scheint ja die entscheidende Wendung zum Guten im Charakter des Gottes bei der Orphik und den Neuplatonikern erfolgt zu sein, aber alles das sind vorläufig sehr undeutliche Dinge und wir möchten es doch gerne zu einer richtigen Geschichte, die die wesentlichen Punkte bezeichnen kann, ausbauen, nicht aber zu einer absichtlich unscharf gelassenen Skizze (wie es bisher war).

Hinzu kommt, dass wir auch eigentlich für das Mittelalter keine richtigen guten Sammlungen des Materials besitzen. Für Beides möchten wir gerne Ihre Hilfe. Was wir von Saturn bereits haben, schicke ich Ihnen gleichzeitig."

65 DLA, A, KLIBANSKY: Saxl to Klibansky, 4 September 1929: "Raymond, ich hoffe von ganzem Herzen, daß wir auch im weiteren Leben zusammen sein und zusammenarbeiten werden können. Und ich möchte hoffen, daß damit im Zusammenhang sich manches Unsichere in Ihrem Leben befestigt, manches überflüssig Schwere erspart wird."

66 WIA, GC: Saxl to Klibansky, 28 September 1929 (containing a reference, written a few days earlier and sent to Marianne Weber: "Dr. Klibansky hat … mit meinem Freunde Panofsky und mir an dem Problem der Geschichte des Melancholiebegriffes gearbeitet. Seine Arbeitsintensität, wie seine Fähigkeit, philosophie- und religionsgeschichtlichen Gedankengängen nachzugehen, seine natürliche Skepsis gegen alle auf zu schmaler Basis errichteten wissenschaftlichen Gebäude hat uns seine Mitarbeit höchst wertvoll gemacht. Wenn die demnächst erscheinende 2. Auflage unseres Buches zum ersten Mal eine Geschichte des Melancholiebegriffes in der Antike zu geben in der Lage sein wird, verdanken Professor Panofsky und ich das nicht zuletzt dem damaligen Studenten Klibansky.") Cf. Saxl's reference for the Academic Assistance Council (AAC), dated November 1934: "Dr Raymond Klibansky came to Hamburg in 1925 when he was about nineteen years old. Since that time I have always been in contact with him. He already held an exceptional place among his colleagues as a student, as the range of his knowledge and the strength of his criticism at that time were already impressive."

67 WIA, GC: Klibansky to Saxl, 10 August and 26 December 1929.

68 WIA, GC: Klibansky to Panofsky, 8 May 1930.

69 WIA, GC: Klibansky to Saxl, 18 June 1930; DLA, A, KLIBANSKY: Saxl to Klibansky, 22 July 1930.

70 See Burkart, "'Die Träumereien einiger kunstliebender Klosterbrüder,'" 89–119.

71 WIA, GC: Klibansky to Saxl, 2 and 19 September 1931.

72 WIA, GC: Panofsky to Saxl, 25 May, 6 June (cf. Panofsky, *Korrespondenz 1910 bis 1968*, 1:610, 613), 14 July and 15 October 1933.

73 Klibansky, *Le Philosophe et la mémoire du siècle*, 150–1.

74 See, for example, the passage "[F]or, in all this work of critical iconology, we can unveil the Greek archetype only by stripping away layer upon layer of un-

intelligible accretions." GS 2, 467; trans. by David Britt in Warburg, "Pagan-Antique Prophecy," 569. Cf. Giehlow, "Dürers Stich Melencolia I," 2: 34.

75 For his part, Giehlow was aware of Warburg's work. In his last letter to Warburg, he asked whether the latter's highly acclaimed lecture was going to be published. WIA, GC, Giehlow to Warburg, 26 October 1912.

76 Heidt, *Erwin Panofsky*, 238–45, 249–51.

77 Dieter Wuttke observed that in his early texts Panofsky used not only the terms *Typenkunde* and *Typengeschichte* but also "iconography" and "iconology" more or less synonymously. Wuttke, "Einleitung," in Panofsky, *Korrespondenz 1910 bis 1968*, 1: XXII. In 1932, when Panofsky explained his new method of iconography and iconology, he stressed the function of the history of types (*Typengeschichte*) as corrective. Panofsky, "Zum Problem der Beschreibung und Inhaltsdeutung von Werken der bildenden Kunst."

TEN

Melancholie und Saturn: A Long-Term Collective Project of the Warburg Library

PHILIPPE DESPOIX

The Melencolia *is a cursed business*
from beginning to end.[1]

In his preface to the monumental *Saturn and Melancholy* published in 1964, which he co-signed with Erwin Panofsky, Raymond Klibansky writes: "From the remote times when events in the world of man were first held to be linked with the stars, Saturn was thought to retard any undertaking connected with him. No doubt the ancients would have found ample evidence of his sluggish influence in the fate of this book."[2] Klibansky is alluding here to the long postponement of what was originally supposed to be the second and enlarged edition of *Dürers 'Melencolia I'* co-authored in 1923 by Panofsky and Fritz Saxl. This delay of more than a third of a century encapsulates not only the history of a long collective labour but also the vicissitudes that the Warburg Library experienced until after the Second World War – the rise of Nazism and the move to London, war, exile, and the dispersal of a number of the library's collaborators.

We now know that there was in fact a *double* postponement of a project that began in 1913 when Warburg learned of the death of Karl Giehlow, whose pioneering study "Dürers Stich Melencolia I und der maximilianische Humanistenkreis" ("Dürer's Engraving 'Melencolia I' and Maxmilian's Humanist Circle [1903–04)]") he admired. Giehlow had been the first to explore the relationship between this work and the intellectuals who mediated between the German artist and Florentine Neoplatonic conceptions of melancholy. Following Giehlow's death, Warburg enquired about the state of the former's work on Dürer and undertook to buy a part of his collection of reproductions linked to the project.[3] The result was a series of publications culminating, in 1990, with the German edition of *Saturn und Melancholie* that was signed by Klibansky, Panofsky, and Saxl.

Warburg's Impetus: On the Migration of Planetary Images (1913)

During the Akademische Sommerkurse (Academic Summer School) of 1913, a few months after Giehlow's death, Warburg explored the transfers of representations of the heavens from antiquity to the Renaissance, turning his attention specifically to Raphael's frescoes at the Villa Farnese and to Dürer's *Melencolia I*. Relying on Giehlow, Warburg outlined a first detailed analysis of the famous engraving in his slide lecture "Die Planetenbilder auf der Wanderung von Süd nach Nord und ihre Rückkehr nach Italien."[4] The fact that the goal of this lecture was one of oral and visual teaching rather than publication lends Warburg's interpretation an explicit character that is not fully present in his later published essay *Heidnisch-antike Weissagung in Wort und Bild zu Luthers Zeiten* (1920),[5] whose focus on Dürer is slightly different.

Melencolia I (1514) constituted for Warburg a very particular point of crystallization within the "afterlife" of the ancient divinities that had been transmitted by Arab scholars (such as Abu Ma'shar) in the form of planetary demons. For Warburg, it was Dürer's humanization of the terrifying, ambiguous figure of the planetary god Saturn, and the latter's transformation into an emblem of the artist's genius in the modern age, that first revealed traces of a complex transfer arising from Florentine Platonism and the medical writings of Ficino. In order to neutralize the dangerous melancholic effects of a saturnine constitution – affecting particularly scholars – Ficino suggested a number of methods in his *De vita* (1482–89), including hygiene and diet, but also concentration of the mind on a single point in a relation similar to that of the sphere to its own centre. Warburg summarized this state of "inner concentration" depicted by Dürer as follows in his lecture: "The sphere is Ficino's symbol for Melancholy's soul gathered together; this is why it holds the point of the compass in its hand."[6] The compass is not yet used to measure the sphere but is held by one of its points in a way that corresponds to the mind concentrating on its forthcoming task (fig. 10.1). This instrument is no longer a classical attribute of the allegory of Geometry: just like the pose of the head leaning on the fist, the strange holding of the compass reflects for Warburg the dynamic of a potential gesture that is characteristic of inverted energy – the productive side of melancholic genius.

The second register of transfer coined by Warburg in his slide lecture is linked to the tables of numbers on the engraving and belongs to astrological magic (fig. 10.2). Ficino also recommended neutralizing the destructive influx of the planet Saturn by gaining the protection of Jupiter with the help of apotropaic images. As Warburg noted, however: "Ficino only mentions images, not numbers, as an efficient amulet of Jupiter; on the other hand, Agrippa von Nettesheim advises precisely this magic square."[7] This astrological talisman made of sixteen numbers (the sum of which always amounts to thirty-four), evoked in Agrippa's *De occulta philosophia,* is none other than the *mensula Jovis,* which stands for Jupiter's protection. Warburg corrects Giehlow on this point by insisting on its oriental origin, via Arab transmission, and on the protective symbolic conjunction of both planetary gods.[8]

The third dimension highlighted by Warburg refers, this time, to the polyhedron and the rational aspect of numbers, to the *De divina proportione* of the great mathematician Luca Pacioli. This book appears in a painting attributed to Jacopo de' Barbari, who had been in direct contact with Dürer (fig. 10.3).[9] The scholar finds implicit connections between the two artworks by means of precise details: the dodecahedron on the table in Barbari's painting – one of the five Platonic solids depicted in Pacioli's book – and the portable inkwell in the foreground of the Italian painting, which allows the identification of the curious object near the sphere at Melancholy's feet. "That Melancholy intends to write is proved by the portable writing utensil above the sphere," writes Warburg.[10] This inkwell might also refer to the writing of Dürer's own books, then in gestation, on the topic of proportion (and for which Pacioli's work had been one of the models) – a theory of art and linear perspective that would become the book *Underweysung der Messung* (*The Four Books on Measurement,* 1525).

Fig. 10.1 *Above* Melencolia figure with compass. Detail from Dürer's *Melencolia I.*

Fig. 10.2 *Left* "Mensula Jovis," the "magic square." Detail from Dürer's *Melencolia I.*

Fig. 10.3a Jacopo de' Barbari [?], *Ritratto di Frà Luca Pacioli* (c. 1500). Tempera on panel (99 × 120 cm).

Thus, this master etching depicts more than simply a fusion of the traditional iconography of Geometry with that of Melancholy. The hand-held point of the compass (Ficino's concentration exercise), Jupiter's magic square protecting from Saturn's excessive, destructive power (oriental astrological influence), the study of geometric forms with Italian masters (the polyhedron and portable inkwell) are so many decisive details determining the constellation in which Warburg inscribes his inquiry into the major transformation of Saturnine figuration in Dürer's art. It is worth noting that he does not argue from the realm of pure ideas but always from the evidence of symbolic details, whether in the realm of the medicine of humours, astrological magic, or the art of mathematical proportions.

In a more concentrated way, the same registers of interpretation will be found to reappear when Warburg returns to Dürer's engraving in his now classic *Heidnisch-antike Weissagung in Wort und Bild zu Luthers Zeiten,*

Fig. 10.3b The portable inkwell and polyhedron. Detail from Dürer's *Melencolia I.*

which addresses traces of ancient divination in the period of the Reformation. Here, however, Warburg approaches the work of art as a differential element within the larger iconographic corpus of the period, documenting beliefs in the power of the planets. It is in this study that Warburg proposes his well-known formula characterizing Dürer's engraving as a "humanistic comfort against the fear inspired by Saturn" (*humanistisches Trostblatt wider Saturnfürchtigkeit*).[11] Let us recall that this formula aims at highlighting the fundamental difference of orientation between this artwork and other contemporary representations, in particular those illustrating predictions of the influential astrologist Johannes Lichtenberger (fig. 10.4). For Lichtenberger, Saturn and Jupiter's struggle for control over human destiny remains "demonic" with no form of humanization.[12] But the proposed formula also contrasts with Luther's refusal of mythological fatalism, and with his anathema vis-à-vis the power of the stars, which he rejects as diabolical idolatry. The larger context within which Warburg articulates these reflections on Dürer's print is a cultural history of images and representations symbolizing human fate in its relation to gods and the cosmos. For him, the artist's figure of *Melancholy* is still marked by a tension between ancient magic-astrological practices and the mathematization of the world that is characteristic of the Renaissance, as shown in works by Kepler and, later on, Halley. Here, in other words, was already visible the program that the Kulturwissenschaftliche Bibliothek Warburg (KBW) had laid out for the years ahead.

Saxl and Panofsky: *Dürer's 'Melencolia I'* (1923)

Warburg's desire to see Giehlow's work on Dürer in print was unwavering, but after the war he was unable to contribute to its publication, leaving Fritz Saxl to take on this role.[13] After receiving Giehlow's manuscript in 1921 and concluding that the late scholar had, in looking for a hieroglyphic dimension in *Melencolia I*, taken a wrong interpretive path, Saxl intended nonetheless to complete the book. For this, he enlisted Erwin Panofsky's help, and the book was to appear as a double volume, whose first part would contain Giehlow's studies, and the second Saxl and Panofsky's complementary interpretation.[14] However, once it was discovered that Giehlow's typescript had been lost at the *Staatsdruckerei* in Vienna, and moreover that the typeset proofs were rumoured to have been pulped, the original aim was discarded.[15]

The single volume, which was ultimately published in Leipzig by Teubner in 1923, appeared as the second of the *Warburg Studien* series and contains a preface by Giehlow's literary executor, Arpád Weixlgärtner, which retraces the history of obstacles to the publication of Giehlow's study. Forty of the volume's sixty-eight illustrations, printed free of charge by the Viennese Staatsdruckerei,[16] were adopted from Giehlow's work, but his own text is absent from the book, which is authored by Panofsky and Saxl alone and entitled *Dürers 'Melencolia I.' Eine quellen- und typengeschichtliche Unter-*

Fig. 10.4 The conjunction of Saturn und Jupiter. Illustration from Johan Lichtenberger's *Propheceien und Weissagen* ..., Doctoris Paracelsi, Augsburg, 1549.

suchung.[17] Their study returns (as Warburg had in his 1913 lecture) to the textual and visual sources of the representations of melancholy before its renewal by Dürer. Their iconographical analysis of the engraving makes little reference to other works by the artist, as their perspective is one of historical genesis over the very long term. Accompanied by an imposing annex of materials and sources on melancholy and its association with Saturn – pseudo-Aristotle, Abu Ma'shar, astrological representations of the children of the planet, Ficino, among others – which takes up as much space in the volume as does the principal account, the study covers the periods of antiquity, the Middle Ages, and the Florentine Renaissance, before focusing on Dürer and his master engraving.

The collaboration between Saxl, a specialist of astrological manuscripts, and Panofsky, a young *Privatdozent* at the University of Hamburg whose doctoral thesis had been on Dürer's theory of art, seems to have been well balanced – even if Panofsky was largely in charge of writing and editing. Most chapters are divided, reflecting the complementary specializations of the two scholars, with one section focusing on the planetary god and another on the conceptions of melancholy. Through its breadth and erudition, the study is a testament to the importance of the intellectual environment of the KBW: indeed, the four-handed study enlarges Warburg's sketches not only by exploiting the ancient and oriental sources of Saturn and his children but also by drawing from the learned and popular iconography of melancholy up to the intellectual turning point of the fifteenth and sixteenth centuries, taken essentially from Giehlow (figs. 10.5a and 10.5b).

The chapter devoted to Dürer also relies on the analysis made in Warburg's essay on Luther, and when the authors do introduce a judgment that differs from Warburg's, it is done prudently in the footnotes. The principal point of divergence – where one surmises the hand of Panofsky – concerns the magico-astrological dimension of the engraving: *Melencolia I*, we read there, could probably better be understood as a "warning than as comfort" (*Warnungsblatt denn als Trostblatt*) against Saturn's power and his moods.[18] The necessity of assuaging this ambivalent demon by combining his influx with a protection by Jupiter (the magic square), appears here as a minor motif, whereas, for Warburg, it represented one of the *preconditions* for the humanizing metamorphosis at work in Dürer.

The truly new argument in relation to Warburg, however, is the introduction, via Pico della Mirandola, of Henry of Ghent's Neoplatonic conception of melancholy, which informs the book's analytical conclusion. This thirteenth-century philosopher, quoted in Pico's *Apologia*,[19] is invoked as a final interpretive authority to explain the numeral "*I*" of the work's title. Panofsky and Saxl saw in this numeral the first stage of an ascending series (uncompleted by Dürer) that would point to a surpassing of the limitations of the saturnine artist.[20] In his *Apologia* (1489), Pico briefly lays out Henry's conception of a split relation between melancholy and mathematical genius which allows a distinction between the two human types under Saturn's influence: on the one hand, those whose power of representation remain

Fig. 10.5a *Top* Melancolicus, from the first German Calendar, Augsburg c. 1480.

Fig. 10.5b *Bottom* The Melancholic, from Marsilio Ficino's *Das Buch des Lebens*, Strasbourg, Johannes Grüninger, 1508.

linked to imagination in space and, on the other, those with pure metaphysical and theological minds.[21] In contrast to these speculative minds, the "imaginative ones," artists in particular, appear to be unable to free themselves from their specific saturnine side, dependent as they are on spatial representation and geometry.

The complementary stages of melancholy might correspond to this twofold division. Set against a second, higher state – for which the contemporary engraving of *Saint Jerome in His Cell*, with its figure of the translator of the Holy Scripture, could be a counterpart (*Gegenbild*) in Dürer (fig. 10. 6) – *Melencolia I* would symbolize the first stage: namely, necessary resignation vis-à-vis the limits of an art based mainly on mathematical measurement.[22] Without being able to prove that Dürer was aware, through Pico, of this precursor of Renaissance Platonism's conception of melancholy, the authors conclude: "in any case, this line of thought [Henri of Ghent's] leads right into the meaning that we have to give to Dürer's engraving."[23] That is to say that, while not conclusive, this theory of melancholy offers a way of understanding the true signification of *Melencolia I* for the artist himself. In this will to determine in a mainly textual way the ultimate meaning of an individual artwork, we can surely discern more the impetus of Panofsky – the future theoretician of iconology – than that of Saxl. Indeed, this is where the interpretation of the engraving as a confession and a Faustian expression of the impossibility of knowledge particular to the artist takes hold – an interpretation that would, despite some variations, mark the project's subsequent versions.

The Making of a Second Edition: Redefinitions and Controversies (1926–1939)

As has often been noted, it was via Ernst Cassirer's work on his book *Individuum und Kosmos in der Philosophie der Renaissance* that the young Klibansky entered the Warburg circle in 1926. A graduate student at the time, he had been tasked by the philosopher with editing, in an annex of his volume, the *Liber de sapiente* by Charles de Bovelles.[24] In this Latin text, Klibansky came across, probably for the first time, the Renaissance problematic of melancholia.

Fig. 10.6 Albrecht Dürer, *Saint Jerome in His Cell*. Engraving on laid paper (1514). This engraving is evoked as a counterpart to Dürer's *Melencolia I* in Panofsky and Saxl, *Dürers 'Melencolia I.'*

Fig. 10.7 *De quattuor hominum gradibus* from Charles de Bovelles, *Liber de sapiente* (1510).

Charles de Bovelles (or Bovillus) was one of the first thinkers to have assimilated the works of Nicholas of Cusa and also those of the Florentine Platonist Academy: according to Cassirer, his *De sapiente* of 1510 represented a direct prolongation of the liberating language of Pico in *De hominis dignitate* (1486). Thus, among the original engravings reproduced in Klibansky's annexed edition of the text, we can find the scheme *De quattuor hominum gradibus* (fig. 10.7). It still employs the old terminus *acedia* (sloth or torpor), understood as the basest level to which man falls when reduced to pure existence, whereas he could raise himself, as *studiosus*, to the superior level of knowledge of the cosmos.[25] As for the planet Saturn, Bovelles clearly identified it with the powers of imagination.

It is possible that in the course of Klibansky's exchanges with Saxl on this Latin edition, the idea grew of working together on an enlarged version

Gegenstand der Interpretation	Subjektive Quelle der Interpretation	Objektives Korrektiv der Interpretation
1. Phänomensinn (zu teilen in Sach- und Ausdruckssinn)	Vitale Daseinserfahrung	Gestaltungsgeschichte (Inbegriff des Darstellungsmöglichen)
2. Bedeutungssinn	Literarisches Wissen	Typengeschichte (Inbegriff des Vorstellungsmöglichen)
3. Dokumentsinn (Wesenssinn)	Weltanschauliches Urverhalten	Allgemeine Geistesgeschichte (Inbegriff des weltanschaulich Möglichen)

Fig. 10.8 Panofsky's iconologic scheme.

of Saxl and Panofsky's volume on Dürer's *Melencolia*. According to the correspondence between the two – they would become close friends – it is obvious that Klibansky was working from the turn of the year 1927–28 on providing critical notes and materials for a new collective edition that took shape during the following years.[26] The details of his contributions can be reconstructed from the correspondence and from the so-called *Zettel*, the handwritten notes by topics (and chapters) that Klibansky would send – most often from Heidelberg where he was still completing his thesis on Proclus.[27]

An allusion to the preparation of this new enlarged edition can be found in Panofsky's important article "Zum Problem der Beschreibung und Inhaltsdeutung von Werken der bildenden Kunst," which appeared in *Logos* in 1932. In this first systematic attempt to define what would become *his* specific iconological method, Panovsky distinguished between three levels of meaning: phenomenal meaning, meaning dependent on content, and documentary – or intrinsic – meaning (*Phänomen-*, *Bedeutungs-*, *Dokument-* or *Wesenssinn*).[28] (fig. 10.8) At the end of this essay, the art historian mentions specifically the case of Dürer's *Melencolia I* – he refers to the artist's (and his time's) "vision of the world" to exemplify the last interpretive stage of his formalized method – and the footnote associated with this passage encourages the reader to: "Compare the second edition currently in preparation of the study compiled together with Fritz Saxl, *Dürers* 'Melencolia I': Leipzig, 1923."[29] So the bulk of the work had already been done before 1932 and the new "iconological method" had been tested on the *Melencolia I* engraving itself. In 1931–32, Panofsky became visiting professor at New York University, and he rarely returned to Europe before he began to teach at Princeton, where he was to receive a position at the Institute for Advanced Study in 1935.

In 1933 the KBW staff realized they must leave Hamburg because of the Nazis' seizure of power. It is known that Edgar Wind and Klibansky determined the final choice of London,[30] just as it is well known how difficult the subsequent years would be for what was to become the Warburg Institute. When it became possible, after 1935, to return to work on the *Melencolia I* volume and finalize the new edition, a disagreement broke out among the group of authors – one that is well documented in their triangular correspondence.

Panofsky assured Saxl in a letter of December 1937 (quoted by the latter to Klibansky): "I am of course absolutely satisfied with everything you plan to do with respect to the 'Melencolia', including the reformulation of the title. I, too, feel that Klibansky deserves to appear on the title page."[31] There remained, however, tension in the following years regarding who would be named as authors and in what order their names would appear. In particular, and despite the fact that Klibansky had, at Saxl's request, been the decisive editor in the final phase, Panofsky refused to grant him the status of full co-author of the volume.[32]

But controversy also surrounded the possible subtitle, which was meant to clarify the nature of the new work (which still had *Melancholia* as main title), thereby revealing an issue about method and perspective. In the summer of 1938, Panofsky flatly rejected Klibansky's proposition, which was originally: *Studien zur Geschichte der Naturphilosophie, Medizin, Astrologie und deren Einwirkung auf die darstellende Kunst* (*Studies on the History of Natural Philosophy, Medicine, Astrology and their Impact on Visual Art*). He categorically refused any allusion to natural philosophy or to *Geistesgeschichte* and seemed to want, still (and strictly), to locate the enterprise within art history.[33] In this disagreement one can see a revealing question about disciplinary frontiers, with conceptual implications for the relations between the study of art and the history of medical, religious, and scientific representations, which were, however, at the heart of the Warburgian approach.

The Missing Link: *Melancholie und Saturn* (1939)

Recent research in the Warburg Institute Archive and in the Deutsches Literaturarchiv Marbach collections have brought to light different sets of proofs between 1937 and 1939 of the volume in preparation under the new title *Melancholie und Saturn.*[34] This document allows us better to evaluate the profound transformation of the project since 1923. The subtitle (and authorship) on the title page runs: *Studien zur Geschichte der Naturphilosophie, Charakterlehre und bildenden Kunst. Von Erwin Panofsky und Fritz Saxl, unter Mitarbeit von Raymond Klibansky* (*Studies in the History of Natural Philosophy, of the Theory of Character Types and of the Visual Arts. By E. Panofsky and F. Saxl, with the collaboration of R. Klibansky*). (fig. 10.9) If explicit mentions of astrology and medicine were not included in the subtitle,

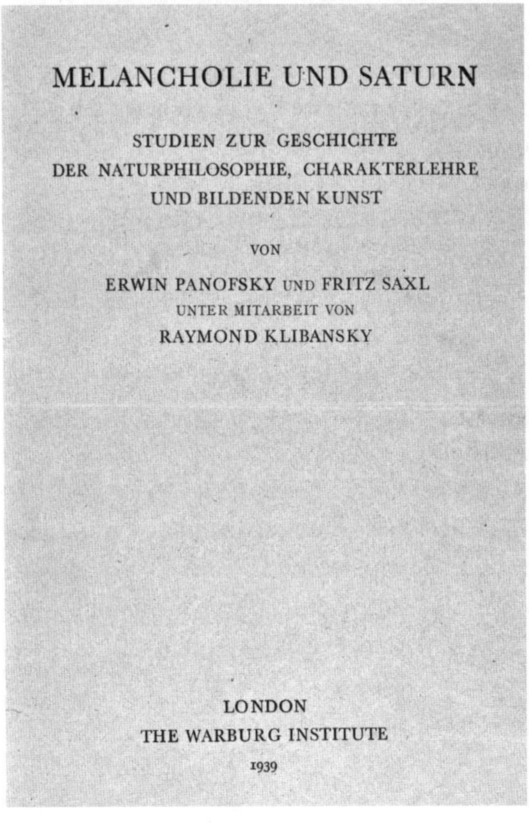

MELANCHOLIE UND SATURN

STUDIEN ZUR GESCHICHTE
DER NATURPHILOSOPHIE, CHARAKTERLEHRE
UND BILDENDEN KUNST

VON

ERWIN PANOFSKY UND FRITZ SAXL
UNTER MITARBEIT VON
RAYMOND KLIBANSKY

LONDON
THE WARBURG INSTITUTE
1939

Fig. 10.9 *Melancholie und Saturn*, proofs [1939], title page.

the collective publication was to carry, even if asymmetrically, the three authors' names (in a formulation that would, however, be rejected by Klibansky in August 1939).[35] With the exception of the introduction, appendices, and the index, the book was effectively completed. On one of the last sets of proofs we can read the date of 2 August 1939 stamped by the German printer J.J. Augustin at Glückstadt. We know that the book never went to print (because of the outbreak of the war) and that the plates disappeared in the Nazi war effort.[36]

The reconstruction of the content from the 1939 proofs runs as follow:

This version of the project develops all the elements that made up the 1923 volume, and integrates into the main "story" the numerous sources and documents that had been previously presented in appendices. The focus is now on retracing the history of melancholy and of the representations of Saturn from ancient medicine, philosophy, mythology, and literature to Florentine Platonism, before arriving at Dürer. The text is almost tripled in volume (from 154 to 424 pages), and the number of visual documents doubled (passing from 68 to 147). Even if the original structure of 1923 remains central to the edifice of the new book, a qualitative shift can be noted. The new edition moves well beyond the original focus on Dürer's art to include a broad cultural history of the relation between discourses on melancholic affect and beliefs attached to the planetary god Saturn. An entire chapter (III.A), written probably at Klibansky's instigation, was added to cover the question of poetic melancholy after the Middle Ages.[38] Dürer's *Melencolia I* does not appear until page 290. The fifth section is also new – "Die künstlerische Nachfolge der 'Melencolia I'" – and it maps the engraving's consequences in the visual arts of the time.

As a history of ideas and representations in medicine, theology, astrology, and literature, Parts One to Three of the book include much that is new and are fairly autonomous from the rest of the volume. The fourth section, on Dürer, has remained relatively stable, but subsection (B), which was devoted to the "new meaning" of *Melencolia I*, clarifies and modifies the 1923 mode of interpretation. Methodically, it is Panofsky's iconological scheme, whose three stages were first laid out in 1932, that now clearly dominates the project. Indeed, Panofsky's three stages correspond to the three subdivisions of section IV.B.ii in the 1939 proofs: 1) The new form of expression (*Ausdruckssinn*), 2) the new notional content (*Begriffsgehalt*), and 3) the new significance (*Dokumentsinn*) of the artwork:[39]

IV. DÜRER

A. DIE MELANCHOLIE AUFFASSUNG DES CONRAD CELTES

B. DER KUPFERSTICH MELENCOLIA I

I. DIE TYPENGESCHICHTLICHEN VORAUSSETZUNGEN DER „MELENCOLIA I.“

II. DER NEUE SINN DER MELENCOLIA I

1. *Der neue Ausdruckssinn*
2. *Der neue Begriffsgehalt*
    a) Saturn- bzw. Melancholiesymbolik
    b) Geometriesymbolik
3. *Der neue Dokumentsinn*

C. *DIE VIER APOSTEL*

As for new material, an example of an interesting contribution is the discussion of the "notional content" of the astrological symbols – such as the controversial magic square. This new element in the study is due to the discovery of a planetary square identical, in every detail, to that of Dürer's engraving in an unpublished mathematical treatise by Luca Pacioli, *De Viribus Quantitatis* (ca. 1500).[40] Chapter 72 from this manuscript, written in the vernacular and entitled "Numeri in quadrato," cites the known Arab sources with the series of numbers attached to the planets Saturn, Jupiter, Mars, and so forth. In the corresponding footnote of *Melancholie und Saturn*, one reads: "It is remarkable that Pacioli deals with the squares simply as a mathematical 'jeu d'esprit,' and merely mentions their astrological and magical significance without going into it: he therefore completely ignores any talismanic virtues of the various squares."[41]

This note is somewhat unsettling, as it shows that the authors were aware, without further exploration or elaboration, that Dürer may well have had direct knowledge of this source through a probable encounter with Pacioli in Bologna.[42] The fact does not deter them, or more likely Panofsky on his own, from reinforcing in the next paragraph the criticism of the importance that Warburg attached to Jupiter's magic square in the engraving:

> All these antidotes are merely a weak makeshift in the face of the real destiny of the melancholy person. Just as Ficino had already realized that selfless and unconditional surrender to the will of Saturn was after all not only the "ultima" but also the "optima ratio" for the intellectual man, so, too, Dürer ... creates a Melencolia whose sad but sublime destiny cannot, and perhaps should not, be averted by palliatives, whether natural or magical.[43]

The discovery that the magic square may have been that of Pacioli could, however, on the contrary, have strengthened Warburg's hypothesis of the metamorphosis in Dürer of the celestial magic of numerals into an art of rational measuring by numbers. This direction seems not to have interested Panofsky, likely because of the demonstrative character he wanted to give to the third level of his new interpretive method.[44] For this ultimate stage provides the title to the last section on the engraving: "*der neue Dokumentsinn*" (The new significance) of *Melencolia I*.

This section, in fact, returns to the philosophical background of melancholy proposed in 1923 in order to *modify* the hypothesis on the enigmatic "*I*" of the title. Neither Ficino's conception, nor the allusion that Pico made to the theory of Henry (of Ghent), could here account in a satisfactory way for the new relation between Geometry and Melancholy in Dürer's allegory. For Ficino, melancholy entertains no particular relation with mathematics; for Henry, that discipline is too narrowly associated with uninspired imagination to explain the "*I*" in the title. It is the esoteric author Agrippa who now takes the role of the main mediator via the *first* unpublished version of *De occulta philosophia*. This manuscript, dated around 1510, and located by the KBW librarian Hans Meier, differs considerably from the known edition printed in 1533. It undertakes a more direct compilation of Ficino's ideas and, significantly, the magic squares of the subsequent version are missing from it.[45]

The elucidation of this earlier doctrine by Agrippa in the section on the new significance of Dürer's engraving culminates in a table visualizing the corresponding gradation *imaginatio – ratio – mens* of the three stages of melancholy, dividing those who are affected by it into: i) artists, ii) scientists and politicians, and iii) theologians and prophets. (fig. 10.10)

The conclusion following this synthetic table could hardly be clearer: "Let us now imagine the task of an artist who wishes to undertake a portrait of the first or imaginative form of melancholy talent and frenzy, in accordance with the theory of Agrippa ... What would he have to represent?"[46] After a long enumeration of the elements belonging to "Agrippian" melancholic imagination, the unequivocal answer comes: "[It] would be what Dürer did in *Melencolia I*."[47] Just as already outlined in the 1923 version, but relying on

Stufe der saturnisch-melancholischen Inspiration.	Vollzugsorgane der saturnisch-melancholischen Inspiration.	Psychologischer Ort der saturnisch-melancholischen Inspiration.	Schöpferisches Auswirkungsgebiet der saturnisch-melancholischen Inspiration	Prophetisches Auswirkungsgebiet der saturnisch-melancholischen Inspiration.
I.	Untere Dämonen.	Imaginatio.	Technische Künste, insbesondere Architektur, Malerei usw.	Elementarereignisse, insbesondere Regengüsse, Hungersnot usw.
II.	Mittlere Dämonen.	Ratio.	Wissen um die natürlichen und menschlichen Dinge, insbesondere Naturphilosophie, Medizin, Staatskunst usw.	Politische Ereignisse, Umsturz und Wiederaufrichtung.
III.	Obere Dämonen.	Mens.	Wissen um die göttlichen Geheimnisse, insbesondere Kenntnis des göttlichen Gesetzes, der Angelogie und Moraltheologie.	Religiöse Ereignisse, insbesondere Auftreten neuer Propheten oder Entstehung neuer Religionen.

Fig. 10.10 "Stufen der saturnischen melancholischen Inspiration," in the *Melancholie und Saturn* proofs [1939].

a different textual source, the engraving is presented as expressing the insurmountable ignorance of Faust, the resignation of he who has to realize the inevitable failure of his artistic skills.[48]

It is rather astonishing that the global interpretation of the engraving remained stable between 1923 and 1939 while the central theoretical reference that was supposed to constitute its horizon of significance changed from one version to another – here, a specifically German esoteric variation on Neoplatonism. In this interpretation we touch on a hallmark particular to the kind of hermeneutics characteristic of Panofsky's iconology: the discursive stabilization of an ultimate meaning, underwritten by a text – marking thus a significant difference from the Warburgian legacy.[49]

Respite and Postponements (1945–1964)

As already mentioned, the outbreak of war postponed *sine die* the perspective of publication for the new book, which should have been printed at the end of 1939. In London, Saxl was still struggling to ensure long-term institutional support for the Warburg Institute. As for Klibansky, he had enlisted – he was active within the Political Warfare Executive – and would finish the war as a colonel in the British Army. Panofsky, for his part, held one of the most prestigious positions in the United States at Princeton. In 1939 he brought out his *Studies in Iconology* in English with an introduction to his new method, this time without alluding to the joint project stemming from the Warburg Library. But he was above all preparing his new monograph, *The Life and Art of Albrecht Dürer*, the first edition of which appeared in 1943.[50]

The largest part of Panofsky's chapter devoted to the master engravings of the artist is on *Melencolia I* – the section being a transposition, into the new framework of the monograph, of the core elements developed in the unpublished German collective volume. In his preface, while mentioning this, Panofsky concedes self-deprecatingly that for this section, "half of the credit, if any, goes to Dr. Saxl and his associates."[51] We can understand that this expression refers not only to the team of the Warburg Institute but also to Klibansky, whose name is not cited. Taking up again the theory of Agrippa's manuscript of the *De occulta philosophia* as the main key, the significance proposed for the engraving was reaffirmed as the first limited stage of the melancholic inspiration: "Here is the inertia of a being which renounces what it could reach because it cannot reach for what it longs."[52]

Only with the end of the war could the project of publishing the collective work be relaunched. When Saxl died in 1948, Klibansky, who had been tasked by him to prepare the English edition, found himself on his own for the final editing work while at the same time involved in two other major Warburg publication projects: the journal *Mediaeval and Renaissance Studies* (which he co-edited with Richard Hunt) and the colossal editorial project on the Latin and Arabic *Corpus Platonicum Medii Aevi*, which would stretch over about twenty years (1941–62). From Montreal where he had in the meantime been appointed to McGill University,[53] Klibansky no longer found the necessary support from the new heads of the Warburg Institute, Henri Frankfort and, after 1959, Ernst Gombrich; on the other hand, he was still coming up against Panofsky's reservations about publishing the volume.

What Gertrud Bing called in a letter to Panofsky of 1949 "the long argument which passed between you and Saxl on this question" was only finally resolved when Klibansky visited Panofsky in Princeton in 1955.[54] That same year, which also saw Panofsky withdrawing his opposition, the fourth edition of his Dürer monograph came out – this time a portable edition "addressed to the student as well as the 'general reader,'"[55] which would not be in competition with the newly published monumental scholarly book written by the three scholars.

Finally, the now well-known collective publication *Saturn and Melancholy*, which carried the names of the three authors (in alphabetical order) and the subtitle *Studies in the History of Natural Philosophy, Religion and Art* appeared in 1964. As a comparison easily shows, this version differs relatively little from the state of the proofs of 1939. The only notable difference in structure is that the fifth and last part of the German version, "Die künstleriche Nachfolge der *Melencolia I*," has been integrated into the fourth, imposing section on Dürer as a final chapter entitled "The Artistic Legacy of *Melencolia I*."[56] The iconographic material remained unchanged, and the English text turns out be a revision of the German that had been translated by Frances Lobb.[57] The central place given to the conception of saturnine melancholy from Agrippa's manuscript has been preserved, and the conclusions about the intrinsic meaning of the engraving have not changed.

Let us now take a retrospective glance along the path we have followed. Warburg's investigation of *Melencolia I* was made at the intersection of a diachronic series in, on the one hand, the transmission of representations of Saturn from antiquity forward and, on the other, a typological comparison with astrological (Lichtenberger) or religious (Luther) conceptions toward divination. Agrippa also played an important role for Warburg in the identification of the astral dimension of Dürer's Melancholy. But *De occulta philosophia* would not determine for him a given (or ultimate) meaning to the engraving; rather, it helped in retracing a visual element of the composition and its function – the *mensula Jovis* as talisman assuaging Saturn.[58] But it was only an element within a greater whole, a condition of the open dynamic of Melancholy's gesture.

The strange holding of the compass as a visual transposition of Ficino's concentration exercises; the portable inkwell pointing toward the writing of the artist's theory of proportions and measurement – these were the other decisive moments for Warburg.[59] This set of elements designed the constellation where he inscribed the *shift* of which the engraving was the trace and the symbol – that is, the metamorphosis of Saturn into a genius. This is particular to the Warburgian understanding of figurative transmission and its specific aesthetic differentiation. Here, the ambivalent polarities of the saturnine-melancholic type are characteristic of a "general" iconology apprehended as a cultural history of representations and images which could not be reduced to a hermeneutics of meaning.

For his part, Panofsky had closed the chapter on Dürer in the unpublished *Melancholie und Saturn* with a treatment of Paul in the artist's late painting *The Four Apostles* (1525–26). In this portrait of Paul – whose figure would become central to the Reformation – the art historian saw the possible incarnation of a *Melencolia III*, the spiritual and prophetic stage in his new interpretative grid. The 1964 English edition would not change this conclusion, which was based on the iconological method that marked Panofsky's postwar success as a leading art historian.

In his new preface to the French and German editions of *Saturn and Melancholy* – which appeared respectively in 1989 and 1990, after Panofsky's death – Klibansky enlarges the perspective of the collective erudite study with an overview on melancholy in philosophy and literature after Dürer.[60] Returning to *Melencolia I*, he still endorses the plausible influence of Agrippa's first *Occulta philosophia* on Dürer, but recalls – as Warburg did – the importance of the magic square in the engraving, nonetheless rejecting any interpretation of an artist drifting toward occult magic.[61] There, he again makes a reference to the complex religious constellation of Dürer's time, pointing to the complementarity between the *Melencolia I*, full of symbols of the pagan world, and *Saint Jerome in His Cell* with its Christian dimension.[62] Klibansky also returns to the subsequent proximity between the artist, Melanchthon, and Luther, recalling Dürer's faith by citing that other formula of melancholic pathos that the young artist presented in *Christ, Man of Sorrows.*[63] Thus, it is likely with irony that the author ultimately expresses doubts about the possibility of deciphering a final, irreducible meaning within the famous engraving.[64]

We know that Panofsky considered the collective volume to be "outdated" from the point of view of his discipline.[65] Today we can certainly see *Saturn and Melancholy* in a different, renewed actuality – despite the criticisms that have been formulated since its publication and the corrections that future research will likely contribute.[66] As the *summa* that it is, the three-authored volume contains, inherent within itself, many paths that could still be followed (such as, for instance, the importance of the possible contact of the artist with the mathematician Pacioli) in order to nuance our approaches and evaluation of the place of Dürer's art at the threshold between the Middle Ages, the Renaissance, and the Reformation. Moreover, the methodological tensions among different parts of the book bear witness to the difficult production of the Warburg Institute and its network in exile. And as a case study, it offers a unique interrogation on the possibility of a long-term history of knowledge and beliefs intersecting with the history of arts, literature, and technologies – all disciplinary domains that were connected within Warburg's programmatic library.

Klibansky, for his part, deemed it important to pursue the publication of the book, including additions, and to have it translated into several languages. With the English version of *Saturn and Melancholy* long out of print, he also – at the age of eighty-seven in 1992–93 – persuaded Yale University Press to republish it. Yet, although it was dispatched, the contract for the new edition was never signed.[67] Thus, the legendary opus once again awaited printing.

NOTES

1 Deutsches Literaturarchiv Marbach, A: Raymond Klibansky (hereafter: DLA, A, KLIBANSKY): Lotte Labowsky to Raymond Klibansky, 25 May 1949, quoted in Weber, "Aktivitäten der Warburg-Bibliothek," 110.

2 Klibansky, Panofsky, and Saxl, *Saturn and Melancholy*, v.

3 WIA, General Correspondence (hereafter GC)/4327: Aby Warburg to Gustav

Glück, 15 December 1913; later on, Warburg even proposed to help Giehlow's literary executor, Arpád Weixlgärtner, to edit the unfinished volume on *Melencolia I* and to put his own research at his disposition; see WIA, GC/12077: Warburg to Arpád Weixlgärtner, 23 March 1915 and WIA, GC/28996: 12 January 1916.

4 Warburg, "Die Planetenbilder auf der Wanderung von Süd nach Nord und ihre Rückkehr nach Italien," 359–65; see also Despoix, "*Translatio* and Remediation."

5 Warburg, *Heidnisch-antike Weissagung in Wort und Bild zu Luthers Zeiten.*

6 "Die Kugel ist das Ficinosymbol der gesammelten Seele der Melencolia; darum hält sie auch die Spitze des Zirkels in der Hand," in Warburg, *Werke in einem Band*, 368. See also "Zirkel und Kreis (und also die Kugel) sind nach der alten Übersetzung des Ficino das Denksymbol der Melancholie," in Warburg, *Heidnisch-antike Weissagung in Wort und Bild zu Luthers Zeiten*, 63; trans. Britt, in Warburg, "Pagan-Antique Prophecy in Words and Images in the Age of Luther," *The Renewal of Pagan Antiquity*, 645.

7 "Ficino erwähnt nur Bilder, nicht Zahlen, als wirksame Jupiteramulette; dagegen empfiehlt Agrippa von Nettesheim eben dieses Zauberquadrat," ibid., *Werke in einem Band*, 369; see also "Der magisch angerufene Jupiter kommt durch seine gütige und besänftigende Wirkung auf den Saturn zu Hilfe. Die Erretung des Menschen durch diesen Gegenschein des Jupiter ist auf dem Bilde gewissermassen schon erfolgt," in Warburg, *Heidnisch-antike Weissagung*, 64, trans. in *The Renewal of Pagan Antiquity*, 645.

8 These tables made their way via Arab treaties and their Latin translations, such as the *Picatrix*, of which Giehlow had no knowledge; see Warburg, "Planetenbilder auf der Wanderung," 369, and *Heidnisch-antike Weissagung*, 60, trans. in *The Renewal of Pagan Antiquity*, 643.

9 See slide 30 of the lecture's typescript, WIA, III.87.1.2: "Abbildungen."

10 "Dass die Melencolia selbst auf schreiben sinnt, beweist das Gürtelschreibzeug über der Kugel," Warburg, "Planetenbilder auf der Wanderung," 368; and "auf dem Bilde wird Luca Pacioli als Entdecker des Buches über die regelmässigen Körper gefeiert … vor ihm liegt … ein Gürtelschreibzeug, das uns das Gerät neben der Kugel erklärt," ibid., 369. This point was not taken over into *Heidnisch-antike Weissagung*. Giehlow, for his part, had seen in the inkwell a hieroglyphic emblem.

11 Warburg, *The Renewal of Pagan Antiquity*, 644 (modified translation); see *Heidnisch-antike Weissagung*, 61: "Der recht eingentlich schöpferischer Akt, der

Dürers 'Melencolia I' zum humanistischen Trostblatt wider Saturnfürchtigkeit macht, kann erst begriffen werden, wenn man diese magische Mythologik als eigentliches Objekt der künstlerisch-vergeistigenden Umformung erkennt."

12 Ibid., 63, trans. in *The Renewal of Pagan Antiquity*, 645.

13 In the fall of 1920, Saxl wrote to Weixlgärtner offering to prepare Giehlow's 'Melencolia I' manuscript for print, see: WIA, GC/12657: Saxl to Arpád Weixlgärtner, 30 September 1920. See also Claudia Wedepohl, chapter 9 in this volume.

14 WIA, GC/13342: Saxl to Warburg, 21 November 1921, and WIA, GC/13775: Saxl to Weixlgärtner, 7 January 1922.

15 WIA, GC/13776: Weixlgärtner to Saxl, 29 January 1922. Saxl then suggests everything that has been added to Giehlow's material should be published in the "Warburg Studien," printed by Teubner in Leipzig, see: WIA, GC/13778: Saxl to Weixlgärtner, 7 March 1922.

16 The Staatsdruckerei was also to provide the paper for the illustrations, cf. WIA, GC/13785.

17 Panofsky and Saxl, *Dürers 'Melencolia I'*; see also Weixlgärtner, "Zum Geleite," and "Einleitung," 1n1, which mentions the series of preliminary materials that had been gathered by Giehlow and by Warburg.

18 "Trotz Giehlows und Warburgs scharfsinniger Argumentation ... möchte das Dürerische Blatt – auf die dunkle Seite auch der 'melancholia generosa' mit mindestens der gleichen Eindringlichkeit hinweisend, wie auf ihre lichte – noch eher als 'Warnungsblatt,' denn gerade als 'Trostblatt' zu bezeichnen sein," *Dürers 'Melencolia I,'* 54n1.

19 A work that Dürer could have known through Pirckheimer, who had been in Padua under the spell of Pico and whose nephew became his friend; see Campbell Hutchison, *Albrecht Dürer: A Biography*, 52.

20 Heinrich Wölfflin, the author of an important monograph on Dürer (1904), would imagine – in the same year, 1923 – a (lost) *Melencolia II* representing a victory of his depressive and morbid side; see Wölfflin, "Zur Interpretation von Dürers 'Melancholie,'" 105.

21 See the quotation from Pico's *Apologia* (*Opera omnia*, Basel, 1572, vol. 1, 133, VD 16 P 2580) in Panofsky and Saxl, *Dürers 'Melencolia I,'* 72–3n3: "unde tales melancholici sunt, et optimi fiunt mathematici, sed sunt naturales inepti. Haec Henricus ad verbum. Ex quibus sequitur, quod secundum Henricum iste Magister sit male dispositas ad studium philosophiae naturalis, peius ad studium Meta-

physicae, pessime ad studium Theologiae, quae etiam est de abstractionibus: relinquitur ei solum. aptitudo ad Mathematica."

22 "Insofern ist die 'Melancholie' in der Tat ein Gegenbild zum 'Hieronymus,' dem die metaphysisch-religiöse Spekulation eine Befriedigung gewährt, wie sie die rational-mathematische niemal gewähren kann." *Dürers 'Melencolia I,'* 73–4; see also: n. 1: "man [hat] bei diesem Gegesatz – der gerade bei Pico sehr klar und mit deutlichster Zuspitzung auf die Theologie zum Ausdruck kommt – nicht etwa an ein 'Pendant'-Verhältnis im äusserlichen Simme zu denken."

23 "Jedenfalls führt jener Gedanke [Heinrich von Gents] tief hinein in das, was wir als den Sinn des Dürer Stiches empfinden dürfen." Ibid., 73.

24 Carolus Bovillus [Charles de Bovelles] (ed. Klibansky), *Liber de sapiente.*

25 See Cassirer, *Individuum und Kosmos*, 95–6: "Wie das Sein sich in das *Esse, Vivere, Sentire und Intelligere* abstuft, so kann der Mensch nach freier Wahl entweder das Ganze dieser Stufenreihe durchmessen, oder aber auf einer einzelenen Stufe verharren und stehen bleiben. Er kann, wenn er dem Laster der Trägheit, der mittelalterlichen '*acedia*,' verfällt, bis zur Stufe absinken, auf der ihm nur noch das nackte Dasein … bleibt – er kann bis zur höchsten sich erheben, auf der er durch das Medium der eigenen Selbsterkenntnis die Erkenntnis des Kosmos gewinnt."

26 WIA, GC/20548 f: Saxl to Klibansky, 12 January and 7 February 1928.

27 WIA holds in the Saxl papers more than twenty short documents in Klibansky's hand (about eighty pages with quotations and commentaries on different topics related to melancholy).

28 The article dates back to a talk to the Kiel section of Kant Society in May 1931; see Panofsky, "Zum Problem der Beschreibung und Inhaltsdeutung von Werken der bildenden Kunst," 118; in English: trans. Elsner and Lorenz, "On the Problem of Describing and Interpreting Works of the Visual Arts," 482.

29 Ibid, 117 and 118n1; see trans.: "So, for example, art historians use the intellectual testimonia of the Renaissance (among which naturally the writings of Dürer himself must be included) to show the worldview within which Dürer's Melancholia united a *typus Acediae* with a *typus Geometriae* and thus for the first time brought together in a single conception the sufferings of creatures with a sense of fateless agency," ibid. 480 and 481n21. Note Panofsky's handwritten dedication of this article to Klibansky in 1932 (in the Raymond Klibansky Collection (RKC), Rare Books and Special Collections (RBSC), McGill University Library).

30 Saxl, "The History of Warburg's Library," 336.

31 Letter from Saxl to Klibansky, 8 December 1937 (RKC, RBSC, McGill University Library).

32 Weber, "Aktivitäten der Warburg-Bibliothek," 108.

33 DLA, A, KLIBANSKY: Klibansky to Saxl, 17 August 1928, and Weber, ibid., 107–8. On Panofsky's answer to Saxl from 2 September 1938, see also Davide Stimilli's chapter 11 in this volume, note 49.

34 I would like to thank Claudia Wedepohl at the WIA in London and Regina Weber at the DLA for their help in tracing the different proofs.

35 See WIA, Fritz Saxl Papers, boxes "Saturn und Melancholie": "Titelzeug und neues Vorwort."

36 Klibansky, *Le Philosophe et la mémoire du siècle*, 151.

37 See WIA, Fritz Saxl Papers, boxes "Saturn und Melancholie." I thank Elisabeth Otto for helping with this reconstruction.

38 Raymond Klibansky will later return to this topic; see, for example, Raymond Klibansky, "Le avventure della malinconia."

39 They are introduced in English as early as 1939, in Panofsky, "Introductory," in *Studies in Iconology*, 3–17, and will be transposed subsequently into the 1964 edition of the collective work: Klibansky, Panofsky, and Saxl, *Saturn and Melancholy*.

40 See WIA, Fritz Saxl Papers, boxes „Saturn und Melancholie": proofs [1939], 343–4; see, for the English translation, *Saturn and Melancholy*, 326–7. One must also remember that Pacioli is the same author featured in the Barbari painting cited by Warburg in his 1913 lecture.

41 Quotation according to the 1964 edition *Saturn and Melancholy*, 327n147; see also WIA, Fritz Saxl Papers, boxes "Saturn und Melancholie," proofs [1939], 344n3: "Bemerkenswert ist, daß Pacioli die Quadrate nur als mathematisches jeu d'esprit handelt, und ihre astrologisch-magische Bedeutung zwar erwähnt, aber nicht weiter berücksichtigt: daher von den talismanhaften Leistungen der einzelnen Quadrate mit keinem Worte die Rede ist … Agrippa von Nettesheim hat die Planetenquadrate erst in der Druckausgabe (II, 22), während sie, was Giehlow freilich nicht wissen konnte, in der Urfassung noch fehlen."

42 On Dürer's possible contact with Pacioli in Bologna, see Campbell Hutchison, *Albrecht Dürer*, 74, and also Schuster, *Melencolia I. Dürers Denkbild*, I, 32–3.

43 Quotation according to the 1964 edition *Saturn and Melancholy*, 327–8; see also: WIA, Fritz Saxl Papers, boxes "Saturn und Melancholie," proofs [1939], 344–5:

"All diese Gegenmittel aber sind nur ein schwacher Notbehelf gegen das, was nun einmal die *eimarmenê* des melancholischen Menschen ist. Wie schon Ficino einsah, daß die selbstlose und bedingungslose Ergebung in den Willen des Saturn im Grunde nicht nur die 'ultima,' sondern auch die 'optima ratio' des geistigen Menschen sei, so hat auch Dürer (das lehrt ja schon das 'schwarze Gesicht' und die 'geballte Faust') die 'Melencolia' zu einem Wesen gemacht, das natürliche und magische Palliative vor seinem traurig erhabenen Schicksal nicht schützen können, und vielleicht nicht schützen sollen: Der kosmische Konflikt zwischen Saturn und Jupiter kann, wenn er überhaupt jemals zum Austrag gebracht werden wird, jedenfalls nicht mit einem Siege des Jupiter enden." The same criticism was made in a more circumspect way in the 1923 version; see 54n1.

44 See WIA, Fritz Saxl Papers, boxes "Saturn und Melancholie," proofs [1939], 345n1, and *Saturn and Melancholy*, 327: "We can associate ourselves with [Warburg's] description only with many reservations, since we cannot imagine the 'demoniac conflict' between Saturn and Jupiter ending in a victory for the latter: nor can we accord it that prime significance for the interpretation of Dürer's engraving which Warburg attributes to it. The 'mensula Jovis,' after all, is only one of many motifs, and by no means the most important. Despite Giehlow's and Warburg's acute arguments, the relevance of the engraving for Maximilian I cannot be proved; and even if it could, *Melencolia I* would have been a warning rather than a consolation to him."

45 Dürer could have known the first version through the humanistic circle around Maximilian before completing the engraving, but not the printed one, as it appeared after his death. On Agrippa of Nettesheim's manuscript see WIA, GC/21131, Aby Warburg to Erwin Panofsky, 9 August 1928, and WIA, Fritz Saxl Papers, boxes "Saturn und Melancholie," proofs [1939], 344n3; trans. *Saturn and Melancholy*, 327n147: Agrippa's work contains the planetary squares only in the printed edition; they were absent in the original version.

46 Quotation according to the 1964 edition *Saturn and Melancholy*, 359; see also: WIA, Fritz Saxl Papers, boxes "Saturn und Melancholie," proofs [1939], 382: "Versuchen wir nun, uns die Aufgabe eines Künstlers vorzustellen, der es unternehmen würde, im Anschluß an diese Theorie des Agrippa von Nettesheim der 'ersten', imaginativen Form der melancholischen Begabung und 'Begeisterung' anschauliche Gestalt zu geben. Was hätte er darzustellen gehabt? Ein Wesen, das verdüstert ist – denn sein Geist ist melancholisch; ein Wesen das

sowohl schöpferisch als prophetisch ist – denn sein Geist hat Anteil am 'inspiratorischen Furor'; ein Wesen, dessen Erfindungsgabe sich auf den Bereich der räumlichen Anschauung, d.h. auf das Gebiet der 'technischen' Künste beschränkt und dessen seherischem Blick nur drohende Elementarkatastrophen zugänglich sind – denn sein Geist ist ganz auf das Vermögen der 'Imaginatio' gestellt; und ein Wesen endlich, das sich der Unvollkommenheit seines Erkenntnisvermögens ahnend bewußt ist – denn seinem Geiste ist die Fähigkeit versagt, die höheren Seelenkräfte wirksam werden zu lassen und andere als die 'unteren' Dämonen in sich aufzunehmen. Mit andern Worten: was jener Künstler darzustellen gehabt hätte, wäre die 'Melencolia I' von Albrecht Dürer."

47 Ibid.

48 WIA, Fritz Saxl Papers, boxes "Saturn und Melancholie," proofs [1939], 388.

49 It is now possible to make the hypothesis that the research on *Melencolia I* undertaken in this context was one of the workplaces through which Panofsky definitively formulated the iconological method that would mark his post-war success. It is therefore not astonishing that the founder of the Warburg Library became here a minor reference.

50 Panofsky, *The Life and Art of Albrecht Dürer*. On Saxl's reaction to this publication see Davide Stimilli, chapter 11 in this volume.

51 See Panofsky, "Preface to the first edition," *The Life and Art of Albrecht Dürer*, xi: "The writer must apologize … for having incorporated in the section on the engraving *Melencolia* the more important results of the as yet unpublished second edition of his and his friend Dr. Saxl's previous book on the subject (Dürers *Melencolia I*, 1923). Its publication having been prevented by the War, he could not help anticipating it ... but he wants to make it perfectly clear that half of the credit, if any, goes to Dr. Saxl and his associates."

52 Ibid., 169 and 171 for the quotation: "Dürer's engraving is, at the same time, the objective statement of a general philosophy and the subjective confession of an individual man ... It typifies the artist of the Renaissance who respects practical skills, but longs … for mathematical theory ... It epitomizes the Neo-Platonic theory of Saturnian genius as revised by Agrippa … But in doing all this it is in a sense a spiritual self-portrait of Albrecht Dürer."

53 Klibansky also taught for several years at Université de Montréal (1947–68).

54 See Gertrud Bing to Panofsky, 12 April 1949, in Panofsky, *Korrespondenz 1910 bis 1968*, 2: 1071, and Elsner and Lorenz in their commentary to "On the Problem of Describing and Interpreting Works of the Visual Arts," 481n21: "This sorry

saga, which may be traced in Panofsky's ... correspondence, does not show him in a very generous light."

55 Panofsky, "Preface," (1954) ix.

56 This section (Part IV, Chapter III) features a discussion of Cranach's *Melancholies.*

57 See the acknowledgments ("Preface," *Saturn and Melancholy*, v f.) to Frances Lobb (for preparing the first draft of the translation from the German), to the staff of the Warburg Institute (for procuring the photographs for illustrations and assistance in the earlier stages of the proofs), to the late Hans Meier (who discovered the original version of Agrippa's *De occulta philosophia*), to Gertrud Bing and Rosemary Woolf (for collaboration in revising the translation) and to Lotte Labowsky (for helping in establishing the Greek text of pseudo-Aristotelian Problem XXX, I, likely by Theophrastus).

58 See Warburg's reaction *after* reading the 1923 Dürer's *Melencolia I* study in his letter draft to Panofsky from 21 January 1924: "Ich bin doch der Meinung, dass man die Metamorphose des Saturn ins Genie durch das [Jupiter] Amulett belegen kann. Bis zum Faust alla Hamlet"; quoted in Wedepohl, "Warburg, Saxl, Panofsky and Dürer's *Melencolia I*," 44n1.

59 Let's remember that the last point was not explicitly included in the 1920 Luther study, which was for a long time the only published text of Warburg dealing with *Melencolia I* – and calling explicitly for an "iconological science of civilisation" (*The Renewal of Pagan Antiquity*, 651).

60 See Jean-Philippe Uzel, chapter 12 in this volume.

61 See "Avant-Propos," in Klibansky, Panofsky, and Saxl, *Saturne et la Mélancolie*, 14 and 17; and "Vorwort zur deutschen Ausgabe" in Klibansky, Panofsky, and Saxl, *Saturn und Melancholie*, 25 and 21: "Gewiss ... das magische Quadrat stellt einen Talisman dar, der Jupiter Schutz vor unheilvollen Strahlen verbürgt. Hingegen weisen seine [Dürers] zahlreichen gesammelten Schriften keinerlei Spuren von Dämonologie oder Kabbala auf; sie zeigen, dass er im künstlerischen Verfahren allenthalben nach der Exaktheit von Zahl und Mass strebt." This is somehow a critique of the argument developed in chapter 6 of Frances Yates, *The Occult Philosophy in the Elizabethan Age*, and in her article "Chapman and Dürer on Inspired Melancholy."

62 Klibansky, Panofsky, and Saxl, *Saturne et la Mélancolie*, 18; *Saturn und Melancholie*, 27–8.

63 Dürer, *Christus als Schmerzensmann,*1st version as a painting, ca. 1493–94, 2nd version as a woodcut, 1511; ibid. resp. 19 and 28.

64 Ibid., resp. 19 and 28: "In seinem Zauber liegt ein für jede historische Deutung irreduzibles Moment."

65 DLA, A, KLIBANSKY: Panofsky to Klibansky, 9 November 1964, quoted in Regina Weber, "Aktivitäten der Warburg-Bibliothek," 112.

66 See among other critics: Schuster, *Melencolia I. Dürers Denkbild*, I, 131–3, and Part 1, chaps. I–III, in Agamben, *Stanzas: Word and Phantasm in Western Culture.*

67 See DLA, A, KLIBANSKY: VI, 2.

ELEVEN

The Melancholy of the (Co-)Author: Panofsky and the Authorship of *Saturn and Melancholy*

DAVIDE STIMILLI

Finis laudat opus
Aby Warburg, 28/IV/1929, Rome
Tagebuch der KBW.[1]

No author is immune to the melancholy realization that other writers may be better poised to handle a task at hand. In this case, I am aware that other contributors might do a more thorough job at presenting the history of *Saturn and Melancholy* than I may manage in these pages, but I nonetheless outline that history again, and ask for readers' patience, should they encounter any reiterations. I am particularly interested in the question of the book's authorship, a question that may be explored, and possibly settled, either by collating the different versions, which may be attempted if all versions are known and available, or by collating statements by the putative authors on their participation and contribution. A combination of the two methods is even more desirable, and may indeed be necessary. For this discussion, I limit myself to a consideration of author claims, which allows me in turn to claim some completeness, since at least one of the protagonists, Erwin Panofsky, has left a quite substantial and virtually exhaustive record and paper trail on the subject in his correspondence.[2]

A recurrent and influential *topos* in Panofsky's statements, in the mold of the post-classical *habent sua fata libelli*[3] – and one that Raymond Klibansky appropriated in the opening sentence of his preface to the 1964 edition of *Saturn and Melancholy* – is that of the *livre maudit*: "our ill-fated *Melencolia I*."[4] Panofsky used the phrase when he wrote to Saxl on 9 May 1942[5] and ten years earlier, in a letter written 20 November 1933 to Walter Friedländer, he had already predicted that "the unhappy Melencolia II [would] never see the light of day."[6] As this very volume confirms, however, the book has on the contrary experienced a remarkable longevity, if not yet an afterlife, and may be regarded as an exemplary case study of the peculiar melancholy that authors are liable to the moment a book is out of their hands and they abandon it to its fate – if it is true, as Paul Valéry suggested, that there are no complete, or completed, works, but only abandoned ones.[7]

In a letter from 19 April 1949, Panofsky invites Gertrud Bing to assess Klibansky's actual contribution to the book by looking with her own eyes: "in case the voluminous raw material of the book is still preserved at the Warburg Institute the amount of the notes and excerpts contributed by Dr. Klibansky could easily be ascertained. I am sure that it would not exceed the 10 to 15 per cent at which I estimated it in my last letter, and I certainly know that not a sentence in the German version as set up in type in Glücksburg was phrased by anyone but Saxl and myself."[8] While consideration of archival evidence is obviously indispensable, my suspicion is that the available record will probably not solve once and for all the questions on the book's authorship; it certainly could not dispel the broader anxieties about authorship that are evident in Panofsky's statements on the genesis of the book.

The Third Man

In the same letter to Bing, Panofsky refers ironically to the association of the three co-authors as a "Trinity."[9] *Tertium non datur* is Panofsky's consistent position all along, since he becomes aware in June 1939 that the book is announced as forthcoming under the joint authorship of "E. Panofsky, R. Klibansky and F. Saxl" in the Warburg Institute prospect of publications (fig. 11.1).[10] He writes to Saxl:

MYTH AND ALLEGORY IN ANCIENT ART. By ROGER HINKS. (*Studies of the Warburg Institute, No.* 6.) With 41 illustrations on 32 plates. 18s. Ready in April.

A study of mythology and allegory in Greek art in terms of the philosophical ideas which underlie them. Mr. Hinks considers particularly those features in the thought of the Greeks, such as their conception of time and their views on the relation of man to the physical universe, which led them to a method of artistic expression not always intelligible to the modern mind.

INFLUENCES ANTIQUES DANS L'ART DU MOYEN AGE FRANÇAIS. By JEAN ADHÉMAR. (*Studies of the Warburg Institute, No.* 7.) With 127 illustrations on 40 plates. 18s. In French. Ready in April.

It is now generally admitted that Roman culture was by no means forgotten during the Middle Ages, but that on the contrary it was one of the most important formative influences on mediaeval art. In order to define this influence more exactly, M. Adhémar has tried to find out what works of ancient art were accessible to French artists before the fifteenth century. He has also examined the use to which they put their knowledge, and has shown that the attitude of artists and writers towards antiquity varied considerably during different centuries of the Middle Ages.

ALLEGORIES OF THE VIRTUES AND VICES IN MEDIAEVAL ART. By ADOLF KATZENELLENBOGEN. (*Studies of the Warburg Institute, No.* 10.) With 76 illustrations on 48 plates. 18s. Ready in April.

Mediaeval artists loved to depict the struggle between Good and Evil in the form of a battle in which the Virtues and Vices personified were the combatants. Dr. Katzenellenbogen has shown how artists adapted scenes of combat in Roman reliefs to suit their new theme. In certain cases only the final victory of the Virtues is shown, without the combat; in others the Vices are accompanied by characters from the Bible. These variations are traced by Dr. Katzenellenbogen up to the middle of the thirteenth century, and illustrated by a series of plates after miniatures and sculptures.

LA SURVIVANCE DES DIEUX ANTIQUES. By JEAN SEZNEC. Essai sur le rôle de la tradition mythologique dans l'humanisme et dans l'art de la Renaissance. (*Studies of the Warburg Institute, No.* 11.) 18s. In French. Ready in May.

Nothing shows more clearly the close link which unites the Middle Ages to the Renaissance than the survival in the culture of the latter of the mythological ideas current during the former. M. Seznec has followed the fate of the pagan Gods from classical antiquity up to the sixteenth century. He shows how they were moralized and forced into the service of the Catholic Church, and particularly studies their survival in the mythological handbooks of Italian Renaissance scholars.

MELANCHOLIE UND SATURN. By E. PANOFSKY, R. KLIBANSKY and F. SAXL. Studien zur Geschichte der Naturphilosophie, Charakterlehre und bildenden Kunst. (*Studies of the Warburg Institute, No.* 13.) A second edition of Erwin Panofsky's and Fritz Saxl's *Dürer's Melencolia I*, enlarged and entirely re-written, with 146 illustrations on 88 plates. 25s. In German. Ready shortly.

The first edition, which was devoted to explaining Dürer's enigmatic engraving, has been re-written on an entirely new basis. Now the ideas involved have been treated in a much broader way, and the book contains a general study of the philosophical and medical theories on which the conception of the Temperaments was based, and an inquiry into the origin and development of astrological ideas and religious conceptions since antiquity. These ideas are traced in literature and the fine arts up to the sixteenth century, and their later development is also indicated.

REMBRANDT'S SACRIFICE OF MANOAH. By FRITZ SAXL. (*Studies of the Warburg Institute, No.* 9.) With 40 illustrations on 5 plates. 5s. 6d. Ready in April.

A study of Rembrandt's painting in the Dresden Gallery. Dr. Saxl analyses particularly the method of representation of the supernatural event chosen by Rembrandt. In the various stages of the design, which can be traced in drawings, he depicts either an unwinged angel or a flash of light. Dr. Saxl has been able to clarify the evolution of the picture on the basis of X-ray photographs.

DIE AUSDRUCKSFUNKTION EXTREM VERKUERZTER FIGUREN. By KURT RATHE. (*Studies of the Warburg Institute, No.* 8.) With 32 illustrations on 16 plates. 6s. In German. Ready in April.

It is usually assumed that the emotional effect of a painting or a bas-relief is produced by the gestures and facial expressions represented in it, but certain purely formal pictorial devices have an equally strong value as means of expression. Taking his instances from a number of little-known works of art, Dr. Rathe studies the effect produced on the spectator by figures which appear at right-angles to the plane of the picture.

Fig. 11.1 The new book is announced, in the Prospect of Publications, 1939, under the title *Melancholie und Saturn. Studien zur Geschichte der Naturphilosophie, Charakterlehre und bildenden Kunst* as "[a] second edition of Erwin Panofsky's and Fritz Saxl's *Dürers Melencolia I*, enlarged and entirely rewritten, with 146 illustrations on 88 plates."

> It horrifies me to see that the book is announced in your prospect as authored by you, me *and Klibansky*. I must protest against it in the sharpest possible way, as there has never been a discussion in such terms. You asked me whether I had anything against the appearance of Klibansky's name on the title page with the formula "*in collaboration with*" … and I had, of course, nothing against it. But rightful co-author K. is *not*, and the form that was originally proposed ("by E.P. and F.S., with the collaboration of R.K.") expresses the amount of his participation completely correctly. The book, as book, is *our* book, and must remain such.[11]

Panofsky threatens to withdraw his name if his wish is not fulfilled. "It has particularly bothered me," he adds with a well-calculated appeal to his older friend's self-esteem (vanity is probably a term one should not apply lightly to Saxl),[12] "that K. in that announcement is even mentioned before you, breaking the alphabetical order."[13] Even in response to Bing's request of a financial contribution toward the publication of Saxl's *Lectures*, almost an exact year to his death on 3 March 1948, Panofsky cannot but react angrily to the Annual Report 1947/48 of the Warburg Institute that announces the book again under their joint authorship. He writes to Bing on 4 April 1949:

> As you know, the book is *not* by "Klibansky, Panofsky and Saxl." The material exceeding that already used in the first edition was very largely discovered and "processed" by Saxl. The ideas, such as they are, were developed by Saxl and myself. And the verbal formulation of the book was largely incumbent upon myself. Dr. Klibansky contributed extensively (but not, I should estimate, to an extent of more than fifteen or twenty per cent) to the material. He played no appreciable part in the discussions preceding the final formulation, and no part whatever in the final formulation itself … So far as I recall, Saxl never took a definite stand in the matter, and the next thing I heard about the enterprise was that an English translation was planned. I consented to this under the assumption that Saxl had accepted either the one or the other of the above alternatives … This whole discussion may be quite academic because thus far a publisher has not been found and the publication itself is thus very much in doubt. I thought it wise, however, to make an unequivocal statement before a fait accompli has been created. As you see, I have no interest to see my name on the title at all; only, if it does appear, I do not wish it to imply my sanctioning a by-line which does not do justice to the actual division of responsibility.[14]

In her reply on 12 April 1949, Bing begs Panofsky to relent; indeed, she goes as far as "to throw [herself] on [his] mercy,"[15] convinced as she declares to be that the matter had been in principle resolved by Saxl's American trip and meeting with Panofsky in 1945: "Saxl came back highly delighted with what he regarded as your kind, generous and very sensible new view of the question. He told us that you had consented to allow the book to appear under the three names as joint authors, provided 'you had nothing more to do with the matter.'"[16]

Bing's dramatic plea is, however, to no avail: Panofsky continues to resist the inclusion of Klibansky's name as a co-author until Henri Frankfort, new director of the Warburg Institute after Saxl's premature death, announces a few months later, on 19 July 1949, that an "agreement has been reached on the wording of the title page of the *Melencolia*,"[17] and that Klibansky's contribution is to be demoted to a collaboration. Only after Klibansky visits Panofsky in Princeton, as we learn from a letter dated 20 June 1955 to Bing, who had become director of the Warburg Institute earlier that year, does Panofsky's attitude ostensibly change for good:

> I received a visit from our friend Dr. Klibansky, as a result of which I feel bound to confess that I seem to have done him an injustice when I so strongly objected to his name's appearing on the title page of the unfortunate book on melancholia *pari passu* with Saxl's and mine. When I became so furious some years ago, I imagined that the English edition would be a straight translation of the German text as established by Saxl and myself and was, therefore, very much surprised to see the controversial by-line … I have now come to see that Mr. Klibansky did in fact much more for the English edition than he had done for the German version, and the former thus seems to differ more emphatically from the latter than I knew. I therefore withdraw my original objection and, if and when the book gets published, you may formulate the by-line as you please.[18]

Panofsky's detachment and reiterated distancing from the book remains, however, a constant, and his final stance on the matter appears to be more a capitulation tinged by bitter resignation than a wholehearted acceptance of the outcome: he writes again to Bing shortly thereafter, on 30 July 1955, in lapidary fashion: "I am now so much 'out of it' and have accepted Dr. Klibansky as a full-fledged co-author."[19] On 6 September 1962, he transmits to yet another director of the Warburg Institute, E.H. Gombrich, a formal agreement to the now impending publication and gives the institute "*plein pouvoir*" on the matter;[20] that same day, in response to Klibansky's proposal on 30 August 1962 that Panofsky's name should come first on the title page, in accordance with "Saxl's original draft,"[21] Panofsky replies magnanimously that the sequence should be alphabetical so as not to discriminate against Saxl, stating in no uncertain terms that "so complete is my detachment from it that I do not even care for the sequence in which the names of the authors will appear."[22]

By signing the preface to *Saturn and Melancholy*, Panofsky implicitly agreed to its wording, which he must have regarded as a misrepresentation, if measured by all his recorded statements: once "the framework of the monograph on Dürer's engraving" had to be abandoned, Klibansky writes, "the plan of a new book on Saturn and Melancholy emerged to be undertaken by the three authors whose names now appear on the title-page."[23] The story is, at the very least, greatly simplified.

The preface is interesting for other reasons as well. For instance, Klibansky mentions among the remaining lacunae the lack of a treatment of the Hellenistic legend of Democritus and the Abderites – which resurfaces in the preface to *The Anatomy of Melancholy* by "Democritus Junior" – and the lack of a treatment of Burton's work itself, notwithstanding the homage paid to "the great 'melancholizer' by prefixing his effigy to the present volume."[24] (fig. 11.2) The book is thus buried under two additional layers of authorship: those of Burton and his pseudonym. The choice of Burton's sepulchral monument as the book's frontispiece is perhaps meant to solve symbolically the question of authorship by pointing out, as Burton does in his preface, that the book, and possibly any book, is only "a Cento collected from others" ("le texte est un tissu de citations," Roland Barthes will later echo);[25] or maybe, too, because of its epigraph: *cui vitam dedit et mortem melancholia* ("to whom melancholy gave life and death").

Panofsky's most sustained statement about the history of the book, which he describes as "truly Saturnian," is to be found in a letter of 27 April 1966 to Carl Nordenfalk:

> The book was completed and set in type in 1940 [1939]. Then the whole edition was bombed out of existence and I should have wished that it should never have been revived since Saxl died a few years later and I lost touch, so to speak, with the whole enterprise. As a result, the final redaction was done by Dr. Klibansky who, however, is a medievalist rather than an art historian. In its present form the new edition is therefore entirely out of date as far as our literature is concerned … and

Fig. 11.2 Frontispiece to *Saturn and Melancholy*: Tomb of Robert Burton (died 1640), author of *Anatomy of Melancholy*. Christ Church Cathedral, Oxford.

although the book has been treated with undeserved leniency, it really should be judged by the standards of 1940 rather than those of 1964.

Panofsky concludes with a disturbing simile (and one he has used before)[26] to describe the book: "It reminds me of those petrified embryos known as *lithopaedia* which died and crystallized in their mothers' wombs and are occasionally removed about thirty years after conception."[27]

The Prussian Ultimatum

As we have seen, Panofsky was at least clear about whose wombs the embryo of *Saturn and Melancholy* had died and crystallized in. If *maternitas semper certa*, however, *paternitas incerta*. It is highly ironic that Panofsky had staked a similarly confident claim to authorship, on his and Saxl's behalf, at the time of the hard-nosed negotiations over the 1923 edition of their study, *Dürers Melencolia I*, which followed the inaugural volume by Ernst Cassirer, *Die Begriffsform im mythischen Denken*, in the new series of *Studien der Bibliothek Warburg*. While not as ill-fated as the second edition, the genesis and publication history of the first *Melencolia* is equally fraught and indeed "Saturnian," to use Panofsky's coinage.

In the 1915 *Nachwort* to Karl Giehlow's *Die Hieroglyphenkunde des Humanismus in der Allegorie der Renaissance*, Arpád Weixlgärtner, the executor of Giehlow's *Nachlass*, had announced a forthcoming expanded edition of the deceased's groundbreaking study on *Dürers Stich "Melencolia I" und der maximilianische Humanistenkreis*.[28] According to Weixlgärtner's "Zum Geleite" prefacing the 1923 Saxl-Panofsky volume, it was then Friedrich Dörnhöffer, *Generaldirektor* of the *Bayerische Staatsgemäldesammlungen* in Munich, who had suggested Aby Warburg as the person ideally suited to revise and bring to completion Giehlow's book, which was finished except for its tenth and final chapter on "Die hieroglyphische Symbolik der Melencolia I" and the necessary updating to contemporary scholarship. Warburg was, however, prevented from taking up the task "because of several circumstances" (*durch mannigfache Umstände*),[29] as we are told with the necessary discretion. At this juncture enter Saxl and Panofsky, who were working on an essay for Max Dvorak's *Jahrbuch für Kunstgeschichte*, based partly on

Giehlow's pioneering contribution and partly on new astrological sources. Weixlgärtner had reached an agreement with them to replace Warburg and to publish the book by having their new work follow "as supplement and conclusion" (*als Ergänzung und Abschluß*) to Giehlow's work.[30] This plan was, however, pre-empted by the circumstance (eerily anticipating the fate that was to befall the "standing type"[31] of the revised 1939 version during the Second World War) that the proofs were pulped "during the collapse" (*während des Umsturzes*)[32] of the Habsburg empire. Thus both books share also the fate of being casualties of war.

We must assume that this "Zum Geleite" text is the fruit of a compromise, as in a letter of 18 May 1923 Panofsky thanks Weixlgärtner for it, but requests changes, as he does not agree with Weixlgärtner's explanation of the genesis of the book and rejects in very blunt terms any acknowledgment of Giehlow's authorship on the shared title-page: Panofsky and Saxl's research was completed before the plan was devised to combine it with Giehlow's research, Panofsky argues, and they were only marginally influenced by Giehlow's material, which they received after completing their own research. Panofsky concludes by suggesting that Weixlgärtner modify his text accordingly and that he add a passage on the good services rendered by the Bibliothek Warburg in financing the publication of the research.[33] Weixlgärtner had no choice but to yield again to this "Prussian ultimatum,"[34] as he had already done when faced with the lack of financial resources in Vienna. Weixlgärtner's preface is an extremely interesting, but also an uneasy text for the reader, with the palpable feel of a humiliating surrender to an enemy power: after the Bibliothek Warburg had taken on the costs of publication, the most the Austrian Staatsdruckerei could offer by way of reparation for the disaster was to print fifteen photos and to take on at least partially the cost of image reproduction.[35]

While Panofsky is eager to diminish the importance and indebtedness of his and Saxl's works to Giehlow's study, it is remarkable that later on, in a letter to William Heckscher on 23 November 1955, he does not hesitate to mention Giehlow along with Richard Förster and Warburg as "our real 'founders,'" adding:

> That my name has come to be so closely associated with iconological studies is only due to the fact that when I appeared in this country in

> 1931, the work of those three men was largely unknown, so that their achievement was more or less credited to one who tried to *transmit* their point of view and thereby to counteract to some extent the over-emphasis on stylistic analysis and preoccupation with attributions.[36]

Even more disturbing in light of this posthumous tribute is the refusal to dedicate the work to Giehlow and Warburg, one an already dead scholar and one who was terminally ill, as Panofsky unceremoniously pairs them, though he is only hinting at what was then the widespread belief among Warburg's family and circle of disciples and collaborators that the latter was no longer capable of a full recovery, a *restitutio ad integrum*:[37]

> A dedication of the whole book to Giehlow's *manes* appeared to us not really doable, since our new work is based in an equally large part on Aby Warburg's researches as on Giehlow's researches and material. And a double dedication to a dead and a living sick person would have been impossible. In addition, we share a general dislike against dedications to great scholars.[38]

Weixlgärtner plaintively points out that Ludwig Volkmann's essay "Bilderschrift der Renaissance"[39] was published with a dedication to Giehlow.[40] In lieu of the dedication brutally refused by Panofsky, Weixlgärtner provides a biography and a bibliography,[41] but this is the most he is able to wring out of his adversaries, who clearly have the upper hand. He also refers the reader to a beautiful but not easily accessible obituary published in the *Zeitschrift des Nordböhmischen Gewerbemuseums* by the director of that institution, Ernst Schwedeler-Meyer.[42] Warburg, who was obviously very fond of Giehlow, to the point one may argue that the latter's premature death in 1913 had on him a similar effect to that of Franz Boll's death in 1924,[43] received the obituary directly from Schwedeler-Meyer, a mutual friend: without naming Warburg, Schwedeler-Meyer had touchingly paired him with the deceased, describing him as a scholar blazing new trails in the study of the Italian Renaissance in the same way that Giehlow had for the German Renaissance.[44] In his letter of thanks on 9 April 1913, Warburg mentions for the first time his interest in helping with the disclosure of Giehlow's *Nachlass*[45] that he would then communicate directly to Weixlgärtner on 23 March 1915.[46]

Panofsky and Saxl's own introduction to the work includes the not very sincere sounding acknowledgment that the two authors "have done nothing else than to pursue the paths mapped and in large part opened by two great scholars – Giehlow and Warburg – a bit farther than it appeared necessary or possible to the pathfinders themselves."[47] In spite of this (half-hearted) *captatio benevolentiae*, Giehlow's name has been successfully erased from the title-page, where it was initially supposed to appear first. Klibansky's name will eventually replace Giehlow's, but, we may add, it is Giehlow's name that Panofsky and Saxl[48] wanted to remove in the first place, and they succeeded in achieving that goal.

Saxl's Dream

What takes place over time is not only the return of the repressed third author but also the duplication of the protagonists, as the title *Melancholia*, on which Panofsky and Saxl had agreed (according to Panofsky), and under which the book was announced at least on a few occasions, doubles to become *Saturn and Melancholy*. Like Mnemosyne to Warburg's "Atlas," Melancholia was to be the patron goddess of the book. Panofsky proposes the title *Melancholia* in a letter to Saxl of 7 February 1936,[49] and on 2 September 1938 reiterates that:

> We had at that time decided to call our unlucky creature (*Unglückswurm*) MELANCHOLIA, with a subtitle … The best solution seems to me:
>
> MELANCHOLIA,
> A Study on the Literary and Visual Sources
> Of the Saturnian Melancholic Type.
>
> As far as the subtitle is concerned, I would like to grant you freedom … But the simple "*Melancholia*" seems good to me as main title, and I have already quoted us this way proleptically [*here Panofsky is referring to his* Studies in Iconology, *whose bibliography lists the book as "in print*"],[50] (fig. 11.3) since we had already agreed on this point at that time in a definitive way.[51]

252 Panofsky, E., and F.Saxl, *Dürers "Melencolia I", eine quellen- und typengeschichtliche Untersuchung*, Berlin and Leipzig: 1923 (Studien der Bibliothek Warburg, 2)
253 Panofsky, E., and F.Saxl, *Melancholia*, Second edition of *Bibl.*252 *(in print)*

Fig. 11.3 *Melancholia* listed as "Second edition" of item 252 in "Bibliography of References Cited" under Erwin Panofsky, *Studies in Iconology.*

Suddenly, however, Saturn appears on the title page, and this apparition coincides with Klibansky's rising: as a *paranatellon*, Klibansky ascends along with the planet. Even more so, one may say, Saturn is Klibansky himself, and the digger with the spade, as the god was represented in the astrological iconography, turns out to be an author equally entitled and legitimately claiming that title, and not just a pretender, or, even worse, a mere *Quellensucher*[52] – as the missing chapter, the chapter on Saturn, is the one that drags on the longest and only Klibansky can complete, even in Panofsky's estimation.[53]

Meanwhile Panofsky announces to Saxl on 17 October 1942 the forthcoming publication of his influential Dürer monograph,[54] which was to include and first unveil the results of their research:[55] "I hope you will not mind my anticipating our *Melencolia II* in my book. But I had naturally to discuss that fateful print, and I really do not think that the German version will ever see the light."[56] The extraordinary dream that Saxl relates to Panofsky on 13 April 1943 is in direct response to this announcement. Disingenuously, Panofsky suggests not to interpret it in a Freudian fashion:[57]

> My dear Pan, I had a dream the other day about you: you arrived at a London station; I was expecting you, and saw you walking along the platform. I came up from behind and touched your shoulder, and realized that your hair had gone grey on the temples. We then did not look for a hotel for you because I lived in one of the Parks, and so I

offered you my bed in the open. We slept there but realized that it was too narrow and went in search of a hotel for you. – This I dreamt when I was in the country last week.

Saxl continues by expressing his own anticipation of his friend's book and especially of its chapter on Melencolia, but sets up an implicit and unflattering comparison to Panofsky's behaviour. He reports that, after "a lecture on the subject" to the Royal Society of Medicine, he was asked to publish it: "I refused," Saxl remarks matter-of-factly, "because I did not want to divulge our common secret." As a justification, but even more damningly for Panofsky, Saxl adds: "It is of course different when you have to write a book about Dürer, you cannot avoid dealing with Melencolia. I came to slightly different results then from those we had in the book; and I wish I had known in time about your Dürer book so that I could have sent you my lecture." The letter concludes with the remark: "Alas, I cannot say as you do in your letter that I am leading the life of a small-time country gentleman."[58] Saxl's ambivalence toward the country gentleman that Panofsky had become in Princeton is evident, and the reproach to Panofsky that he did not wait to reveal their secret only thinly veiled. It is plain that the relationship between the two was no longer as intimate as it had been in "that unforgettable period of close association between 1921 and 1934," as Panofsky writes to Rudolf Wittkower on 23 April 1948, when asked by the latter to contribute a short biography of Saxl that he never produced.[59]

The melancholy of the author, or Panofsky's melancholy, if we accept his claim to that role as the most grounded and legitimate among the three, may be ultimately due to the sobering realization that "even in Arcadia there is death" – even in such an enviable Arcadia as the American exile turned out to be for Panofsky – and the completion of one's work cannot but be a prefiguration and anticipation of one's own death. The motto "Et in Arcadia ego," the visual and conceptual centre of Nicholas Poussin's famous Louvre painting, is, in addition to the title, also the enigma at the centre of the essay that Panofsky wrote for Cassirer's sixtieth anniversary *Festschrift*, edited by Klibansky (with H.J. Paton) in 1936.[60] This version of the essay, however, is very different from its reworking for publication in the influential 1955 collection *Meaning in the Visual Arts*, and has Watteau as a second focus besides Poussin, as reflected by the subtitle: "On the Conception of Transience in

Poussin and Watteau." The later version eliminates entirely the Poussin-Watteau bifocalism.[61] What attracted Panofsky in Watteau's art, we learn, is that "even the border-line between a preparatory and a final stage of execution is abolished. The creative process does not lead to a stage of finality, but continues throughout, so that the very paintings are still subject to the principle of fluctuation."[62] It may be perhaps in the name of such a principle that Panofsky was finally willing to acknowledge, though grudgingly, Klibansky's contribution.[63]

Tombeaux

Roland Barthes's famous essay "The Death of the Author" was published only three years after the release of *Saturn and Melancholy*,[64] and thanks to, rather than in spite of its delayed publication, a book that may have fallen on deaf ears or only attracted a highly specialized readership had it been published in the 1930s, enjoyed a warm reception in the 1960s; one may even argue that it became almost a post-structuralist book *avant la lettre* rather than the neoclassical *tombeau* it was perhaps intended to be. Walter Benjamin's concurrent renaissance in the early 1960s may paradoxically also have contributed to the success of the book, as he quoted extensively its precursor, the 1923 Panofsky-Saxl study, in his German Baroque drama *Habilitationsschrift*, which greatly contributed, at the same time, to the rediscovery of Warburg and his school.

Benjamin's assessment comes closer, also, to recognizing Giehlow's true stature and literary merit and paying him the homage that Panofsky and Saxl had ungraciously withheld: "with the Renaissance the whole wealth of ancient meditations re-emerged from the sources. The great achievement of Giehlow and the superior beauty of his work [*das hohe Verdienst und die höhere Schönheit*] consist in the discovery of this turning point and the way it is presented with all the force of a dramatic *peripeteia*."[65] It may not be far-fetched to imagine that Panofsky was not pleased by this assessment, and Giehlow's ranking above his and Saxl's re-writing may have played a role in his dismissive response to Benjamin's book.[66] The only melancholy tribute Panofsky is willing to concede is by way of quoting Benjamin's groundbreaking study in "Et in Arcadia ego," though hiding its mention in the crypt of a footnote.[67]

While Klibansky is eventually granted the exalted status of co-author on the title page of the 1964 *Saturn and Melancholy*, as we have seen, and the story ends well, as far at least as he is concerned, Giehlow's name is already obliterated from the 1923 study, and the memory of Weixlgärtner's valiant effort to prevent that outcome similarly fades away in subsequent editions. And yet, in another unexpected turn of this Viennese-Hamburguese waltz, Panofsky was chosen to write the foreword to Weixlgärtner's last book, a monograph on Grünewald, published posthumously in 1962. Perhaps under no other pressure than the "presence of the forgotten" that is tradition, in Adorno's formulation,[68] rather than the remorse of a bad conscience, Panofsky declares that he had felt bound "in gratitude and admiration for half a century to the twenty-year older scholar," who shared with other representatives of the Viennese school of art history "the veneration for the detail" (*die Ehrfurcht vor dem Detail*), the proverbially Warburgian virtue.[69] We may well conclude with Francis Bacon (and Saxl): *Recte enim Veritas filia Temporis dicitur, non Auctoritatis.*[70]

NOTES

1 Warburg, *Tagebuch*, 443.

2 We are especially fortunate to be able to rely on Dieter Wuttke's monumental edition, from which I quote: Panofsky, *Korrespondenz 1910 bis 1968*. Translations from the German originals are mine.

3 The wingèd words occur in the treatise of the late Latin grammarian and poet Terentianus Maurus, *De litteris, de syllabis, de metris* (ca. 300 CE), v. 1286, and are quoted by Robert Burton in *The Anatomy of Melancholy* (1621) in its context: *Pro captu lectoris habent sua fata libelli*, which he paraphrases: "Our writings are as so many dishes, our readers guests, our books like beauty, that which one admires, another rejects; so are we approved as men's fancies are inclined." Burton, *The Anatomy of Melancholy*, 13.

4 Klibansky, Panofsky, and Saxl, *Saturn and Melancholy*, v: "From the remote times when events in the world of man were first held to be linked with the stars, Saturn was thought to retard any undertaking connected with him. No doubt the ancients would have found ample evidence of his sluggish influence in the fate of this book." (The preface is signed by R.K. and E.P., but it was written by Klibansky alone, as we learn from a letter from Panofsky to Klibansky on 12 February 1964: "I personally should think it justifiable if you, 'the only begetter' of the *Preface*, were to sign it alone; but if you think otherwise, I have no objection at all": Panofsky, *Korrespondenz*, 5: 447.)

5 Ibid., 2: 344.

6 "Die unglückliche 'Melencolia II,' die nun wohl nie das Tageslicht erblicken wird." Ibid., 1: 674.

7 Valéry, *Tel Quel*, 154 and 160.

8 Panofsky, *Korrespondenz*, 2: 1075. As Wuttke points out, Panofsky meant Glückstadt, where the printing house J.J. Augustin was located.

9 Ibid., 2: 1074.

10 Reproduced in Panofsky, *Korrespondenz*, 2: 203. The book is announced under the title *Melancholie und Saturn. Studien zur Geschichte der Naturphilosophie, Charakterlehre und bildenden Kunst* as "[a] second edition of Erwin Panofsky's and Fritz Saxl's *Dürers Melencolia I*, enlarged and entirely rewritten ... In German. Ready shortly. The first edition, which was devoted to explaining Dürer's enigmatic engraving, has been re-written on an entirely new basis. Now the ideas involved have been treated in a much broader way, and the book contains a general study of the philosophical and medical theories on which the conception of the Temperaments was based, and an inquiry into the origin and development of astrological ideas and religious conceptions since antiquity. These ideas are traced in literature and the fine arts up the sixteenth century, and their later development is also indicated."

11 4 June 1939: "Ich sehe zu meinem Entsetzen, dass das Buch als von Ihnen, mir *und Klibansky* verfasst in Ihrem Prospekte angezeigt wird. Dagegen muss ich aufs schärfste protestieren, da davon nie die Rede gewesen ist. Sie fragten mich, ob ich etwas dagegen hätte, wenn Klibanskys Name mit einem '*in collaboration with*' auf dem Titelblatt erscheinen würde ... und ich hatte selbstverständlich nichts dagegen. Aber vollberechtigter Mitverfasser ist K. nicht, und die ursprünglich vorgeschlagene Form ('by E.P. and F.S., with the collaboration of

R.K.') drückt das Mass seiner Beteiligung vollständig richtig aus. Das Buch, qua Buch, ist *unser* Buch, und soll es bleiben." Panofsky, *Korrespondenz*, 2: 204 (italics are underlinings in the original typescript and are preserved as such in Wuttke's edition.)

12 On Saxl's self-effacing personality, see Gertrud Bing's moving tribute, "Fritz Saxl (1890–1948): A Memoir."

13 "Besonders geärgert hat mich, dass K. in jener Anzeige, unter Durchbrechung der alphabetischen Reihenfolge, sogar vor Ihnen genannt ist." Panofsky, *Korrespondenz*, 2: 204.

14 Ibid., 2: 1068.

15 Ibid., 2: 1071.

16 Ibid., 2: 1071–2.

17 Ibid., 2: 1085.

18 Ibid., 3: 779–80.

19 Ibid., 3: 794.

20 Ibid., 5: 251.

21 Ibid., 5: 253.

22 Ibid., 5: 257.

23 Klibansky, Panofsky, and Saxl, *Saturn and Melancholy*, v.

24 Ibid., vi.

25 Burton, *Anatomy of Melancholy*, 1: 112; Barthes, "La mort de l'auteur," 494.

26 In a letter to Robert Klein on 27 September 1965. Panofsky, *Korrespondenz*, 5: 701.

27 Ibid., 5: 829.

28 Weixlgärtner, *Nachwort*, 232.

29 Weixlgärtner, "Zum Geleite," IX. Weixlgärtner is hinting at Warburg's mental breakdown and hospitalization in the aftermath of Germany's own *Umsturz*. See my edition (with Chantal Marazia) of Warburg's clinical history, *Ludwig Binswanger-Aby Warburg, Die unendliche Heilung*.

30 Weixlgärtner, "Zum Geleite," X.

31 Klibansky, Panofsky, and Saxl, *Saturn and Melancholy*, v.

32 Weixlgärtner, "Zum Geleite," X.

33 "Tatsächlich war ja unsere Arbeit, bevor der Plan einer Zusammenlegung mit der Giehlow'schen auftauchte, vollständig abgeschlossen und Sie wissen ja selbst, da Sie das Vergleichsmaterial zur Hand haben, wie relative wenig die später er-

langte Kenntnis des Giehlow'schen Nachlasses uns zu einer Änderung oder Erweiterung unserer Ausführungen genötigt hat." Panofsky, *Korrespondenz*, 1: 124.

34 Warburg Institute Archive (hereafter WIA), General Correspondence (hereafter GC): Arpád Weixlgärtner to Fritz Saxl, 8 July 1922.

35 Weixlgärtner, "Zum Geleite," X.

36 Panofsky, *Korrespondenz*, 3: 860.

37 See my introduction, "Tinctura Warburgii," to Marazia and Stimilli, *Binswanger and Warburg: Die unendliche Heilung*, 7–11.

38 "Eine Widmung des ganzen Buches an die Manen Giehlows schien uns deswegen nicht wohl tunlich, weil unsere neue Arbeit zu einem eben so grossen Teil auf den Forschungen und dem material A. Warburgs beruht wie auf den Forschungen und dem material Giehlows. Und eine doppelte Widmung an einen Toten und einen lebenden Kranken unmöglich gewesen wäre. Hinzukommt, dass wir überhaupt eine gemeinsame Abneigung gegen Dedikationen an grosse Gelehrte haben." Panofsky, *Korrespondenz*, 1: 124–5.

39 Volkmann, *Bilderschriften der Renaissance*.

40 WIA, GC: Weixlgärtner to Erwin Panofsky, 16 April 1923.

41 Weixlgärtner, "Zum Geleite," XII–XV.

42 Schwedeler-Meyer, "Karl Giehlow †," [1r–1v].

43 See my *Einleitung* to Warburg, *"Per Monstra ad Sphaeram,"* especially 20–5.

44 "Auch unter seinen gleichaltrigen Fachgenossen ist es nur Einer, der in gleicher Weise für die italienische Renaissance eine ähnliche Aufgabe zu lösen sucht, wie Giehlow es für die deutsche tat." Schwedeler-Meyer, "Karl Giehlow," [1v].

45 WIA, GC: Aby Warburg to Ernst Schwedeler-Meyer, 9 April 1913.

46 WIA, GC: Warburg to Weixlgärtner, 23 March 1915.

47 "[Sie haben] dabei nichts anderes getan, als die von zwei großen Gelehrten – Giehlow und Warburg – gewiesenen und großenteils geebneten Wege um ein Stück weiter zu verfolgen, als es den Pfadfindern selbst notwendig oder möglich erschien." Panofsky and Saxl, *Dürers 'Melencolia I,'* 1.

48 Saxl had issued the original "Prussian ultimatum" in a letter to Weixlgärtner on 24 June 1922 (WIA, GC), threatening to publish the book in the *Studien der Bibliothek Warburg* if no answer was received by 10 July.

49 Panofsky, *Korrespondenz*, 1: 873.

50 *Melancholia* is listed as "Second edition" of item 252 (Panofsky and Saxl, *Dürers 'Melencolia I'*) and "*in print*" in the "Bibliography of References Cited" to Panofsky, *Studies in Iconology: Humanistic Themes in the Art of the Renaissance*, 244.

51 "Wir hatten damals beschlossen, unser Unglückswurm MELANCHOLIA zu nennen, mit einem Untertitel … Am besten scheint mir:

MELANCHOLIA,

Eine quellen- und bildgeschichtliche Studie

über den Typus des saturnischen Melancholikers.

Ich möchte in Bezug auf den Untertitel Ihnen Freiheit lassen … Das einfache '*Melancholia*' als Haupttitel aber erscheint mir gut, und ich habe uns auch proleptischer Weise schon so zitiert, da wir uns damals über diesen einen Punkt definitive geeinigt hatten." Panofsky, *Korrespondenz*, 2: 138.

52 Dieter Wuttke attributes the role of *Quellensucher* to Saxl vis-à-vis Panofsky as the author (*Verfasser*). Panofsky, *Korrespondenz*, 3: 693.

53 See Panofsky's letter to Saxl on 14 July 1936, where he avows to have nothing more to add to the Saturn section and recommends to Saxl to trust "in the favour of God and Klibansky" (*deo et Klibansko favente*). Panofsky, *Korrespondenz*, 1: 910.

54 Panofsky, *The Life and Art of Albrecht Dürer*.

55 "The analysis given in the text includes some of the material and conclusions to be submitted in the second edition of E. Panofsky and F. Saxl, *Dürers Kupferstich Melencolia. I, Studien der Bibliothek Warburg*, II, Leipzig 1923. The publication of this second edition – parts of which were prepared with the assistance of Dr. Raymond Klibansky – has thus far been prevented by the political circumstances." Panofsky, *Albrecht Dürer*, 2: 26.

56 Panofsky, *Korrespondenz*, 2: 379.

57 Panofsky to Saxl, 21 May 1943: "Dear, old Sassetto [*Saxl's nickname, first coined by Warburg*]. Thanks a lot – as we Yankees say – for your kind letter. It is good to feel that old friendships can outlast so many years of separation, and your dream – as far as I can see, without compromising Freudian connotations for either of us – may still come true." Panofsky, *Korrespondenz*, 2: 400.

58 Ibid., 2: 394.

59 Ibid., 2: 931.

60 Panofsky, "*Et in Arcadia Ego*: On the Conception of Transience in Poussin and Watteau," 223–54.

61 Panofsky, "*Et in Arcadia Ego*: Poussin and the Elegiac Tradition," 295–320.

62 Panofsky, "*Et in Arcadia Ego*: On the Conception of Transience in Poussin and Watteau," 251.

63 Klibansky himself described his contributions as relating primarily to ancient

Greek and Latin philosophy, literature, and medicine, as well as medieval thought up to Marsilio Ficino: see "Raymond Klibansky, philosophe et historien. Entretien avec Yves Hersant et Alain de Libera," 132.

64 Barthes, "La mort de l'auteur."

65 Benjamin, "Ursprung des deutschen Trauerspiels (1928)," 328; also in *The Origin of German Tragic Drama*, 150. (The book was first republished in 1963 by Suhrkamp in a "revised edition" curated by Rolf Tiedemann.) In equally unflattering terms, Benjamin writes that "in their discovery of this most vital function of the Saturn-image Panofsky and Saxl have, in their fine study, *Dürers Melencolia I*, completed and perfected the discoveries made by their predecessor, Giehlow, in his remarkable studies," or, more literally: "the discoveries of their extraordinary model, Giehlow's studies" (*die Entdeckungen ihres außerordentlichen Vorbildes, den Studien Giehlows*): Benjamin, *Ursprung des deutschen Trauerspiels*, 327 (English version: *Origin of German Tragic Drama*, 149).

66 Sigrid Weigel has outlined the "odyssey of the *Trauerspielbuch* in the *Kulturwissenschaftliche Bibliothek Warburg*" and published the relevant correspondence in her *Walter Benjamin. Die Kreatur, das Heilige, die Bilder* (Frankfurt: Fischer, 2008), 228–64.

67 Panofsky, "*Et in Arcadia Ego*: On the Conception of Transience in Poussin and Watteau," 234; Panofsky, "*Et in Arcadia Ego*: Poussin and the Elegiac Tradition," 309.

68 "Tradition is the presence of the forgotten" (*das gegenwärtige Vergessene*): Adorno, *Philosophie der neuen Musik*, 117; *Philosophy of New Music*, 95.

69 Panofsky, "Zum Geleit," 5.

70 "Truth is rightly called the daughter of time, not of authority." Saxl discusses the shorter version of the motto, originating with Aulus Gellius, under the title "Veritas Filia Temporis" in the same Cassirer *Festschrift* (*Philosophy & History*) edited by his "learned friend Klibansky" (200); Bacon's interpretation is on p. 220.

TWELVE

The Theme of Melancholy in Raymond Klibansky's Work after 1964

JEAN-PHILIPPE UZEL

It would be no exaggeration to say that Raymond Klibansky worked on the theme of melancholy all his life. The first evidence of this work appears a few months after his entry into the "working community" (*Arbeitsgemeinschaft*) of the Kulturwissenschaftliche Bibliothek Warburg in 1926. Indeed, Klibansky's first publication, written in the context of the KBW, addresses the question of melancholy and its allegorical representation from different angles. The *Liber de sapiente* (or *Book of the Wise*, 1511) by the sixteenth-century French philosopher and disciple of Nicholas of Cusa, Charles de Bovelles (Carolus Bovillus), which appears in appendix to Ernst Cassirer's *Individuum und Kosmos in der Philosophie der Renaissance* (1927),[1] is an exemplar of French humanism. Bovelles's book deals repeatedly with the question of *acedia*, the name Christian monks gave to melancholy during the Middle Ages. It was considered one of the seven deadly sins, and Bovelles warned that it reduced its sufferer "to the very lowest rank," making him "similar to minerals."[2]

Some contemporary authors, like Peter-Klaus Schuster,[3] maintain that Bovelles's book is closely linked with Dürer's engraving *Melencolia I*. Schuster asserts that Dürer could have been inspired by an engraving in *Liber de sapiente* which illustrates the antithesis *virtus/fortuna*, a recurring theme in humanist thinking of the Renaissance. These two images, the one by Dürer and the one in Bovelles's book, would both have aimed at exhorting melancholic beings to virtue. Regardless of the veracity of this hypothesis, Klibansky's edition of the *Liber de sapiente* shows that he was familiar with issues related to melancholy and its representation before working with Panosfky and Saxl on *Saturn and Melancholy.*[4] The early nature of this interest is important, because it shows that his attention to the topic was not only a product of his collaboration with the two art historians, but may have been a pre-existing personal concern.

Just as it would be a mistake to believe that Klibansky's interest in melancholy grew merely out of his collaboration with Panofsky and Saxl, it would be wrong to believe that it ended there. Indeed, during the four decades following the publication of *Saturn and Melancholy*, Klibansky continued to focus on this issue, pursuing new research directions, including medical literature, modern philosophy, and French poetry. But he also continued to work on other aspects and major themes that traverse the book. In the 1989 French edition, for instance, he provided a new translation of the pseudo-Aristotelian Problem XXX.1 (probably authored by Theophrastus). The foreword he wrote for the French (1989) and German (1990) translations of the book also offers an interesting reflection on its scientific method, which is often seen, rightly or wrongly, as the culmination of the "Warburg method." Distancing himself from Panofsky's iconographic approach, Klibansky defends a more open conception of art history, one that recalls the *Kulturwissenschaft* proposed by Aby Warburg.[5] His foreword thus highlights disagreements between Warburg and his successors, including the authors of *Saturn and Melancholy.*

A Persistent Interest in Problems Related to Melancholy

After 1964 Klibansky continued to research melancholy in ways that extend well beyond the scope of *Saturn and Melancholy*. His foreword to the French and German translations of the book attests to his unwavering commitment to the subject, and shows that he carefully followed publications on the theme for many years: "Just think of the growing number of books published during the quarter century since the publication of our book, in fields ranging from history and philosophy to medicine and psychiatry, religion and theology, astrology and alchemy, literature and art. It would take a whole new book to do them justice."[6]

While Klibansky evidently did not wish to write a new book, he did feel compelled to make a number of additions and corrections to the French and German translations. The most obvious of these is the new translation of Problem XXX.1,[7] to say nothing of several expanded footnotes that are listed in an appendix at the end of each.[8] The German translation also contains a new "selected bibliography"[9] (*Auswahlbibliographie*) organized around themes such as "Ancient," "Medieval," "Dürer," and "Psychiatry and psychoanalysis."

In addition to supplementing the French and German translations of *Saturn and Melancholy*, Klibansky continued to devote original research to melancholy. His most developed scholarly article, "Le avventure della malinconia," was published in 1996 in the Italian journal *Dianoia*. It mentions many authors whose works both deepen and complement the analyses of *Saturn and Melancholy*, including Giovanni Manardo (1462–1536), a doctor from Ferrara who helped Pico della Mirandola with his criticism of astrology. Klibansky refers to Manardo as "one of the glories of Italian medicine," and quotes a letter from him to a friend suffering from the "black bile." In it, the doctor advises his friend to stay away from all magical cures. "The necessary antidotes are within you; no one better than you can be your doctor ... you have your healing in your hands."[10] This attitude vis-à-vis melancholy, notes Klibansky, contrasts surprisingly with the pessimistic position of the doctor's contemporary, Marsilio Ficino, the most famous representative of Florentine Neoplatonism.

Klibansky's paper also focuses on modern and contemporary authors interested in melancholy. In addition to Enlightenment philosophers (Shaftesbury, Diderot, Kant) and their successors (Kierkegaard, Nietzsche), he pays particular attention to nineteenth-century French poets such as Charles Baudelaire and Gérard de Nerval. More surprisingly, he also considers fourteenth-century French poetry, which he sees as inaugurating "a new historical era." Indeed, in contrast to most manuals on the subject, Klibansky sees the emergence of modern subjectivity in the verses of *De nature suis merancolieux*, by Eustache Deschamps (1346–1406), a senior official of the court of Charles V, rather than in fifteenth-century Florentine poetry.[11]

It is, however, Klibansky's interest in medical literature on melancholy that is most visible in "Le avventure della malinconia." We know that it was one of his principal contributions to *Saturn and Melancholy*, since he was responsible for the chapters "Melancholy in the Physiological Literature of the Ancients" and "Medieval Medicine, Science and Philosophy." While also referring to more contemporary authors, Klibansky's article makes several references to Robert Burton's book *Anatomy of Melancholy*, which is mentioned only briefly in *Saturn and Melancholy*. In addition, Klibansky criticizes German psychiatrists for continuing to use the term "melancholy" instead of "depression," which had been adopted long ago by their colleagues in the United Kingdom. "In our time, the term has been the subject of numerous studies of German-speaking psychiatrists who believe they have found the solution using the philosophy of Heidegger to define the 'endogenous psychoses.'"[12]

Another way to gauge Klibansky's interest in melancholy is to consider his personal library, preserved today in the Rare Books and Special Collections at McGill University. In consulting this collection, it becomes clear that Klibansky acquired books on this theme throughout his lifetime. The most recent title is *Melancholy: Die traurige Leichtigkeit des Seins*, by Josef Zehentbauer, which was published in 2001, when Klibansky was ninety-six years old. By studying the composition of his library, it also becomes apparent that all his life Klibansky nourished a passion for scientific and medical treatises dealing with melancholy. This collection starts with various editions of *Anatomy of Melancholy* by Robert Burton (originally published in 1621), but also extends to the contemporary period; his library includes, for example, Alfred Winterstein's *Dürers "Melancholy" im Lichte der Psychoanalyse* (1929), as well as more recent works by the French author Jean Starobinski. Klibansky also had a passion for Dr William Osler's library, which is also preserved in the McGill Library.

As this material shows, the issue of melancholy in both its modern and ancient dimensions was of interest to Klibansky throughout his life, and while *Saturn and Melancholy* is undoubtedly his most important contribution to the topic, it is far from being his only one.

Limits of the Iconographic Method

In his book *Le Philosophe et la mémoire du siècle*, Klibansky explains how, in 1923, Panofsky and Saxl invited him to work on a new version of their book *Melencolia I*.

> They [Panofsky and Saxl] had written a book in 1923 on the engraving *Melencolia* by Dürer, a beautiful book, very interesting. At my own risk, I took the liberty of criticizing it, because it seemed not to take sufficient account of the philosophical and theological roots of the different conceptions of melancholy. To my surprise, they recognized that my criticisms were not unfounded and invited me to formulate them. Thus was born the desire for a new book.[13]

If Saxl immediately agreed to include the young Klibansky as third author of the book, things were not so simple for Panofsky. Let us recall, for example, that in a note appearing in an article published in 1932, Panofsky briefly discusses the significance of *Melencolia I* by Dürer and then refers the reader "to the second edition in preparation of the study published in common with F. Saxl in 1923"[14] without mentioning Klibansky. Panofsky's letters to Saxl also show that he was more than reluctant to consider the young art historian as a third co-author of the book.[15] He eventually allowed Klibansky's name to appear on the cover of the version of the book to be published in 1939, with the proviso that his role as collaborator be made explicit (the cover reads, "by Erwin Panofsky and Fritz Saxl with the cooperation of Raymond Klibansky"); only after Klibansky's 1955 visit to Panofsky in Princeton did the latter agree to have the names of all three authors appear on an equal footing and in alphabetical order.[16] This saga recalls the scathing response Panofsky wrote to Walter Benjamin after reading *Ursprung des deutschen Trauerspiels* (1928), in which the philosopher quotes recent works on melancholy by Giehlow, Warburg, and Panofsky and Saxl.[17]

Beyond issues of personality and authorship, it is also possible to see in these disagreements a more scientific argument concerning methodological approaches to iconology. Indeed, distancing himself from Panofsky's method of iconographic analysis, in his 1989 foreword to *Saturn and Melancholy* Klibansky hints at something new concerning the interpretation of *Melencolia*

I. The pages devoted to the analysis of Dürer's engraving in *Saturn and Melancholy* are indeed very close to those found in the book that Panofsky published on the artist in 1943.[18] The wingèd figure is an allegory for the melancholic type of Geometry, which symbolizes the new spirit of the Renaissance artist, who feels both inspired by celestial influences and constrained by the limits of his mind. *Melencolia I* is thus seen as a warning against the despair of melancholic genius, which is unable to reach higher states of knowledge. This interpretation, which is at the heart of *Saturn and Melancholy*, had therefore already been formulated in 1932, as the following passage shows: "[A]rt historians use the intellectual testimonia of the Renaissance (among which naturally the writings of Dürer himself must be included) to show the worldview within which Dürer's *Melancholia* united a *typus Acediae* with a *typus Geometriae* and thus for the first time brought together in a single conception the sufferings of creatures with a sense of fateless agency."[19]

For Panofsky, who authored *Studies in Iconology* in 1939, iconographical interpretation was not supposed to leave room for suspicion. Its aim was to reveal the "intrinsic meaning" of the work of art, to decipher the "worldview" (*Weltanschauung*) it carried. This ultimate meaning was, according to Panofsky, "apprehended by ascertaining those underlying principles which reveal the basic attitude of a nation, a period, a class, a religious or philosophical persuasion – unconsciously qualified by one personality and condensed into one work."[20]

The question thus arises: what is the purpose of all this in-depth analysis, if the final results are always the same? Indeed, the 1932, 1943, and 1964 interpretations of *Melencolia I* remain identical. The reader cannot help feeling that subsequent research should result in a more nuanced interpretation, and that the many pages devoted, for example, to artistic genius in Renaissance Neoplatonism, should impart a deeper meaning to the melancholy main figure of the engraving. In this sense, pages 345 and 346 of the 1964 *Saturn and Melancholy* are quite significant. While the doctrine of Marsilio Ficino is here recognized as the "foundation" of Dürer's ideas, a more detailed link is not only rejected, but seen as contradictory to the "intrinsic meaning" of the engraving. The passage in question deserves to be reproduced in its entirety:

> But beyond this general connexion the *De vita triplici* can hardly have had any influence on the composition of the engraving, for the very idea which is most essential to Dürer's composition of the engraving, namely the integral interpenetration of the notions of melancholy and geometry (in the widest sense), was not only foreign to Ficino's system, but actually contradicts it.[21]

There is indeed a kind of gap between the accumulated knowledge and the always-identical meaning of the engraving. Robert Klein pointed this out, noting in his 1964 review: "When we finally arrive at Dürer's engraving, we learn that all this historical background is insufficient to explain it, because the large wingèd woman is not, iconographically, a Melancholy, but a Liberal Art, especially a Geometry."[22]

It is possible to see, in Panofsky's insistence that the 1932 interpretation remain definitive, a fear of undermining the whole structure of his system. Carlo Ginzburg critiques the circular nature of this method in a 1966 article concerning the self-sufficiency of iconographical research. In it, he notes the following about Panofsky's essay "The Neoplatonic Movement and Michelangelo":[23] "The scholar might be lured either to involuntarily slant texts … or to discard the documentation that does not square with the predetermined scheme of interpretation."[24] In this article, Ginzburg is one of the very first scholars to oppose Warburg's method to Panofsky's; this opposition has since been explored in greater detail by several authors, most recently Georges Didi-Huberman.[25]

Without explicitly naming Panofsky, Klibansky devotes a small, interesting paragraph in his 1989 foreword to the limits of iconographic analysis. In his words, "The iconographic method is vital and valuable as an auxiliary science, but instead of considering the place due to the fundamental unity of the work, it may reduce it to the sum of its details."[26] Adding that any interpretation of *Melencolia I*, however rich, will ultimately fail to unravel its mystery,[27] Klibansky seems to be asserting that there is no such a thing as an "intrinsic meaning" to the work of art. He thus seems to favour a more open reading of visual art, one that seems to revive the spirit and method of Aby Warburg's *Kulturwissenschaft* against the shortcomings he sees as inherent in Panofsky's iconographic method. We know that iconographic analysis was first put into practice by Warburg in his magisterial 1912 lecture on the frescoes of the Palazzo Schifanoia in Ferrara. Warburg never intended this new method of analysis to solve a "pictorial riddle for its own sake,"[28] but rather to revive the understanding and knowledge of images. Panofsky expanded upon this method in hopes of systematizing its application. In so doing, he abandoned its more experimental aspects.

Revival of the *Kulturwissenschaft*

Saturn and Melancholy is inseparable from the Warburg Library and its project to establish a "science of culture" (*Kulturwissenschaft*). In the words of historian Robert Klein, "I do not think the 'Warburgian spirit' was ever better illustrated."[29] The version of the book that finally appeared in 1964 is indeed very different from the original study of 1923, and the contribution of Klibansky certainly played a key role in these changes. According to Klein:

> [The] first book was for the authors only the first step; they were joined by Raymond Klibansky, a historian of ideas who had thoroughly studied the transmission of philosophical and scientific thought from antiquity to the Renaissance; together, they decided to broaden the subject in a general history of Saturn and Melancholy up to and beyond Dürer.[30]

It is important to keep in mind that Warburg had already proposed an interpretation of Dürer's engraving in his 1920 essay *Heidnisch-antike Weissagung in Wort und Bild zu Luthers Zeiten*. Arguing against Karl Giehlow's posthumously published writings, he asserted that *Melencolia I* did not praise the saturnine genius, but sought rather to counteract the harmful effect of Saturn in opposition to the beneficial effect of Jupiter.[31] Warburg rested his argument on the presence of the magic square of Jupiter, a legacy of magical astrology dating back to late antiquity and which appears to be built into the wall above the engraving's main figure. According to Warburg, this *Mensula Jovis* (the seal of Jupiter) operated as an anti-Saturnian talisman.[32] But the authors of *Saturn and Melancholy* do not believe in this comforting aspect of the engraving. In a footnote, they explicitly cite Warburg's description, declaring: "We cannot imagine the 'demoniac conflict' between Saturn and Jupiter ending in a victory for the latter; nor can we accord it the prime significance for the interpretation of Dürer's engraving which Warburg attributed to it."[33] For them, the ultimate significance of *Melencolia I* is that it serves as a warning against the despair of melancholic genius and its inability to reach higher states of knowledge.

With this conflict of interpretation in mind, it is interesting to note that in his 1989 foreword Klibansky actually returns to this point and seems to rehabilitate the importance of the magic square. "Dürer shared the ideas of his time on the influence of planets and temperaments. The Magic Square is a talisman that ensures the protection of Jupiter against the harmful rays [of Saturn]."[34] He also opens another avenue of interpretation linked to Dürer's knowledge of the book *De vita* by Marsilio Ficino.[35] *Saturn and Melancholy* mentions the possibility that Dürer became aware of this book on his second trip to Italy.[36] According to Giehlow, Dürer's writings during his Italian time seem to adopt the assumptions of the Florentine humanists concerning melancholy, including the notion that melancholy can be cured by "pleasant tunes on the lute."

Yet, this interpretation is rejected by the authors of *Saturn and Melancholy*, who note that the melancholy effects of music were known during the Middle Ages, as evidenced by engravings of the thirteenth century. In his foreword, Klibansky seems instead to give credence to Giehlow's thesis, claiming that Dürer did indeed have direct contact with Florentine humanism during his journey to Italy, where he befriended Giovanni Francesco, nephew of Pico della Mirandola. Klibansky also asserts that Dürer could have had direct access to the *De vita* through the German translation of Johannes Adelphus Muelich without recourse to *Occulta philosophia* by Cornelius Agrippa of Nettesheim, which, according to the authors of *Saturn and Melancholy*, was the key to the interpretation of *Melencolia I*.

This hypothesis deserves, of course, to be verified, but it would certainly revive the interpretation of the engraving. I do not wish at this point to confirm or disprove the validity of Klibansky's assertions. Rather, I would simply like to note that he never stopped questioning the conclusions of *Saturn and Melancholy* during the decades following its publication. Perhaps this ongoing questioning can be seen as a legacy of the "Warburg method," which Ernst Gombrich once beautifully defined in the following way: "I believe that the only method which would deserve the name [the Warburg method] is the willing suspension of belief … For without such willingness to distrust one's own assumptions, iconology is subject to the same dangers to which the interpretation of styles had been so prone, the danger of circularity."[37]

In conclusion, I would like to underscore once more the fact that Klibansky never ceased to keep abreast of new works related to melancholy, but also that he continued to question and build upon the conclusions of *Saturn and Melancholy* (1964). Perhaps it is possible to see in this commitment the influence of Saturn, whose planet slows any undertaking connected with him, while also fuelling it for the long term.

NOTES

1 Carolus Bovillus [Charles de Bovelles] (ed. Klibansky), *Liber de sapiente.*

2 Bovelles, *Le livre du sage*, 27. Translations from French originals are mine unless otherwise specified.

3 Schuster, *Melencolia I. Dürers Denkbild.*

4 Klibansky, Panofsky, and Saxl, *Saturn and Melancholy.*

5 See also Philippe Despoix, chap. 10 in this volume.

6 Klibansky, "Avant-propos" in Klibansky, Panofsky, and Saxl, *Saturne et la Mélancolie*, 7.

7 Klibansky, Panofsky, and Saxl, *Saturne et la Mélancolie*, 49–75.

8 Ibid., 676–9.

9 Klibansky, Panofsky, and Saxl, *Saturn und Melancholie*, 573–84.

10 Klibansky, "Le avventure della malinconia," 17–18. Translations from Italian originals are mine unless otherwise specified.

11 Ibid., 25.

12 Ibid., 24. This ironic remark was intended for the psychiatrist Hubertus Tellenbach who, in his book *Melancholie. Zur Problemgeschichte, Typologie, Pathogenese und Klinik*, used the Heideggerian concept of *Geworfenheit* (thrownness). This reminds us of the deep aversion Raymond Klibansky felt for Martin Heidegger, an aversion that extended to all those who knew the philosopher. For example, when Georges Leroux asked him what he remembered of Hannah Arendt, he offered the following amazing response: "I knew her as student, when she was attracted to Heidegger, and she was certainly a woman of great intelligence, but the reputation she enjoys now seems exaggerated to me. She found good for-

mulas, but if one looks closely, her thinking is not deep." Klibansky and Leroux, *Le Philosophe et la mémoire du siècle*, 26.

13 Ibid., 35.

14 Panofsky, "Zum Problem der Beschreibung und Inhaltsdeutung von Werken der bildenden Kunst" (1932, cited here from its 1964 reprinting in *Aufsätze zu Grundfragen der Kunstwissenschaft*, ed. Oberer and Verheyen), 97n15.

15 See also Davide Stimilli, chap. 11 in this volume.

16 Concerning this episode, which is not very flattering to Panofsky, see the comprehensive note of the translators of the 1932 Panofsky article. Panofsky, "On the Problem of Describing and Interpreting Works of the Visual Arts," trans. Elsner and Lorenz, 481n21.

17 Brodersen, "Wenn Ihnen die Arbeit des Interesses wert erscheint." On this point, see also Davide Stimilli's contribution to this volume, chap. 11.

18 Panofsky, *The Life and Art of Albrecht Dürer*, 157–71.

19 Panofsky, "On the Problem of Describing and Interpreting Works of the Visual Arts," 480–1.

20 Panofsky, *Studies in Iconology*, 7.

21 Klibansky, Panofsky, and Saxl, *Saturn and Melancholy*, 364.

22 Klein, "Saturne: croyances et symboles (1964)," 227. The English translation of the book [Robert Klein, *Form and Meaning* (New York: Viking Press, 1979)] does not include this essay.

23 Panofsky, *Studies in Iconology*, 171–233.

24 Ginzburg, "From Warburg to E.H. Gombrich: A Problem of Method (1966)," in *Clues, Myths, and the Historical Method*, 36.

25 Didi-Huberman, *L'Image survivante*, 91–102.

26 Klibansky, "Avant-propos" in Klibansky, Panofsky, and Saxl, *Saturne et la Mélancolie*, 16.

27 Ibid., 19.

28 Warburg, "Italian Art and International Astrology in the Palazzo Schifanoia, Ferrara," 585.

29 Klein, "Saturne: croyances et symboles," 224.

30 Ibid., 224–5.

31 Giehlow, "Dürers Stich 'Melencolia I' und der maximilianische Humanistenkreis."

32 Warburg, "Pagan-Antique Prophecy in Words and Images in the Age of Luther (1920)," 645–7.

33 Klibansky, Panofsky, and Saxl, *Saturn and Melancholy*, 327n148.

34 Klibansky, "Avant-propos" in Klibansky, Panofsky, and Saxl, *Saturne et la Mélancolie*, 14.

35 Ibid., 17.

36 Klibansky, Panofsky, and Saxl, *Saturn and Melancholy*, 281–2.

37 Gombrich, "Art and Scholarship," 116.

AFTERWORD

Through these chapters, conceived as complementary to each other, this collective volume has proposed a new perspective on Raymond Klibansky's enduring ties with the group of scholars who pursued, within the Warburg Institute, the programmatic studies developed from the founding of the eponymous library in Hamburg. We have not limited ourselves here to the intellectual wanderings of Klibansky from Heidelberg to London, and later Montreal but have concentrated on what links him most closely to the Warburg circle as a whole. Various other intellectual contexts could be further explored: from the more individual angle of his relationship to the philological tradition of his university studies director, Ernst Hoffmann; to the more strictly philosophical tradition of Ernst Cassirer; or the articulation of the relationship between ancient source transmission and a commitment to the tradition of tolerance, which characterizes so much of Klibansky's later work. What this volume reveals most particularly is the eminently collective character of the Warburg Institute projects carried out by Klibansky – whether the edition of the *Corpus Platonicum* (*Plato Latinus* and *Arabus*), the periodical *Mediaeval and Renaissance Studies*, or the iconic *Saturn and Melancholy* – and their paradigmatic value of research that transcends disciplinary boundaries, in the very spirit of its founder, for the reconstituted institution in London.

There is perhaps, here, a new form of intellectual history emerging, focusing less on individual authorial attributions than on group interactions, less on the formalization of research methods than on their transposition into new political, cultural, and media environments ... all elements of what could become a microhistory of scholarly institutions and their constituent networks. The network of the Warburg Institute remains an exemplary case for study toward such a history.

In this sense, it is our hope that the research carried out here will continue, and that subsequent studies will be undertaken in a similar vein on the individual and collective involvement of, in particular, Fritz Saxl, Gertrud Bing, and Edgar Wind with respect to other major projects of the Warburg Institute's redevelopment phase, among them the *Bibliography on the Survival of the Classics*, the *Journal of the Warburg and Courtauld Institutes*, and the *Studies of the Warburg Institute*. Only through such a series of investigations might the specificity of the multiple Warburgian heritage ultimately appear. And this all the more so if such a study could be complemented by a more systematic examination of the significance of a role played by the immigration – to the United Kingdom, the United States, and Canada – of such a group of scholars in the further development and institutionalization of the humanities and social sciences. Such investigations would contribute to a renewal, through new perspectives, of classic network studies.

Finally, we can see in Raymond Klibansky's *oeuvre* how the philosophical analysis developed in his work is essentially linked both to philological considerations and to the material bibliographical examination of texts in all their historical variants. This in fact characterizes the Warburg network itself, in which geographical transmission and historical transmission meet – and it is from this essential base that Klibansky deploys a true ethics of transmission. Today, as we witness so many instances of ancient heritage being threatened or even destroyed, as in Palmyra, it would be pertinent to resume, in contrast, Klibansky's work and that of the Warburg network to re-emphasize the decisive importance of the Arab world in the transmission of ancient knowledge and in the recycling of that knowledge in new contexts. By intimately linking the material evidence of the library with reflective methods of intellectual study and intensive exchange, the great originality of the Warburg network helps us also to conceive of new and constructive scholarly uses of electronic and digital media in this still young twenty-first century.

Philippe Despoix and Eric Méchoulan

BIBLIOGRAPHY

Archives

Austrian National Library, Vienna
Bundesgymnasium Vienna 9, Wasagasse, archive
Deutsches Literaturarchiv Marbach
Ernst Cassirer Papers, Addition, General Collection, Beinecke Rare Book and Manuscript Library, Yale University
Ernst Kris Papers, Library of Congress, Washington, DC
Heckscher-Archiv im Warburg-Archiv des Kunstgeschichtlichen Seminars der Universität Hamburg
Hudson's Bay Company Archives, Archives of Manitoba, Winnipeg, London
Meyer Schapiro Collection, Rare Book and Manuscript Library, Columbia University
Oxford University Press Archive
Raymond Klibansky Collection, Rare Books and Special Collections, McGill University Library
The Society for the Protection of Science and Learning (SPSL) Papers, Bodleian Library, Oxford
Warburg Institute Archive, London
Webb Diaries, Bodleian Library, Oxford
Wind Papers, Bodleian Library, Oxford

Publications by Raymond Klibansky: Principal Works in Chronological Order

Carolus Bovillus [Charles de Bovelles]. *Liber de sapiente.* Edited by Raymond Klibansky. In Ernst Cassirer, *Individuum und Kosmos in der Philosophie der Renaissance*, 299–458. *Studien der Bibliothek Warburg* 10. Leipzig and Berlin: Teubner, 1927.

Ein Proklos-Fund und seine Bedeutung. Sitzungsberichte der Heidelberger Akademie der Wissenschaften 1928–29, Philosophisch-Historische Klasse, 5. Abhandlung. Heidelberg: Winter, 1929.

Cusanus-Texte, I: Predigten, 1, Dies Sanctificatus vom Jahre 1439. Edited by Raymond Klibansky and Ernst Hoffmann. Heidelberg: C. Winter, 1929. "Bernhard und Thierry von Chartres." *Habilitationsschrift*, University of Heidelberg, 1932.

Nicolai de Cusa [Nicholas of Cusa]. *Opera omnia (issu et auctoritate Academiae Litterarum Heidelbergensis edita)*. Leipzig: Meiner, 1932–83:

1932. Vol. I, *De docta ignorantia.* Edited by Raymond Klibansky with Ernst Hoffmann.

1934. Vol. II, *Apologia doctae ignorantiae.* Edited by Raymond Klibansky.

1959. Vol. VII, *De pace fidei*. Edited by Raymond Klibansky with Hildebrandus (Hildebrand) Bascour OSB. Second edition, 1970. First published in London by the Warburg Institute, 1956. Reprint of Warburg edition: Nendeln, Liechtenstein: Kraus International, 1977.

1982. Vol. XII, *De venatione sapientiae. De apice theoriae*. Edited by Raymond Klibansky and G.H. Senger.

1983. Vol. V, *Idiota de sapientia. Idiota de mente*. Edited by R. Steiger. With two appendices by Raymond Klibansky: I: *De memoria librorum Idiotae*. II: *De dialogis De vera sapientia Francisco Petrarcae addictis*. Hamburg: Meiner, 1983.

Magistri Eckardi [Meister Eckhart]. *Opera Latina (auspiciis Instituti S. Sabinae in Urbe ad codicum fidem edita)*. Fasc. I: *Super oratione dominica*, edidit Raymundus Klibansky. Leipzig: Meiner, 1934.

Magistri Eckardi. *Opera Latina (auspiciis Instituti S. Sabinae in Urbe ad codicum fidem edita)*. Fasc. XIII: *Quaestiones Parisienses*, edidit Antonius Dondaine OP; *Commentariolum de Eckardi Magisterio*, adiunxit Raymundus Klibansky. Leipzig: Meiner, 1936.

Philosophy and History: Essays Presented to Ernst Cassirer. Edited by R. Klibansky and H.J. Paton. Oxford: Clarendon Press, 1936. Reprinted Gloucester, MA: Peter Smith, 1975.

"The Philosophical Character of History." In *Philosophy and History*, 323–37.

The Continuity of the Platonic Tradition During the Middle Ages: Outlines of a Corpus Platonicum medii aevi. London: Warburg Institute, 1939. Reprinted London: Warburg Institute, 1950. Reissued ...*with a New Preface and Four Supplementary Chapters, Together with Plato's Parmenides in the Middle Ages and the Renaissance.* Munich: Kraus International, 1981; reprinted Millwood, NY: Kraus International, 1982.

Corpus Platonicum Medii Ævi. Auspiciis Academiæ Britannicæ. Edidit Raymundus Klibansky. London: Warburg Institute, 1940–62.

Volumes published:

1940. *Plato Latinus I:* Meno, *Interprete Henrico Aristippo.* Ed. Victor Kordeuter. Recognovit et praefatione instruxit Carlotta Labowsky.

1943. *Plato Arabus II: Alfarabius de Platonis Philosophia.* Ed. Franciscus Rosenthal et Richardus Walzer.

1950. *Plato Latinus II:* Phaedo, *Interprete Henrico Aristippo.* Ed. et praefatione instruxit Laurentius Minio-Paluello.

1951. *Plato Arabus I: Galeni Compendium* Timaei *Platonis.* Edd. Paulus Kraus et Richardus Walzer.

1952. *Plato Arabus III: Alfarabius Compendium* Legum *Platonis.* Ed. Franciscus Gabrieli.

1953. *Plato Latinus III: Platonis* Parmenides *usque ad finem primae hypothesis nec non Procli Commentarium in Parmenidem, pars ultima adhuc inedita, interprete Guillelmo de Moerbeka.* Ediderunt, praefatione adnotationibusque illustraverunt Raymundus Klibansky et Carlotta Labowsky.

1962. *Plato Latinus IV:* Timaeus, *a Calcidio translatus commentarioque instructus.* Ed. Jan Hendrick Waszink.

Reprint of *Plato Latinus I–III and Plato Arabus I–III.* Nendeln, Liechtenstein: Kraus-Thomson, 1973. Second edition of *Plato Latinus IV.* Leiden: Brill, 1975.

Medieval and Renaissance Studies. Edited by Raymond Klibansky and Richard Hunt. 1941–1943–1968. 6 vols. + 3 supplements. Vols. 4–6 (1959–68) also co-edited by Carlotta (Lotte) Labowsky. (Vols. 1–3, and supplements 1 and 3 reprinted, Nendeln, Liechtenstein: Kraus Reprint, 1970–77).

Includes Klibansky's:

"Leibniz's Unknown Correspondence with English Scholars and Men of Letters." Vol. I, no. 1 (1941–43): 133–49.

"Plato's *Parmenides* in the Middle Ages and the Renaissance." Vol. I, no. 2 (1943): 281–330.

"The Rock of Parmenides: Medieval Accounts of the Origins of Dialectic." Vol. I, no. 2 (1943): 171–86.

Mussolini, Benito. *Memoirs: 1942–1943, with Documents Relating to the Period.* Translated by Frances Lobb. Edited with commentary by R. Klibansky. London: Weidenfeld and Nicolson, 1949. Reprinted New York: Fertig, 1975.

Croce, Benedetto. *My Philosophy and Other Essays on the Moral and Political Problems of Our Time.* Edited by R. Klibansky. London and New York, 1949. Reprinted Oxford, 1969; New York, 1983.

New Letters of David Hume. Edited with E.C. Mossner. Oxford: Clarendon Press, 1954. Reprinted Oxford, 1969. Reprinted New York: Garland, 1983. Paperback ed., Oxford, 2011.

Plato. *Philebus and Epinomis.* Translation and introduction by A.E. Taylor. Edited by Raymond Klibansky with the co-operation of Guido Calogero and A.C. Lloyd. London: Nelson, 1956.

Philosophy in the Mid-Century / La Philosophie au milieu du vingtième siècle. Edited by Raymond Klibansky. Florence: La Nuova Italia, 1958–1959. 4 vols. Reprinted Nendeln, Liechtenstein: Kraus International, 1967–1976.

"The School of Chartres," in *Twelfth-Century Europe and the Foundations of Modern Society*, edited by Marshall Clagett, Gaines Post, and Robert Reynolds, 3–14. Madison: University of Wisconsin Press, 1966. First published in 1961 as conference proceedings (University of Wisconsin Press).

Locke, John. *Lettera sulla tolleranza, testo latino e versione italiana.* Latin text edited with a preface by Raymond Klibansky. Philosophy and World Community series. Florence: La Nuova Italia, 1961. This is the first publication of Klibansky's edition of the Latin text, which was subsequently printed in several bilingual editions.

– *Lettre sur la tolérance. Texte latin et traduction française.* Critical edition and preface by Raymond Klibansky. Translation and introduction by Raymond Polin. Montreal: Casalini, 1964. Also published at Paris: Presses universitaires de France, 1965; 2nd ed. Paris: Presses universitaires de France, 1967.

– *Epistola de tolerantia: A Letter on Toleration.* Latin text edited with a Preface by Raymond Klibansky. English translation with an introduction and notes by J.W. Gough. Oxford: Clarendon Press, 1968.

Plato. *The Sophist and the Statesman.* Translation and introduction by A.E. Taylor. Edited by Raymond Klibansky and Elizabeth Anscombe. London: Nelson, 1961.

Saturn and Melancholy: Studies in the History of Religion, Art, and Natural Philosophy. Co-authored with Erwin Panofsky and Fritz Saxl. London: Nelson; New York: Basic Books, 1964. Reprinted Nendeln, Liechtenstein: Kraus International, 1979.
Subsequent editions:
Saturno e la melanconia. Studi su storia della filosofia naturale, medecina, religione e arte. Translated by Renzo Federici. Torino: Einaudi, 1983.
Saturne et la mélancolie. Études historiques et philosophiques: Nature, religion, médecine et art. Translated by Fabienne Durand-Bogaert and Louis Évrard. Augmented edition with an introduction by Raymond Klibansky. Bibliothèque illustrée des histoires series. Paris: Gallimard, 1989.
Saturn und Melancholie. Studien zur Geschichte der Naturphilosophie und Medizin, der Religion und der Kunst. Translated by Christa Buschendorf. Frankfurt: Suhrkamp, 1990.
Translated into Spanish (1991), Japanese (1991), Romanian (2002), Polish (2009), Slovenian (2013).

Contemporary Philosophy. Edited by Raymond Klibansky. 4 vols. Florence: La Nuova Italia, 1968–71.

Philosophy and Science in the Middle Ages. Contemporary Philosophy: A New Survey, vol. VI. Edited by G. Floistad and R. Klibansky. 2 vols. Dordrecht: Kluwer, 1990.

Die Handschriften der philosophischen Werke des Apuleius. Ein Beitrag zur Überlieferungsgeschichte. Co-authored with Frank Regen. Göttingen: Vandenhoeck & Ruprecht, 1993.

La Philosophie en Europe. Edited by Raymond Klibansky and David Pears. Folio Essais 218. Paris: Gallimard, 1993.

La Pensée philosophique d'expression française au Canada. Le rayonnement du Québec. Edited by Raymond Klibansky and Josiane Boulad-Ayoub. Quebec: Presses de l'Université Laval, 1998.

Le Philosophe et la mémoire du siècle: Tolérance, liberté et philosophie. Entretiens avec Georges Leroux. Paris: Belles Lettres, 1998; Also published in Montreal: Boréal, 2000.
Translations:
El filósofo y la memoria del siglo: Tolerancia, libertad, filosofía. Conversaciones con Georges Leroux. Barcelona: Península, 1999.
Erinnerung an ein Jahrhundert. Gespräche mit Georges Leroux, translated from the French by Petra Willim. Frankfurt: Insel, 2001.

Idées sans frontières. Histoire et structures de l'Institut international de philosophie. With the collaboration of Ethel Groffier. Paris: Belles Lettres, 2005.

[posthumous] *Tradition antique et tolérance moderne.* Texts selected and introduced by Philippe Despoix and Georges Leroux. Montreal: Presses de l'Université de Montréal, 2016.

General Bibliography

Adorno, T.W. *Gesammelte Schriften.* Vol. 20, Bd. 1, *Vermischte Schriften I.* Frankfurt: Suhrkamp, 1997.

– *Philosophie der neuen Musik.* Frankfurt: Suhrkamp, 1978. Published in English as *Philosophy of New Music*, trans. Robert Hullot-Kentor (Minneapolis and London: University of Minnesota Press, 2006).

– Review of *Cassirer Festschrift. Zeitschrift für Sozialforschung* 6 (1937, published 1938): 657–61.

Agamben, Giorgio. *Stanzas: Word and Phantasm in Western Culture.* Minneapolis: University of Minnesota Press, 1992.

Al-Farabi. *Alfarabius. Compendium Legum Platonis.* Edited by Francesco Gabrieli. *Corpus Platonicum Medii Aevi, Plato Arabus*, 3. London: Warburg Institute, 1952.

– *Alfarabius. De Platonis philosophia.* Edited by Franz Rosenthal and Richard Walzer. *Corpus Platonicum Medii Aevi, Plato Arabus*, 2. London: Warburg Institute. 1943.

Arendt, Hannah. *Between Past and Future.* New York: Viking Press, 1961.

Aristotle. *Selecta ex Organo Aristoteleo capitula. In usum scholarum academicarum.* Oxford: Clarendon Press, 1902.

Bakhouche, Béatrice, ed. *Calcidius, Commentaire au* Timée *de Platon. Édition critique et traduction française.* 2 vols. Paris: Librairie philosophique J. Vrin, 2011.

Balavoine, Claudie. "Edgar Wind. Itinéraire d'un philosophe historien de l'art. Entretien avec Raymond Klibansky." *Préfaces. Les idées et les sciences dans l'édition européenne* (June 1992): 28–32.

Barthes, Roland. "La mort de l'auteur." In *Œuvres complètes II: 1966–1973*, 491–95. Paris: Seuil, 1994.

Baudelaire, Charles. "Correspondances." In *Les Fleurs du mal et autres poèmes*, 39–40. Paris: Flammarion, 1964.

Benjamin, Walter. *The Origin of German Tragic Drama.* Translated by John Osborne. London: Verso, 1998.

– "Ursprung des deutschen Trauerspiels (1928)." Vol. I, pt. 1 of *Gesammelte Schriften*. Frankfurt: Suhrkamp, 1974.

Biester, Björn. *Der innere Beruf zur Wissenschaft. Paul Ruben (1866–1943)*. Berlin-Hamburg: Reimer, 2001.

Bing, Gertrud. "A.M. Warburg." *Journal of the Warburg and Courtauld Institutes* 28 (1965): 299–313.

– "Aby Warburg. Vortrag von Frau Professor Dr. Gertrud Bing anlässlich der feierlichen Aufstellung von Aby Warburgs Büste in der Hamburger Kunsthalle am 31. Oktober 1958." In Aby Warburg, *Ausgewählte Schriften und Würdigungen*, edited by Dieter Wuttke, 455–64. Baden-Baden: Verlag Valentine Koerner, 1979; third edition 1992.

– "Der Begriff des Notwendigen bei Lessing. Ein Beitrag zum Geistesgeschichtlichen Problem Leibniz-Lessing." PhD diss., University of Hamburg (1921).

– "Fritz Saxl 1890–1948: A Memoir." Offprint by the Warburg Institute from *Fritz Saxl 1890–1948: A Volume of Memorial Essays*, edited by D.J. Gordon, 1–46. London: Nelson, 1957.

– "The Warburg Institute." *Library Association Record* 4, no. 1 (August 1934): 262–6.

Bloch, Marc. *Apologie pour l'histoire ou le métier d'historien*. Paris: Armand Colin, 1997 [1941].

– *Les Rois thaumaturges*. Paris: Albin Michel, 1923.

Bock, C.V. "First Report on the Gundolf Papers at the Institute of Germanic Languages and Literatures in the University of London." *German Life and Letters: A Quarterly Review* 15 (October 1961): 16–20.

Bovelles, Charles de. *Le Livre du sage*. Translated by Pierre Magnard. Paris: Vrin, 2010.

Braudel, Fernand. "L'Histoire, mesure du monde." In *Les Ambitions de l'histoire*, 11–83. Paris: Éditions de Fallois, Livre de poche, 1997 [1943].

Bredekamp, Horst. "Ex nihilo. Panofskys Habilitation." In *Erwin Panofsky, Beiträge des Symposions Hamburg 1992*, edited by Bruno Reudenbach, 31–47. Berlin: Akademie Verlag, 1994.

Brisson, Luc. *Le Même et l'autre dans la structure ontologique du Timée de Platon. Un commentaire systématique du Timée de Platon*. Paris: Klincksieck, 1974.

British Academy. Proceedings of the British Academy [1937–59].

Brodersen, Momme. "Wenn Ihnen die Arbeit des Interesses wert erscheint ... Walter Benjamin und das Warburg-Institut: einige Dokumente." In *Aby Warburg. Akten des Internationalen Symposiums, Hamburg 1990*, edited by Horst Bredekamp et al., 87–94. Weinheim: VCH, 1991.

Burkart, Lucas. "'Die Träumereien einiger kunstliebender Klosterbrüder …' Zur Situation der Kulturwissenschaftlichen Bibliothek Warburg zwischen 1929 und 1933." *Zeitschrift für Kunstgeschichte* 63 (2000): 89–119.

Burton, Robert. *The Anatomy of Melancholy*. London: W.J. Widdleton, 1875.

Calcidius. *Commentario al Timeo di Platone*. Translated and edited by Claudio Moreschini from the Latin edition made by J.H. Waszink for the *Corpus Platonicum Medii Aevi, Plato Latinus* 4. Milan: Bompiani, 2003.

Campbell Hutchison, Jane. *Albrecht Dürer: A Biography*. Princeton, NJ: Princeton University Press, 1990.

Cassirer, Ernst. *A Commentary on Kant's Critique of Judgment*. London: Methuen, 1938.

– *Ausgewählter wissenschaftlicher Briefwechsel*. Edited by John Michael Krois, *Ernst Cassirer – Nachgelassene Manuskripte und Texte* (ECN) 18. Hamburg: F. Meiner, 2009.

– "Descartes et l'idée de l'unité de la science." *Revue de Synthèse* 14, no. 1 (April 1937): 7–28.

– "Ficino's Place in Intellectual History." Review of *The Philosophy of Marsilio Ficino* by Paul O. Kristeller, *Journal of the History of Ideas* 6, no. 4 (October 1945): 483–501.

– *Freiheit und Form. Studien zur deutschen Geistesgeschichte*. Berlin: B. Cassirer, 1916.

– "Freiheit und Notwendigkeit in der Philosophie der Renaissance." *Inaugural lecture, 1 May 1926*. Published in *Individuum und Kosmos in der Philosophie der Renaissance*, chap. 3. Leipzig: Teubner, 1927.

– *Idee und Gestalt. Goethe/Schiller/Hölderlin/Kleist*. Berlin: B. Cassirer, 1921.

– *The Individual and the Cosmos in Renaissance Philosophy*. Translation and introduction by Mario Domandi. New York: Harper & Row, 1964.

– *Individuum und Kosmos in der Philosophie der Renaissance. Studien der Bibliothek Warburg* 10. Leipzig: Teubner, 1927.

– *Kleinere Schriften zu Goethe und zur Geistesgeschichte*. Edited by Barbara Naumann. *Ernst Cassirer – Nachgelassene Manuskripte und Texte* (ECN) 10. Hamburg: F. Meiner, 2006.

– *Philosophie der symbolischen Formen*. Vol. 3, *Phänomenologie der Erkenntnis*. Berlin: B. Cassirer, 1929.

– *Die platonische Renaissance in England und die Schule von Cambridge. Studien der Bibliothek Warburg* 24. Leipzig: Teubner, 1932.

– *Zur Einstein'schen Relativitätstheorie. Erkenntnistheoretische Betrachtungen.* Berlin: B. Cassirer, 1921.

Cassirer, Ernst, and Ernst Hoffmann. "Die Geschicht der antiken Philosophie." In *Lehrbuch de Philosophie*, vol. 1, *Die Geschichte der Philosophie*, edited by Max Dessoir, 7–256. Berlin: Ullstein, 1925.

Cassirer, Toni. *Mein Leben mit Ernst Cassirer.* Hamburg: F. Meiner, 2003.

Certeau, Michel de. *The Writing of History*. Translated by Tom Conley. New York: Columbia University Press, 1988.

Char, René. "Feuillets d'Hypnos (1943–44)." In *Fureur et mystère*, 83–150. Paris: Gallimard, 1967.

Chernow, Ron. *The Warburgs: The Twentieth-Century Odyssey of a Remarkable Jewish Family.* New York: Random House, 1993.

Classical Association. *Proceedings of the Classical Association* 32 (1935); 36 (1939).

De Burgh, William. Review of *Philosophy and History: Essays Presented to Ernst Cassirer*, edited by R. Klibansky and H.J. Paton. *Mind* 45, no. 180 (October 1936): 514–25.

Despoix, Philippe. "*Translatio* and Remediation: Aby Warburg, Image Migration and Photographic Reproduction." *SubStance* 44, no. 2 (2015): 129–50.

Dessoir, Max. *Beiträge zur allgemeinen Kunstwissenschaft.* Stuttgart: F. Enke, 1929.

Didi-Huberman, Georges. *L'Image survivante.* Paris: Minuit, 2003.

– "Die leichtfüßige Dienerin (Wissen der Bilder, Wissen von außen)." In *Warburgs Denkraum. Formen, Motive, Materialien*, edited by Martin Treml, 259–72. Munich: Fink, 2014.

Dilly, Heinrich, et al., eds. "Chronik des Kunsthistorischen Seminars der Hamburgischen Universität." Unpublished material of the Warburg Haus, Hamburg, 1989.

Dronke, Peter, ed. *A History of Twelfth Century Western Philosophy.* Cambridge: Cambridge University Press, 1988.

Eckhart, Meister. *Die deutschen und lateinischen Werke.* Herausgegeben im Auftrage der Deutschen Forschungsgemeinschaft. 11 vols. Stuttgart and Berlin: Verlag W. Kohlhammer, 1936.

Eijk, Philip J. van der. "Aristoteles über die Melancholie." *Mnemosyne* 43 (1990): 33–72.

– *Medicine and Philosophy in Classical Antiquity: Doctors and Philosophers on Nature, Soul, Health and Disease.* Cambridge: Cambridge University Press, 2005.

Euripides. *Fragments: Aegeus – Meleager:* Vol. 7 of *Euripides*, translated by Christopher Collard and Martin Cropp. Loeb Classical Library. Cambridge, MA: Harvard University Press, 2008.

Febvre, Lucien. *Combats pour l'histoire*. Paris: Armand Colin, 1992 [1952].

Flasch, Kurt. "Der Hüter des Erbes. Zum 90. Geburtstag von Raymond Klibansky." *Frankfurter Allgemeine Zeitung*, 14 October 1995: 31.

Flashar, Helmut. *Melancholie und Melancholiker in den medizinischen Theorien der Antike*. Berlin: De Gruyter, 1966.

Fleck, Ludwik. *The Genesis and Development of a Scientific Fact*. Edited by T.J. Trenn and R.K. Merton. Chicago: University of Chicago Press, 1979.

Foucault, Michel. *The Care of the Self*. New York: Random House, 1988.

– "The Order of Discourse. Inaugural Lecture at the Collège de France, December 2, 1970." In *Untying the Text: A Post-Structuralist Reader*, edited by Robert Young, 48–76. London: Routledge & Kegan Paul, 1981.

Friedman, Michael. "Ernst Cassirer." *The Stanford Encyclopedia of Philosophy*, edited by Edward N. Zalta (Spring 2011). http://plato.stanford.edu/archives/spr2011/entries/cassirer/, accessed 5 October 2015.

Gawronsky, Dimitry. "Ernst Cassirer: His Life and Work." In *The Philosophy of Ernst Cassirer*, edited by Paul Arthur Schlipp, 1–38. Evanston, ILL: Library of Living Philosophers, 1949.

Gay, Peter. *A Godless Jew: Freud, Atheism, and the Making of Psychoanalysis*. New Haven: Yale University Press, 1987.

– *Weimar Culture: The Outsider as Insider*. New York: W.W. Norton & Company, 2001.

Gersh, Stephen. *Middle Platonism and Neoplatonism: The Latin Tradition*. Notre Dame, IN: Notre Dame University Press, 1986.

Gerson, Lloyd P., ed. *The Cambridge History of Philosophy in Late Antiquity*. Cambridge: Cambridge University Press, 2010.

Giehlow, Karl. "Dürers Stich 'Melencolia I' und der maximilianische Humanistenkreis." *Mitteilungen der Gesellschaft für vervielfältigende Kunst* 2 (1903): 29–41; 4 (1904): 6–18, and 57–78.

– "Die Hieroglyphenkunde des Humanismus in der Allegorie der Renaissance." *Jahrbuch der Kunsthistorischen Sammlungen des Allerhöchsten Kaiserhauses* 32, no. 1 (1915): 1–232. Published in Italian as *Hieroglyphica. La conoscenza umanistica dei geroglifici nell'allegoria del Rinascimento*. Edited by Maurizio Ghelardi and Susanne Müller. Turin: Aragno, 2004.

Ginzberg, Carlo. "Aby Warburg to E.H. Gombrich: A Problem of Method." In *Clues, Myths, and the Historical Method*, translated by John and Anne C.

Tedeschi, 17–59. Baltimore, MD: Johns Hopkins University Press, 1989. The book was published in the UK as *Myths, Emblems, Clues*. London: Hutchinson Radius, 1990. The essay was first published in Italian in 1966.

Gombrich, Ernst. *Aby Warburg: An Intellectual Biography, with a Memoir on the History of the Library by F. Saxl*. 2nd ed. Oxford: Phaidon, 1986. First published London: Warburg Institute, 1970.

– "Art and Scholarship." In *Meditations on a Hobby Horse and Other Essays on the Theory of Art*, 106–19. London: Phaidon, 1963.

Gordon, D.J., ed. *Fritz Saxl (1890–1948): A Volume of Memorial Essays from his Friends in England*. London: Nelson, 1957.

Grabmann, Martin. *Mittelalterliche lateinische Ubersetzungen von Schriften der Aristoteles-Kommentatoren Johannes Philoponos, Alexander von Aphrodisias und Themistios*. Sitzungsberichte der Bayerischen Akademie der Wissenschaften. Philosophisch-Historische Abteilung (1929, no.7). Munich: Bayerische Akademie der Wissenschaften, 1929.

– Review of Nicolai de Cusa *Opera omnia*, vol. 1: *De docta ignorantia*, edited by Ernst Hoffmann and Raymond Klibansky, and vol. 2: *Apologia doctae ignorantiae*, edited by Raymond Klibansky. *Deutsche Literaturzeitung* 15 (1933): 685–91.

Groffier, Ethel. "De l'amour des livres à l'amour des bibliothèques." In Georges Leroux, *Raymond Klibansky, 1905–2005 – La bibliothèque d'un philosophe*, 151–61.

– "Raymond Klibansky et la quête de l'objectivité." In *Aesthetics in Contemporary Philosophy: Proceedings of the International Institute of Philosophy Conference*, edited by Tomonobu Imamichi and Hans Lenk, 259–73. Tokyo: IIP, 2006; Vienna: Lit Verlag, 2009.

Grolle, Joist. *Bericht von einem schwierigen Leben. Walter Solmitz (1905 bis 1962), Schüler von Aby Warburg und Ernst Cassirer*. Berlin-Hamburg: Dietrich Reimer Verlag, 1994.

– *Der Hamburger Percy Ernst Schramms. Ein Historiker auf der Suche nach der Wirklichkeit*. Hamburg: Verein für Hamburgische Geschichte, 1989.

– "Percy Ernst Schramm – Fritz Saxl. Die Geschichte einer zerbrochenen Freundschaft." In *Aby Warburg. Akten des internationalen Symposiums Hamburg 1990*, edited by Horst Bredekamp, Michael Diers, and Charlotte Schoell-Glass, 95–114. Weinheim: VCH, 1991.

Gundolf, Friedrich. *Anfänge deutscher Geschichtschreibung*. Edited by Elisabeth Gundolf and Edgar Wind. Amsterdam: Elsevier, c. 1938.

Günther, Horst. "d'anima Fiorentino." In *'Ekstatische Nymphe ... trauernder Flußgott.' Porträt eines Gelehrten,* edited by Robert Galitz and Brita Reimers, 32–51. Hamburg: Dölling & Galitz, 1995.

Hamesse, J. and M. Fattori, eds. *Rencontres de cultures dans la philosophie médiévale. Traductions et traducteurs de l'Antiquité tardive au XIVème siècle.* Actes du Colloque international de Cassino, 15–17 June 1989. Louvain-la-Neuve: Publications de l'Institut d'études médiévales de l'Université catholique de Louvain, 1990.

Hankins, James. *Plato in the Italian Renaissance.* 2 vols. Leiden: Brill, 1990.

Heckscher, William S. "The Genesis of Iconology." Reprinted in his *Art and Literature: Studies in Relationship*, edited by Egon Verheyen, 2nd ed., 253–80. Baden-Baden: V. Koerner, 1994.

Hegel, Georg Wilhelm Friedrich. *The Phenomenology of Mind.* Translated by J.B. Baille. Mineaola, NY: Dover, 2003.

Heidt, Renate. *Erwin Panofsky: Kunsttheorie und Einzelwerk.* Cologne and Vienna: Böhlau, 1977.

Hoffmann, Ernst. "Platonismus und Mittelalter." *Vorträge der Bibliothek Warburg.* Vol. 3, *1923–1924*, 17–82. Leipzig and Berlin: Teubner, 1926.

– *Platonismus und Mystik im Altertum.* Heidelberg: Winter, 1935.

Holst, Niels von. *Creators, Collectors, and Connoisseurs: The Anatomy of Artistic Taste from Antiquity to the Present Day.* New York: Putnam, 1967.

Hume, David. *New Letters of David Hume.* Edited by Raymond Klibansky and Ernest Mossner. Oxford: Oxford University Press, 2011 [1954].

Hunt, R.W. *The Schools and the Cloister: The Life and Writings of Alexander Nequam, 1157–1217.* Edited and revised by Margaret Gibson from the author's unpublished doctoral dissertation. Oxford: Clarendon Press, 1984.

Idel, Moshe. *Hasidism: Between Ecstasy and Magic.* Albany, NY: State University of New York Press, 1995.

– *Saturn's Jews: On the Witches' Sabbat and Sabbateanism.* London and New York: Continuum, 2011.

Imamichi, Tomonobu and Hans Lenk. eds. "À la mémoire de Raymond Klibansky." Special section in *Aesthetics in Contemporary Philosophy: Proceedings of the International Institute of Philosophy, Tokyo*, 231–73. Vienna: LIT Verlag, 2009.

John of Salisbury. *Ioannis Saresberiensis episcopi Carnotensis Policratici ... libri VIII.* Edited by C.C J. Webb. Oxford: Clarendon Press, 1909.

– *Ioannis Saresberiensis episcopi Carnotensis Metalogicon … libri IIII*. Edited by C.C.J. Webb. Oxford: Clarendon Press, 1929.

Josephus. *The Jewish War*. Vol. 1: Books I–II. Edited by Henry St. John Thackeray. Cambridge: Harvard University Press, 1927.

Kafka, Franz. *Letters to Milena*. New York: Schocken, 1953.

Kannicht, Richard, ed. *Tragicorum Graecorum fragmenta*. Vol. 5, *Euripides*. Göttingen: Vandenhoeck and Ruprecht, 2004.

Klein, Robert. "Saturne: croyances et symboles." In *La Forme et l'intelligible*, 224–30. Paris: Gallimard, 1970. First published in *Mercure de France*, 1964.

Klibansky, Raymond. "Le avventure della malinconia." *Dianoia* 1 (1996): 11–27.

– "La Découverte d'un texte platonicien inconnu de l'Antiquité classique," in *Témoignages: Reflections on the Humanities*, 41–51. Ottawa: Fédération canadienne des études humaines, 1993.

– "Erinnerungen an Ernst Cassirer. Raymond Klibansky im Gespräch mit Thomas Göller," *Internationale Zeitschrift für Philosophie* 2 (1999): 275–88.

– "Die Grenzen des akademischen Lebens sprengen. Ein Gespräch über Ernst Cassirer und die Bibliothek Warburg," *Merkur. Deutsche Zeitschrift für europäisches Denken* 50, no.3 (March 1996).

– "La Notion de *Kulturwissenschaft*." RACAR (Revue d'art canadienne / Canadian Art Review) 27, nos. 1–2 (2000 [2003]): 144–6. Reprinted in *Tradition antique et tolérance moderne*, edited by Philippe Despoix and Georges Leroux, 339–45. Montreal: Presses de l'Université de Montréal, 2016.

– "Rapports annuels sur le progrès du *Corpus platonicum*." In *Compte-rendu de la session annuelle* of the Union Académique Internationale. Bruxelles: Academie Royale de Belgique, [for the years of] 1937–39, 1958–59, 1961–64 and 1969–1979.

– "Raymond Klibansky, philosophe et historien. Entretien avec Yves Hersant et Alain de Libera." *Préfaces. Les idées et les sciences dans la bibliographie de la France*, 13 (May–June 1989): 132–42.

– "Report on the progress of the *Corpus Platonicum medii aevi*." Reprinted from the *Warburg Institute Annual Report*, vols. 1946/47: 1947–58.

– "L'Université allemande dans les années trente. Notes autobiographiques." *Philosophiques* 18, no. 2 (1991): 139–57.

Kristeller, Paul Oskar. Review of *The Continuity of the Platonic Tradition During the Middle Ages: Outlines of a Corpus Platonicum Medii Aevi*, by Raymond Klibansky. *Journal of Philosophy* 37, no. 15 (1940): 409–11.

– Review of *Corpus Platonicum Medii Aevi*, vols. 2 and 3, general editor Raymond Klibansky. *Journal of Philosophy* 53, no. 5 (1956): 196–201.

Labowsky, Carlotta. *Bessarion's Library and the Biblioteca Marciana: Six Early Inventories*. Rome: Edizioni di Storia e Letteratura, 1979.

– "Der Begriff des Prepon in der Ethik des Panaitios. Mit Analysen von Cicero *De officiis I, 93–49* und Horaz *Ars poetica*" (PhD Diss., University of Heidelberg, 1932).

Leroux, Georges, ed. *Raymond Klibansky 1905–2005. La Bibliothèque d'un philosophe*. Catalogue of the exhibition curated by Leroux at Bibliothèque et Archives nationales du Québec, 13 November 2012–25 August 2013. Montreal: BANQ, 2013.

Liebeschütz, Hans. "Obituary" [for Fritz Saxl]. *The Synagogue Review* (May 1948): 138.

Lloyd-Jones, Hugh. "A Biographical Memoir." In *The Eloquence of Symbols: Studies in Humanist Art*, by Edgar Wind, xiii–xxxvi, edited by Jaynie Anderson. Oxford: Oxford University Press, 1993.

Locke, John. *Ein Brief über Toleranz*. Translation and introduction by Julius Ebbinghaus. Philosophie et communauté mondiale 1, general editor Raymond Klibansky. Hamburg: Meiner, 1957.

Luna, Concetta and Alain-Philippe Segonds, eds. *Proclus: Commentaire sur le* Parménide *de Platon*. Paris: Belles Lettres, 2007–2010.

Mansion, Auguste. "Les progrès de l'*Aristoteles Latinus*." *Revue Philosophique de Louvain* 54, no. 41 (1956): 90–111.

Marazia, Chantal and Davide Stimilli, eds. *Ludwig Binswanger / Aby Warburg. Die unendliche Heilung. Aby Warburgs Krankengeschichte*. Zürich-Berlin: Diaphanes, 2007.

McEwan, Dorothea. *Fritz Saxl: Eine Biografie. Aby Warburgs Bibliothekar und erster Direktor des Londoner Warburg Institutes*. Vienna: Böhlau, 2012.

– "Gegen die 'Pioniere der Diesseitigkeit.'" *Trajekte. Zeitschrift des Zentrums für Literaturforschung Berlin* 4, no. 8 (2004–2005): 9–11.

– "Saxl and Boll." *Journal of Art Historiography* 5 (December 2011): (14 pages; online) https://arthistoriography.files.wordpress.com/2011/12/mcewan.pdf

McTaggart, John. "The Unreality of Time." *Mind* 17 (1908): 456–73.

Meier, Hans, Richard Newald, and Edgar Wind, eds. *Kulturwissenschaftliche Bibliographie zum Nachleben der Antike*. General editor, the Kulturwissenschaftliche Bibliothek Warburg. Vol. 1, *Die Erscheinungen des Jahres 1931*. Leipzig and Berlin: Teubner, 1934.

– *A Bibliography on the Survival of the Classics.* General editor, Warburg Institute. Vol. 1, *The Publications of 1931.* The text of the German edition with an English introduction. London: Cassell, 1934 [i.e., 1935].

– *A Bibliography on the Survival of the Classics.* General editor, Warburg Institute. Vol. 2, *The Publications of 1932–1933.* London: Warburg Institute, 1938.

Meyer, Thomas. *Ernst Cassirer.* Hamburg: Ellert & Richter, 2006.

Meyer, Thomas, and Martin Treml. "Gertrud Bing – ein intellektuelles Porträt." *Trajekte. Zeitschrift des Zentrums für Literaturforschung Berlin* 5, no. 10 (2004–2005): 18–22.

Mitchison, Naomi. *You May Well Ask: A Memoir 1920–1940.* London: Gollancz, 1979.

Mittig, Hans-Ernst. "Ein Residuum der Unzufriedenheit. Kunstwissenschaft der 1960er Jahre in der Bundesrepublik Deutschland und Berlin-West." *Kritische Berichte* 18, no. 3 (1990): 53–65.

Mrazek, Wilhelm. "Giehlow, Johann Carl Friedrich." *Neue deutsche Biographie.* Edited by the Historical Commission of the Bayerische Akademie der Wissenschaften, 6, no. 371. Berlin: Duncker & Humblot, 1964.

Müller, Susanne. "Introduzione." In *Hieroglyphica. La conoscenza umanistica dei geroglifici nell'allegoria del Rinascimento*, by Karl Giehlow, VII–XIX.

Naber, Claudia. "'… die Fackel deutsch-jüdischer Geistigkeit weitertragen.' Der Hamburger Kreis um Ernst Cassirer und Aby Warburg." In *Die Juden in Hamburg 1590 bis 1990*, 393–406. Hamburg: Dolling & Galitz, 1991.

Neschke-Hentschke, Ada Babette, ed. *Le Timée de Platon. Contributions à l'histoire de sa réception.* Leuven: Éditions Peeters and Éditions de l'Institut supérieur de philosophie, 2000.

Nicholas of Cusa. *De pace fidei.* Edited by Raymond Klibansky and Hildebrand Bascour. Mediaeval and Renaissance Studies, Supplement 3. London: Warburg Institute, 1956.

Norden, Eduard. *Die Geburt des Kindes. Studien der Bibliothek Warburg* 3. Leipzig: Teubner, 1924.

Norton, Robert. *Secret Germany: Stefan George and his Circle.* Ithaca, NY: Cornell University Press, 2002.

Osterkamp, Ernst. "Art History and Humanist Tradition in the George Circle." *Comparative Criticism* 23 (2001): 211–30.

Ott, Martin. *Die Entdeckung des Altertums. Der Umgang mit der römischen Vergangenheit in Süddeutschland im 16. Jahrhundert.* Kallmünz: M. Lassleben, 2002.

Panofsky, Erwin. "*Et in Arcadia Ego*: On the Conception of Transience in Poussin and Watteau." In *Philosophy and History: Essays Presented to Ernst Cassirer*, edited by Raymond Klibansky and H.J. Paton, 223–54. Oxford: Clarendon Press, 1936.

– "*Et in Arcadia Ego*: Poussin and the Elegiac Tradition." In *Meaning in the Visual Arts: Papers in and on Art History*, 295–320. Garden City, NY: Doubleday, 1955.

– *Korrespondenz 1910 bis 1968. Eine kommentierte Auswahl in fünf Bänden*. 5 vols. Edited by Dieter Wuttke. Wiesbaden: Harrassowitz, 2001–2011.

– *The Life and Art of Albrecht Dürer*. Vol. 1 of *Albrecht Dürer*. 2 vols. Princeton, NJ: Princeton University Press, 1943.

– "On the Problem of Describing and Interpreting Works of the Visual Arts." English edition of "Zum Problem der Beschreibung und Inhaltsdentung von Werken der bildenden Kunst," translated by Jaś Eisner and Katharina Lorenz. *Critical Inquiry* 38, no. 3 (March 2012): 467–82.

– "Preface to the First Edition." *The Life and Art of Albrecht Dürer*, xi–xii. 4th ed. Princeton, NJ: Princeton University Press, 1955.

– *Studies in Iconology: Humanistic Themes in the Art of the Renaissance*. New York: Oxford University Press, 1939.

– "Zum Geleit." In *Grünewald*, by Arpád Weixlgärtner, 5–6. Wien: Anton Schroll, 1962.

– "Zum Problem der Beschreibung und Inhaltsdeutung von Werken der bildenden Kunst." *Logos* 21 (1932): 103–19. Reprinted in *Aufsätze zu Grundfragen der Kunstwissenschaft*, edited by Hariolf Oberer and Egon Verheyen (Berlin: Bruno Hessling, 1964), 85–97.

Panofsky, Erwin, and Fritz Saxl. *Dürers 'Melencolia I.' Eine quellen- und typengeschichtliche Untersuchung*. Leipzig and Berlin: Teubner, 1923.

– *La 'Melencolia I' di Dürer. Una ricerca storica sulle fonti e i tipi figurativi*. Edited by Emiliano de Vito, with an introduction by Claudia Wedepohl and a preface by Arpád Weixlgärtner. Macerata: Quodlibet, 2016.

Papapetros, Spyros. *On the Animation of the Inorganic: Art, Architecture, and the Extension of Life*. Chicago: University of Chicago Press, 2012.

Park, Désirée. "Humanité et tolerance chez Raymond Klibansky. Une anthologie." In Leroux, *Raymond Klibansky 1905–2005. La Bibliothèque d'un philosophe*, 141–9.

Patschovsky, Alexander. "Nachwort des Herausgebers." In *Synagoge und Ecclesia. Religionsgeschichtliche Studien über die Auseinandersetzung der Kirche mit dem Judentum im Hochmittelalter*, by Hans Liebeschütz, 237–44. Heidelberg: L. Schneider, 1983.

Pellegrin, Élisabeth, ed. *Fonds Paletta et fonds de la Reine*. Vol. 2, pt. 1 of *Les Manuscrits classiques latins de la Bibliothèque Vaticane*. Paris: CNRS, 1978.

Petropoulos, Jonathan. *The Faustian Bargain: The Art World in Nazi Germany*. Oxford: Oxford University Press, 2000.

Peutinger, Conrad. *Briefwechsel*. Edited by Erich König. Munich: Beck, 1923.

Pfizer, Gustav. *Der Welsche und der Deutsche. Aeneas Sylvius Piccolomini (Pabst Pius II) und Gregor von Heimburg: historisch-poetische Bilder aus dem fünfzehnten Jahrhundert*. Stuttgart: Rieger, 1844.

Pico della Mirandola, Giovanni. *Apologia*. In *Opera omnia Ioannis Pici Mirandulae Concordiaeque comitis, theologorum et philosophorum, sine controversia, principis*. P. I, II. Basileae [Basel], ex officina Henricpetrina, 1572; 1573.

Plato. *Euthyphro, Apology, Crito, Phaedo, Phaedrus*. Translated by Harold North Fowler. Loeb Classical Library 36, Plato 1. Cambridge, MA: Harvard University Press, 1914.

– "Summarium Platonis librorum atque placitorum" in *Codex Vaticanus reginensis lat*. 1572, 77r–86r.

Proclus. *Commentaire sur le* Parménide *de Platon. Traduction de Guillaume de Moerbeke*. Edited by Carlos Steel. 2 vols. Leuven, Belgium: Presses de l'Université de Louvain, 1982–1985.

– *Procli in Platonis Parmenidem commentaria*. Edited by Carlos Steel, 3 vols. Oxford: Clarendon, 2007–09. Vol. 1, *Tomus I, Libros I–III continens*, edited by Carlos Steel, Caroline Macé, and Pieter d'Hoine (2007); Vol. 2, *Tomus II. Libros IV–V continens*, edited by Carlos Steel, C. Gribomont, and Pieter d'Hoine (2008); and Vol. 3, *Tomus III Libros VI–VII et indices continens*, edited by Carlos Steel and Leen Van Campe (2009).

– *Procli opera inedita*. Edited and revised by Victor Cousin. Paris: Durand, 1864.

Rajak, Tessa. *Josephus: The Historian and His Society*. London: Duckworth, 1983.

Randall, J.H. "Cassirer's Theory of History as Illustrated in his Treatment of Renaissance Thought." In *The Philosophy of Ernst Cassirer*, edited by Paul Arthur Schilpp, 691–728. Evanston, ILL.: Library of Living Philosophers, 1949.

Rasch, Martin. "Juden und Emigranten machen deutsche Wissenschaft." *Völkischer Beobachter* (North German edition), 5 January 1935. Reprinted in Wuttke, *Kosmopolis der Wissenschaft*, 295–8.

Reinhardt, Karl. *Kosmos und Sympathie: Neue Untersuchungen über Poseidonios*. Munich: C.H. Beck, 1926.

– *Poseidonios*. Munich: Oskar Beck, 1921.

Rieff, Philip. *Charisma: The Gift of Grace, and How It Has Been Taken Away from Us*. New York: Vintage, 2008.

Rose, William, ed. *An Outline of Modern Knowledge*. London: Gollancz, 1931.

Rosenberg, Alfred. *Der Mythos des 20. Jahrhunderts. Eine Wertung der seelisch-geistigen Gestalten-Kämpfe unserer Zeit*. 3rd. ed. Munich: Hoheneichen, 1932.

Rosenstock Huessy, Eugen. *Out of Revolution: Autobiography of Western Man*. New York: Morrow, 1938.

Saalmann, Timo. *Kunstpolitik der Berliner Museen 1919–1959*. Berlin: de Gruyter, 2014.

Saxl, Fritz. "Aller Tugenden und Laster Abbildung." Offprint from *Festschrift für Julius Schlosser*, edited by A. Weixlgärtner, and L. Planiscig, 103–21. Zürich: Amalthea Verlag, 1927.

– *Gebärde, Form, Ausdruck. Zwei Untersuchungen*. Presented by Pablo Schneider. Zürich: Diaphanes, 2012.

– *A Heritage of Images: A Selection of Lectures*. Edited by Hugh Honour and John Fleming. Harmondsworth: Penguin Books, 1970.

– "The History of Warburg's Library." In Ernst Gombrich, *Aby Warburg: An Intellectual Biography*, 325–38. 2nd ed. Chicago: University of Chicago Press, 1986.

– *Lectures*. London: The Warburg Institute, 1957.

– "The Origin and Survival of a Pictorial Type (the Mithras Reliefs)." *Proceedings of the Classical Association* 32 (May 1935): 32–5.

– "Veritas Filia Temporis." In Klibansky and Paton, *Philosophy and History*, 197–222.

– *Verzeichnis astrologischer und mythologischer illustrierter Handschriften des lateinischen Mittelalters*. Vols. 1 and 2. Heidelberg: Winter, 1915–27.

– *Vorträge der Bibliothek Warburg, 1930/1931*. Leipzig: Teubner, 1932.

Schäfer, Hans Michael. *Die Kulturwissenschaftliche Bibliothek Warburg. Geschichte und Persönlichkeiten der Bibliothek Warburg mit Berücksichtigung der Bibliothekslandschaft und der Stadtsituation der Freien und Hansestadt Hamburg zu Beginn des 20. Jahrhunderts*. Berlin: Logos, 2003.

Schäfer, Peter. *History of the Jews in Antiquity: Jews of Palestine from Alexander the Great to the Arab Conquest*. Abingdon and New York: Routledge, 1995.

Scholem, Gershom. *Sabbatai Sevi: The Mystical Messiah 1626–1676*. Princeton, NJ: Princeton University Press, 1973.

– *From Berlin to Jerusalem: Memories of My Youth*. New York: Schocken, 1980.

Schuster, Peter-Klaus. *Melencolia I. Dürers Denkbild*. 2 vols. Berlin: Gebrüder Mann, 1991.

Schwedeler-Meyer, Ernst. "Karl Giehlow †." *Zeitschrift des Nordböhmischen Gewerbemuseums* 8 (1913): [1r–1v].

Sears, Elizabeth. "Edgar Wind on Michelangelo." In *The Religious Symbolism of Michelangelo: The Sistine Ceiling*, by Edgar Wind, xvii–xl. Oxford: Oxford University Press, 2000.

– "Kenneth Clark and Gertrud Bing: Letters on 'The Nude.'" *Burlington Magazine* 1301 (August 2011): 530–1.

– "The Warburg Institute, 1933–1944: A Precarious Experiment in Amalgamation." *Art Libraries Journal* 38, no. 4 (2013): 7–15.

– "Warburg Institute Archive, General Correspondence." *Common Knowledge* 18, no.1 (winter 2012): 32–49.

Senger, Hans Gerhard. "In memoriam Raymond Klibansky," *Bulletin de philosophie médiévale* 47 (2005): XI.

– "Zur Geschichte der Edition der *Opera omnia* des Nicolaus Cusanus." In *Nicolai de Cusa Opera omnia: Symposium zum Abschluss der Heidelberger Akademie-Ausgabe; Heidelberg, 11. und 12. Februar 2005*, edited by Werner Beierwaltes and Hans Gerhard Senger, 37–77. Heidelberg: Winter, 2006.

Simon, Ernst. *Aufbau im Untergang. Jüdische Erwachsenenbildung im nationalsozialistischen Deutschland als geistiger Widerstand*. Tübingen: Mohr, 1959.

Singer, Charles. Review of *Verzeichnis astrologischer und mythologischer illustrierter Handschriften des lateinischen Mittelalters*, vols. 1 and 2, by Fritz Saxl. *Times Literary Supplement* 1412 (21 February 1929): 139.

Singer, Dorothea. "Alchemical Texts bearing the name of Plato." *Ambix* 2, nos. 3–4 (December 1946): 115–28.

– *Catalogue of Latin and Vernacular Alchemical Manuscripts in Great Britain and Ireland Dating from Before the XVI Century*. 3 vols. Brussels: Lamertin, 1928–31.

– *Les manuscrits des Îles Britanniques*. Vol. 3 of *Catalogue des manuscrits alchimiques grecs*, edited by J. Bidez et al. Bruxelles: Lamertin, 1924.

Sloterdijk, Peter. *God's Zeal: The Battle of the Three Monotheisms*. Cambridge: Polity, 2009.

Solmitz, David O. *Piecing Scattered Souls: Maine, Germany, Mexico, China and Beyond*. Solon, ME: Polar Bear & Co., 2011.

Solmitz, Walter. "Cassirer on Galileo." In *The Philosophy of Ernst Cassirer*, 731–56. Evanston, ILL: Library of Living Philosophers, 1949.

Southern, Richard William. "Powicke, Sir (Frederick) Maurice (1879–1963)." Revised by Alan Harding. *Oxford Dictionary of National Biography*. http://www.oxforddnb.com/view/article/35596, accessed 15 June 2015.

– "Richard William Hunt (1908–79)." *Proceedings of the British Academy* 67 (1981): 371–97.

Stead, G.C. "A Commentary on Kant's Critique of Judgment." *Mind* 48 (1939): 99–101.

Stebbing, Susan. "Some Ambiguities in Discussions Concerning Time." In Klibansky and Paton, *Philosophy and History*, 107–23.

Stimilli, Davide. Introduction ("*Einleitung*") to "*Per Monstra ad Sphaeram*": *Sternglaube und Bilddeutung. Vortrag in Gedenken an Franz Boll und andere Schriften 1923 bis 1925*, by Aby Warburg, 6–28. Edited by Davide Stimilli with the collaboration of Claudia Wedepohl. Hamburg: Dölling & Galitz, 2008.

Stockhausen, Tilmann von. *Die Kulturwissenschaftliche Bibliothek Warburg: Architektur, Einrichtung und Organisation*. Hamburg: Dölling & Galitz, 1992.

Stover, Justin A. *A New Work by Apuleius: The Lost Third Book of the* De Platone. Oxford: Oxford University Press, 2016.

Taylor, Paul. "Henri Frankfort, Aby Warburg and 'Mythopoeic Thought.'" *Journal of Art Historiography* 5 (December 2010): 1–16.

Tellenbach, Hubertus. *Melancholie. Zur Problemgeschichte, Typologie, Pathogenese und Klinik*. Berlin: Springer, 1961.

Thieme, David. *Percy Ernst Schramm und das Mittelalter*. Göttingen: Vandenhoeck & Ruprecht, 2006.

Thimann, Michael. *Caesars Schatten. Die Bibliothek von Friedrich Gundolf: Rekonstruktion und Wissenschaftsgeschichte*. Heidelberg: Manutius, 2003.

Tocqueville, Alexis de. *Democracy in America*. Indianapolis: Liberty Fund, 2010 [1840].

Treml, Martin. "Dionysos, Luther und der Teufel im Denkraum. Zu Warburgs Theorie, betrachtet mit Freud." In *Warburgs Denkraum. Formen, Motive, Materialien*, edited by Martin Treml, Sabine Flach, and Pablo Schneider, 51–70. Munich: Fink, 2014.

– "Flavius Josephus im Jüdischen Krieg. Zur Archäologie des Märtyrers." In *Tinte und Blut. Politik, Erotik und Politik des Martyriums*, edited by Andreas Krasz and Thomas Frank, 75–94. Frankfurt: Fischer Taschenbuch, 2008.

– "Nachleben als Programm und Methode der Kulturwissenschaftlichen Bibliothek Warburg." *Trajekte. Zeitschrift des Zentrums für Literaturforschung Berlin* 9, no. 18 (2008–2009): 14–17.

– "Warburgs Nachleben. Ein Gelehrter und (s)eine Denkfigur." In *Nachleben der*

Religionen. Kulturwissenschaftliche Untersuchungen zur Dialektik der Säkularisierung, edited by Daniel Weidner, 25–40. Munich: Fink, 2007.

Trendelenburg, Adolf. *Erläuterungen zu den Elementen der aristotelischen Logik. Zunächst für den Unterricht in Gymnasien*. Berlin: G. Bethge, 1861.

Turner, John D., and Kevin Corrigan, eds. *Plato's Parmenides and Its Heritage*. Atlanta: Society of Biblical Literature, 2010.

Valéry, Paul. *Tel Quel*. Vol. 1. Paris: Gallimard, 1941.

Vidal-Naquet, Pierre. "Du bon usage de la trahison." In *La guerre des Juifs*, by Flavius Josephus, translated from the Greek by Pierre Savinel. Paris: Editions de Minuit, 1977.

Volkmann, Ludwig. *Bilderschriften der Renaissance. Hieroglyphik und Emblematik in ihren Beziehungen und Fortentwicklungen*. Leipzig: Hiersemann, 1923.

Warburg, Aby. "The Art of Portraiture and the Florentine Bourgeoisie." In *The Renewal of Pagan Antiquity*, 185–221.

– *Der Bilderatlas Mnemosyne*. Edited by Martin Warnke with the collaboration of Claudia Brink. Berlin: Akademie Verlag, 2000.

– "Dürer and Italian Antiquity." In *The Renewal of Pagan Antiquity*, 553–8.

– "Dürer und die italienische Antike." *Verhandlungen der 48. Versammlung deutscher Philologen und Schulmänner in Hamburg vom 3. bis 6. Oktober 1905* (1906): 55–60.

– "Francesco Sassetti's Last Injunctions to His Sons." In *The Renewal of Pagan Antiquity*, 223–62.

– *Fragmente zur Ausdruckskunde*. Edited by Ulrich Pfisterer and Hans Christian Hönes. Studienausgabe 4. Berlin: De Gruyter, 2015.

– *Gesammelte Schriften, Die Erneuerung der heidnischen Antike. Kulturwissenschaftliche Beiträge zur Geschichte der europäischen Renaissance*. Edited by Gertrud Bing with Fritz Rougemont. 2 vols. Leipzig: Teubner 1932.

– *Heidnisch-antike Weissagung in Wort und Bild zu Luthers Zeiten*. Edited by Franz Boll, 57–65. Heidelberg: Carl Winters Universitätsbuchandlung, 1920. Reprinted in *Ausgewählte Schriften und Würdigungen*, edited by Dieter Wuttke, 199–304, Baden-Baden: Verlag Valentine Koerner, 1979.

– "Italian Art and International Astrology in the Palazzo Schifanoia, Ferrara." In *The Renewal of Pagan Antiquity*, 563–91.

– "Italienische Kunst und internationale Astrologie im Palazzo Schifanoja zu Ferrara [1912–22]." In *Werke in einem Band. Auf der Grundlage der Manuskripte und Handexemplare*, 373–402. Berlin: Suhrkamp, 2010.

– *"Per Monstra ad Sphaeram": Sternglaube und Bilddeutung. Vortrag in Gedenken an Franz Boll und andere Schriften 1923 bis 1925*. Edited by Davide Stimilli with the collaboration of Claudia Wedepohl. Hamburg: Dölling & Galitz, 2008.
– "Pagan-Antique Prophecy in Words and Images in the Age of Luther [1920]." In *The Renewal of Pagan Antiquity*, 597–667.
– "Die Planetenbilder auf der Wanderung von Süd nach Nord und ihre Rückkehr nach Italien [1913]." In *Werke in einem Band auf der Grundlage der Manuskripte und Handexemplare*, 349–72.
– *Il primo Rinascimento italiano. Sette conferenze inedite*. Edited by Giovanna Targia. Turin: Aragno, 2013.
– *The Renewal of Pagan Antiquity: Contributions to the Cultural History of the European Renaissance*. Edited by Julia Bloomfield et al. Translated by David Britt, with an introduction by Kurt W. Foster. Los Angeles: Getty Research Institute, 1999.
– *La rinascità del paganesimo antico. Contributo alla storia della cultura*. Compiled by Gertrud Bing. Translated by Emma Cantimori. Florence: La Nuova Italia, 1966.
– *Sandro Botticellis "Geburt der Venus" und "Frühling". Eine Untersuchung über die Vorstellungen von der Antike in der italienischen Frührenaissance*. Hamburg/Leipzig: Leopold Voss, 1893. Reprinted in *Gesammelte Schriften I.1*; published in English as "Sandro Botticelli's Birth of Venus and Spring," in *The Renewal of Pagan Antiquity*, 89–156.
– *Tagebuch der Kulturwissenschaftlichen Bibliothek Warburg mit Einträgen von Gertrud Bing und Fritz Saxl*. Edited by Karen Michels and Charlotte Schoell-Glass. Berlin: Akademie Verlag, 2001.
– *Werke in einem Band auf der Grundlage der Manuskripte und Handexemplare*. Edited with a commentary by Martin Treml, Sigrid Weigel, and Perdita Ladwig. Berlin: Suhrkamp, 2010.
Warburg Institute. *Annual Report* 1934/35–1958/59. London: Warburg Institute.
Warnke, Martin. "Aby Warburg (1866–1929)." In *Altmeister moderner Kunstgeschichte*, edited by Heinrich Dilly, 117–30. Berlin: D. Reimer, 1999 [1990].
Watanabe, Morimichi. "An Appreciation." In *Introducing Nicholas of Cusa: A Guide to a Renaissance Man*, edited by Christopher M. Bellitto, Thomas M. Izbicki, and Gerald Christianson, 16–17. New York: Paulist Press, 2004.
– "The Origins of Modern Cusanus Research in Germany and the Establishment of the Heidelberg '*Opera omnia*.'" In *Nicholas of Cusa in Search of God and Wis-*

dom: Essays in Honor of Morimichi Watanabe by the American Cusanus Society, edited by Gerald Christianson and Thomas M. Izbicki, 17–42. Leiden and New York: E.J. Brill, 1991.

Webb, C.C.J. *God and Personality* [Gifford Lectures 1918 and 1919, first course]; *Divine Personality and Human Life* [Gifford Lectures 1918 and 1919, second course] . London: Allen & Unwin, 1919–20.

– *Kant's Philosophy of Religion*. Oxford: Clarendon Press, 1926.

– Review of *Magistri Eckardi Opera Latina Auspiciis Instituti Sanctae Sabinae ad Codicum fidem edita. I. Super oratione Dominic*, edited by Raymond Klibansky. *Philosophy* 10 (1935): 228–9.

Weber, Regina. "Aktivitäten der Warburg-Bibliothek, gespiegelt im Marbacher Nachlass Raymond Klibansky." In *Exilforschung. Ein internationales Jahrbuch*, edited by Claus-Dieter Krohn and Lutz Winckler (by commission of the Gesellschaft für Exilforschung/Society for Exile Studies) 29 (2011): 100–14.

– *Lotte Labowsky (1905–1991), Schülerin Aby Warburgs, Kollegin Raymond Klibanskys. Eine Wissenschaftlerin zwischen Fremd- und Selbstbestimmung im englischen Exil*. Berlin: Reimer, 2012.

Wedepohl, Claudia. "Warburg, Saxl, Panofsky and Dürer's *Melencolia I*." *Schifanoia* 48–9 (2015): 27–44.

– "Critical Detachment: Ernst Gombrich as Interpreter of Aby Warburg." In *Vorträge aus dem Warburg-Haus* 12. Special issue: *The Afterlife of the Kulturwissenschaftliche Bibliothek Warburg*, edited by Uwe Fleckner and Peter Mack. (2015): 134–64.

Weigel, Sigrid. *Walter Benjamin. Die Kreatur, das Heilige, die Bilder*. Frankfurt am Main: Fischer, 2008.

Weiss, Roberto. Review of *Medieval and Renaissance Studies* (MARS) 1, no. 1, edited by Richard Hunt and Raymond Klibansky. *Modern Language Review* (MLR) 36, no. 4 (1941): 520–2.

– Review of MARS 1, no. 2, edited by Richard Hunt and Raymond Klibansky. MLR 39, no. 2 (1944): 186–8.

Weixlgärtner, Arpád. "Zum Geleite." In *Dürers 'Melencolia I.' Eine quellen- und typengeschichtliche Untersuchung*, by Erwin Panofsky and Fritz Saxl, IX–XV. Leipzig: Teubner, 1923.

– "Nachwort." In "Die Hieroglyphenkunde des Humanismus in der Allegorie der Renaissance," by Karl Giehlow. *Jahrbuch der kunsthistorischen Sammlungen des Allerhöchsten Kaiserhauses* 32 (1915): 232.

Wind, Edgar. *Das Experiment und die Metaphysik. Zur Auflösung der kosmologischen Antinomien.* Berlin: Suhrkamp, 2001. First published Teubingen: Mohr, 1934.

– Review of *Aby Warburg: An Intellectual Biography,* by Ernst Gombrich. *Times Literary Supplement* (25 June 1971): 735–6. Reprinted in Wind, *The Eloquence of Symbols*, 106–13.

– "The Warburg Institute Classification Scheme." *The Library Association Record*, 4th ser., 2 no. 37 (May 1935): 193–5.

Wölfflin, Heinrich. *Die Kunst Albrecht Dürers* (1904). 2nd ed. Munich: F. Bruckmann, 1908.

– "Zur Interpretation von Dürers 'Melancholie.'" *Jahrbuch für Kunstwissenschaft* I, 1923. Reprinted in his *Gedanken zur Kunstgeschichte. Gedrucktes und Ungedrucktes*, 96–105. Basel: Benno Schwabe, 1941.

– *Worte zur Beisetzung von Professor Dr. Aby M. Warburg: geboren am 13. Juni 1866 / gestorben am 26. Oktober 1929.* Hamburg: Roetherdruck, 1929.

Wuttke, Dieter, ed. *Kosmopolis der Wissenschaft: E.R. Curtius und das Warburg Institute: Briefe 1928 bis 1953 und andere Dokumente.* Saecvla Spiritalia 20. Baden-Baden: V. Koerner, 1989.

Yates, Frances. "Chapman and Dürer on Inspired Melancholy." *University of Rochester Library Bulletin* 34 (1981): 25–34.

– *The Occult Philosophy in the Elizabethan Age.* London: Routledge, 2001 [1979].

Zimmerman, David. "The Society for the Protection of Science and Learning and the Politicization of British Science in the 1930s," *Minerva* 44 no. 1 (2006): 25–45.

Zinn, Ernst. *Der Wortakzent in den lyrischen Versen des Horaz.* PhD diss., University of Munich, 1940. Published Munich: Filser, 1940.

CONTRIBUTORS

PHILIPPE DESPOIX is professor of comparative literature and director of the Centre of Intermedial Research in Arts, Literatures and Technologies (CRIalt) at the Université de Montréal. Former director of the Canadian Centre for German and European Studies, he has been (2009–14) editor-in-chief of the journal *Intermédialités* and a fellow at Kolleg-Forschergruppe BildEvidenz of the Freie Universität Berlin (2014). His recently published works include: "Traverser/Crossing" (co-editor, *Intermédialités* 20, 2013); "Diaprojektion mit freiem Vortrag. Warburg und der Mythos von Kreuzlingen" (*Zeitschrift für Medienwissenschaft* 2, 2014); Siegfried Kracauer, *The Past's Threshold: Essays on Photography* (ed., Diaphanes, 2014); "*Translatio* and Remediation: Aby Warburg, Image Migration and Photographic Reproduction" (*SubStance* 44, 2, 2015); and *Raymond Klibansky, Tradition antique et tolérance moderne* (ed. with Georges Leroux, Presses de l'Université de Montréal, 2016).

GEORGES LEROUX is professor emeritus in the Department of Philosophy at Université du Québec à Montréal, where he taught Greek philosophy and philology from 1969 to 2006. He is the author of many works on Greek philology, aesthetics, and the history of ideas. He equally developed a career as translator, which led him to publish translations of Plato, Marcus Aurelius, and Plotinus. Leroux is a member of the Académie des Lettres du Québec and the Royal Society of Canada and has, among others, edited Raymond Klibansky, *Le Philosophe et la mémoire du siècle. Entretiens avec Georges Leroux* (Belles Lettres, 1998) and, with Philippe Despoix, a collection of papers by Raymond Klibansky, *Tradition antique et tolérance moderne* (Presses de l'Université de Montréal, 2016). His most recent essay is an autobiographical conversation with Christian Nadeau, *Entretiens* (Boréal, 2017)

ERIC MÉCHOULAN is professor in the Department of French Literature at the Université de Montréal. He was also program director at the Collège international de philosophie (Paris) and is currently head of the Centre de recherche sur les documents et la culture numérique. He recently published *La Culture de la mémoire, ou comment se débarrasser du passé?* (Presses de l'Université de Montréal, 2008), *D'où nous viennent nos idées? Métaphysique et intermédialité* (VLB Éditeur, 2010), *La Crise (du discours) économique. Émancipation et travail immatériel* (Éditions Nota bene, 2011), and *Lire avec soin. Amitié, justice et médias* (Presses de l'École normale supérieure de Lyon, 2017). Eric Méchoulan founded the review *Intermédialités* and directed it until 2006. Since 1996 he has been co-editor of the American journal *SubStance*.

ELISABETH OTTO is a PhD candidate in art history at the Université de Montréal, where she is finishing her dissertation, "Art Histories of Unlearning: Emily Carr (1871–1945) and Gabriele Münter (1877–1962)." In the first year of her PhD, she was a fellow in Canadian art at the National Gallery of Canada, Ottawa. Since 2015 she has been the scientific coordinator of the research and inquiry group CIÉCO: Collections et impératif évènementiel / The Convulsive Collections (SSHRC). In 2014 she joined the Warburg Library Network project as a research assistant. Besides her research on the interrelations between European and North American art and art histories, she is interested in the work of Indigenous contemporary women artists. Her most recent article: "The Affect of Absence: Rebecca Belmore and the Aesthetico-politics of 'Unnameable Affects,'" *Affecting Feminist Literary and Cultural Production / Affects féministes dans les productions littéraires et culturelles. Atlantis: Critical Studies in Gender, Culture, & Social Justice* 38, no. 2.

ELIZABETH SEARS is George H. Forsyth Jr. Collegiate Professor of History of Art at the University of Michigan and current chair of her department. Trained in the Warburgian tradition, she specializes in Western medieval art – especially manuscript illumination – and disciplinary historiography. In a long series of studies, she has investigated the life and work of figures including Aby Warburg, Adolph Goldschmidt, Erwin Panofsky, Edgar Wind, Jean Seznec, W.S. Heckscher, and H.W. Janson, and she is now completing a book, *Warburg Circles*, set in the years 1929–64, treating the intellectual movement that traced its origins to the Kulturwissenschaftliche Bibliothek Warburg in Hamburg. Her recent work has been supported by a Guggenheim Fellowship and residential fellowships in Rome (British School), Hamburg (Warburg Haus), Berlin (American Academy), and Washington (Center for Advanced Study in the Visual Arts).

DAVIDE STIMILLI (Yale, PhD, comparative literature) is associate professor of German, comparative literature, and Jewish studies at the University of Colorado, Boulder. He is the author of *Fisionomia di Kafka* (Bollati Boringhieri, 2001) and *The Face of Immortality: Physiognomy and Criticism* (SUNY Press, 2005), and the editor of Aby Warburg's clinical history, *Die unendliche Heilung. Aby Warburgs Krankengeschichte* (Diaphanes, 2007) and a selection of his unpublished writings, *"Per Monstra ad Sphaeram": Sternglaube und Bilddeutung. Vortrag in Gedenken an Franz Boll und andere Schriften 1923 bis 1925* (Dolling & Galitz, 2008). Recent publications on Warburg and the Warburg Library network include: "La lealtà della memoria: Warburg, Vöge, Panofsky, e il *Timoteo* di Van Eyck," in *Energia e Rappresentazione. Warburg, Panofsky, Wind*, eds. Alice Barale, Fabrizio Desideri, and Silvia Ferretti (*Mimesis*, 2016): 149–65; "Dream Bodies: On the Iconography of the Dreamer," in *The Art of Dreams: Reflections and Representations*, eds. Barbara Hahn and Meike G. Werner (De Gruyter, 2016): 97–119; and "L'énigme de Warburg," *Revue française de psychanalyse* 79 (2015): 1100–14.

JILLIAN TOMM joined the Warburg Library Network project as a postdoctoral researcher in 2016. Transition advisor to Alberto Manguel at the Biblioteca Nacional (Argentina) in 2016–17, she was previously assistant head librarian at Rare Books and Special Collections, McGill Library. Her doctoral work focused on McGill's Raymond Klibansky Collection. Publications include *Meetings with Books: Special Collections in the 21st Century* (McGill University Library, 2014). On Klibansky in particular she co-authored with Georges Leroux "La collection Raymond Klibansky conservée à l'Université McGill. Présentation de la bibliothèque d'un humaniste montréalais," *Mémoires du livre* 5, no. 1 (fall 2013); and contributed "La Bibliothèque de Raymond Klibansky. Une ouverture sur le monde," in *Raymond Klibansky, 1905–2005. La bibliothèque d'un philosophe*, ed. by Georges Leroux (BANQ, 2013).

MARTIN TREML, PhD, historian of religion and Jewish studies, has worked at the Center for the Study of Literature and Culture (ZfL) in Berlin since 2000. His main fields of research are theories and figures of Western religions, German-Jewish cultural history since 1750, and reception of Antiquity. His recent publications include: *Grenzgänger der Religionskulturen. Kulturwissenschaftliche Beiträge zu Gegenwart und Geschichte der Märtyrer*, with S. Horsch (Fink, 2011); Aby Warburg, *Werke*, with S. Weigel and P. Ladwig (Suhrkamp, 2010); *Nachleben der Religionen. Kulturwissenschaftliche Untersuchungen zur Dialektik der Säkularisierung*, with D. Weidner (Fink, 2007); *Warburgs Denkraum. Formen, Motive, Materialien*, with Sabine Flach and Pablo Schneider, eds. (Fink, 2014); and Jacob Taubes, *Apokalypse und Politik. Aufsätze, Kritiken und kleinere Schriften*, with Herbert Kopp-Oberstebrink, eds. (Fink Wilhelm GmbH + CompanyKG, 2017).

JEAN-PHILIPPE UZEL is a professor of art history at the Université du Québec à Montréal. His research focuses on the issue of cultural exchanges, both in the field of historiography of art (Winckelmann, Warburg, Klibansky ...) and in contemporary visual creation, particularly Indigenous contemporary art. His most recent article summarizes these two fields: "Déni et ignorance de l'historicité autochtone dans l'histoire de l'art occidentale," *RACAR* 42, no. 2 (2017). Articles on Klibansky in particular include "Sous le signe de Saturne. Raymond Klibansky et la mélancolie," in *Raymond Klibansky, 1905–2005. La bibliothèque d'un philosophe*, ed. by Georges Leroux (BAnQ, 2013); and "Raymond Klibansky et l'histoire de l'art du XXe siècle," *RACAR* 27, no. 1–2 (2000/2003).

REGINA WEBER, PhD, studied Germanistik, Romanistik, and Kunstgeschichte in Bonn and Tübingen. From 1986 to 1993 she was "wissenschaftliche Mitarbeiterin" at the Deutsche Literaturarchiv Marbach. From 1989 to 1993 she participated in the research project of the Deutsche Forschungsgemeinschaft on "Wissenschaftsemigration aus dem 'Dritten Reich'" – publications on the emigration of German literature scholars to the USA. Since then she has made several contributions on emigrated scholars, among them Richard Alewyn, Werner Vordtriede, Bernhard Blume, Karl Vietor, Heinz Politzer, Raymond Klibansky, and Lotte Labowsky. Her most recent published book is *Lotte Labowsky (1905–1991) – Schülerin Aby Warburgs, Kollegin Raymond Klibanskys* (Dietrich Reimer, 2012)

CLAUDIA WEDEPOHL (DPhil, University of Hamburg) is an art historian who joined the staff of the Warburg Institute in 2000. Since 2006 she has been the institute's archivist. Her research focuses on two fields: the reception of late antique models in fifteenth-century Italian art and architecture, and the genesis of Aby Warburg's cultural theoretical notions. She is the author of *In den glänzenden Reichen des ewigen Himmels. Cappella del Perdono und Tempietto delle Muse im Herzogpalast von Urbino* (Scaneg, 2009); co-author of *Warburg, Cassirer und Einstein im Gespräch. Kepler als Schlüssel der Moderne* (Wagenbach, 2015); co-editor of the multi-volume edition of Aby Warburg's collected writings *Gesammelte Schriften. Studienausgabe* (Gruyter, 2010–); and author of the article "Aby Warburg" in Oxford Bibliographies (2016).

GRAHAM WHITAKER is an honorary research fellow in classics, University of Glasgow, Scotland. His special interests include the history of classical studies, with particular reference to publishing and biography. He is co-editor of *Brill's Biographical Dictionary of Women Classicists* (forthcoming) and also of *Classics in Practice: Studies in the History of Scholarship* (London: Institute of Classical Studies, 2015). His work on cultural studies has included papers on the Warburg Institute's *Nachleben der Antike* bibliography (1934–38), and a recent chapter on Cassirer and Klibansky in *Ark of Civilization: Refugee Scholars and Oxford University, 1930–1945* (Oxford University Press, 2017).

INDEX